W9-BPM-999

Our People

Carpatho-Rusyns and Their Descendants
in North America

OTHER BOOKS BY PAUL ROBERT MAGOCSI

Let's Speak Rusyn—Bisidujme po-rus'kŷ (1976)
The Shaping of a National Identity (1978)
Let's Speak Rusyn—Hovorim po-rus'kŷ (1979)
The Rusyn-Ukrainians of Czechoslovakia (1983)
Galicia: A Historical and Bibliographic Guide (1983)
Ukraine: A Historical Atlas (1985)
Carpatho-Rusyn Studies, 3 vols. (1988, 1998, 2005)
The Russian Americans (1989, 1996)
The Carpatho-Rusyn Americans (1989, 2001)
The Rusyns of Slovakia (1993)
Historical Atlas of East Central Europe (1993, 2002)
A History of Ukraine (1996)
Let's Speak Rusyn and English—Besheduime po angliiski i po ruski (1997)
Of the Making of Nationalities There Is No End, 2 vols. (1999)
The Roots of Ukrainian Nationalism (2002)

EDITED BY PAUL ROBERT MAGOCSI

The Ukrainian Experience in the United States (1979)
Wooden Churches in the Carpathians (1982)
Morality and Reality: Andrei Sheptyts'kyi (1989)
The Persistence of Regional Cultures (1993)
A New Slavic Language Is Born (1996)
Encyclopedia of Canada's Peoples (1999)
Canada's Aboriginal Peoples (2002)
Encyclopedia of Rusyn History and Culture (2002, 2005)
Rusyns'kŷi iazŷk (2004)
Galicia: A Multicultured Land (2005)

Our People

Carpatho-Rusyns and Their Descendants in North America

Paul Robert Magocsi

Bolchazy-Carducci Publishers, Inc.
Wauconda, Illinois USA

Library of Congress Cataloguing-in-Publication Data
Magocsi, Paul R.
    Our people : Carpatho-Rusyns and their descendants
in North America / Paul Robert Magocsi ; with prefaces
by Oscar Handlin and Michael Novak. — 4th rev. ed.
    p. cm.
Includes index.
ISBN-13: 978-0-86516-611-0 (hardbound : alk. paper)
ISBN-10: 0-86516-611-0 (hardbound : alk. paper)
1. Carpatho-Rusyn Americans—History. 2. Carpatho-Rusyn Americans
—Social conditions. 3. Carpatho-Rusyns—Canada—History.
4. Carpatho-Rusyns—Canada—Social conditions. I. Title.

E184.U5M33 2005
973'.0491791—dc22   2005012971

Preface to the First Edition

The revival of interest in ethnicity in the United States during the 1970s had both beneficial and damaging aspects. Insofar as the motivations behind it were political or sprang out of the desire for competitive advantage in the struggle for a place in the American educational and occupational orders, the quest for ethnic identity generated divisive and exclusive tendencies. People swayed by narrow feelings of group pride often cherished delusive myths about their own past and emphasized the differences that set them apart from others. Insofar, however, as the search for identity welled up out of an authentic desire to understand a distant heritage, out of a wish for intellectual, emotional and cultural roots, it offered individuals creative opportunities for personal and social expression. The associations thus formed reinforced the self in dealing with the complexities of modern life and enriched the experience of the group members and of their neighbors.

The people who are the subjects of this volume were hardly recognized by Americans in the period of their arrival. Immigration officials whose categories were set by political boundaries could not take account of the Carpatho-Rusyns—no Carpatho-Rusyn state appeared on the map of Europe. In the census these newcomers were lost among the much larger count of speakers of Slavic languages. And the peasants who came to the mines and the mills were themselves more likely to think of their affiliations in terms of their native villages than in terms of any larger unit. To a very considerable extent, the Carpatho-Rusyns discovered their identity after they had settled in the United States. Moreover, they did so through the process of learning in a world wider than that of their ancestral homes, what they shared with others and what was unique to themselves.

Hence, the interest of this volume to anyone concerned with the development of American ethnic groups and with their place in the social history of the United States. The book treats the social, religious, and cultural aspects of a complex problem, and it should prove a point of departure for further explorations of a subject rich in significance.

Oscar Handlin
Harvard University
Cambridge, Massachusetts

Preface to the Second Edition

The world is fuller of peoples than of states. This circumstance often means that descendants of peoples who have no single state of their own cannot simply identify themselves by relying on the general knowledge of others or by pointing to a state outlined on a world map. Such is the lot of the Carpatho-Rusyns, particularly in America, far from their homeland in central Europe.

Many Americans will recognize the names of the actresses Lisabeth Scott and Sandra Dee, thinking of them as typical American women; they would not be so likely to recognize their names at birth—Emma Matzo and Alexandra Zuk. Many, too, will have heard of the artist Andy Warhol ("Everyone is famous for fifteen minutes"). A few might recall, if prodded, that one of the Marines immortalized in the famous statue of the raising of the U.S. flag on Iwo Jima was the Carpatho-Rusyn, Michael Strank. Most, though, will know of Carpatho-Rusyns through the brilliant film, *Deerhunter,* a tale set in Clairton, Pennsylvania, although partially filmed in St. Theodosius Orthodox Cathedral and in the Lemko Hall in Cleveland.

It has been the fate of this mostly rural, village-bound people to inhabit a region politically divided at times by Ukraine, Slovakia, Poland, and Hungary—perched across the top portion of the eastern tail, as it were, of Czechoslovakia—and tipping southward into western Ukraine. In religion, this people has for a thousand years turned eastward toward Byzantium. Its language, while related to other Slavic tongues, is distinctive. On the other hand, its geographical proximity to western Europe and to Roman Catholic populations has tied it clearly to the West, as has become yet more evident in the significant migrations of its peoples to the United States and Canada during the past century.

This book is an unusually beautiful and clear account of that relatively small but still self-conscious people. It is a welcome addition to our knowledge of the peoples of America and of the world. It sets a model for other peoples, so that they too might tell the story of "our people," "our memories," while looking toward "our future." It is an honor to have been asked to contribute to it.

The honor is all the more poignant, since the town of my own birth—Johnstown, Pennsylvania—has been a distinctive place of settlement for Carpatho-Rusyns (or Ruthenians as many prefer to say) in America, and since the town near which all four of my grandparents were born abroad—Prešov in Slovakia—has played so pivotal a cultural role in the history of Carpatho-Rusyns. I can say that I have felt spiritually related to this people all my life, and that, indeed, in my lifetime members of my family (as perhaps more than once before in history) have married into Carpatho-Rusyn families.

In a sense, the "Our People" of the title of this volume suggests, too, that the people of this story are part of "our people"—the pluralistic, planetary people of the United States and Canada. It is good to see this story told so well.

Michael Novak
George Frederick Jewett Chair
in Religion and Public Policy
American Enterprise Institute
Washington, D.C.

Contents

Maps

Text Inserts and Charts

List of Photographs

To my father

ALEXANDER B. MAGOCSI

a second-generation American who
believed in the cultural similarities
and avantages of cooperation
among all immigrants
from the Danubian Basin

Introduction

Whenever you drive through the northeastern and north-central states of Connecticut, New York, New Jersey, and Pennsylvania and proceed on to Ohio, Indiana, Michigan—even as far west as Minnesota— you are likely to notice that the often nondescript and grimy urban landscape through which you pass is punctuated from time to time by strange-looking gilded domes topped by equally unusual multi-barred crosses. These architectural surprises belong to the so-called "Russian" churches—churches that still function and even thrive as places of worship in the otherwise blighted downtown areas of many American inner cities. Your curiosity is whetted and you are prompted to ask: what are these strange and even exotic looking structures and who are the people that still flock to them in large numbers?

What you are seeing in these churches is a reflection of the long tradition of Eastern Christianity, in both its Byzantine Catholic and Orthodox variants. The people who attend them are first-generation immigrants or more likely their second-, third-, fourth-, and even fifth-generation descendants. The immigrants are mainly Slavs from the Carpathian Mountain regions in east-central Europe, men and women who were originally known as Rusyns or Rusnaks but who through the centuries acquired a whole host of names given to them by others or adopted by themselves, especially in America. Thus, while throughout their history the Carpatho-Rusyns may have been deprived of many things, including political independence and a reasonable standard of living, they were never at a loss for names. Among the more common ones were Rusyn,

Rusnak, Uhro-Rusin, Carpatho-Russian, Ruthenian, Carpatho-Ukrainian, Lemko, Slavish, Byzantine, or simply the *"po-našomu"* people (literally people like us or who speak our language—that is, "our people"). This, then, is the story of the *"po-našomu* people," whom we will call by their most commonly accepted name—Carpatho-Rusyns.

To be sure, Carpatho-Rusyns cannot be counted among the world's more numerous peoples. In the European homeland, there are about 1.2 million people who inhabit Carpathian Rus', the traditional Rusyn ethnolinguistic territory on both sides of the Carpathians. But for various reasons alluded to in the first chapter of this book, by the second half of the twentieth century fewer and fewer identify themselves as Rusyns. An active sense of Rusyn national and ethnic identity was only maintained among a small group (25,000), whose ancestors emigrated in the eighteenth century to what today is the country of Serbia and Montenegro (its historic region of the Bačka or Vojvodina). As for the later and larger group of emigrants who left the Carpathian Mountains for the United States during the late nineteenth and early twentieth centuries, there are perhaps 600,000 people who can be counted as having at least one parent or grandparent of Rusyn background.

Only a certain percentage of North America's Carpatho-Rusyns continue to maintain a clear sense of their European heritage. This portion of the group, however, which is on the increase among the younger generations, appears to be quite determined to distinguish its heritage as Carpatho-Rusyn, especially in contrast to neighboring or related European heritages in North America, such as Slovak, Hungarian, Russian, Ukrainian, or Polish. It is perhaps the need to have some "ethnic label" other than simply American or Canadian, combined with a growing sense that there are an ever decreasing number of Rusyns in the European homeland that has made some of the American descendants of the group feel that they are the "last Mohicans" of a people whose name and traditions would otherwise completely disappear unless preserved in some way on this continent. How else can one explain the "minor renaissance" of Rusyn identity which has occurred in the United States since the mid-1970s?

This book will attempt, albeit indirectly, to provide an explanation for the recent surge of interest in things Rusyn. This is not its main purpose, however. Rather, it has been written to provide a relatively detailed description of the multifaceted nature of the Carpatho-Rusyn experience in North America from its beginnings close to a century ago to the present. The book is thematic in structure, beginning with the origins of the group in Europe and its migration and settlement in the New World. This discussion is followed by an examination of religious, organizational, cultural, and political institutions and issues, and it concludes with a discussion of the efforts to preserve a sense of group identity and cohesiveness.

This study does not pretend to be definitive. Many questions and problems remain to be researched more thoroughly. But before that research is undertaken, it seemed necessary first to outline the boundaries of the subject—to identify who Carpatho-Rusyns in America actually are and to determine what religious, fraternal, cultural, and political organizations should be considered part of the experience of this particular American ethnic group. This book, then, is intended as a first step in the process of helping interested Rusyns understand where they belong within the North American mosaic. It is hoped also that it will stimulate other researchers to study in detail many of the issues touched on only briefly here. The author will have fulfilled his purpose if the book's various readers may recall something they already know, perhaps learn something new, or be stimulated to want to learn even more.

Throughout the text, the reader will encounter names of numerous individuals who have been or who are still active in the community. These are rendered in the form most commonly used in Latin-alphabet publications and documents. Other Rusyn and East Slavic names or terms in the text are rendered from the Cyrillic alphabet using the international transliteration system, which is similar to the popular standard used in Rusyn-American publications. The Cyrillic publications listed in the bibliography, however, are transliterated according to the Library of Congress system. This will make it easier for the interested reader to find such publications in some of the leading research libraries (Library of Congress, New York Public Library, Harvard College Library, Hoover Institution Library, Immigration History Research Center) in the United States and in Canada (University of Toronto).

The author is extremely grateful to various individuals and institutions who have helped and encouraged the completion of this book. Much of the photographic material and hard-to-obtain data was supplied by the Most Reverend Michael J. Dudick, DD (Bishop of the Byzantine Ruthenian Catholic Diocese of Passaic); Professor John H. Erickson (chairman, Department of History and Archives of the Orthodox Church in America); Dr. Joseph M. Kirschbaum (executive vice-president, Slovak World Congress); the Most Reverend Stephen J. Kocisko, DD (Metropolitan Archbishop of the Byzantine Ruthenian Catholic Church); Michael Logoyda (editor, *Karpatska Rus'*); Michael Lucas (general secretary, Society of Carpatho-Russians in Canada); Frederick Petro (editor, *GCU Messenger* and head of public relations, Greek Catholic Union); and Dr. M. Mark Stolarik (director, Balch Institute for Ethnic Studies). The technical preparation for the publication of the generally old and poor-quality photographs has been skillfully supervised by Karen Hendrick (Photoduplication Department, University of Toronto Library).

The manuscript was read in full and benefited enormously from the criticisms and suggestions of Jerry Jumba (SS Cyril and Methodius Byzantine Catholic Seminary), Edward Kasinec (Chief of Slavonic Division, New York Public Library), the Reverend Brian Keleher (Ukrainian Catholic Eparchy, Toronto), Steve Mallick (business manager, *Carpatho-Rusyn American),* Professor Vasyl Markus (associate editor, *Encyclopedia of Ukraine),* Orestes Mihaly (former editor, *American Carpatho-Russian Youth Guardian*), Professor Bohdan Procko (specialist on Ukrainian-American religious history), Michael Roman (former editor, *Amerikansky Russky Viestnik* and *Greek Catholic Union Messenger),* Professor Richard Renoff (specialist on the celibacy controversy), and Monsignor John Yurcisin (chancellor and historian, American Carpatho-Russian Orthodox Greek Catholic Church). The texts for the insert on Carpatho-Rusyn in the Context of Neighboring Languages and Dialects were provided by Mary Haschyc (Toronto), Stefanie Hurko (University of Toronto), Dr. Joseph M. Kirshbaum (Slovak World Congress), Anna Magocsi (Fairview, New Jersey), Dr. Mykola Mušynka (Prešov, Slovakia), and Professor Gleb Žekulin (University of Toronto).

The editing and production aspects of the book were enhanced by Ann Orlov (managing editor, *Harvard*

Encyclopedia of American Ethnic Groups) and Dr. Robert Harney (director, Multicultural History Society of Ontario), while George Shanta (Toronto, Ontario) assisted in compiling the invaluable list of Carpatho-Rusyn villages in the homeland. Finally, Ruth C. Cross once again has increased the usefulness of yet another manuscript by this author with the preparation of a comprehensive index, while Geoff Matthews (director, Cartographic Office of the University of Toronto's Department of Geography) supervised preparation of the attractive maps. Despite the efforts and experience of the aforementioned individuals, any shortcomings that may still be found in this book are the responsibility of the author alone.

PRM
Toronto, Ontario
April 1984

A Note on the Second Edition

The author is gratified to learn that within the initial four months of this book's appearance (December 1984), the first edition of 2,000 copies went out of print. In preparing this second printing of *Our People,* a few corrections and additions have been made that reflect comments from readers and recent developments in the community. Four photographs have also been replaced. I am particularly thankful to Michael Novak, noted syndicated columnist and fellow of the American Enterprise Institute in Washington, D.C., for his perceptive remarks in the book's new preface.

The speed with which the first edition of *Our*

People was sold out underscores the continuing interest of members and non-members alike in the fate of Carpatho-Rusyns in America. Let us hope that the book's enthusiastic reception will also lead to the fulfillment of another eventuality called for in the original introduction—that *Our People* "will stimulate other researchers to study in detail many of the issues touched on only briefly here."

PRM
Toronto, Ontario
March 1985

A Note on the Third Revised Edition

Although nearly a decade has passed since *Our People* first appeared, the book is still sought out by interested readers. That same decade has also witnessed several changes in the community in North America. It is in the European homeland, however, where truly profound transformations have taken place, most especially following the Revolution of 1989 which ended

Communist rule in East Central Europe.

These changes are reflected in the revised third edition of *Our People*. The text has been substantially emended and brought up to date where necessary. I am especially grateful to several readers of previous editions who provided more precise information on the photographs; to Richard D. Custer (Pittsburgh,

Pennsylvania), David G. Felix (Johnstown, Pennsylvania), Jerry Jumba (Herminie, Pennsylvania), Father Evan Lowig (Vancouver, British Columbia), Alexis Liberovsky (archivist, Orthodox Church in America), Frederick M. Petro (Communications director, Greek Catholic Union), John Righetti (Mars, Pennsylvania), Reverend Jaroslav Roman (Niagara Falls, New York), and John Ryzyk (Yonkers, New York) who helped with some of the changes in the text of this edition; and to Olena Duc'-Fajfer (Jagiellonian University, Cracow), who supplemented data on Lemko villages in the Root Seeker's Guide to the European Homeland. The chapter on Group Maintenance has, in particular, been expanded to reflect the new relationship and mutual influences between the North American community and the European homeland. The previous information on Rusyns in Canada has been supplemented and placed in a new concluding chapter. All the maps have been updated or emended and a dozen new photographs added. The Root Seeker's Guide has been entirely revised with the addition of 35 villages and each name has been supplemented with linguistic variants in seven languages for the entire list. Over fifty new entries have been added to the bibliography. The updated bibliography confirms what was hoped for in the first edition—that Our People might "stimulate other researchers to study in detail many of the issues touched on only briefly here."

Yet despite the recent advances in knowledge about Carpatho-Rusyns in whatever country they live, and despite the greater availability of books and articles on the subject, I continue to receive letters similar in content to one from Cleveland, Ohio that arrived as recently as December 14, 1992, and which read in part:

To begin with, I admit I was ashamed of my parents because I didn't know who they were or where they came from. They taught and spoke Slovanic [sic] and we tried to learn English. … My wife and I are 77 and 76 years of age. I am pleading with you. Please help me if you can with my problem. I remember hearing my parents discussing their young days in Telepovce. … and mentioning Vyšná Jablonka and Hostovice. … I will gladly pay you anything if you can help me to know where my parents came from.

The villages this distraught inquirer mentions are all listed in the Root Seeker's appendix to Our People and, therefore, the Cleveland request can easily be resolved. This letter does reveal, however, the ongoing need that continues to be expressed by Americans of Carpatho-Rusyn background, whether young or old, to know who they are and where they fit into the larger scheme of things. Hopefully, Our People will continue to reach such distraught individuals and help them to fulfill their need.

PRM
Toronto, Ontario
July 1993

A Note on the Fourth Revised Edition

Another decade has gone by and Our People is still in demand. The entire text has been substantially revised with updating and data on new developments within Carpatho-Rusyn communities in both the United States and Canada. Several photographs have been replaced, the bibliography supplemented, and hundreds of new places with linguistic variants added to the Root Seeker's Guide to the Homeland.

The author is particularly grateful to several friends and colleagues, who provided critical remarks and factual data that have definitely improved the text. In particular, I have in mind Richard D. Custer, Bogdan Horbal, Jerry Jumba, and John Righetti, to whom I express deep appreciation. Finally, the complicated technical aspects of producing this volume are largely the result of the inputting and design skills of Nadiya Kushko, Julie Lu, and Gabriele Scardellato, all of the University of Toronto.

PRM
Toronto, Ontario
March 2004

Our People

CARPATHIAN RUS', BEFORE WORLD WAR I

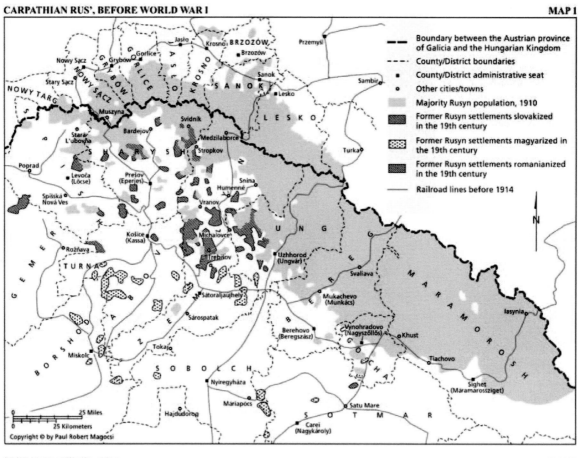

MAP 1

Legend:
- Boundary between the Austrian province of Galicia and the Hungarian Kingdom
- County/District boundaries
- County/District administrative seat
- Other cities/towns
- Majority Rusyn population, 1910
- Former Rusyn settlements slovakized in the 19th century
- Former Rusyn settlements magyarized in the 19th century
- Former Rusyn settlements romanianized in the 19th century
- Railroad lines before 1914

Copyright © by Paul Robert Magocsi

CARPATHIAN RUS', 2004

MAP 2

Legend:
- International boundaries
- Transcarpathian oblast (Subcarpathian Rus')
- Carpatho-Rusyn settlement, 1920
- District centers in Poland (powiat), Slovakia (okres), and Ukraine (raion)
- Settlements with Rusyn minority self-government

Copyright © by Paul Robert Magocsi

Chapter 1

Origins

Carpatho-Rusyns live in the center of the European continent. Looking at a map of Europe as it stretches from the tip of Norway in the north to the isle of Crete in the south, and from the coast of Ireland in the west to the Ural Mountains in the east, the exact geographic midpoint, which was carefully calculated in the late nineteenth century and marked by a monument, is south of the Carpatho-Rusyn town of Rachiv. (see Map 2)

The Carpatho-Rusyn homeland, known as Carpathian Rus', is situated at the crossroads where the present-day borders of Ukraine, Slovakia, and Poland meet. There are also smaller numbers of Carpatho-Rusyns in Romania, Hungary, and Serbia. In no country do Carpatho-Rusyns have an administratively distinct territory, although the lands where they form the majority population have come to be known by different names: Subcarpathian Rus' (Transcarpathia) in far western Ukraine; the Prešov Region in northeastern Slovakia; the Lemko Region in southeastern Poland; the Maramureş Region in northcentral Romania; and the Vojvodina (Bačka and Srem) in northern Serbia. Parts of the Carpatho-Rusyn homeland have been known by different names in the past, including Carpatho-Ruthenia, Carpatho-Russia, Carpatho-Ukraine, or simply Ruthenia.

Subcarpathian Rus' and the Prešov Region, located south of the Carpathian Mountain crests, formed since the Middle Ages the northern borderland of the Kingdom of Hungary. Hungarian rule over these regions was to remain firmly in place until the end of World War I, when all "Rusyns living south of the Carpathians" were joined to the newly created republic of Czechoslovakia. In Czechoslovakia, about 360,000 Carpatho-Rusyns lived in the theoretically autonomous province of Subcarpathian Rus' (in Czech: Podkarpatská Rus) and 100,000 or so in the Prešov Region of northeastern Slovakia. Hungary reannexed Subcarpathian Rus' in 1939 and held it until 1944; at the close of World War II in 1945 the province was ceded by Czechoslovakia to the Soviet Union. It formed the Transcarpathian oblast of the Ukrainian Soviet Socialist Republic (Soviet Ukraine), and since 1991 is part of independent Ukraine. The Carpatho-Rusyns farther west in the Prešov Region continue to live in the northeastern corner of Slovakia, which since early 1993 has become a state independent of the former Czechoslovakia. By 2001, in Ukraine's Transcarpathian oblast, the East Slavic Rusyns (designated as Ukrainians) numbered about 800,000 while in the Prešov Region 63,000 people declared that they speak Rusyn or Ukrainian, the two names by which the East Slavs identify themselves in Slovakia.

As for those Rusyn Americans who call themselves Lemkos, their ancestors came from just north of the Carpathian crests in what is today the far southeastern corner of Poland. The Lemko Region consists of several villages within the mountainous foothills bordered in the west by the Dunajec River; in the east by the San River; in the north by the towns of Nowy Sącz, Grybów, Gorlice, Sanok, and Lesko, and in the south by the crests of the Carpathian Mountains. Originally part of the Galician principality within the medieval Kievan Rus' federation, the Lemko Region came under Polish rule in the fourteenth century and then was part of the Austrian Habsburg province of Galicia from 1772 to 1918. Since World War I, with only a brief interruption during World War II (1939-1944), the Lemko Region again has been part of Poland.

The Lemkos themselves numbered about 250,000 on the eve of World War II. After a new Polish-Soviet border was established in 1945 along the upper San River, the following year close to 80 per cent of the Lemkos resettled eastward in the Soviet Ukraine as part of an international agreement between Poland and the Soviet Union regarding the voluntary exchange of minority populations. At the very same time, the whole Carpathian region became the center of anti-Communist and anti-Soviet activity led by Ukrainian nationalist partisans. In retaliation, the Communist Polish government in 1947 forcibly deported the remaining Lemkos during the so-called Vistula Operation, and settled them in western and north-central Poland on territories that had until the end of the war been part of Germany. Thus, the Lemko homeland was stripped of its Carpatho-Rusyn inhabitants, with Lemko homes and fields given to Polish newcomers. Since the 1960s, however, some Lemkos (about 10,000) have been permitted to return to their old Carpathian villages, although today the Lemko Region is still inhabited mostly by Poles.

Carpatho-Rusyn civilization has its origins in the Eastern Orthodox cultural sphere, but because the Carpathian region is a border zone, it has also been strongly influenced by western European and Roman Catholic cultural and religious developments. Slavic peoples appeared in the Carpathian region already in the fifth century AD as part of their settlement of the Danubian Basin. Between the seventh and twelfth centuries, small groups of migrants continued to arrive from Galicia and Volhynia and from Podolia, territories to the northeast and southeast beyond the Carpathian Mountains in what is today Ukraine. Further waves of migrants arrived especially from Galicia between the thirteenth and the eighteenth centuries. The language or, more precisely, the variety of dialects spoken by Carpatho-Rusyns belong to the eastern branch of the Slavic languages. For the longest time Rusyn dialects were classified as Ukrainian, but since 1989 there exist several variants of literary Rusyn, which is today recognized by an increasing number of linguists as a distinct Slavic language.

MAP 3

Where Did the Rusyns Come From and From Whom Did They Receive Christianity?

These two questions have been researched for decades by scholars in the European homeland, and they have also been of great interest to Carpatho-Rusyns in America. Definitive answers have yet to be found. Instead, numerous and often conflicting hypotheses abound.

The question of where Rusyns came from is closely related to the famous controversy in the study of early eastern European history known generally as the problem of the origin of Rus'. There are at least three explanations favored by various Rusyn and other eastern European scholars: (1) that the Rus' derive from a Varangian (Scandinavian) tribe or group of leaders who made Kiev their political center in the mid-ninth century AD—the so-called Normanist theory; (2) that the Rus' or Ros were an indigenous Slavic tribe who were already settled just south of Kiev by the fourth century AD, later giving their name to the Scandinavian conquerors—the so-called anti-Normanist theory; and (3) that the Rus' came from Scandinavia, but were not associated with any particular Varangian tribe. Instead, they were part of an international trading company that plied the North and Baltic seas. The company, which comprised various peoples, traced its roots to the city of Rodez (Ruzzi) in what is today southern France—a city whose inhabitants were called Ruteni or Ruti, and who today are known as rutenois.

As for the first Rus' in the Carpathians, there are also numerous theories. For many years, scholars thought that the Carpathian region was the original homeland of all the Slavs. Today, however, it is generally felt that the original Slavic homeland was just north of the Carpathians, in what is today eastern Poland, southwestern Belarus, and northwestern Ukraine. Archaeological remains indicate that human settlement in the Rusyn region south of the Carpathians goes back over a million years, but it is still not certain when the ancestors of the Rusyns first made their appearance. Some writers—who support the so-called autochthonous theory—argue that Rusyns were already in the Carparthians in the fifth and sixth centuries AD and that they had a state ruled by a Prince Laborec' which was "independent" until its destruction by the Magyars at the very end of the ninth century. Others—who support the so-called colonization theory—state that the Rusyns began to arrive with the Magyars at the end of the ninth century, although only in small groups; larger numbers did not come until after the thirteenth century.

Faced with these varying interpretations from "European authorities," Rusyn-American writers have favored one or more of the above theories and some have even added other less convincing explanations, seeking Asiatic roots for Rusyns either in the Urals, the Caucasus, or the Himalayas.

In reality, the origins of the Carpatho-Rusyns are complex. They were not, as is often asserted, associated exclusively with Kievan Rus'. Rather, the ancestors of the present-day Carpatho-Rusyns are: (1) early Slavic peoples who came to the Danubian Basin with the Huns in the fifth century AD and Avars in the sixth century AD; (2) the Slavic tribe of White Croats who inhabited both slopes of the Carpathians and in the sixth and seventh centuries built several hill-forts in the region, including Hungvar (modern-day Užhorod) ruled by the semi-legendary Prince Laborec'; (3) shepherds known as Vlachs who came from present-day Romania in the late thirteenth to fifteenth centuries and settled throughout what became the Carpatho-Rusyn homeland; and (4) Rusyn migrants from Galicia and Podolia in present-day western Ukraine who between the twelfth and six-teenth centuries were invited by the Hungarian authorities to settle along the kingdom's northern Carpathian frontier. The most famous of these invitees was the Lithuanian Prince Fedor Koriatovyč from Podolia, later Duke of Mukačevo and the legendary founder of the nearby Monastery of St. Nicholas on Monk's Hill (Černeča Hora).

The problem of when and from whom Rusyns received Christianity also remains an unresolved question. One major concern with respect to this question has to do with the issue of a western or an eastern orientation in Rusyn religious culture.

Traditionally, Rusyn historians have argued that their people received Christianity from the "Apostles to the Slavs," Cyril and Methodius, as part of their mission from the Byzantine Empire to the state known as Greater Moravia in 863. Although based in former central Czechoslovakia (Moravia, eastern Bohemia, and western Slovakia), the Moravian sphere of influence—and therefore Christianity—reached farther northward, southward, and eastward. Ostensibly one of the original Methodian dioceses was based in the Rusyn center of the Mukačevo. It should be mentioned that although the Cyril-Methodian mission brought Christianity according to the eastern Byzantine rite, it came "from the west" and was recognized by the Pope. The Universal Church had, of course, not yet become divided into "western Roman" and "eastern Orthodox" Christian spheres.

Another theory basically rejects or minimizes the importance of the Cyril-Methodian mission, and instead associates Christianity in the Carpathians with the arrival of Rusyns (that is, the Rus' people or those of the Orthodox faith) from the east, most especially after the conversion of Rus' to Christianity in 988 carried out by the Kievan grand prince Vladimir (Volodymyr). This "eastern theory" is used to justify the "Orthodox origin" of Carpatho-Rusyns.

The newest theory, proposed in the 1980s by the late Greek Catholic priest and historian from Slovakia, Stepan Pap, suggests that on their way to Greater Moravia Cyril and Methodius stopped first in the Rusyn homeland where they converted the local populace. And as for Kievan Rus' in the east, it was Rusyns from the Carpathians who, according to Pap, brought Christianity to Kiev during the following century and not the other way around.

With regard to the traditional interpretations, it is not surprising that the Byzantine Ruthenian Catholic Church favors the "western" Cyril-Methodian view. The Byzantine Catholic Metropolitanate of Pittsburgh sees itself as the successor to the Eparchy of Mukačevo, which in turn evolved from the ostensible presence of the Methodian mission in the Carpathian region in the ninth century. For this reason, the Byzantine Metropolitanate participated fully in the 1963 celebration to honor SS. Cyril and Methodius and their missionary work in Greater Moravia 1,100 years ago. It did not join the millennium celebrations of the Christianization of Kievan Rus' in 1988.

As for the Carpatho-Russian Orthodox (Johnstown) Diocese, it accepts both the "western" and "eastern" views; that is, it recognizes the importance of the Cyril-Methodian mission as well as the Kievan Prince Vladimir's conversion as contributing factors to the Carpatho-Rusyn religious tradition. On the other hand, the Orthodox Church in America and Patriarchal Exarchate (in which Carpatho-Rusyns are members) emphasize the "eastern theory" and, therefore, they participated fully in the millennium celebrations in 1988 to honor the Christianization of Kievan Rus' ("Kievan Russia").

As far as religion, there is still much controversy regarding the source of Christianity in the Carpathians. Popular tradition, still maintained by many in the United States, considers that Eastern Christianity was received by Carpatho-Rusyns some time in the late ninth century from the "Apostles to the Slavs," Cyril and Methodius, who at the time were on a mission to Moravia. It is more likely, however, that Christianity came with the colonizers who crossed the mountains from the East. The term Rusyn actually derives from the word Rus', a name applied to all East Slavic ad-herents of Orthodoxy who lived within the cultural sphere of the loosely knit political federation known as Kievan Rus'. While the name Rusyn was initially used to describe all East Slavs in the Middle Ages, gradually they were differentiated as Russians, Belarusans, and Ukrainians, so that only in the Carpathian region did the name Rusyn persist down to the mid-twenti-eth century. After World War II, the term Ukrainian was administratively imposed upon all East Slavs in the Carpathian homeland. Some welcomed the move, but among large segments of the population the name

---

What's in a Name?

The terms Rusyn/Rusnak have come to be a source of contro-versy not only in the European homeland (especially along the Rusyn/Slovak/Magyar ethnolinguistic border area south of the Carpathians) but also among immigrants and their de-scendants from those areas in the United States. Originally, the terms Rusyn/Rusnak were used simply to designate an ad-herent of Eastern Christianity, whether of Orthodox or later, as we shall see, of Greek Catholic persuasion. Beginning in the last decades of the nineteenth century, however, the in-habitants were called upon to identify themselves not simply according to religious affiliation, but also according to their language and/or nationality.

During this procedure (often related to decennial censuses), some leaders argued that all Greek Catholics—notwithstand-ing what Rusyn or transitional Rusyn/East Slovak dialects they may have spoken—were originally called Rusyns/Ru-snaks and therefore should be considered of Carpatho-Rusyn nationality. The Greek Catholic-equals-Rusyn viewpoint was also applied to Slovak-speaking and Magyar-speaking Rus-yns/Rusnaks who were considered slovakized or magyarized Rusyns. Not surprisingly, Slovak and Hungarian publicists re-jected such an interpretation, arguing instead that East Slovak or Hungarian-speaking Greek Catholics should be considered respectively as either Slovak or Magyar Greek Catholics. Later, some of these spokesmen went so far as to conclude that Rusyns or Rusnaks did not form a distinct ethnolinguistic or national group at all; rather, they were simply Slovaks or Magyars of the Greek Catholic faith.

While still in Europe, the peasant masses before World War I remained essentially immune to what seemed to them to be "politicking" among their intellectual and clerical leaders. Therefore, the vast majority came to America simply as Rus-yns or Rusnaks, that is, Slavs and in a few cases Magyars of the Greek Catholic faith. After their arrival in America, how-ever, they often were called on to identify with some ethno-linguistic or national group and, besides the Rusyn, Slovak, or Hungarian options, the Russian or Ukrainian options were now added.

The identity problem has been especially acute among those Americans whose ancestors came from the ethnolinguis-tic border area of eastern Slovakia—that is, villages around Prešov, Bardejov, Košice, Humenné, Trebišov, and even as far east as Užhorod. As a result, it is not surprising to find some people who will adamantly argue that they are Slovak, while others from the same village, even the same family, will state they are Carpatho-Rusyn or sometimes its derivative, Car-patho-Russian. It is also interesting to note that the Slovak self-identifier will often deny that Carpatho-Rusyns exist as a distinct group.

As problematic is the nomenclature and identity problem among those Americans whose ancestors came from Galicia, where the term Rusyn as a self-identifier was also widespread until as late as the third decade of the twentieth century. In the United States, these Galician-Rusyn immigrants and their descendants, often from the same village or even same fam-ily, have identified themselves either as Carpatho-Russians, Russians, or Ukrainians. These varied identities are also found among Galicians and their descendants from villages in the Lemko Region, who have interacted particularly closely in America with Rusyns from south of the Carpathians. There-fore, one can encounter in the immigration Rusyn Lemkos, Russian Lemkos, Ukrainian Lemkos, or those who simply identify as Lemkos.

How to resolve these problems? In one sense, each person has the right to claim whatever ethnic identity he or she wishes, regardless if the claim has any relationship to objective crite-ria, such as geographical origin, spoken language, or customs. Moreover, identity is always a problem in border areas. The Rusyn/Slovak/Magyar ethnolinguistic boundary south of the Carpathians has, in particular, changed often during the last century with the Rusyn area generally receding northward in the face of Slovak and Magyar assimilatory trends.

Yet the situation is not entirely fluid. There are observable linguistic and ethnographic characteristics which differentiate Rusyn villages from Slovak and Magyar villages in the Eu-ropean homeland. These characteristics have been mapped in linguistic atlases and ethnographic maps more than once dur-ing the past century, thereby making it possible to define the ethnolinguistic make-up of these borderland villages at differ-ent points in time. The root-seeker simply has to know what village his or her parents or grandparents came from. With such information, ethnic background can be determined. For a list of all Rusyn villages in the European homeland, see the Root Seeker's Guide to the homeland at the back of this book.

Rusyn (in some cases Rusnak) remained common. Since 1989, the name Rusyn is again recognized as the official designation in most countries where the group lives.

The eastern ethnolinguistic and religious origins and inclinations of the Carpatho-Rusyns for several centuries were counterbalanced by strong influences from western and, in particular, Roman Catholic Europe. Both Hungary and Poland were predominantly Roman Catholic countries in which the East Slavic Orthodox Rus' inhabitants increasingly were treated as second-class citizens. The desire to alter their own unfavorable sociocultural status, combined with varying forms of official pressure on the part of the Hungarian and Polish governments and Roman Catholic Church, prompted several Orthodox Rus' hierarchs and some priests to accept the idea of union with Rome. Consequently, declarations of church union were proclaimed first in Poland (Union of Brest, 1596) and then in Hungary (Union of Užhorod, 1646). The result, however, was not conversion to Roman Catholicism, but rather the creation of a new institution known as the Uniate and later as the Greek Catholic Church. According to the acts of union, the Uniate or Greek Catholic Church was permitted to retain its Eastern-rite liturgy in the Slavonic tongue and its traditional customs (including the Julian calendar, communion in two species, and

married clergy). On the other hand, the new church recognized as its ultimate head the Pope in Rome and not—as had previously been the case—the Ecumenical Patriarch in Constantinople.

To be sure, the official acts of union promulgated during the late sixteenth and mid-seventeenth centuries were not accepted universally by the Rus' population, and Orthodox adherents with their own hierarchs continued to function for several more decades, most especially far eastern regions of Carpathian Rus'. By the outset of the eighteenth century, however, Greek Catholicism had become the religion of most Carpatho-Rusyns, and at the popular level it functioned as a cultural attribute to distinguish them as a group from the Roman Catholic Poles and Roman Catholic or Protestant Slovaks and Magyars.

During the nineteenth century, when Carpatho-Rusyns, like other national minorities in Europe, experienced a national awakening, the Greek Catholic Church became the primary vehicle for maintaining the traditional culture, and its priests provided the leadership for the small clerically-oriented nationalist movement. Many of the elementary schools that existed before World War I were operated by the Greek Catholic Church, and the few newspapers, books, and cultural societies were almost all dominated by Greek Catholic clergymen. It was during this period that the

1. Carpatho-Rusyn homestead in the old country, circa 1910 (photo by Josef Zeibrdlich).

Greek Catholic priest Aleksander Duchnovyč, known as the "national awakener of the Carpatho-Rusyns", was most active.

As for the Carpatho-Rusyn masses, their socioeconomic status remained basically unchanged from the medieval period until the twentieth century. Because they inhabited mountainous and generally infertile valleys, they were forced to struggle in order to eke out a subsistence-level existence from their tiny plots and small herds of cows, sheep, and goats. Almost without exception, Carpatho-Rusyns inhabited small villages and worked as serfs for Hungarian or Polish landlords until 1848, and then as poorly paid and/or indebted agricultural laborers under the same landlords for several more decades after their "liberation" from serfdom. The few nearby towns—Prešov, Bardejov, Humenné, Užhorod, Mukačevo, Sanok—were inhabited by Slovaks, Magyars, Poles, Jews, and Germans, so that Rusyns generally experienced small-town life only as visitors to the markets and shops or as domestic help and urban laborers.

Until the twentieth century, social and even geographic mobility was uncommon. Although some railroad lines passed through the region, most Carpatho-Rusyns spent their entire lives within their native or neighboring villages, where their life cycle was dominated by the demands of the agricultural seasons and the church calendar. Indeed, as high as 97 per cent of Carpatho-Rusyns were born and died in the same village and were married to someone of the same religion. To be sure, seasonal migration in search of work did occur, especially during the summers, when Carpatho-Rusyn males found employment farther south as agricultural laborers on the Hungarian plain. Such migration lasted only as long as the harvest season, however. Thus, subsistence-level farming in small mountainous villages; cultural and religious identity as defined by membership in the Greek Catholic Church; and the lack of any distinct political life even at the local level were the main characteristics of Carpatho-Rusyn society on the eve of the initial Rusyn emigration to the United States.

2. Working the fields in Užok, Subcarpathian Rus', circa 1920 (photo by Themac).

Chapter 2

Migration

As is typical for people who live in traditional peasant societies, Carpatho-Rusyns were very attached to the land. Acquiring more land was therefore an important status symbol. The immigrants and their descendants in the United States continued to hold to this tradition. Owning one's own house and piece of surrounding property became (and still remains) an important life goal, which if achieved was expected to provide both financial and psychological security. It was precisely the lack of available land in the European homeland, caused in part by population increases and in part by the continual subdivision of landholdings and inefficient agricultural practices, that forced the Rusyns to live in severe poverty. These conditions, sometimes combined with the threat of being drafted into the military, prompted many to emigrate.

The immediate stimulus to leave may have been provided by letters from neighbors and relatives who were already in America earning dollars, or from steamship agents who sometimes toured European villages acting as middlemen for American factory owners looking for cheap labor. Not surprisingly, it was young males, single or recently married, who made up almost three-quarters of the Carpatho-Rusyn emigrants before World War I. The desire to earn funds with which to buy land, to prepare for marriage, or to support a young family and perhaps to pay off a mortgage, prompted what seemed at times to be a large-scale flight to America—an America that was still believed to be a land of milk and honey where the streets were ostensibly paved with gold.

To be sure, such fantasies were quickly destroyed by the turn-of-the-century realities that faced the American worker—long, hard, and often monotonous hours of work for little pay. While some immigrants were unable to cope with the gruelling conditions they encountered in the New World, others were able to meet the challenge. They earned the highly praised dollars; they wrote glowing letters encouraging fellow-countrymen to make the journey; and they returned to their native villages where they were able to buy land and play the role of the wealthy "relative" who had struck it rich in America.

After the initial decision to leave home was made, an often heart-rending departure was accompanied by weeping relatives and a final blessing under the wayside cross at the head of the village. A slow, bumpy ride on a horsedrawn cart provided much time to reflect about family, friends, and loved ones left behind as the prospective immigrant made his or her way to the nearest rail terminal in order to board a train that eventually provided transport to the coast. There were also numerous cases in which villagers walked most of the way to major cities before boarding trains for the faraway ports. This was often the case with the large number of young men, who on the eve of World War I feared induction into the Austro-Hungarian army. Flight from military authorities as well as from civil authorities, who during certain periods feared the depopulation of certain Rusyn-inhabited districts, led to periodic government restrictions on emigration, which in turn prompted illegal as well as legal departures.

3. Typical wayside cross, often the last sight of the native village seen by departing emigrants. At Koločava-Horb, Subcarpathian Rus', 1925 (photo by Florian Zapletal).

The number of illegal departures by far outweighed legal departures.

Of all the regions in the Austro-Hungarian Empire, it was precisely those inhabited by Carpatho-Rusyns which provided among the highest proportion of emigrants. Those from the Lemko Region of the Austrian province of Galicia came from the districts of Nowy Sącz, Grybów, Gorlice, Jaslo, Krosno, Sanok, and Lesko. They generally travelled toward the northwest and left from Germany's North Sea ports of Bremen or Hamburg. Carpatho-Rusyns from Hungary originated in the main from the counties of Szepes (Rusyn: Spiš), Sáros (Šaryš), Zemplén (Zemplyn), Ung (Už), Bereg, Ugocsa (Ugoča), and Máramaros (Maramoroš). There was also a small number who came from the southern Hungarian counties of Bács-Bodrog (Bačka) and Szerém (Srem); that is, the Rusyns of a region in present-day Serbia called the Vojvodina. The largest number, however, came from the counties of Ung and Bereg, followed by Máramaros, Zemplén, and Sáros. These "Hungarian" Rusyns (or Uhro-

Rusyns as they sometimes were known) also generally travelled north and left from the ports of Bremen and Hamburg on German ships, although after 1903 many—at the encouragement of the government—went south instead and left from Hungary's port on the Adriatic Sea, Fiume (today Rijeka in Croatia), or across the border into Romania and its Black Sea port of Constanța.

From these various ports, the emigrants boarded ships packed with other eastern and southern Europeans and began the long three- to four-week journey across the Atlantic. They had never seen the ocean and in most cases had previously never left the immediate surroundings of their native village. For some, the ocean voyage produced fear of the unknown, while for others it contributed to the spirit of adventure that led to new and exciting experiences, friendships, even unplanned marriages. Also, the experience of the first ocean voyage did not deter many, now described as sojourners, who after a few years of working decided to return home and then again to re-emigrate. Hard times in the American economy, as in late 1907, encouraged many Carpatho-Rusyns to Europe, so that the average number of returnees each year during the decade before 1914 was nearly seventeen percent the number arriving. Thus, in the decades before World War I, some immigrants came, returned, and came again, so

4. View from the steerage on an immigrant ship as it enters New York City harbor, ca. 1905.

that movement back and forth across the Atlantic from rural Rusyn villages to the industrial centers of the northeast United States was quite common.

Almost without exception the immigrant ships headed for New York City, passed the Statue of Liberty, and docked along the wharves of the world's largest urban complex. Immediately, the immigrants were transferred to small ferries and taken to Ellis Island on the New Jersey side of the harbor. There, in isolation from the mainland, they were inspected primarily for potential health problems. In most, but not all, cases they received a stamp of approval, and some were even given a new name by immigration officers unsympathetic to or impatient with the strange sounding Slavic names. After passing these hurdles, they were released to find their way to waiting friends, relatives, or prospective employers.

As might be expected, the Carpatho-Rusyn newcomers were, in the main, members of the working class. According to United States statistics for the years 1900 through 1914, of the 254,000 "Ruthenians" who came from Austria-Hungary during those years, 41 percent were engaged in agriculture, 22 percent were laborers, and 20 percent were domestic servants. Only 2 percent were skilled artisans, less than 1 percent professionals, and even fewer were merchants. To complete the demographic picture, 13 percent were women and children without occupational status. During these years, 71 percent of "Ruthenian" immigrants were males, and only 33 percent of the total population over 14 years of age was literate.

While these figures may give us some idea of the socioeconomic character of the immigration, it is difficult, if not impossible, to determine the exact number of Carpatho-Rusyns who came to the United States. Official reports are not much help. Nonetheless, by extrapolating from various sources, it is reasonable to say that before 1914 approximately 225,000 Carpatho-Rusyns emigrated to the United States. While a few individuals had begun to arrive as early as the 1860s, it was not until the late 1880s and 1890s that substantial numbers came, the movement reaching its height during the first decade of the twentieth century.

This pre-World War I influx of Carpatho-Rusyns was not to be repeated. The war years (1914-1918) put a virtual halt to all emigration. Then, after 1920, when the political situation stabilized and Carpatho-Rusyns found themselves within two new states—Czechoslovakia and Poland—migration resumed. The composition of these immigrants differed at least initially from the pre-1914 group in that women and children now predominated, as they joined husbands and fathers who had already left before the war. Before long, however, there were new impediments to what had become the somewhat common bidirectional movement of people between east-central Europe and America. This time the restrictions were imposed by the United States, which enacted in 1924 a national quota system that was highly unfavorable to the further entry of immigrants from eastern and southern Europe. Therefore, as a result of the 1924 quota system and world economic depression in the 1930s, which reduced further the ability to find the means to travel and the possibility of finding jobs, only 8,000 Carpatho-Rusyns left Czechoslovakia for the United States and 10,000 from Poland between 1920 and 1938. Faced with these American restrictions, many Carpatho-Rusyns from Czechoslovakia went instead (generally as sojourning

5. Slavic immigrant awaiting processing at Ellis Island, circa 1908 (photo by Lewis Hine).

THE PROBLEM OF STATISTICS

It is impossible to know the number of Americans of Carpatho-Rusyn background in the United States. Among the reasons for this lack of information are: (1) inadequate or non-existent statistical data, whether from sending countries or from the United States; and (2) the decision of many of the first-generation immigrants and their descendants not to identify themselves as Rusyns. The latter problem is typical for many peoples who do not have their own states.

Most often, when traveling or living abroad, "stateless peoples" identify with the country in which they were born, even if their own nationality or ethnocultural background may be different from the dominant one in their home country. Thus, numerous immigrants from the pre-World War I Austro-Hungarian or Russian Empires identified—or were identified by others—as Austrians, Hungarians, or Russians, even though ethnically they were not Austrian, Hungarian, or Russian.

There is also the question of what is meant by the term Rusyn American. Does this refer to a person of Carpatho-Rusyn background who has immigrated to the United States, or can it refer as well to the offspring of such a person? If the latter, do both parents or grandparents have to be of Carpatho-Rusyn background, or is one ancestor sufficient? For our purposes, a Rusyn American is defined as any person born in the European homeland or born in the United States of at least one parent, grandparent, or other generational ancestor who came from one of the 1,101 Rusyn villages listed in the Root Seeker's appendix to this volume or, if born elsewhere (in a nearby town), someone who chooses to self-identify as a Rusyn.

Why are official or governmental statistics not helpful? First of all, it was not until as recently as 1980 that the United States Census Bureau recognized the name Rusyn, although it was to be still another decade—the census of 1990—before the census data actually indicated Americans who identified themselves as Carpatho-Rusyns. Prior to 1990, Rusyns were classified in many other ways.

Between 1899 and 1914, which coincides with the heaviest period of Carpatho-Rusyn immigration, United States statistics reported the arrival of 254,000 Ruthenians/Russniaks. Since there was an average annual return migration of 16.7 percent, this left 212,000 Ruthenians in the United States.

That figure needs to be revised, however. First of all, the terms Ruthenian/Russniak are not entirely helpful, because many Ukrainians—at least before 1914—also identified themselves as Ruthenians. Nonetheless, informed observers suggest that during the pre-World War I period, at least 60 percent of immigrants classified as Ruthenians/Russniaks were from Carpatho-Rusyn inhabited villages in northeastern Hungary and the Lemko Region of Galicia. Therefore, between 1899 and 1914, at least 152,000 immigrants classified as Ruthenians/Russniaks arrived in the United States from the Carpatho-Rusyn homeland. We also know from 1910, 1920, and 1930 U.S. census reports that an average of 32 percent of Carpatho-Rusyn immigrants from Hungary (and later Czechoslovakia) described themselves as "Russians." This means another 73,000 must be added for a total of 225,000.

Yet even this figure has its limitations, because it does not include immigration before 1899 nor those Rusyns who chose to identity—or who were identified by others—as Austrians, Hungarians, Poles, Slovaks, or simply as "Slavish." We know from other sources that the use of the name "Slavish" was particularly widespread. Nonetheless, by reworking official United States data, it can be concluded that before World War I at least 225,000 Carpatho-Rusyns immigrated to the United States.

Statistics from the sending countries have some value but limitations as well. For instance, Hungarian records indicated that 55,000 Rusyns left Hungary between 1889 and 1913; while official and unofficial sources suggest that for the longer period between 1880 and 1913 as many as 62,000 emigrated. Since 97 percent of Hungary's Rusyn emigrants went to the United States, the corrected figure would be 60,000.

The problem with these statistics is that they record only legal departures. Records from German ports, the preferred route for departure, show that only half of the immigrants who passed through those ports had left Hungary legally. Thus, it is reasonable to assume that they were twice as many Carpatho-Rusyns—120,000—who emigrated to the United States from Hungary alone before World War I. In the absence of equivalent emigration statistics specifically from Rusyn villages in the Lemko Region of Galicia, we can only provide a rough estimate. Since Lemko region villages comprise 31 percent of the total number of Carpatho-Rusyn inhabited villages, this would suggest that perhaps 55,000 Lemkos left for the United States before World War I.

Based on such limited data from the United States and sending countries, it is reasonable to assume that during the height of immigration from central and eastern Europe between the years 1880 and 1914, no less than 225,000 Carpatho-Rusyns immigrated to the United States. Subsequent immigration was on a much smaller scale, consisting of about 18,000 newcomers from Czechoslovakia and Poland during the interwar years and another 7,000 from those two countries and the Soviet Ukraine in the nearly half century after World War II.

Despite such immigration figures totaling over 250,000 for the period both before and after World War I, not to mention natural demographic growth rates that by the 1990s should have produced through offspring about two and one-half times the number of original immigrants, the present figures for Carpatho-Rusyns are wholly inadequate. In 1980, the United States Census Bureau recorded only 8,485 Ruthenians (at that time persons who answered Rusyn were classified as Russian). Then, in 1990, the census recorded a total of 12,946 persons who classified themselves in five categories: Carpatho-Rusyn (7,316), Ruthenian (3,776), Rusyn (1,357), Carpathian (266), and Lemko (231). It is also likely that many Americans of Carpatho-Rusyn background are among the 315,285 persons who described themselves as Czechoslovakian, or the 122,469 Eastern Europeans, or the 70,552 Slavics/Slavish.

How, then, is it possible to obtain a more realistic estimate of the number of Americans today of Carpatho-Rusyn background? We may begin with the conservative estimate of 225,000 immigrants for the pre-1914 period. To this must be added the post-World War I immigration—primarily in the 1920s—of 8,000 from Czechoslovakia and 10,000 from the Lemko Region of what was then Poland. (Because of the world economic crisis of the 1930s and changing goals among immigrants no more than a few hundred returned home). This gives us 243,000.

Since the general population growth in the United States between 1930 and 1990 was 2½ fold, the pre-1930 first generation immigrants and their descendants should number today around 607,000. To these must be added several smaller waves of new arrivals that came after World War II: 4,000 who came in the wake of the war before 1950; 1,000 following the crisis in Czechoslovakia in 1968; and 2,000 in the course of political changes in Poland during the 1980s. Together with their descendants, the post-World War II group includes about 15,000, leaving a total of 622,000 Carpatho-Rusyns. While it is impossible to know the precise number of Americans of Carpatho-Rusyn background, a reasonable estimate would place the figure in 2000 somewhere between 600,000 and 625,000.

SOURCES: *13th, 14th and 15th Census of the United States* (Washington, D.C., 1913-33); Oleksander Mytsiuk, "Z emihratsïï uhro-rusyniv pered svitovoiu viinoiu," *Naukovyi zbirnyk tovarystva 'Prosvita'*, XIII-XIV (Užhorod, 1938), pp. 21-32; Wasyl Halich, Ukrainians in the United States (Chicago, 1937), esp. pp. 150-153; Julianna Puskás, *From Hungary to the United States, 1880-1914* (Budapest, 1982); Julianna Puskás, ed., *Overseas Migration from East-Central and South-Eastern Europe 1880-1940* (Budapest, 1990), esp. pp. 46-58.

workers who planned to return home after a few years) to Argentina or Uruguay, while about 10,000 from the Lemko Region—in what was by then Poland—went to settle permanently in Canada.

World War II interrupted the normal if limited flow of people, but it did lead to the phenomenon of displaced persons who for political reasons were unable or unwilling to return to their homeland. About 4,000 of these "DPs" were Carpatho-Rusyns who, between 1945 and 1950, eventually found their way, often via displaced persons camps in Germany and Austria, to the United States or Canada. By 1950, the Soviet Union and the east-central European countries under its political control effectively barred emigration from the Carpatho-Rusyn homeland for most of the four decades of Communist rule that lasted until 1989-1991.

The only exceptions were the brief periods of political liberalization in Czechoslovakia (1968) and Poland (1980-1981), which produced in their wake the arrival of about 5,000 new Carpatho-Rusyn immigrants to the United States and Canada.

Because of the lack of reliable statistics from Europe, the specific character of United States statistics, and the tendency of many immigrants to describe themselves in a manner other than Carpatho-Rusyn, we cannot know with any certainty the number of Carpatho-Rusyn Americans. Nonetheless, estimates based on United States census data, on statistics from sending countries, and on membership in churches suggest that by the early 1990s there were approximately 600,000 Carpatho-Rusyns and their descendants in the United States.

Carpatho-Rusyn Church Statistics in the United States

Church	Membership ca. 2000	Carpatho-Rusyn Membership (estimate)
Byzantine Ruthenian Catholic Metropolitan Archdiocese	99,000	80,000
American Carpatho-Russian Orthodox Diocese	20,000	18,000
Orthodox Church in America	115,000*	60,000
Russian Orthodox Church in the U.S.A. —the Patriarchal Parishes	10,000 (1985 figure)	8,000
Other Orthodox, Ukrainian Catholic, Roman Catholic, and Protestant denominations	—	150,000
Total		316,000

*Traditionally, figures for all Orthodox jurisdictions have been inflated, with the Orthodox Church in America claiming 1,000,000 members. Recent data supplied by the church itself suggests the numbers provided above. These include dues-paying registered members (just over one-third the total number) and adherents, that is, those who attend only sporadically.

SOURCE: *The Official Catholic Directory 2004* (New Providence, N.J., 2004); Alexei D. Krindatch, "Orthodox (Eastern Christian) Churches in the United States at the Beginning of the New Millennium," *Journal for the Scientific Study of Religion*, XLI, 3 (2002), pp. 533-563.

Chapter 3

Settlement Patterns and Economic Life

The initial and subsequent geographical distribution of Carpatho-Rusyn immigrants in the United States reflects their socioeconomic background, their goals, and the needs of American society in the decades before World War I, a time when the vast majority arrived. The newcomers were for the most part poor peasants, 65 percent of whom arrived before 1914 with less than $30 in money and belongings. With meagre financial resources, they were in no position to buy the relatively expensive land in the northeastern states near the port of their arrival—Ellis Island in New York City's harbor—nor to travel long distances by train to the west where cheap land was still available.

In any case, most did not plan to make the United States their permanent home. Their stay was to be merely for a few years, or as long as it took to earn enough money in order to return home and buy that all-important peasant commodity—land. Because most were temporary sojourners, they were interested in finding whatever jobs would pay the most. As for American society, it was going through a period of rapid industrial expansion, especially in the northeast, and was therefore in need of a large, unskilled industrial work force to man its mines and factories. Thus, the needs of American industry and the desires of Carpatho-Rusyn immigrants complemented each other.

Carpatho-Rusyn immigrants settled for the most part in the northeast. The first center to attract the newcomers during the 1880s and 1890s was the coal-mining belt in eastern Pennsylvania, near Scranton and Wilkes-Barre, and in smaller coal towns like Hazleton, Freeland, Mahanoy City, and Olyphant. The industrial plants of New York City and its suburb Yonkers, as well as the southern Connecticut city of Bridgeport and the northern New Jersey factories and oil refineries in Passaic, Bayonne, Elizabeth, Rahway, Perth Amboy, and Manville also attracted Carpatho-Rusyn immigrants in search of work. But by the outset of the twentieth century, the newest center of settlement became western Pennsylvania, most especially Pittsburgh and its suburbs like Homestead, Munhall, McKeesport, McKees Rocks, Monessen, Braddock, Clairton, and Duquesne. In these places, as well as in Johnstown about 75 miles to the east, it was the steel mills and related industries that provided jobs for Rusyns and other immigrants of Slavic background.

Soon concentrations of Carpatho-Rusyns were found in other industrial centers: Binghamton, Endicott, and Johnson City in south-central New York; Cleveland, Parma, and Youngstown in Ohio; Gary and Whiting in Indiana; Chicago and Joliet in Illinois; Detroit and Flint in Michigan; and Minneapolis in Minnesota. It is not surprising, therefore, that in the decade 1910-1920, as high as 79 percent of the Carpatho-Rusyns lived in the urban areas of the Middle Atlantic states. This included 54 percent in Pennsylvania, 13 percent in New York, and 12 percent in New Jersey, followed by Ohio, Connecticut, and Illinois. Despite this basic settlement pattern centered in the northeast industrial belt, it is interesting to note that some Carpatho-Rusyns ventured to a few out-of-the-way and unexpected places. Thus, the marble industry attracted

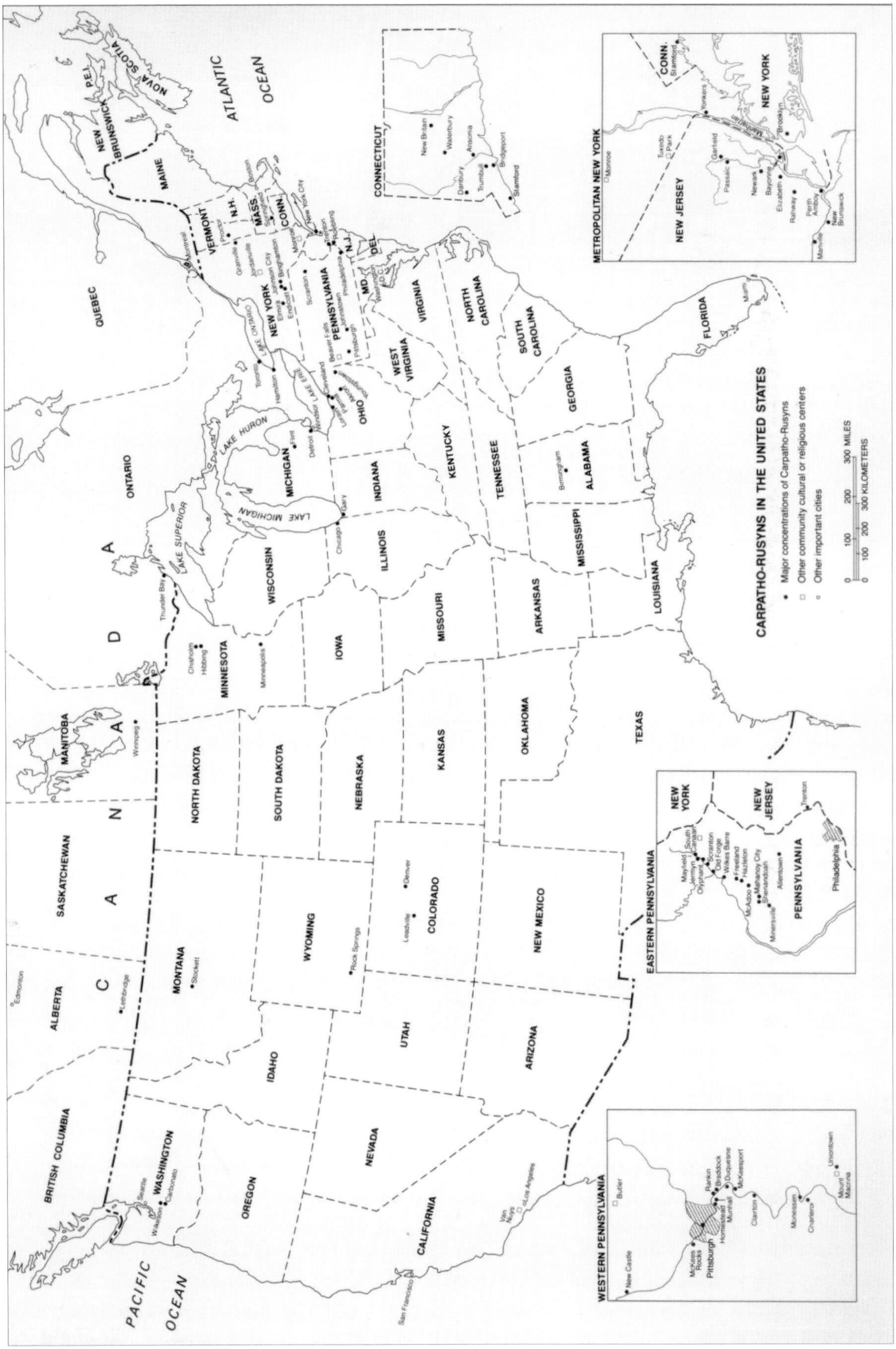

CARPATHO-RUSYNS IN THE UNITED STATES

- ● Major concentrations of Carpatho-Rusyns
- □ Other community cultural or religious centers
- ○ Other important cities

MAP 4

6.   Workers on their way to the coal mines in Lattimore, Pennsylvania, circa 1900 (photo by Rise and Gates).

a small group who established a community in Proctor, Vermont, while some went south to start farms in Virginia or to work in the steel mills of Birmingham, Alabama. In the mid-west, Carpatho-Rusyns were drawn to the coal mines around Royalton in southern Illinois; to the varied industries of St. Louis, Missouri and the steel mills of nearby Granite City, Illinois; to the lead mines around Bonne Terre and Desloge, Missouri; to the coal mines near Hartshorne and Haileyville, Oklahoma; and farther north to the iron mines of Chisholm and Hibbing in upstate Minnesota. Some even ventured as far west as the gold, silver, and lead mines in Leadville, Colorado; the railroad in Rock Springs, Wyoming; the copper mines in Stockett, Montana; and the coal mining settlements of Carbonado and Wilkeson in the Carbon River valley just south of Seattle, Washington.

In view of the temporary nature of their intended stay in the New World, Carpatho-Rusyns often moved into company-owned houses and tenements near the mines or factories where they worked. A high percentage of single males (which characterized the group before World War I) lived in boardinghouses often supervised by the wife of a Carpatho-Rusyn or fellow

Slavic immigrant. While these early living quarters were often overcrowded and polluted with industrial smoke and noise—a far cry from the placid rural environment of the Carpathian mountain homeland—they nonetheless did provide a certain degree of psychological security in an otherwise strange land in that the majority of their neighbors were Rusyns or other Slavic immigrants from central and eastern Europe.

By the 1920s, political conditions in Europe (including the upheaval of World War I that had cut off migration across the Atlantic) as well as adaption to American life (enhanced by a gradual increase in monetary savings and the establishment of family life through marriages in the New World or the arrival of wives and children from the Old) were factors which convinced many Carpatho-Rusyns that their temporary work visits might preferably become permanent. When, by the 1950s, Carpatho-Rusyns had become psychologically as well as physically established in America, some first-generation immigrants, and certainly their second- and third-generation descendants, began to move out of the company-owned houses and inner-city tenements to the surrounding suburbs. With the decline of American inner cities, especially during the 1970s, the traditional "Carpatho-Rusyn ghettos" all but disappeared in the downtown areas of cities like New York, Passaic, Pittsburgh, and Cleveland. The churches do remain, however, and are attended mainly by parishioners who arrive in cars to spend a few hours each Sunday morning before returning to their suburban homes.

While the desire to remain in or near one's original birthplace in the northeastern United States continued to be strong, by the 1970s a new trend had developed. Following general demographic and settlement patterns in the United States, Carpatho-Rusyns began moving to the sun-belt states of Florida, California, and Arizona. Those who have chosen this route include the original first-generation immigrants and their now also elderly second-generation offspring who fear the dangers of urban life in the northeast and who, at their advanced age, prefer the warmer climates of the south and west, as well as second-, third-, and fourth-generation professionals who are forced to move at the behest of their employers.

Despite these relatively recent demographic developments, the majority of the Carpatho-Rusyns as well as their religious and secular organizations remain within the industrial cities of the northeastern and north-central states. For instance, of the 300 parishes in the Byzantine Ruthenian Catholic Church and the American Carpatho-Russian Orthodox Diocese, 80 percent are still located in four states: Pennsylvania (50 percent), Ohio (13 percent), New Jersey (11 percent), and New York (6 percent).

Since the vast majority of Carpatho-Rusyns who arrived in the United States were poor peasants, it is not surprising that, with few exceptions, they were forced to seek their livelihood among the ranks of unskilled laborers. Thus, the first generation found employment in the factories, mines, and steel mills of the northeast United States. In the coal industry, where many obtained their first jobs, they began as miner's helpers usually receiving no more than a third of the miner's

7.   Women workers, including many Carpatho-Rusyns, on the assembly line at the Endicott-Johnson Shoe Company Jigger Factory, Johnson City, New York, circa 1930.

normal wage, while in factories and steel mills they were first hired to do the most menial tasks. Gradually, they moved up to become miners or semi-skilled and skilled factory laborers in their own right. Because they generally were at the lowest end of the working man's income level, it was not surprising to find Carpatho-Rusyns taking part in the many strikes that rocked the industrial and coal mining regions of Pennsylvania and neighboring states, especially in the decades before World War I. Still, it must be admitted that because Rusyn workers were primarily concerned with earning quick cash in order to return to the European homeland, they were likely to accept harsher work conditions and to avoid strike and anti-company activity which might jeopardize their goals.

Carpatho-Rusyn women, who began to come in larger numbers just before and after World War I, often found employment—especially if they were single—as servants or maids in the households of wealthy Americans and the increasing number of well-to-do eastern European Jews and Slavs. As they became more adjusted to the American environment, Carpatho-Rusyn women began to work as waitresses or retail salespersons and in light industries such as shoe, soap, and cigar factories, or in laundries and garment works. Those women who were already or who became married were expected to remain at home and care for the children and household. Besides these onerous tasks, however, they often had to supplement their husband's income—especially in times of economic hardship or strikes—by hiring themselves out as domestics or by working part-time in stores or mills.

There were, of course, among Carpatho-Rusyns, a small number of more ambitious individuals who from the earliest years of the immigration tried their luck at founding and operating small businesses. Among the most popular outlets were enterprises that served the needs of their fellow immigrants, such as butcher shops, groceries, taverns, and small restaurants. Some even entered the ranks of white-collar businessmen, as operators of funeral homes, travel and package-sending agencies, or as editors and officers in community organizations, most especially the fraternals. Women also expanded their economic potential by turning their residences into boardinghouses, where they provided rooms and cooked meals for single male workers.

As individuals whose original peasant mentality placed great importance on acquiring material security and a modicum of wealth, Carpatho-Rusyns could accept quite easily the American mainstream ideology which promised rewards for those who worked hard and lived a "decent," even frugal life. The same peasant mentality also contained, however, an undisciplined come-what-may attitude, which sometimes led to an unending cycle of hard work (according to the merciless clock of modern industry and not the more humane "sun clock" of nature) followed by "relief" in heavy drinking. Not surprisingly, frequent and often daily visits to the local tavern (korčma) on the way home from work would cut deeply into whatever savings had been acquired. Alcoholism, especially in the early years, became a problem for many Carpatho-Rusyn workers, although they soon learned that if they wanted to improve their financial status they would have to become more disciplined and to give up the tradition of less structured work and living habits.

It seems that the American environment and the attraction of potentially improved living circumstances proved to be the stronger force. Even in the early years, official United States statistics (1904-1905) reported that along with Bulgarians and other South Slavic immigrants, "Ruthenians" had the lowest proportion (.04 percent) of people in public charities and, for that matter, in penal institutions. Subsequently, the few statistics that are available show a distinct rise in the economic status of Carpatho-Rusyns. By the second generation, that is, among the American-born who began their working careers after World War I, the majority of Carpatho-Rusyns had become skilled and semi-skilled workers, foremen, or clerical workers. By the third generation, there was a marked increase in managerial and semi-professional occupations.

Nonetheless, it seems that the socioeconomic structure of third- and fourth-generation Carpatho-Rusyns is not as oriented toward upward social mobility as that of other groups—Jews, Italians, Greeks, Hungarians—whose parents and grandparents also arrived in large numbers at the outset of the twentieth century. To be sure, there were a few large companies founded by Carpatho-Rusyns who became wealthy through business skills, such as the Peerless Aluminum Foundry in Bridgeport, Connecticut of the Peter Hardy family, the Manhattan Building Supply in New York City of the

8.   Coal miner families relaxing on a Sunday afternoon in eastern Pennsylvania, circa 1900.

Mahonec family, and the Liberty Tool Corporation in Bridgeport, Connecticut of John Cipkala. There was even a Hungaro-Russian Slavonic State Bank that operated during the first decades of this century in Johnstown, Pennsylvania under the direction of George Kondor.

Particularly successful in the business world was the son of Lemko immigrants to Canada and later the New York investor, Paul M. Fekula. Raised in the Orthodox religious tradition, Fekula was embued with a Russian identity and Pan-Slavic spirit which led him to amass the largest private collection of Slavic books and old manuscripts in North America. But by far the most successful private entrepreneur was Stephen B. Roman, a native of the Prešov Region in Slovakia and a self-professed "Rusnak Slovak." Roman was one of the earliest developers of uranium mining in Canada. He founded and until his death in the late 1980s headed Denison Mines Limited, a multimillion dollar con-

glomerate based in Toronto, Ontario with several subsidiary companies in oil, gas, coal, potash, and banking located in Canada and other countries. Aside from his business interests, Roman was a fervent community activist and especially instrumental in the creation in 1982 of the Slovak Byzantine-rite Catholic Diocese of Canada.

The Carpatho-Rusyn immigration has also produced a small but steadily increasing number of professionals—lawyers, physicians, dentists, university professors, and, in particular, school teachers and nurses—most of whom are from the second, third, and fourth generation. Nonetheless, the ultimate goal for most Rusyns is to attain a place in "middle-class" America and to be satisfied with working for an established company which provides limited advancement but a measure of financial security that will permit the ownership of one's own home and a modest bank account.

Chapter 4

Religious Life

Another part of the cultural traditions or collective psyche that Carpatho-Rusyns brought to America was their attitude toward religion. Religion, in the form of Eastern Christianity, had always been an integral part of Carpatho-Rusyn community life, at least until the advent of Communist-dominated governments in their homeland after 1945. The whole village life-cycle used to be governed by the church. The traditional peasant mode of existence, determined by the climatic changes of the agricultural seasons, was interspersed by numerous religious holidays, including workless Sundays and other feast days of the church calendar, baptisms, marriages, and funerals—all carried out according to the fixed guidelines of the church. Since religious life was so bound up with the Carpatho-Rusyn mentality, it was only natural that the first immigrants attempted to recreate for themselves a similar environment in the United States. In this they were quite successful, so that even after three, four, and five generations, Carpatho-Rusyn community life in the United States continues to rely almost exclusively on an individual's relation to the church.

In essence, the history of Carpatho-Rusyns in the United States is virtually synonymous with the group's religious development. And this development has been the story of the successes and failures of the Greek (later known as the Byzantine Ruthenian) Catholic Church in its attempts to maintain its traditional rights and privileges in the face of encroachments by the dominant Roman Catholic hierarchy. Nonetheless, at various times the Greek (Byzantine Ruthenian)

Catholic Church has had to forfeit certain traditions. This has led to rebellion on the part of many Carpatho-Rusyn priests and parishioners, who consequently left their original church and either joined existing religious bodies, especially various Orthodox churches, or set up new ones.

The organizational history of the Greek Catholic Church began with the establishment of its very first parishes, including three in eastern Pennsylvania—Shenandoah (1884), Freeland (1886), Hazleton (1887)—and one in Minneapolis, Minnesota (1887). For nearly three decades, these and other early parishes included Greek Catholics not only from the Hungarian Kingdom (Carpatho-Rusyns as well as Slovaks and some Magyars), but also those from north of the Carpathian Mountains in Austrian Galicia, including Rusyns who called themselves Lemkos and those who after living in America began to identify themselves as Ukrainians or as Russians.

It was the people themselves who took the initiative to organize parishes, build churches, and request priests from Europe. The very first Greek Catholic priest to arrive in America was Father John Volansky, who in 1884 came to Shenandoah, Pennsylvania. He was followed by Zenon Liakhovych and Constantine Andrukhovych, both of whom were also from Galicia. The next priest to arrive, in 1889, was Father Alexander Dzubay, who was the first to come from Rusyn lands south of the Carpathians in Hungary. From then on, the majority of priests came from Hungary, so that by 1894, out of more than 20 Greek Catholic priests,

9.   St. Mary's Greek Catholic Church, Freeland, Pennsylvania, built 1887. This is the original church of the oldest parish still within the Byzantine Ruthenian Catholic Church.

10.   One of the earliest group photographs in the United States of Byzantine Rite (Greek) Catholic priests, Wilkes Barre, Pennsylvania, 1890. Seated left to right: Gabriel Vislocky, Ivan Zapotocky, Alexis Toth, Theofan Obushkevich; standing left to right: Eugene Volkay, Alexander Dzubay, Stefan Jackovics, Gregory Hrushka

only 4 were from Galicia.

These early priests arrived in an environment that was not hospitable to Greek (Byzantine-rite) Catholicism. Volansky, for instance, was not recognized by the Latin-rite Archbishop of Philadelphia, Patrick J. Ryan, who forbade him to perform his priestly functions. Not only was the Irish-dominated Roman Catholic hierarchy unsympathetic, but fellow Slavic Catholic priests, especially Poles, also scorned these seemingly strange Eastern-rite Catholics.

The main reason for the generally cold reception was the ignorance that prevailed among American Catholic leaders about anything other than the Latin rite within their own "universal" church. Another factor was the trend in certain Catholic circles and public life in general known as Americanization. There was even a National Americanization Committee, which was engaged in an effort to make the foreign-born "give up the languages, customs, and methods of life which they have brought with them across the ocean, and to adopt instead the language, habits, and customs of this country, and the general standards and ways of American living."[1] And if the habits of immigrants from the old country might be difficult to change, then for sure their American-born or acculturized children must become fully assimilated. The best way to achieve that goal and the process of Americanization in general was through the school system, which should instill "an appreciation of the institutions of this country and absolute forgetfulness of all obligations or connections with other countries, because of descent or birth."[2]

In this connection, it should be remembered that the Catholic Church in the United States had, since colonial days, experienced varying kinds of discrimination and lingering social intolerance, the kind of intolerance encountered by all religious groups that did not belong to mainstream Protestantism. Although the Roman Catholic Church officially condemned Americanization, a few Catholic leaders welcomed certain aspects of it in the hope that their church would finally be accepted fully into American society. Hence, in an attempt to prove their "Americanness," Catholic leaders headed by Bishop Ryan in Philadelphia and Bishop John Ireland in St. Paul, Minnesota were anxious to remove all ethnic distinctions within the Roman Catholic Church. The church was simply to became an American institution and an instrument of assimilation. Through such a "progressive" policy, these Catholic leaders hoped finally to have Catholicism fully accepted in American life.

It was into such an environment that Greek or Byzantine-rite Catholics arrived. While it is true that the ethnic Poles or Slovaks—even the "racially" more acceptable Germans—may have used their native languages and still have followed certain Old-World religious practices, they at least were of the Latin rite. The Carpatho-Rusyns, on the other hand, were of the Byzantine rite; therefore, they used Church Slavonic instead of Latin in their liturgies and they observed the Julian calendar (about two weeks later) instead of the "normal" Gregorian calendar. And as if that was not bad enough, their priests could be married. For the Roman Catholic prelates this seemed the ultimate anathema! Not surprisingly, therefore, Bishop Ryan's rejection of Father Volansky was repeated time and again toward other Greek Catholic priests. They were often forbidden to issue the sacraments, to bury their parishioners in Roman Catholic cemeteries, and they were snubbed by the Roman Catholic clergy in the communities where they lived.

Left to its own devices, the community and its few priests took matters into their own hands. Often with the help of Carpatho-Rusyn businessmen, parishes bought property and built their own churches, which might include a meeting hall and school below the sanctuary or in a separate building. Because of the initiative of laymen in organizing church life, these early years set a pattern whereby secular leaders felt they had the right as well as obligation to be concerned with the religious developments of the community. For instance, church property was often not registered in the name of the bishop representing a diocese (as was to become standard Catholic practice), but rather in the name of a board of lay trustees within each individual parish. The existence of this legal arrangement subsequently

---

[1] From a leaflet published by the National Americanization Committee, cited in Milton M. Gordon, *Assimilation in American Life* (New York, 1964), p. 101.

[2] Statement in 1918 by the Superintendent of the New York Public Schools, cited in Gordon, *Assimilation*, pp. 100-101.

11. The existence of married priests was to cause great difficulties for Byzantine Rite (Greek) Catholics in America. Here the wedding of Emil Gulyassy (to the right of the bride with flowers, Lily Mihalich) before his ordination to the priesthood. Father Anthony Mhley (on the far right) was the officiating priest at Holy Ghost Greek Catholic Church, Charleroi, Pennsylvnia, 1922.

12. Secular trustees were to control many of the early Rusyn-American churches. The trustees together with three priests—top row, left to right: Fathers Nicholas Szabados, Thomas Szabo, and Cornelius Laurisin of St. Michael's Church, St. Clair, Pennsylvania, circa 1912.

was to have serious consequences for the church.

It was not long before the Vatican became aware of the difficulties that had developed between the Roman and rapidly growing Greek Catholic communities in the United States. In an attempt to clarify the situation, on October 1, 1890, the Vatican issued its first decree concerning the Greek Catholic Church in America. The decree specified that newly arriving Greek Catholic priests were to report to, receive jurisdiction from, and remain under the authority of the local Latin-rite bishop. Moreover, all priests had to be celibate and married priests were to be recalled to Europe. As an addendum, another Vatican decree in 1895 declared that in areas where there were no Greek Catholic churches, the parishioners could become Roman Catholic.

As might be expected, many Greek Catholic priests felt that their century-old traditions dating back to the Union of Brest (1596) and Union of Užhorod (1646) were not being honored by Rome and were being directly undermined by an unsympathetic American Catholic hierarchy. Thus, already in late 1890 and

13. Father Alexis G. Toth

again in late 1891 groups of Greek Catholic priests met and concluded that their increasingly unfavorable plight would not improve until they had their own bishop. In the interim, they requested the appointment of a Carpatho-Rusyn vicar general who, in the person of Father Nicephor Chanat, was chosen to act as an intermediary between Greek Catholic priests and Latin-rite bishops.

More serious was the case of Father Alexis G. Toth. Toth was a respected seminary professor and chancellor of the Eparchy of Prešov in the Carpatho-Rusyn region of Hungary who, in 1889, was sent to the United States to serve in the parish in Minneapolis. Upon his arrival, Toth reported as expected to the local Latin-rite ordinary, Archbishop John Ireland of St. Paul. Ireland was the foremost spokesman of the Americanization movement, and because of his desire to eliminate ethnic differences, it is not surprising that he was already negatively disposed toward this new priest from east-central Europe. Because of the importance of Toth's later activity, it would be useful to quote him directly about the fateful meeting with Bishop Ireland. The following is taken from Toth's courtroom testimony delivered in 1894:

> As an obedient Uniate [Greek Catholic], I complied with the orders of my Bishop, who at the time was John Valyi [of the Eparchy of Prešov] and appeared before Bishop Ireland on December 19, 1889, kissed his hand according to custom and presented my credentials, failing, however, to kneel before him, which, as I learned later, was my chief mistake. I remember that no sooner did he read that I was a 'Greek Catholic', his hands began to shake. It took him fifteen minutes to read to the end after which he asked abruptly—we conversed in Latin:
>
> 'Have you a wife?'
>
> 'No.'
>
> 'But you had one?'
>
> 'Yes, I am a widower.'
>
> At this he threw the paper on the table and loudly exclaimed: 'I have already written to Rome protesting against this kind of priests being sent to me!'
>
> 'What kind of priests do you mean?'
>
> 'Your kind.'
>
> 'I am a Catholic priest of the Greek rite. I am a Uniate and was ordained by a regular Catholic Bishop.'
>
> 'I do not consider that either you or this bishop of yours

are Catholic; besides, I do not need any Greek Catholic priests here; a Polish priest in Minneapolis is quite sufficient; the Greeks can also have him for their priest.'

'But he belongs to the Latin rite; besides our people do not understand him and so they will hardly go to him; that was the reason they instituted a church of their own.'

'They had no permission from me and I shall grant you no jurisdiction to work here.'

Deeply hurt by the fanaticism of this representative of Papal Rome, I replied sharply: 'In that case, I know the rights of my church, I know the basis on which the Union was established and shall act accordingly.'

The Archbishop lost his temper. I lost mine just as much. One word brought another, the thing had gone so far that our conversation is not worth putting on record.[3]

Despite Bishop Ireland's refusal to recognize Father Toth, the latter continued to serve his Carpatho-Rusyn parish and hope for some favorable intervention from his bishop in Europe. When no help was forthcoming, Toth felt that the centuries-old traditions of his church, recognized by Rome as canonically legal, were being violated in the New World. He therefore decided to abjure the Catholic church altogether and to convert to Orthodoxy. He travelled to San Francisco, where a Russian Orthodox bishop was residing. The result was that on March 25, 1891, Father Toth and his community of 365 Carpatho-Rusyns were formally accepted by Bishop Vladimir Sokolovsky into the Russian Orthodox Diocese of Alaska and the Aleutian Islands.

For its part, the Russian Orthodox Church was only too willing to accept Toth and his flock, for at the time Russia's tsarist government was supporting liberally the spread of Orthodoxy both in Europe and the New World. The talented Toth was before long sent on missionary work to Pennsylvania, where he succeeded in converting many more Carpatho-Rusyns to the Orthodox faith. It has been estimated that by the time of his death in 1909, this energetic priest "brought back" more than 25,000 Carpatho-Rusyns (three-quarters of whom were from the Lemko Region in Galicia) into the fold of Orthodoxy. These converts and their de-

scendants have since then formed the largest portion of the membership in the Russian Orthodok Greek Catholic Church in America (later the "Metropolia" and now the Orthodox Church in America). For his services, Toth has been hailed by the church as the "father of Orthodoxy" in the United States and in 1994 was proclaimed a saint.

Toth's proselytizing efforts did not end with his passing from the scene. They were, in fact, increased in intensity under the energetic Archbishop Platon Rozhdestvensky, who headed the Russian Orthodox Church in North America from 1907 to 1914. During his tenure, no less than 72 parishes or communities were received into Orthodoxy, most of them containing "Carpatho-Russian" Greek Catholics who were being urged to seek their "true home" in the Russian Orthodox Church.

In addition, Toth and Platon's missionary work was also felt beyond the borders of the New World. Some of his immigrant converts, who had returned temporarily or permanently to Europe, often brought Orthodox literature (published in Russia and the United States) and dollars back to the Rusyn homeland. In fact, the first revival of Orthodoxy among Carpatho-Rusyns in Europe began during the 1890s and was the result

[3]Cited in Keith S. Russin, "Father Alexis G. Toth and the Wilkes-Barre Litigations," St. Vladimir's Theological Quarterly, XVI, 3 (Crestwood, N.Y., 1972), pp. 132-133.

14. The original building of St. Mary's Church, Minneapolis, built 1888, the first Greek Catholic parish to join the Orthodox Church.

15. Brotherhood of the Apostles Peter and Paul, Minneapolis, founded 1891, composed of laymen from the parish of Father Alexis Toth (bottom center), who helped him in the struggle to join the Orthodox Church

of the confluence of American immigrant dollars and Russian "rolling rubles" (funds supplied by the tsarist government) meeting in the valleys of the Carpathians.

Faced with these difficulties, the Vatican agreed in 1902 to appoint an apostolic visitor in order to study conditions among Greek Catholics in the United States. The individual chosen was Father Andrew Hodobay from the Prešov Eparchy, who after five years returned to Europe with recommendations for the appointment of a Greek Catholic bishop. From the beginning, however, Hodobay received little cooperation from Rusyn-American priests, a situation that illustrates another aspect of difficulties within the immigrant community.

Initially, all Carpatho-Rusyn and other Eastern-rite immigrants, whether from Galicia or northeastern Hungary, were united in the same Greek Catholic churches and, as we shall see, they belonged to the same frater-nal organizations. But almost from the outset, regional and national differences made it impossible to maintain this arrangement. From the Carpatho-Rusyn point of view, the problem arose when young priests from Galicia (Nestor Dmytriw, John Ardan, Stephan Makar, Anton Bonchevsky among others), who were embued with Ukrainian national feeling, tried to ukrainianize their parishes. The Galician Ukrainians looked, in turn, at their fellow Carpatho-Rusyn Lemkos from Galicia as Russophiles constantly susceptible to the Orthodox "schism," and at Carpatho-Rusyns from Hungary as Magyarones who, if they did not succumb to russification, were ever ready to sell out their Slavic heritage and to magyarize their parishes. Hence, by the 1890s each newly arrived Greek Catholic priest was scrutinized by community leaders to see whether he was from Galicia or from Hungary and whether he was a Ukrainophile, a Russophile, or a Magyarone.

The apostolic visitor was suspected of serving the magyarizing policy of the Hungarian government, and for that reason he was immediately boycotted by the Galicians (both Ukrainophile and Russophile) and later as well by many Carpatho-Rusyns (especially secular leaders) from Hungary. And if regional and national divisions were not enough, Rusyn priests were also divided along eparchial lines. This was especially prevalent among priests from Hungary, with the "aristocratic" clergy from the Mukačevo eparchy looking down on their brethren from the Prešov eparchy as being little more than uncouth "peasant types." Finally, added to the rivalries and bickering among priests was the increasingly strong influence of lay leaders, especially those associated with the first Carpatho-Rusyn fraternal organization known as the Greek Catholic Union (*Sojedinenije*) of Russian Brotherhoods. Secular community leaders were well aware that they were the ones who had paid for and built the churches, rectories, and schools and who supported the priests financially. Influenced by the new American environment in which they lived, they were not about to be "subjects as it is in the Old Country . . . . to pay, support, be silent, and obey." "In the land of the free," these lay leaders argued, "it would be ridiculous to support and work for a cause without representation."[4]

These varying levels of antagonism became especially apparent in 1907, when the Vatican finally appointed a bishop for America's Greek Catholics.

Ea Semper Decree

(Excerpts from *Acta Sancta Sedis*, Vol. XLI, Rome, 1908, pp. 3-12, trans. from Latin by Eric Csapo)

It has always been the special and proper concern of the Apostolic See that the various and diverse rites which adorn the Catholic Church be carefully preserved. Many provisions and statutes of our predecessors make clear declarations to this effect, especially as regards the venerable liturgies of the Eastern churches.

. . . . The rite of the Ruthenians could best be preserved unchanged and appropriately administered, and the Ruthenian faithful could with the approval of this council arm themselves more effectively against the dangers to which they lay exposed by the acts of schismatic citizens if a bishop were given to them. . . . We have taken counsel for the selection and nomination of a bishop who, invested with the necessary authority, will make every effort to see that the Ruthenian Greek rite be preserved unaltered in the various missions in the United States.

Article 1. The nomination of the bishop of the Ruthenian rite for the United States is a task fully reserved for the Apostolic See.

Article 2. The bishop of the Ruthenian rite is under the immediate jurisdiction and power of the Apostolic See and is to be overseen by the Apostolic Delegate in Washington. Moreover, he is to have no ordinary jurisdiction, but only that delegated to him by the respective bishops of the [Latin-rite] diocese in which the Ruthenians reside.

Article 3. The bishop of the Ruthenian rite will be able to visit his parishes provided he has the written permission of the [Latin-rite] bishop. The latter will confer such powers as he deems fit.

Article 4. When the bishop of the Ruthenian rite visits his parishes, he will ask for an account of the property of that parish from the respective rector, and he will see that the rector does not hold in his own name and right items acquired with the help of contributions made in any way by the faithful. . . . Title to such goods shall be either transferred to the local [Latin-rite] bishop as soon as possible or be firmly assigned in any secure and legal fashion approved by the same bishop and thereby remain in support of the parish.

Article 10. Since there are not yet any Ruthenian priests who were either born or even educated in the United States, the bishop of the Ruthenian rite, in consultation with the Apostolic Delegate and the local [Latin-rite] bishop, will make every effort to establish seminaries to educate Ruthenian priests in the United States as soon as possible. In the meantime, Ruthenian clergymen will be admitted to the Latin seminaries in the area

where they were born or in which they are domiciled. But only those who are celibate at present and who shall remain so may be promoted to the sacred orders.

Article 14. It is strictly forbidden Ruthenian priests who are resident in the United States to consign the baptized with holy chrism. It they do so despite the prohibition, they should know that their actions are invalid.

Article 17. All rectors of Ruthenian parishes in the United States are subject to dismissal at the discretion of the local [Latin-rite] bishop. The bishop of the Ruthenian rite is to be informed in good time. No dismissal, moreover, should be ordered without serious and fair cause.

Article 21. The Ruthenian faithful in those localities where no church nor priest of their rite is available will conform to the Latin rite. The same concession applies to those who are unable to go to their churches without great inconvenience because of distance, although no one should be induce to change rites by the provision.

Article 27. Marriage between Ruthenian and Latin Catholics is not prohibited, but a husband of the Latin rite may not follow the rite of his Ruthenian wife, nor a wife of the Latin rite follow the rite of her Ruthenian husband.

Article 34. Children born in the United States of America of a father of the Latin rite and a mother of the Ruthenian rite are to be baptized according to the Latin rite because offspring should follow the rite of their father in all respects if he is of the Latin rite.

Article 35. If the father should be of the Ruthenian rite and the mother of the Latin rite, the father is free to choose whether the child should be baptized by the Ruthenian rite or by the Latin rite, in case he so decides in consideration of his Latin-rite wife.

In the love of Christ, by which we the faithful of all rites are permanently bound, we consider these decisions necessary for the spiritual good and the health of the souls of the Ruthenian faithful residing in the United States of America. We have no doubt that they will receive these decisions taken on their behalf with gratitude and with perfect obedience.

The present letter and its every statute and content is not to be censured, impugned, called into question, or subjected to scrutiny for any reason, whatsoever. . . .

Dated at Rome, in Saint Peter's, in the year of our Lord 1907, on the fourteenth day of June, the festal day of Saint Basil the Great, in the fourth year of our [Pius X] papacy.

Actually, even before the appointment was made, Carpatho-Rusyn clergy and lay leaders wanted the nominee to be from Hungary, while the Ukrainophile priests and their supporters quite naturally wanted their own. In the end, the advice of the influential Greek Catholic Metropolitan from Galicia, Andrej Šeptyc'kyj, seemed to have been decisive, because in 1907 the Vatican appointed a priest from Galicia, Soter Ortynsky, to be the first Greek Catholic bishop in America. Instead of improving the situation, however, Ortynsky's appointment only added more fuel to a fire that had already alienated most Carpatho-Rusyns from their Galician Ukrainian co-religionists.

Because he was from Galicia and seemed to associate himself with Ukrainians, Bishop Ortynsky was opposed by many Carpatho-Rusyns from Hungary, who almost immediately began an "anti-Ortynsky" campaign. Their opposition took on particular intensity when Ortynsky, although against his personal convictions, was called upon to enforce the provisions of the latest Vatican decree. This was contained in a papal letter known as the *Ea Semper*, which was made public less than one month after the bishop's arrival in the United States on September 16, 1907. The document was intended to regulate relations between Latin- and Greek (Byzantine)- rite Catholics, with the intention to preserve the "venerable liturgies of the Eastern churches." It also became clear, however, that a separate American Greek Catholic diocese was not to be established and that the first bishop, Ortynsky, was in effect to be only an auxiliary to the Latin-rite bishops where Rusyns lived. Furthermore, Greek Catholic priests were not to administer the sacrament of confirmation, married seminarians were not to be ordained, and new priests were not to be sent to the United States without the advance approval of the American Catholic hierarchy. To the accusations that Ortynsky was a Ukrainian, another epithet was added: that he was a Latinizer ready to give in to every wish of Rome.

16. Bishop Soter Ortynsky.

In actual fact, Ortynsky protested to the Vatican, urging the repeal of the decree. Although his demand was ignored, those provisions of the *Ea Semper* decree which concerned traditional Greek Catholic practices, while left on the books, were not enforced. Nonetheless, several Carpatho-Rusyn priests and lay leaders, most especially from the influential Greek Catholic Union fraternal society, remained profoundly angered with the decree and continued to heap abuse on Ortynsky in their publications. They were in particular critical when Ortynsky attempted to enforce one provision of the *Ea Semper* decree—abandonment of the trustee system of church ownership, whereby all title to church property would be deeded to the bishop. Most Carpatho-Rusyn parishes simply refused to do this and some even went to court over this issue.

The attacks on the unfortunate bishop did not subside, even after the Vatican passed two more favorable decrees. In May 1913, Ortynsky was finally given full episcopal power, and in August 1914, according to a new Vatican decree, the *Cum Episcopo*, jurisdic-

---

[4] Michael Yuhasz in the *Amerikansky russky viestnik*, July 4, 1902, cited in John Slivka, *Historical Mirror: Sources of the Rusin and Hungarian Greek Rite Catholics in the United States of America 1884-1963* (Brooklyn, N.Y., 1978), p. 32.

Major Carpatho-Rusyn Religious Affiliations in the United States

Church	Diocese / Eparchy	Founding date	First hierarch	Present hierarch	Publications	Carpatho-Rusyn membership (estimate)
Byzantine Ruthenian Catholic Metropolitan Archdiocese (formerly Greek Catholic Exarchate of Pittsburgh)	Pittsburgh, Pennsylvania Passaic, New Jersey Parma, Ohio Van Nuys, California	1916/1924	Basil Takach	Basil Schott Andrew Pataki John Kudrick William Skurla	*Byzantine Catholic World* *Eastern Catholic Life* *Horizons*	80,000
American Carpatho-Russian Orthodox Diocese (formerly Carpatho-Russian Greek Catholic Diocese of the Eastern Rite)	Johnstown, Pennsylvania	1937	Orestes Chornock	Nicholas Smisko	*Church Messenger*	18,000
Orthodox Church in America (formerly Russian Orthodox Greek Catholic Church of America—the Metropolia)	Washington, All America, and Canada Pittsburgh, and Western Penn. New York and New Jersey Dallas and the South Detroit (and Romanian) Chicago and the Mid-West San Francisco and the West Ottawa and Canada Sitka, Anchorage, and Alaska Boston (and Albanian)	1794 1916—Carpatho-Russian Exarchy (Stephen Dzubay) 1951—Carpatho-Russian People's Church (Andrew Šlepecky)	Ioasaf Bolotov	Herman Swaiko Kyrill Yonchev Peter L'Huillier Dmitri Royster Nathaniel Popp Job Osacky Tikhon Fitzgerald Seraphim Storheim Nikolai Soraich Nikon Liolin	*Orthodox Church*	60,000
Russian Orthodox Church in the USA and Canada—the Partiarchal Parishes	New York, New York	1933 1943—Carpatho-Russian administration (Adam Philipovsky)	Benjamin Fedchenkov	Mercurius Ivanov	*One Church*	8,000

tional relations between Roman and Byzantine-rite Greek Catholics were clarified. The intention was to safeguard Greek Catholics from the predominantly American Roman Catholic environment in which they operated. Then, in an attempt to quell further discontent arising from regional rivalries, Bishop Ortynsky appointed two Carpatho-Rusyns from Hungary, Father Alexander Dzubay as his vicar-general and Father Augustine Komporday as his chancellor.

None of these acts, however, seemed to allay the fears of the Carpatho-Rusyns. Led by lay leaders from the Greek Catholic Union, they continued to argue that they form a distinct nationality. "The Uhro-Rusins have wholly different customs from the Galicians; their church hymns are different; and even in the performance of ceremonies there are noticeable differences."[5] Furthermore, Galician Ukrainians were accused of putting "nationalistic aims" above religious concerns. Arguments such as these were used not only in 1913, they have been used ever since by Carpatho-Rusyn secular and clerical spokesmen as justification for maintaining their distinctiveness and distance from Ukrainian Americans. Therefore, the Carpatho-Rusyns could "under no consideration renounce their intention of having their own Uhro-Rusin bishop" nor "acquiesce to being ecclesiastically united with the Galician Ukrainians," in order that "under the guise of the Catholic Church they might be thrown into the slavery of Ukrainianism."[6]

In the midst of an increasingly tense atmosphere within the Greek Catholic Church, Bishop Ortynsky unexpectedly died in 1916. Realizing the regional qua national divisions between the Carpatho-Rusyns and Galician Ukrainians who, if "they were to be forcibly united, there would be no peace and order but perpetual wrangling through which the Catholic Church would lose considerably,"[7] the Vatican decided to create two ecclesiastical administrations for Eastern-rite Catholics in the United States. Thus, instead of a single episcopal successor to Ortynsky, two administra-

17. Father Gabriel Martyak.

tors were appointed: Father Gabriel Martyak for the Greek Catholics from Hungary and Father Peter Poniatyshyn for Greek Catholics from Galicia. Indeed, no parish was composed exclusively of families from one region or the other, so that there were some Rusyns from Hungary in Galician parishes and vice-versa. Moreover, those Lemkos who remained Greek Catholics came under the Galician jurisdiction.

Eventually, this division along regional lines came to be associated as well with self-imposed ethnonational distinctions. Thus, while the "Hungarian" Greek Catholic administrative jurisdiction included Slovaks as well as a few Magyars and Croats, it soon came to be ethnically associated with its Carpatho-Rusyn majority and was to be known as the Byzantine Ruthenian Catholic Church. Similarly, while the Galician Greek Catholic administrative jurisdiction included Lemkos and some others who continued to identify themselves as Rusyns, sometimes even as Russians, the vast majority increasingly identified themselves ethnically as Ukrainians, so that the institution came to be known as

---

[5] Petition of the Greek Catholic Union to the Apostolic Delegate to the United States (1913), cited in Slivka, *Historical Mirror*, p. 105.

[6] Slivka, *Historical Mirror*, p. 106.

[7] Slivka, *Historical Mirror*, p. 105.

18. Bishop Stefan (Alexander) Dzubay upon consecration in 1916.

very least to be appointed administrator for Carpatho-Rusyns from Hungary. When he was passed over in favor of Martyak, the discontented Dzubay decided to leave the Catholic church altogether and to become an Orthodox monk. In rapid succession, he entered a monastery and took the name Stephen (July 30, 1916); he was elevated the very next day to archimandrite (July 31); he then agreed to be appointed bishop of a "Carpatho-Russian Subdiocese in Pittsburgh," and in the presence of the head of the Russian Orthodox Church in America and other Orthodox bishops was consecrated at St. Nicholas Orthodox Cathedral in New York City (August 20).

As Bishop Stephen, Dzubay established his residence in Pittsburgh and immediately began a campaign to convert Byzantine Ruthenian Catholics to Orthodoxy. He was able to convince several churches in the Pittsburgh area to go over to Orthodoxy, but he was less successful in obtaining a jurisdictionally-independent Carpatho-Russian diocese within the Russian Orthodox Church. Foreseeing this unlikelihood, Dzubay decided in late 1922 to consecrate Father Adam Philipovsky as archbishop of Philadelphia and Carpatho-Russians, with jurisdiction over 30 to 40 parishes of mostly recent converts to Orthodoxy from among Lemko immigrants from Galicia. Following an independent course, this "Carpatho-Russian Exarchy" never grew in size, and Bishop Philipovsky was from the outset plagued by involvement in the jurisdictional disputes that characterized Russian Orthodoxy in America during the years after World War I. The outcome of those disputes was the eventual creation of three separate jurisdictions: (1) the Russian Orthodox Greek Catholic Church, which remained loyal to the mother church in Russia, although it insisted on the status of autonomy, thereby becoming popularly known as the Metropolia; (2) the Russian Orthodox Church Outside Russia, which refused to recognize the patriarch in Soviet Russia and prefered to be ruled in the traditional collegial or synodal manner, thereby becoming popularly known as the Synod Abroad; and (3) the Russian Orthodox Church in the U.S.A., comprised of parishes which remained directly under the authority of the patriarch in Moscow, thereby becoming popularly known as the Patriarchal Exarchate. As we shall see, it was not uncommon for parishes, priests, and hierarchs to move from one Orthodox ju-

the Ukrainian Catholic Church. Thus, the administrative division of 1916 was, in a sense, a latent recognition of the deep ethnic, cultural, and psychological differences that had existed from the very beginning among America's Eastern-rite Catholics. This move toward separation ushered in a new period of peace and stability within the two branches—Byzantine Ruthenian and Ukrainian—of the Greek or Byzantine-rite Catholic Church.

Not that this was the end of problems which could still deeply effect the church's development. In fact, already by 1916, a new crisis arose within the Byzantine Ruthenian administration. The vicar-general, Alexander Dzubay, was a leading candidate for bishop after Ortynsky's death. Moreover, Dzubay had the support of the powerful Greek Catholic Union. And as the senior member of the clergy, he expected at the risdiction to another, moves that were often accompanied by great controversy and that in some cases led to legal battles in the American court system.

As for Bishop Dzubay, he soon became frustrated with the failure to create a distinct Carpatho-Rusyn Orthodox diocese which he expected to head. Consequently, he turned his attention to the Russian Orthodox Church as a whole. Taking advantage of the breakdown in communications with the Russian homeland (ruled after 1917 by a Soviet regime) and the resultant confusion within the Orthodox movement in the United States, Dzubay convoked an Orthodox Council (sobor) in October 1922 and proclaimed himself to be "acting head" of the entire Russian Orthodox Church in America. Although followed by several priests, in early 1924 Dzubay relinquished his claims and recognized the newly elected Orthodox Metropolitan Platon. Frustrated at every turn in his overambitious bid for power, by late 1924 Dzubay renounced his Orthodox bishopric, begged for forgiveness, and returned to the fold of Byzantine-rite Catholicism. He spent the last eight years of his life as a secluded penitent in a Roman Catholic monastery.

Dzubay's career is of interest because it reveals a pattern that began to take shape already in 1891 with Father Toth. It is a pattern which has continued in some cases down to the present day. In essence, Orthodoxy became a safety-valve for discontented Greek/Byzantine Ruthenian Catholics, both among the clergy and lay parishioners. Whenever there was reason for discontent and for whatever the cause, whether threats to Eastern religious tradition, refusal to relinquish parish-owned church property, frustrated personal ambition, or simply dislike for the local priest, Byzantine Ruthenian Catholics could always count on being accepted (and in the case of some priests often being given high posts) within one of the Orthodox churches.

Having reviewed these early years of the Carpatho-Rusyn religious community, one might conclude that because the Greek (Byzantine-rite) Catholic Church was being constantly rent by internal regional and national divisions and by external pressure from an antagonistic American Catholic clergy, the number of its adherents was continually on the decline. At the same time, its Orthodox rivals—not to mention the Latin-rite churches and Protestant sects—were gaining at the expense of the Greek Catholics. In order not to get the wrong impression, one should remember that all these developments were taking place precisely at a time when Carpatho-Rusyns were flocking to the United States in larger numbers than ever before or after. The result was that, despite defections, the Greek Catholic Church did actually continue to grow, so that by the time Ortynsky received full episcopal powers in 1913, he had jurisdiction over 152 churches, 154 priests, and 500,000 communicants from Galicia, Bukovina, and Hungary.

The next important development came in 1924, when the Vatican decided to replace the temporary Byzantine-rite administrators with bishops. Father Basil Takach from the Eparchy of Mukačevo, which at the time was within the borders of the new republic of Czechoslovakia, was named bishop of the newly created Pittsburgh Exarchate. The exarchate was to have jurisdiction over all Byzantine-rite Catholics from the former Kingdom of Hungary. Upon its establishment, the exarchate comprised 155 churches, 129 priests, and 288,000 parishioners. Simultaneously, Father Constantine Bohachevsky was named bishop for

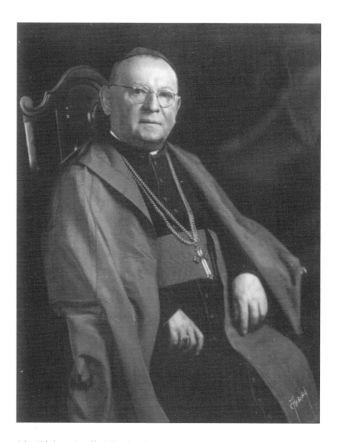

19. Bishop Basil Takach (photo by Parry).

Cum Data Fuerit Decree

(Excerpts from the first published version in the *Leader/Vožď*, II, 12, December 1930, pp. 20-23)

Article 1. The nomination of the bishops is reserved to the Apostolic See.

Article 6. In order to safeguard the temporal goods of the Church, the bishops shall not permit rectors of the churches or boards of administrators to possess in their own right goods contributed in any manner by the faithful. They shall insist that the property be held in a manner that makes it safe for the church according to the laws of the various States. They shall issue rules concerning the administration of the church property.

Article 12. Before the Greek-Ruthenian Church has a sufficient number of priests educated in the United States, the bishops may through the Sacred Congregation for the Oriental Church ask the Greek-Ruthenian bishops of Europe to send them priests. Priests who are not called by the bishops or sent by the Sacred Congregation, but come to the United States of their own accord, cannot be given faculties by the Greek-Ruthenian bishops in the United States, either for saying Mass, or for the administration of the Sacraments, or for any ecclesiastical work. **The priests who wish to come to the United States and stay there must be celibates.**

Article 37. Associations of the faithful of the Greek-Ruthenian rite shall be under the vigilance of the bishops, who shall name the priest who is to have charge of these associations, in order to avoid any abuses with regard to faith, morals, or discipline. Hence it is praiseworthy on the part of the faithful to join associations which have been formed, or at least approved, by ecclesiastical authority. **The faithful should be on their guard, however, against associations which are secret, condemned, seditious, suspect, or which seek to elude the supervision of lawful ecclesiastical authority.**

Likewise Catholic newspapers, magazines, and periodicals are under the supervision of the bishop, and without his permission priests should neither write in them nor manage them.

His Holiness, Pius XI, ratified and confirmed all the above provisions in the audience of 9 February 1929, and ordered the present Decree to be issued, to be effective for ten years.

Byzantine-rite Catholics from Galicia and Bukovina. His diocese, soon to be called the Ukrainian Catholic Church, had its seat in Philadelphia and jurisdiction over 144 churches, 129 priests, and 237,000 parishioners. With this move, Byzantine-rite Catholics gained the legal and structural institutions they had so long desired, although they were split into two jurisdictions depending on whether they originated from north or south of the crest of the Carpathians. This meant that the Lemkos who came from Galicia (that is, those who did not already convert to Orthodoxy) were now split from their fellow Carpatho-Rusyns from former Hungary and instead were jurisdictionally united with other Byzantine-rite Catholics from Galicia, who more and more identified with a Ukrainian ethnic identity. On the other hand, the regional qua national dissention that had marked Greek (Byzantine-rite) Catholic church life until World War I seemed to be overcome, since the bulk of the Carpatho-Rusyns were now separated from the Galician Ukrainians.

This promising beginning toward stability was shattered as early as 1929, however, when in February of that year the Vatican issued (but did not make public) a new decree, the *Cum Data Fuerit*. This decree basically reiterated many of the provisions of the 1907 *Ea Semper*, which in any case had never been strictly enforced. For instance, Bishop Takach had consecrated married priests during the early years of his episcopacy. The *Cum Data Fuerit* was, therefore, an attempt to assure that the Vatican's legal norms be followed, and this time the bishop decided to try to enforce the decree's provisions. Of the several jurisdictional and administrative matters that were dealt with in the *Cum Data Fuerit*, it was the reaffirmation of celibacy, the attack on the trusteeship system of holding church property, and the ban against interference in church affairs by fraternal organizations which led to almost immediate conflict with several priests and lay leaders, especially in the powerful Greek Catholic Union.

For the next eight years, 1930 to 1938, the Byzantine Ruthenian Catholic Church (as the Pittsburgh Exarchate later came to be known) was rent by an almost unending series of conflicts that set priests, fraternal societies, parishioners, even family members against each other in what came to be known as the celibacy controversy. In fact, celibacy was only one of the issues, the other causes of the controversy being the problem of ecclesiastical discipline, rivalry between clergy originating from differing eparchies in Europe (Mukačevo versus Prešov), interference of secular societies in church affairs, and the trustee system of holding church property.

The trouble began when three Rusyn-American seminarians, having completed their studies in the European homeland and having married, returned to the United States. They requested ordination, but Bishop Takach refused. An inquiry made by Father Orestes Chornock of Bridgeport, Connecticut (the parish priest of one of the seminarians) as to why ordination was denied led to friction with the bishop, to the publication in late 1930 of the *Cum Data Fuerit* decree, and to the call by some priests, joined by the laity and the Greek Catholic Union, to struggle against the "unjust" denial of Greek Catholic (Byzantine Ruthenian) religious tradition. Because of his insubordination, Father

Chornock together with four other priests, including the Greek Catholic Union's editor, the Father Stefan Varzaly, were suspended from the priesthood and then excommunicated. These acts only added more fuel to an expanding fire that grew in intensity after the Greek Catholic Union and its so-called Committee for the Defense of the Eastern Rite (KOVO, established 1932) joined the fray, and after individual parishes refused to turn over their property to the bishop.

The next few years were marked by often harsh and libellous charges and countercharges in the fraternal and religious press between the "rebellious" or "tradition-minded" priests around Chornock and Varzaly on the one hand, and the Byzantine Ruthenian hierarchy and priests loyal to Bishop Takach on the other. With no solution in sight, the dissident priests, led by Chornock, Varzaly, and Peter Molchany, met in early 1936 to set the groundwork for a church body that would be independent of Rome. In November 1937, they were joined by several laymen, and meeting in Pittsburgh they formed a church council which declared its abro-

20. Church Congress in Pittsburgh, November 22-24, 1937, which proclaimed the existence of an independent diocese that became the Carpatho-Russian Orthodox Greek Catholic Diocese. Seated in the front row: the Reverend Orestes Chornock (behind the flowers), flanked by the Reverend Ireneus Dolhy (on the left) and the Reverend Stephen Varzaly (on the right).

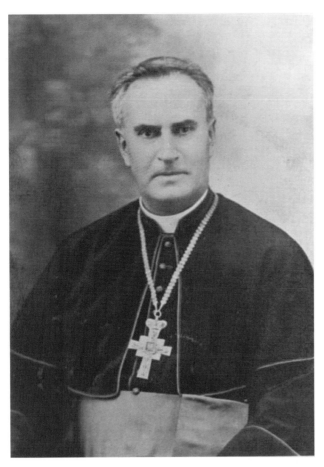

21. Bishop Orestes Chornock upon consecration in 1938

22. St. John the Baptist Church, Arctic Street, Bridgeport, Connecticut. First episcopal residence of the American Carpatho-Russian Orthodox Greek Catholic Church.

gation of union with Rome and its return to the "ancestral faith" of the Carpatho-Rusyn people. The new organization, which initially attracted about 30,000 former Byzantine Catholics, was called the Carpatho-Russian Greek Catholic Diocese of the Eastern Rite of the U.S.A.

This body claimed to be the "true," or Orthodox, Greek Catholic church, which was simply maintaining or restoring traditional Eastern-rite practices. The next question concerned jurisdictional affiliation. Having just rejected Rome, the new diocese was not about to ally itself with the Russian Orthodox Church either. Its leaders were well aware of the difficulties encountered by Bishop Dzubay and his successor in trying to maintain Rusyn religious traditions and a distinct Carpatho-Russian diocese within the Orthodox Metropolia. In fact, the protest movement of the 1930s was heralded by the slogan: "ani do Rimu, ani do Moskvi" (neither Rome nor Moscow). Instead, the new church received its canonical jurisdiction directly from the Ecumenical

Patriarch in Constantinople, a development that was made possible through the good offices of the Greek Orthodox Archbishop of New York, Athenagoras, who later liked to refer to himself as the "godfather of the Carpatho-Russian diocese." Thus, in 1938, Father Chornock travelled to Constantinople, where he was consecrated bishop. Although technically subordinate to the Greek Orthodox Archbishop of America, the Carpatho-Russian Greek Catholic Diocese of the Eastern Rite became, in fact, an independent and self-governing body. Bishop Chornock chose his own parish in Bridgeport, Connecticut as the first diocesan seat, but in 1950 (after a particularly bitter court battle in which the parish was lost) the headquarters were transferred to Johnstown, Pennsylvania. Officially known today as the American Carpatho-Russian Orthodox Diocese of the U.S.A., in Carpatho-Rusyn circles it has come to be popularly known as the "Johnstown Diocese."

Because fractionalization seemed to have become endemic in Carpatho-Rusyn church life, it is hardly surprising that a few parishes led by the Reverend Stefan Varzaly broke with Bishop Chornock already in 1946. By the 1940s, Varzaly had rejected his own earlier slogan—"neither Rome nor Moscow"—and he urged the Johnstown Diocese to join the parishes of the Orthodox Patriarchal Exarchate directly under the jurisdiction of the Patriarch in Moscow. When Bishop Chornock refused to do this Varzaly and a few other discontented priests from the Johnstown diocese called a congress, which claimed itself to be the "true" Carpatho-Russian Orthodox Greek Catholic Diocese. Known popularly as the Carpatho-Russian People's Church, in 1949 the group elected an administrator, the Reverend Andrew Šlepeckij, and intended to place itself under the jurisdiction of the Patriarch in Moscow. But during the height of the Cold War and the Red Scare of the early 1950s, the Un-American Activities Committee of the United States Senate claimed that Varzaly and his church newspaper, *Vistnik* (McKees Rocks, Pa., 1936-55), were being subsidized by Communist funding from abroad. Not wanting to compromise his followers any further, Varzaly turned to the Russian Orthodox Metropolia, which in 1951 accepted into its jurisdiction the 14 parishes of the People's Church. By the 1960s, however, these parishes began one by one to return to the Johnstown Diocese, so that today the Carpatho-Russian People's Church has ceased to exist.

Meanwhile, Bishop Dzubay's original Carpatho-Russian Exarchy dating back to 1916 had, under his successor Bishop Philipovsky, rejoined in 1935 the other Russian Orthodox parishes that by then were known as the Metropolia. Although Philipovsky remained the head of a distinct Carpatho-Russian exarchal administration, it was not long before fellow bishops in the Metropolia began to absorb several of his parishes. Dismayed by this turn of events, Philipovsky with a few of his parishes placed themselves in 1943 under the jurisdiction of the Russian Orthodox Patriarchal Exarchate (that is, under the jurisdiction of Moscow), where they formed a small Carpatho-Russian administration. As for the remaining Carpatho-Russian parishes in the Metropolia, during the 1950s, some switched over to the Johnstown Diocese, the rest were incorporated into the Metropolia's existing diocese. The result was the end of any distinct Carpatho-Rusyn administrative entity within the Russian Orthodox Metropolia,

now the Orthodox Church in America.

The religious dissensions of the 1930s and 1940s carried over into the next decade and proved to be damaging to the Carpatho-Rusyn community. Parishes, even individual families, were split over the "celibacy issue"; fraternal organizations were locked in battle with each other and with the church; and United States district, state, and federal courts were called upon to decide on the legal ownership of church property. These struggles affected both the Byzantine

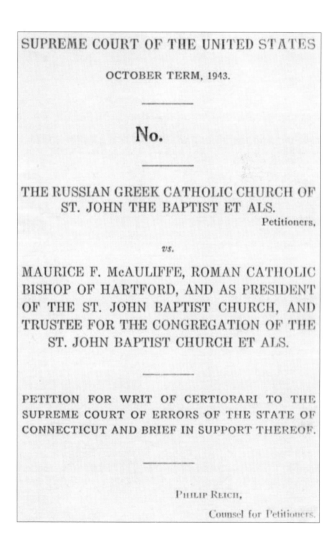

SUPREME COURT OF THE UNITED STATES

OCTOBER TERM, 1943.

No.

THE RUSSIAN GREEK CATHOLIC CHURCH OF ST. JOHN THE BAPTIST ET ALS.
Petitioners,

vs.

MAURICE F. McAULIFFE, ROMAN CATHOLIC BISHOP OF HARTFORD, AND AS PRESIDENT OF THE ST. JOHN BAPTIST CHURCH, AND TRUSTEE FOR THE CONGREGATION OF THE ST. JOHN BAPTIST CHURCH ET ALS.

PETITION FOR WRIT OF CERTIORARI TO THE SUPREME COURT OF ERRORS OF THE STATE OF CONNECTICUT AND BRIEF IN SUPPORT THEREOF.

PHILIP REICH,
Counsel for Petitioners.

23. Title page of one of the many documents from court cases that resulted from the struggle for control over Rusyn-American churches. This 1943 appeal to the United States Supreme Court was part of an unsuccessful attempt begun in 1936 by the Carpatho-Russian Orthodox Greek Catholic Church to maintain custody over Bishop Chornock's cathedral church on Arctic Street in Bridgeport, Connecticut. The Supreme Court upheld the decision of the Connecticut Supreme Court, by which the Bridgeport church was recognized as belonging to the Byzantine Ruthenian Catholic Church and, therefore, was surrendered to them in 1944.

Ruthenian Catholic Church as well as the various Orthodox churches that received Carpatho-Rusyn converts. In the end, many people, whether or not they remained active parishioners, became disgusted with an atmosphere dominated by court battles and slanderous attacks in the press against both lay and clerical figures. As a result, many began to withdraw from their community. By using even more English speech and other "American habits," they hoped to forget the unpleasantness associated with Carpatho-Rusyn ethno-religious life.

Nonetheless, the churches did survive, although they continued to be plagued with serious problems. For instance, the very existence of the Byzantine Ruthenian Catholic Church was threatened in 1954, when papal officials proposed dissolving the Pittsburgh Exarchate and incorporating it within the Ukrainian Catholic jurisdiction of Philadelphia. Such a proposal prompted an immediate response and harsh criticism from Carpatho-Rusyn Catholic clerical and secular leaders, who unequivocally proclaimed: "We are not Ukrainians. . . , and if by means of the church they want to destroy us nationally, we are raising our voice against this and will revolt."[8] Although the proposed merger never came about, the Byzantine Ruthenian Church continued to be troubled by problems at the hierarchal level, with one bishop (Ivancho in 1954) resigning in controversial circumstances and his successor (Elko in 1967) being recalled to Rome and not permitted to head the eparchy any longer.

Orthodox Carpatho-Rusyns also had their problems. The Johnstown Diocese saw the defection of several priests and parishes in the early 1960s after Bishop Chornock appointed a successor without holding elections. One result of these developments was continu-

[8] Michael Roman, "Ukrainization," *Greek Catholic Union Messenger* (Homestead, Pa.), 9 September 1954, p. 1.

24. Byzantine Catholic Seminary of SS Cyril and Methodius, Pittsburgh, Pennsylvania, built 1951 (photo by A. Church).

25. St. John the Baptist Cathedral and Rectory, Munhall, Pennsylvania, the cathedral church of the Byzantine Ruthenian Catholic Archdiocese of Pittsburgh, KSBH Architects, built 1995.

ing friction between various churches as certain parishes changed their allegiances. This took the form of Orthodox Johnstown Diocese parishes returning to the Byzantine Catholic Church, or Orthodox parishes moving from one jurisdiction to another: the Metropolia, Patriarchal Exarchate, and Johnstown Diocese. Yet in spite of these various difficulties lasting from the late 1940s until the mid-1960s, this same period also witnessed signs of growth and stability that were to reach fruition in the late 1960s, when the old fierceness of the interdenominational battles finally began to die down. The stabilizing trend was particularly evident in organizational changes and expansion.

In 1950, the Byzantine Ruthenian Catholic Church constructed its own seminary in Pittsburgh, where it could train future priests without having to send them to the European homeland (by then controlled by antagonistic Communist governments) or to Latin-rite American seminaries. Cut off from the Communist-controlled homeland, Byzantine Ruthenian Catholic leaders realized that their church must survive as an American institution, and so they slowly but surely embarked on a policy of disassociation with its ethnic

and even religious traditions. This policy of "Americanization" was to have its greatest success between 1948 and 1967 under Bishop Daniel Ivancho and his successor Bishop Nicholas T. Elko, the first American-born head of the church. In its attempt to be like other American Catholic churches, the traditional iconostases (screens decorated with icons separating the altar from the congregation) were removed and English more and more replaced Church Slavonic and Carpatho-Rusyn in the liturgy and homily.

At the same time, the status of the Byzantine Ruthenian Catholic Exarchate was enhanced. In order to express its own viewpoint on religious and community issues, several diocesan newspapers were begun, first the *Byzantine Catholic World* (Pittsburgh, 1956-present), followed by the *Eastern Catholic Life* (Passaic, N.J., 1965-present), and *Horizons* (Parma, Ohio, 1979-present), all primarily or exclusively in English. The church's organizational status was also changed. In 1963, two eparchies, with seats in Pittsburgh and Passaic, New Jersey, were created. Then, in 1969, a new eparchy was created with a seat in Parma, Ohio, and all three eparchies came to comprise

26. Archbishop Basil M. Schott, Metropolitan of the Byzantine Ruthenian Catholic Church. His ancestors came from the Rusyn villages of Beňadikovce and Komloša in Slovakia's Prešov Region.

a metropolitanate, now known as the Byzantine Ruthenian Metropolitan Province of Pittsburgh. Finally, in response to the church's growth, especially in the Far West, a fourth eparchy was created in 1982 in Van Nuys, California. At the time of this writing, Basil M. Schott heads the church as archbishop of the Metropolitan See of Pittsburgh; Andrew Pataki is bishop of Passaic; John Kudrick, bishop of Parma; and William C. Skurla, bishop of Van Nuys.

During the period of stability that marked the reign of Archbishop Stephen J. Kocisko in the 1970s and 1980s, the Byzantine Ruthenian Catholic Church continued to expand, so that by 1982, it had under its jurisdiction 227 parishes, 266 priests, 18 elementary schools, 5 monasteries, 5 convents, 2 homes for invalids and the aged, and 284,000 parishioners. Two decades later, while the number of parishes remained the same, there were significant decreases in the other categories, including a marked loss of 85,000 parishioners which coincides with the general decline in membership within America's established churches.

The post-World War II era also proved to be a period of progress for the younger American Car-

patho-Russian Orthodox Greek Catholic Church—the Johnstown Diocese. In 1951, the diocesan seminary (originally established in 1940) was given a permanent home in Johnstown, Pennsylvania, and three years later an impressive new cathedral was dedicated in the same city. Through these institutions, as well as the diocesan newspaper, *Cerkovnyj vistnik/Church Messenger* (Pemberton, N.J., 1944-present), this diocese feels confident it can preserve the ancient traditions (including married priests and the Slavonic liturgy) of the Carpatho-Rusyn community it serves. In 1965, Bishop Chornock was raised to the rank of metropolitan, a post he held until his death twelve years later. By the year 2000, the Johnstown Diocese counted 92 priests, 78 parishes, and 20,000 parishioners. It is headed since early 1985 by Bishop Nicholas Smisko.

By the 1970s, the era of massive defections from the Byzantine Ruthenian Catholic Church to the various Orthodox churches had ended. Since that time, as the ecumenical movement and discussion about Christian unity become more serious, the issues over which the former antagonistic contenders fought so intensely seem no longer to have any validity.

Any description of religious life among Carpatho-Rusyns would not be complete without a few words about converts to Roman Catholicism and Protestant-

27. Metropolitan Nicholas Smisko, American Carpatho-Russian Orthodox Greek Catholic Diocese. His mother comes from the village of Kal'nyk in Subcarpathian Rus'.

28. Christ the Saviour Cathedral, Johnstown, Pennsylvania, the cathedral church of the American Carpatho-Russian Orthodox Greek Catholic Diocese, built 1954

ism. As we have seen, during the early years of the Greek/Byzantine Ruthenian Catholic Church, many Carpatho-Rusyns—some estimates state as high as one-third of the total number—passed over to the Latin rite. This often occurred because there were no local Byzantine Ruthenian Catholic churches or because in mixed marriages the "more American" Latin rite seemed preferable. It was not until 1929 that this problem was clarified. Actually, the otherwise controversial *Cum Data Fuerit* decree, which fuelled anew the celibacy controversy, was primarily concerned with regulating relations between the Latin and Byzantine rites. Henceforth, it was prescribed that children of mixed Latin and Byzantine-rite parents must follow the rite of the father, and this act largely stemmed the flow of changes to the Latin rite.

Ironically, attitudes toward the two rites of the Catholic Church have changed dramatically in the

past three decades. The reason has to do with Vatican Council II, which between 1962 and 1965 instituted several changes in the Roman Catholic Church, including the replacement of Latin with local languages (generally English in the United States) and the introduction of congregational singing, which until then seemed to be the preserve of Protestants. The ecumenical thrust of Vatican II also helped to end the former condescending attitudes on the part of Latin-rite clergy toward their Byzantine-rite brethren. Since at least the 1970s, some Latin-rite Catholics of various ethnic backgrounds, reacting to what they perceive as a loss of tradition, have begun to attend Byzantine Ruthenian churches which are perceived to be more tradition-minded. Thus, the traditions that the Byzantine Ruthenian Catholics were once so anxious to give up are now seen by many Roman Catholics as an attractive antidote to the otherwise ritualized blandness of

American Catholicism.

In the early years of this century, Protestant missionary activity was widespread among newly arrived immigrants, although it was not particularly successful among Slavs. Moreover, as we have seen, Carpatho-Rusyn Greek Catholics always had the safety-valve of Orthodoxy to turn to whenever their discontent was not allayed. Nonetheless, some Carpatho-Rusyns (the actual number or even an estimate is difficult if not impossible to determine) did join mainstream American Protestant churches, especially Baptist ones, where they became quickly assimilated and losing all ties with the ethnic identity of their forebears. One exception was a group in Proctor, Vermont, which founded a fundamentalist Bible-reading sect with branches in Naugatuck, Connecticut and Passaic, New Jersey. Through its publication, *Proroczeskoe svitlo/The Prophetic Light* (Proctor, Vt., 1921-53), the group was able to maintain for many decades a sense of affinity with its Carpatho-Rusyn origins. Descendants of the original group continue to meet in southern Connecti-

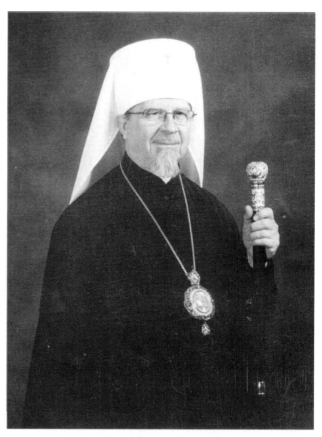

30. Archbishop Herman (Swaiko), Metropolitan of the Orthodox Church in America. His father came from Užok and his mother from Volosjanka, Rusyn villages in Subcarpathian Rus'

cut and the New York City-New Jersey metropolitan area.

The strong religious orientation of the Rusyn-American community has produced individuals who have played a significant role in church affairs beyond as well as within the group's own denominations. Miriam Teresa Demjanovich was the daughter of Rusyn immigrants from the Prešov Region of eastern Slovakia. Before her untimely death at the age of 27, she had become a Roman Catholic Sister of Charity and author of a series of "spiritual conferences" published a year after her death in English and several other languages under the title, *Greater Perfection* (1928). Inspired by her life and writings, a Sister Miriam Theresa League was established in 1945 to work on behalf of her beatification which, should it occur, would make her the first female American saint of Slavic descent in the Catholic Church.

Priests of Carpatho-Rusyn descent still play a leading role in traditional Orthodox churches. Metropolitan Herman (Swaiko), the son of Carpatho-Rusyn immi-

29. Sister Miriam Teresa Demjanovich (by Pino Daeni).

31. Archbishop Laurius (Škurla), Metropolitan and the first Hierarch of the Russian Orthodox Church Abroad—the Synod. He was born in the Carpatho-Rusyn village of Ladomirová in Slovakia's Prešov Region.

grants from Subcarpathian Rus', holds the highest office in the large Orthodox Church in America. Another is Archbishop Laurus (Škurla), who heads the Russian Orthodox Church Abroad—the Synod. Very few Rusyn Americans are members of the Synod Abroad, although Archbishop Laurus became associated with its Holy Trinity Monastery during the 1930s, when it was still located in his native village of Ladomirová in the Prešov Region of Slovakia. The community of monks transferred to Jordanville in upper New York state after World War II. Bishop Laurus is head of the Jordanville monastery, which has become a mecca for Russian Orthodox traditionalists, including fervent supporters like the writer Alexander Solzhenitsyn and the conductor-cellist Mystyslav Rostropovich.

Perhaps the most influential American of Carpatho-Rusyn background active in religious affairs was the evangelist minister Joseph W. Tkach. The son of Rusyn immigrants from the Prešov Region of east-ern Slovakia, Tkach become in 1986 pastor general of the California-based Worldwide Church of God. With 94,000 members in 120 countries, until his death in 1995 Tkach reached his faithful—as well as millions of others—through his role as editor-in-chief of the widely-distributed magazine, *The Plain Truth*, and the syndicated nationwide news-oriented television program, "The World Tomorrow." It is interesting to note that in 1992, when the Worldwide Church of God began to proselytize in the former Soviet Union, it launched its work in Ukraine's Transcarpathia where, as the church's official newspaper reported, "the somber crowd listened with great interest" as the preacher from America "spoke about Mr. Tkach's Rusyn roots."[9]

[9] *The Worldwide News* (Pasadena, Calif.), October 6, 1992, p. 2.

32. Joseph W. Tkach, Pastor General of the Worldwide Church of God.

Chapter 5

Organizational Life

Thrust into a world that was politically, economically, culturally, and linguistically alien, the early Carpatho-Rusyn immigrants, like other newcomers to America's shores, sought ways to cushion the psychological impact of their exposure to a new environment. This is not to say that all Carpatho-Rusyns felt lost and alienated in America. Some, whose intent was often to make money as quickly as possible, adapted easily and achieved their goals. Most, however, tried in some way to interact socially with their fellow immigrants and to recreate, in however rudimentary a fashion, the Old-World environment they had left behind.

At first, the boardinghouses, grocery stores, local taverns, and, of course, the church—at least on Sundays and holidays—provided the setting for social interaction. Next to the church, the most important organizations were the fraternal societies and brotherhoods. Actually, these arose not so much because of their potential social function, but rather for very practical needs. In a foreign land, where most immigrant workers had insufficient funds to protect themselves in case of industrial accidents or other mishaps, the fraternal organizations were able to provide a minimal but nonetheless important source of financial help in times of distress. While life insurance policies and workmen's compensation programs provided some financial security, the newspapers, youth clubs, sports organizations, and social gatherings sponsored by the fraternals created a measure of psychological security for immigrants in the company of their fellow-countrymen. Thus, it was

not long before the fraternal societies saw themselves as defenders of Carpatho-Rusyn culture and religion, so that next to the churches they were to become the most influential force directing the destiny of the community in the United States.

Initially, all Greek (Byzantine-rite) Catholic immigrants, whether they were from the pre-World War I Hungarian Kingdom or Austrian Galicia, belonged to the same fraternals. But before long friction developed among the varying factions. Among the several kinds of differences were: (1) regional differences—Galicians vs. the *uhorci* (those from old Hungary); (2) religious differences—Greek/Byzantine Catholics vs. Orthodox; and (3) national differences—Rusynophiles vs. Russophiles, Ukrainophiles, Slovakophiles, or Magyarones. Splits resulted and new fraternals were created to represent each of the many orientations that evolved in the community. This fragmentation actually occurred rather quickly, so that by the 1890s each of the various regional, religious, and national groups had its own distinct fraternal organization. Moreover, the rather rapid growth of fraternal societies seemed to be a particularly American phenomenon, which was especially important for Carpatho-Rusyns, who with very few exceptions did not have similar organizations in the European homeland before 1918.

The first fraternal organization was the St. Nicholas Brotherhood, founded in 1885 in the coal mining town of Shenandoah, Pennsylvania by the pioneer Greek Catholic priest in America, Father John Volansky. Although the brotherhood was short-lived, lasting only until 1889 when Father Volansky returned to Europe, it nonetheless was part of an active community which also published the first newspaper, *Ameryka* (Shenandoah, Pa., 1886-90), as an "organ for Rusyn immigrants from Galicia and Hungary."

Following the demise of the St. Nicholas Brotherhood, parish-based lodges did continue to survive, although many Carpatho-Rusyns began to join recently founded Slovak fraternals, such as the First Catholic Slovak Union Jednota (est. 1890) and the Pennsylvania Slovak Roman and Greek Catholic Union (est. 1891). It was in part the movement of Rusyns into Slovak Roman Catholic fraternals that highlighted the need for a specific Carpatho-Rusyn organization. During a meeting of 14 Greek Catholic priests who in December 1891 had gathered to protest their treatment by the Vatican and by the American Roman Catholic Church, it was decided to establish a single fraternal society and to publish a newspaper. This goal came to fruition a few months later, when a group of 6 Greek Catholic priests, joined by representatives of 14 local brotherhoods, met in Wilkes Barre, Pennsylvania to form one body that would unite them all. They named it the Greek Catholic Union of Russian [Rusyn] Brotherhoods (Sojedinenije Greko-Kaftoličeskich Russkich Bratstv), and according to its founding charter of February 14, 1892, set as its goals: to strive for unity among the majority of "Greek Catholics who speak Rusyn"; to provide insurance for its members; to encourage education and promote the construction of schools and churches; and to provide a plan to protect widows, orphans, and the indigent. The first chairman was John Žinčak Smith, and the first editor of its newspaper, the *Amerikansky russky viestnik* (Wilkes Barre, Scranton, New York, Pittsburgh, and Homestead, Pa., 1892-1952), was Pavel Zatkovich, both Carpatho-Rusyns from Hungary. The Greek Catholic Union (hereafter GCU) began in 1892 with 743 members in 14 lodges. During the next two decades, which coincided with the height of immigration from Europe, the GCU grew accordingly, and by 1929, at its height, it counted 133,000 members in 1,719 lodges. In 1905, it opened new headquarters with offices and printing facilities in Homestead, Pennsylvania. To this day, the GCU has remained the largest Carpatho-Rusyn fraternal

33. John Žinčak-Smith.

34. Pavel Zatkovich.

35. Insurance policy of the Greek Catholic Union, dated 1927. This attractively designed policy, measuring 14 x 24 inches, included texts in English and Rusyn, both in the Latin alphabet and Cyrillic alphabet.

organization, and during the last three decades it has maintained a steady membership while increasing substantially its financial base. By the time of its 110th anniversary in 2002, the GCU had 40,000 members (holding 50,000 certificates) in 96 lodges and assets of 530 million dollars.

Because of its rapid growth, the GCU had to accommodate Byzantine-rite Catholics of various backgrounds, and its newspaper, the *Amerikansky russky viestnik,* was even published for several decades in two editions, a Carpatho-Rusyn edition in the Cyrillic alphabet, and a so-called "Slavish" edition in the Latin alphabet with a language that was a transitional Eastern Slovak/ Carpatho-Rusyn dialect. From the very beginning, however, the leadership and activity of the GCU was basically concerned with Greek (Byzantine-rite) Catholics of Rusyn background from south of the Carpathian Mountains. Consequently, many neighboring Slovaks of the Byzantine-rite avoided the GCU and instead joined the First Catholic Slovak Union Jednota and the Pennsylvania Slovak Roman and Greek Catholic Union.

The next group to defect were the Galicians, who became disenchanted with what they called the Magyarone-dominated leadership of the GCU. Upon the initiative of four priests from Galicia— Gregory Hrushka, Ivan Konstankevych, Theodore Obushkevych, and Ambrose Poliansky—a new "Russian," later Rusyn National Association (Russkij/ Rus'kyj Narodnyj Sojuz) was founded in Shamokin, Pennsylvania in 1894. Hrushka became the founding editor of its newspaper, *Svoboda* (Jersey City, N.J., 1894-present), and by the turn of the century this organization was reinforced by nationally-conscious Galician-Ukrainian immigrants who, in 1914, changed its name to the Ukrainian National Association. This body is today the largest secular Ukrainian organization in the United States.

As a result of the increasing Ukrainophile orientation of the Rusyn National Association, discontented Galician-Lemko Russophiles like Father Theodore Obushkevych were joined by sympathizers in the GCU who met in Mahanoy City, Pennsylvania, in September 1900, to form the Russian Brotherhood Organization (Obščestvo Russkich Bratstv). John Žinčak-Smith, the first chairman of the GCU, was chosen to head this new group, while another Lemko

and former member of the Rusyn National Association, Victor P. Hladick, became founding editor of the society's newspaper, *Pravda/The Truth* (New York, Olyphant, Philadelphia, Pottstown, Pa., Mogodore, Oh., 1902-present). At the height of its growth in the 1940s, the organization, made up mostly of Lemkos, had around 16,000 members in nearly 300 lodges. By the end of the century, membership decreased to a few thousand; however, those numbers increased somewhat following a merger in 2002 of the Russian Brotherhood Organization with the Russian Orthodox Fraternity Lubov.

Finally, those parishes which Father Alexis Toth brought over to Orthodoxy felt the need for their own organization. Led by Toth and laymen like Ivan Repa and Ivan Pivovarnik, a small group met in Wilkes Barre in April 1895 to form the Russian Orthodox Catholic Mutual Aid Society (Russkoe Pravoslavnoe Obščestvo Vzaimopomošči). Led for many years by the determined Russophile, Father Peter Kohanik, this group through its newspaper *Svit/The Light* (Wilkes Barre, 1894-present) and its annual almanacs tried to offset the Greek Catholic societies and to preserve the "Orthodox faith and Russian nationality" of its Carpatho-Rusyn membership. The society never regained the nearly 10,000 members it had in 1918, and by 1992, it had only 2,300 members in 100 lodges.

Thus, already at the beginning of the twentieth century, several insurance and fraternal organizations existed which represented the various national, regional, and religious affiliations of the Carpatho-Rusyn immigrant community. The Greek Catholic Union was to include primarily Carpatho-Rusyns and some Slovaks from the pre-1918 Hungarian Kingdom and was to follow either a separatist Rusyn or, especially during the 1930s, a Russophile national orientation. The other groups initially attracted immigrants from Galicia, including many Lemkos, and were to identify either with the Russian nationality (Society of Russian Brotherhoods, Russian Orthodox Mutual Aid Society) or Ukrainian nationality (Rusyn/Ukrainian National Association).

Through its financial power and newspaper circulation (at one time as high as 120,000), the Greek Catholic Union was to wield great influence over Carpatho-Rusyn religious and political activity. In general, the GCU defended what it considered to be the

36. Headquarters of the Greek Catholic Union, Beaver, Pennsylvania, opened 1987

religious and cultural interests of the Carpatho-Rusyn community and it adopted a traditionalist position, avidly opposing the "Latinizing" decrees passed down by the Vatican. Although during the 1890s the GCU worked to counteract the Orthodox "schism" led by Father Toth, by the early twentieth century it had already begun unwittingly to aid that movement by its opposition to many of the policies of the Greek Catholic hierarchs, especially those of the first bishop, Soter Ortynsky. In fact, from the very first day of his arrival in America in 1907, Ortynsky and *Amerikansky russky viestnik* editor Pavel Žatkovich became alienated from each other, thereby initiating a pattern of friction between the GCU and the church that it ostensibly defended. From the pages of its official newspaper, the GCU led an almost unending attack against the policies of the new bishop, holding him accountable for enforcing the provisions of the Vatican's 1907 *Ea Semper* decree and accusing him of supporting, with the help of his fellow Galician priests and lay supporters, the Ukrainian "separatist movement."

It was precisely the GCU's antagonistic policy toward the Greek Catholic Church leadership that contributed to the growth of another Carpatho-Rusyn fraternal, the United Societies of Greek Catholic Religion (Sobranije Greko-Katholičeskich Cerkovnych Bratstv). This fraternal had actually come into being as early as 1903, when parishioners of the St. Nicholas parish in the Pittsburgh suburb of McKeesport, Pennsylvania broke away from the GCU. Although initially a local organization, after 1909 lodges were established outside of McKeesport (ironically, the first of these was as far away as Stockett, Montana), so that by 1915 there were 73 lodges with over 2,000 members. From the beginning, the United Societies included primarily Carpatho-Rusyns from the pre-World War I Hungarian Kingdom. But unlike its older and larger rival, the GCU, the United Socities remained loyal to Bishop Ortynsky and staunchly supported him, his successors, and the official policies of the Greek Catholic Church. This approach was elaborated upon in the newspapers of

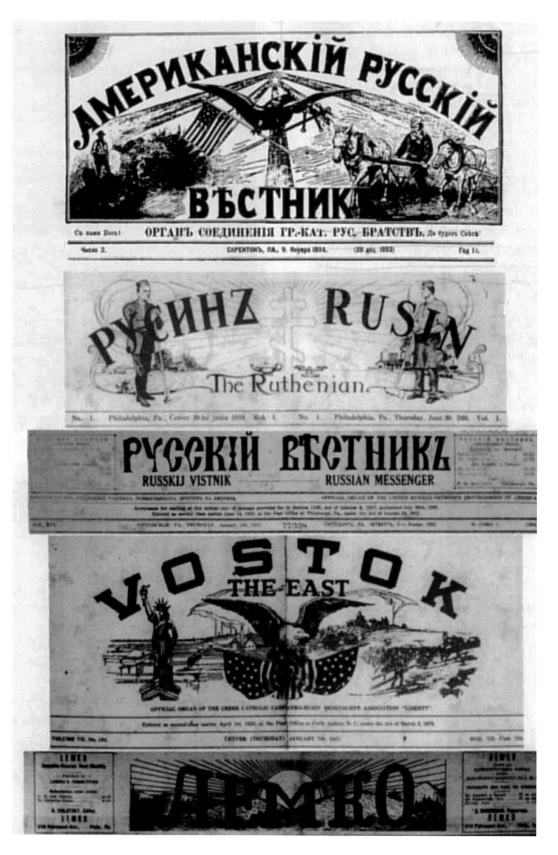

37. Early mastheads of Rusyn-American fraternal newspapers.

the United Societies, including *Rusin/The Ruthenian* (Philadelphia and Pittsburgh, 1910-16), edited by Father Joseph Hanulya, and its succesor *Prosvita/The Englightenment* (McKeesport, Pa., 1917-2000), edited for its first 15 years by Father Valentine Gorzo. By 1992, the United Societies claimed 3,970 members in 40 lodges, but eight years later these were merged, or rather absorbed, by the organization's former rival, the GCU.

Meanwhile, throughout the whole pre-World War I period, the GCU remained in opposition to the Greek Catholic Church leadership under Bishop Ortynsky. It even contributed indirectly to Father Dzubay's defection to Orthodoxy. The GCU had touted Dzubay as the most able candidate to succeed Bishop Ortynsky after his death in 1916. When that did not happen, the discontented priest, who was convinced that he was supported by the community, turned to the Russian Orthodox Church where, as we have seen, he obtained an appointment as bishop. While the GCU did not follow Dzubay's example of defection from the Greek Catholic Church, it nonetheless remained ready to react whenever it perceived that the religious and cultural interests of the Carpatho-Rusyn community were threatened. For a while at least, interest (or interference) in church affairs in America was replaced by a growing concern with the fate of the homeland, and as we shall see in Chapter 8 below, the GCU was particularly influential during the international events of 1918-1919, which resulted in the incorporation of Rusyns living south of the Carpathians into Czechoslovakia.

By the 1930s, religious questions were once again the focus of attention, and it was during that decade that the GCU was to play its last truly dominant role in the life of Carpatho-Rusyns in America. The organization had been badly hit by the effects of the economic depression after 1929, when the failure of banks where it had invested funds threatened the fraternal's very existence. In this period of uncertainty and economic crisis, the GCU needed something to rally the support of its leaders and membership, and it seemed that that something was the celibacy issue. Whatever the motivation, the GCU soon found itself again embroiled in religious issues as it took up the defense of the married priesthood and other traditions it felt were unjustly undermined by the

38. Michael Yuhasz, Sr.

39. Dr. Peter I. Zeedick.

40. Dr. Adalbert M. Smor.

41. Father Stefan Varzaly

Cum Data Fuerit decree of 1929.

The struggle was first carried out through attacks against Bishop Takach on the pages of the GCU's *Amerikansky russky viestnik*, edited at the time by the traditionalist priest, Stefan Varzaly, who ironically had been recommended for the editorial post by the bishop himself. Then in April 1932, the GCU organized a Committee for the Defense of the Eastern Rite (Komitet Oborony Vostočnoho Obrjada) to carry on the struggle. This Committee, headed by GCU president Michael Yuhasz, Sr. and including other influential lay and clerical leaders like Dr. Peter I. Zeedick, Gregory Zatkovich, Adalbert M. Smor, and Father Joseph Hanulya, convened several religious congresses in 1933. In August of that year, a 12-point letter was sent to the Pope urging that non-celibacy and all other rights of the Byzantine Ruthenian Catholic Church be restored immediately, and threatening that if that did not happen within 60 days, the committee would secede from the Catholic Church and form an independent body.

This ultimatum led to almost two years of libellous and often crude attacks by both sides. Angry works appeared on the pages of the GCU's *Amerikansky russky viestnik* and the United Societies' *Prosvita,* as well as in numerous pamphlets intended to defend Byzantine-rite religious traditions (and Carpatho-Rusyn ethnonational distinctiveness), the most well known of which was *Our Stand (Naše stanovišče,* 1934), by the GCU leaders Peter I. Zeedick and Adalbert M. Smor. In the increasingly tense atmosphere that prevailed at the time, Bishop Takach took the unprecedented step in 1935 of excommunicating the GCU as an organization and placing the *Amerikansky russky viestnik* on the Index of forbidden literature. "Consequently," wrote the bishop in a pastoral letter directed at all the faithful, "under strict punishment it is forbidden to any member of this Eparchy to read this newspaper."[10] If any church member disobeyed, he or she would be commiting a "mortal sin."

Not surprisingly, such harsh language caused confusion in the minds of many of the faithful, especially since the attacks on their church were not coming from the Orthodox, but rather from their

[10] Pastoral letter of Bishop Basil Takacs, November 20, 1935, cited in Slivka, *Historical Mirror,* p. 284.

own leading fraternal organization, the GCU. In an attempt to reduce tension, in 1937 the charismatic and traditionalist Varzaly was removed for the second and final time as editor of the *Amerikansky russky viestnik*; he promptly joined with other rebellious priests who founded the independent Carpatho-Russian Greek Catholic Diocese of the Eastern Rite. To be sure, some GCU leaders like Zeedick tried to carry on the struggle. Even the new leadership—John P. Sekerak, elected president of the GCU in 1936, and Michael Roman, appointed editor of the *Amerikansky russky viestnik* in 1937—initially favored Varzaly's traditional "pro-eastern" (*pro-vostočny)* platform. It was not long, however, before there was marked change. Varzaly fell out with the GCU president, while the organization as a whole, concerned with stabilizing its own economic situation exacerbated by the Great Depression and the loss of members who supported the church hierarchy, decided with the full support of the new editor, Michael Roman, to make peace with Bishop Takach and the Byzantine Ruthenian Exarchate.

By the 1940s, not only had the GCU made amends with the Byzantine Ruthenian Church, ever since then it has generally avoided the sensitive issues of religion, nationality, and politics. Symbolic of this change was the adoption in 1953 of an English-language format for its official organ, renamed the *Greek Catholic Union Messenger,* which today only rarely publishes any articles in Carpatho-Rusyn. At present, the GCU functions primarily as an insurance agency, although it also organizes golf and bowling tournaments, provides scholarships for younger members, and contributes $25,000 annually to support the Byzantine Ruthenian Catholic Seminary. In 1987, the GCU opened new national headquarters together with recreational facilities in Beaver, Pennsylvania, a town northwest of Pittsburgh.

Even though the majority of the GCU membership—whether first-generation immigrants or their second-, third-, and fourth-generation descendants—are of Carpatho-Rusyn background, the organization maintains a relatively low profile in terms of specific ethnic identity. It reveals its Carpatho-Rusyn heritage only by publishing a few articles on the history of the "old country," by participating in the annual Byzantine and "Rusyn Day" celebrations held in the Pittsburgh area, by sponsoring excursions to the Carpathian homeland, and by supporting folk ensembles like Slavjane under the direction of Jack and Dean Poloka. A major history published on the occasion of the organization's centenary in 1992 did nonetheless stress the Rusyn origins and basic membership profile of the Greek Catholic Union.

There have also been a host of other fraternal organizations set up during this century to serve the various regional, religious, and national factions of the Carpatho-Rusyn community. From among the converts to Orthodoxy, one group met in Monessen, Pennsylvania, in July 1915, to found the Greek Catholic, later United Russian Orthodox Brotherhood of America—UROBA (Sojedinenije russkich pravo-slavnych bratstv v Ameriki) based in Pittsburgh. Although its members were for the most part Carpatho-Rusyns from pre-World War I Hungary, the fraternal's pro-Orthodox and Russophile orientation was promoted by Nicholas Pachuta, the founding editor of its newspaper, *Russkij vistnik/Russian Messenger/ UROBA Messenger* (Pittsburgh, 1917-92). From a high of nearly 20,000 members on the eve of World War II, the fraternal dropped to only 2,000 in the early 1990s. To avoid further decline, UROBA merged in 1992 with the New Jersey-based Liberty Association to form the Orthodox Society of America based in Lakewood, Ohio. The newly expanded society was able to survive only a decade, however, and in 2003 it ceased to exist as a distinct fraternal association.

Meanwhile, in the New York City metropolitan area, several members of the GCU were unhappy that most of the fraternal's benefits were being paid to lodges in Pennsylvania where the accident rate, especially in the mines, was greater. Not satisfied with the Pittsburgh-based leadership of the GCU, a Byzantine Catholic priest, Peter Kustan, together with John Lucow and John Petrunak, in July 1918 founded in Perth Amboy, New Jersey the Liberty Greek Catholic Carpatho-Russian Benevolent Association (Organizacija Greko Kaftoličeskich Karpatorusskich Spomahajuščich Bratstv Svobody). The Liberty fraternal operated its own print shop where it issued the newspaper *Vostok/The East* (Perth Amboy, N.J., 1919-50), edited by Vasil Izak and Stephen Banitsky. Like the GCU, Liberty's members were mostly Carpatho-Rusyns from Hungary, and also like the older organization, during the 1930s it abandoned a separatist Rusyn (Ruthenian) national orientation for a pro-Russian one.

But in the course of the struggle over celibacy, Liberty remained traditionalist to the end, eventually breaking with the Byzantine Ruthenian Pittsburgh Exarchate and associating instead with the Carpatho-Russian Orthodox Diocese in Johnstown, Pennsylvania. At one time, Liberty claimed to have 100 lodges, but in 1992 the lodges that were left merged with UROBA, which itself became the Orthodox Society of America.

Among smaller fraternal organizations, which included many Russophiles from Galicia as well as Carpatho-Rusyns, was the Cleveland-area American Russian National Brotherhood. It functioned during the 1930s and 1940s under the leadership of William Racine and Father Ivan Ladižinsky. This group sponsored the periodicals *Rodina* (Cleveland, 1927-40) and *Bratstvo/Brotherhood* (Cleveland, 1927-49), and was associated with the Russian Orthodox Church (the Metropolia). Its ideological counterpart in eastern Pennsylvania was the Russian Orthodox Fraternity Lubov (Russka Pravoslavna Ljubov), founded in 1912 by Aleksij Šljanta. As was made clear in the fraternity's monthly magazine *Liubov* (Mayfield, Pa., 1912-57), edited by Stefan F. Telep, it always identified itself as a "Russian" organization associated with the Russian Orthodox Church (the Metropolia), later the Orthodox Church in America. With its approximately 1,000 members in 73 lodges, the Lubov Fraternity merged in 2002 with the Russian Brotherhood Organization.

For the longest time, Carpatho-Rusyn Americans were generally less successful in maintaining cultural organizations. There are several reasons for this. Very few immigrants arrived in this country with a clear sense of national consciousness. Moreover, they often had only a rudimentary level of literacy in their native language, and if they were to improve their education, they generally preferred to do so in English so as to adapt better to their new environment. Finally, the churches, whether Byzantine Ruthenian Catholic or Orthodox, were considered more than sufficient outlets for a Rusyn American's cultural needs.

Nonetheless, there were a few efforts to establish distinct Carpatho-Rusyn cultural organizations. One of the earliest was the Rusin Elite Society, established in 1927 in Cleveland, Ohio at the initiative of Father Joseph Hanulya and under the leadership of Dr. Eugene Mankovich. This society set up ten branches in Ohio and western Pennsylvania and also sponsored

42. Father Joseph Hanulya.

a Rusyn display at Cleveland's All-Nations Exhibition in 1929. From the outset, the Rusin Elite Society had a clear sense that Carpatho-Rusyns formed a distinct nationality, a view that was emphasized on the pages of its English and Rusyn-language monthly, *Vožd/The Leader* (Lakewood, Ohio, 1929-30). The organization got caught up in the celibacy controversy of the 1930s, however, and due to the defection of some of its leaders was forced to reduce its activity.

The Cleveland area was again the basis for another cultural organization, the Rusyn Cultural Garden, which was founded in 1939 to establish a Rusyn presence in the so-called Nationalities Gardens of Cleveland's Rockefeller Park. Dedication ceremonies led by Byzantine Catholic Bishop Basil Takach and Father Hanulya took place in June 1939 and culminated in 1952 with the erection of a commemorative bust of the nineteenth-century Carpatho-Rusyn "national awakener," Aleksander Duchnovyč. Created by the sculptor Frank Jirouch, this was the first (and only) public statue of a Carpatho-Rusyn leader in the United States. The Rusin Cultural Garden was maintained for close to two decades by the Rusin Educational Society and Rusin Day Association of Greater Cleveland,

43.   Rusyn cottage at the All Nations Exposition, Public Auditorium, Cleveland, Ohio, March 1929.

Greek Catholic-oriented cultural organizations which functioned from 1939 to 1961. The public presence of Carpatho-Rusyns as represented by the bust of Duchnovyč was only to last for about two decades, because during the 1970s the statue disappeared—a victim of the deterioration and destruction of America's inner cities. In the 1990s, the Rusin Cultural Garden was restored and since then is maintained as a project of the Cleveland branch of the Carpatho-Rusyn Society.

Carpatho-Rusyns in the Pittsburgh area also tried to foster organized cultural activity. During the 1930s, a Carpatho-Russian Symphonic Choir under the direction of Father Michael Staurovsky became well known in western Pennsylvania for its concerts of religious and secular music. The choir was also used to help raise funds for one of the nationalities' rooms at the University of Pittsburgh's Cathedral of Learning. An organizing committee for the nationality room was set up under the leadership of Dr. Peter Zeedick and other members of the Greek Catholic Union, but because that organization was at the time Russophile in orientation, it joined the smaller Russian-American

community of greater Pittsburgh to create a Russian Nationalities Room. The Russian Room still exists today, and although the bulk of the funds to establish it actually came from the Greek Catholic Union's committee, there are no Carpatho-Rusyn features incorporated into the design. A few decades later, Pittsburgh was also the place where the Bishop Takach Carpatho-Russian Historical Society was organized, but after the publication of two short historical works about the European homeland, it ceased to function.

On the east coast there were also a few shortlived attempts at establishing cultural organizations, with a 150-piece youth orchestra under Andrew Griz in Bridgeport, Connecticut and a Carpatho-Russian Museum under Father Joseph Milly in New York City, both set up in the late 1940s and both affiliated with churches in the Johnstown Diocese. Somewhat later, but again in existence for only a decade or so, were three cultural institutions founded during the 1970s within the framework of the Byzantine Ruthenian Catholic Church: the Archdiocesan Museum of Pittsburgh organized by the Reverend Basil Shereghy; the Heritage Institute of the Passaic Diocese established by Bishop

Michael Dudick; and the library of Carpatho-Rusyn materials at the Benedictine Holy Trinity Monastery in Butler, Pennsylvania set up by Father Stephen Veselenak. The Passaic Heritage Institute, which is now closed to the public, contains especially rich printed material on the history and culture of Rusyns in America and the European homeland, as well as a large collection of Rusyn religious and secular art and ethnographic materials of European and American provenance.

A new infusion of activity on the cultural front followed the arrival of the small group of immigrants who came during the late 1940s and early 1950s as a result of the dislocations caused by World War II. The newcomers left the various regions of Carpathian Rus' during or just after the war and were unwilling to return home after Subcarpathian Rus' was incorporated into the Soviet Union (1945) and Czechoslovakia and Poland came under Communist rule (1945 and 1948). Many first settled in displaced persons camps in the American zone of Germany and, therefore, were part of the so-called DPs who later entered the United States.

Small in number, the post-1945 immigration also differed from the pre-World War I generations in that most were highly educated. Some had even participated in the government and administration of Subcarpathian Rus' when it was within Czechoslovakia (1919-1938) and when it functioned as an autonomous province (1938-1939). Moreover, the majority identified themselves with the Ukrainian nationality.

In 1949, a group led by William Ceresne, Ivan Besaha, and Vincent Shandor founded the Carpathian Alliance (Karpats'kyj Sojuz) in New York City. The Alliance published several pamphlets about the homeland as well as the periodicals, *Karpats'ka zorja/The Carpathian Star* (New York, 1951-52) and *Vistnyk/Bulletin* (New York, 1970-73). By the end of the twentieth century, only its Washington, D.C. branch was active, particularly in publishing the works of the Carpatho-Ukrainian writer, Vasyl' Grendža-Dons'kyj. In 1958, a few Alliance members, led by Julian Revay, Augustine Stefan, and Wasyl Weresh, decided to establish a new organization, the Carpathian Research Center (Karpats'kyj Doslidnyj Centr). During its nearly three decades of existence, the center sponsored many conferences at its headquarters in New York City (until 1978, at the impressive mansion of the Ukrainian Institute on Fifth Avenue) and published several studies about the homeland, especially those dealing with the Ukrainian national movement and the few months of autonomy in 1938-1939.

44. Rusyn Cultural Garden, Rockefeller Park, Cleveland, Ohio, 1952.

The main object of these Ukrainophile organizations has been to promote the Ukrainian viewpoint regarding the history and culture of Carpatho-Rusyns. Though some attempts were made to interact with the older and more established Carpatho-Rusyn religious and lay organizations in America, especially on the part of individuals like the former minister of Carpatho-Ukraine (1938-1939) Julian Revay, these efforts invariably failed because of the antipathy of the older immigrants and their descendants to Ukrainianism. Thus, the Ukrainophiles have remained alienated from the vast majority of the Carpatho-Rusyns and interact instead with the Ukrainian-American community.

Some Russophiles have also tried to set up cultural organizations in the years after World War II. One of these, the Initiative Group for the Organization of Carpatho-Russian Society, was headed by Michael Turjanica, who published *Svobodnoe slovo Karpatskoj Rusi* (Newark, N. J., Mt. Vernon, N.Y., Phoenix, Ariz., 1959-1989), an irregular publication which attacked everything associated with Ukrainianism, Catholicism, and Communism. In the tradition of tsarist pan-Slavism, Turjanica considered Carpatho-Rusyns and their homeland to be part of a supposedly "common Russian" *(obščerusskij)* cultural and linguistic world. A similarly-minded group, the Carpatho-Russian Literary Association, was founded in 1970 in Bridgeport, Connecticut by Peter S. Hardy. Hardy financed the reprinting of four older scholarly studies which stress the Russophile view of Carpatho-Rusyn history. Neither of these groups ever contained more than a handful of supporters and by the 1980s both were for the most part inactive.

During the past three decades, new cultural organizations have been founded by the second-, third-, and fourth-generation descendants of the early immigrants. Born and fully acculturated in the United States, the founders and supporters of these newest organizations are concerned with learning about and propagating the specific features of the Carpatho-Rusyn heritage within the American mosaic. The oldest of these is the Carpatho-Rusyn Research Center, established in 1978 and first based in Fairview, New Jersey. Not affiliated with any religious, fraternal, or political group, the center specializes in the publication and/or distribution of scholarly and popular studies on all aspects of the Carpatho-Rusyn heritage. It also maintains contacts with scholarly institutions and universities in North America and the European homeland and for two decades published an influential quarterly magazine, the *Carpatho-Rusyn American* (Fairview, N.J., 1978-97).

The 1980s also saw the short-lived existence of a Carpatho-Russian Ethnic Research Center in Fort Lauderdale, Florida, which published a bi-lingual (English and "Carpatho-Russian") monthly newspaper, *Carpatho-Russian Echoes/Karpatorusskije otzvuki* (Fort Lauderdale, Flo.; Westmont, W. Va., 1983-89). Somewhat later, Professor Paul J. Best of Southern Connecticut State College established a coordinating center for scholars called the Carpatho-Rusyn (later Carpatho-Slavic) Studies Group, which began a series called *Carpatho-Rusyn Studies* (New Haven, Conn., 1990-present). At the local community level, the Carpatho-Rusyn Cultural Society of Michigan (est. 1979) and the Rusin Association of Minnesota (est. 1983) were founded to rejuvenate and preserve traditional customs among Carpatho-Rusyns in the Detroit and Minneapolis-St. Paul areas. The Minnesota group, founded by Lawrence A. Goga, organizes several social functions, sponsors a Rusyn cultural exhibit at the annual Minneapolis folk festival, and publishes a newsletter, *Trembita* (Minneapolis, Minn., 1987-present). The most recent and dynamic organization is the Carpatho-Rusyn Society/Karpatorusyns'koe obščestvo, founded in 1994 under the leadership of John Righetti. Based in Pittsburgh, Pennsylvania, the society has nine branches in New England, New York City, New Jersey, Washington, D. C., and various places in Pennsylvania, Ohio, and even Tuscon, Arizona. It sponsors a wide variety of cultural programs for its 1,700 members throughout the United States, provides educational and humanitarian aid to the European homeland, and publishes the bi-monthly magazine, *The New Rusyn Times* (Pittsburgh, 1994-present).

Those Carpatho-Rusyn immigrants from Galicia known as Lemkos often felt the need to have their own organizations. A Lemko Committee was established as early as 1922 in New York City by Victor Hladick. It published the magazine *Lemkovščyna* (1922-26) and raised funds to help elementary schools in what was by then the Polish-ruled Lemko Region. More intense organizational activity was not continued in the United States, but first in Canada, where in early 1929 the first Lemko Council came into existence in Winnipeg, Manitoba. Several other branches of such councils were soon formed in Canadian and American cities. By 1931, representatives of the branches met in Cleveland to unite them into a single Lemko Association (Lemko Sojuz) for the United States and Canada, and to adopt as their official organ the newspaper *Lemko* (Philadelphia, Cleveland, and New York, 1928-39), edited by the cultural activists Dr. Simeon Psyh and Dmitry Vislocky (pseudo. Van'o Hunjanka).

By the late 1930s, the focal point for Lemko activity moved eastward from Cleveland to the New York City area. This was also a period when political preferences divided Lemko activists and organizations. Displeased with the increasingly leftist and pro-Soviet orientation of the Lemko Association, Victor Hladick, the popular Lemko cultural figure Stephen Skimba, and several Orthodox priests established in 1935 the Carpatho-Russian National Committee, which for a few years made its views known through the bi-monthly newspaper, *Karpato-russkoe slovo* (New York, 1935-38).

More influential and longer lasting was the Lemko Association. In 1939, it adopted as its mouthpiece

46. Carpatho-Russian American Center, Yonkers, New York, built 1939.

the recently-founded popular newspaper written in Lemko dialect, *Karpatska Rus'* (Yonkers, N.Y., Allentown, N.J., 1938-present), which was to be edited for its first two decades by the group's most prolific postwar spokesperson, Dr. Simeon Pysh. To accommodate the community's increasing social and cultural needs, members of a local branch of the Lemko Association joined with members of the Russian Orthodox Catholic Mutual Aid Society to construct the Carpatho-Russian American Center. Opened in 1938, in the New York City suburb of Yonkers, the C-RA Center was from the outset popularly known as "Lemko Hall," even though it was never owned by the Lemko Association. For six decades the center, with its large banquet hall, performing stage, restaurant-tavern, and picnic grounds, promoted social and cultural activity (including Lemko-Rusyn language classes and theatrical performances) and it housed the Lemko Association and its newspaper, *Karpats'ka Rus'*. The Lemko Association no longer has a building in its original Cleveland home, although smaller Lemko clubs still exist in Ansonia and Bridgeport, Connecticut.

Especially popular was the Lemko Park in Monroe, New York, opened in 1958. With this park, older immigrants obtained what their own symbolic *vatra*, or fireside hearth, where they could spend their retirement years in the warm surrounding of friends. The park also became the site of the Talerhof Memorial, dedicated in 1964 to the "martyrdom" of thousands of Carpatho-Rusyns in Galicia at the hands of Austro-Hungarian authorities during the early years of World War I. As

45. Dr. Simeon Pysh.

47. Lemko Hall, the headquarters of the Lemko National Home in Cleveland, Ohio, from 1947 to 1986.

part of the remembrance, a pilgrimage with religious services (usually led by an Orthodox bishop of the Patriarchal Exarchate) was held annually at Pentecost *(Rusalja)*. Lemko Park also had a resort with hotel facilities and an amphitheater where every summer from 1969 to the 1990s a Carpatho-Russian festival took place.

From the very outset, some Lemko Association spokespersons were anti-clerical in orientation, even though most of its members were and still are Byzantine Catholic or Orthodox parishioners. The organization's publications have also been sympathetic to leftist political ideologies, making it the only segment of the Carpatho-Rusyn immigration to speak—at least until 1989—with sympathy about Communism, the Soviet Union, and its east-central European satellite countries. Pro-Soviet attitudes were especially evident during the 1930s depression and World War II, although since then the group has often altered its views. During the 1960s, for instance, the editor of *Karpatska Rus'*, Stefan M. Kitchura, criticized Communist rule in the homeland and tried to have the Lemko Association co-operate with anti-Soviet, Ukrainian-oriented Lemko-

American groups. As a result, he was removed from the editorship and started instead his own organ, *Lemkovina* (Yonkers, N.Y., 1971-82). The Lemko Association, on the other hand, returned to a pro-Soviet stance. As for the problem of national identity, the group's publications have provided at various times differing and even contradictory explanations: that Lemkos form a distinct Slavic people; that as "Carpatho-Russians" they are part of one Russian nation; or that they are a branch of East Slavs most closely related to Ukrainians.

The seeming contradiction between church membership and the affirmation of pro-Soviet attitudes on the one hand, and confusion with respect to ethnic identity on the other, may possibly be explained by the ideology of Pan-Slavism. Like their nineteenth-century forebears in Europe, Lemko Association spokespersons felt that the unity of all Slavs was the ultimate ideal. In the twentieth century, only the might of the Soviet Union seemed to make such unity possible. Therefore, any threat to Soviet rule in east-central Europe was to be viewed as a potential threat to the greater goal of Slavic unity, which must be preserved at all costs. As a corollary to such views, the Soviet Union was viewed as the embodiment of Russia and of all Rus' peoples, including those from the Carpathians. It is in this sense, therefore, that the Lemko Association remained ideologically pro-Soviet.

The Lemko Association's main goals have been to educate its members about their homeland through the publication of books, annual almanacs, and newspapers. Even after other Rusyn-American periodicals adopted English, the Lemko Association has continued to use the native language (Lemko Region dialect in the Cyrillic alphabet) in some of its publications. For instance, the association's official newspaper only became bi-lingual in the 1980s: *Karpatska Rus'/Carpatho-Rus'*. In an attempt to attract younger members, several exclusively English-language publications were started—the *Lemko Youth Journal* (Yonkers, N.Y., 1960-64), *Carpatho-Russian American* (Yonkers, N.Y., 1968-69), *Karpaty* (Yonkers, N.Y., 1978-79)—but these were unable to survive for long. Young people were also attracted to folk ensembles, the first of which, Karpaty, lasted from 1967 to 1969 under the direction of a recently arrived professional dancer from the Prešov Region in Slovakia, Michael Savčak. In the 1980s, a Karpaty Chorus functioned in Yonkers. Despite these efforts to attract young people, the Lemko Association is today primarily the preserve of first- and second-generation immigrants whose numbers are rapidly decreasing.

A smaller group of Lemkos of pro-Ukrainian orientation felt they had little in common with the policies of the Lemko Association. Led by Mychajlo Dudra and Vasyl' Levčyk, they founded in New York City in 1936 the Organization for the Defense of the Lemko Land (Orhanizacija Oborony Lemkivščyny), which was opposed to the former Polish government's policy of considering Lemkos a nationality distinct from Ukrainians. This group was harrassed by American authorities during World War II and effectively ceased functioning, but in 1958 it was revived in Yonkers, New York under the leadership of Julijan Nalysnyk. By the 1960s, it claimed 1,500 members, and among its publications which have appeared in literary Ukrainian were *Lemkivs'kyj dzvin* (New York, 1936-40) and *Lemkivs'ki visti* (Yonkers, N.Y. and Toronto,

1958-79). A World Lemkos Federation came into being in 1973, which under the leadership of Ivan Hvozda attempted, though unsuccessfully, to function as an umbrella organization for all Ukrainian-oriented Lemko groups. The federation has managed to publish six volumes of a scholarly journal, *Annals* (Camillus, N.Y., 1974-98). Finally, in an attempt to consolidate limited resources, these two organizations also support the Lemko Research Foundation in Clifton, New Jersey, which publishes the Ukrainian-language quarterly, *Lemkivščyna* (New York, Clifton, N.J., 1979-present), and in 1982 they all cooperated to open a Ukrainian Lemko Museum at the headquarters of the Ukrainian Catholic Eparchy in Stamford, Connecticut.

Besides meeting periodically for social and cultural functions, the main activity of these various Ukrainian-oriented Lemko groups seems to be the publication of periodicals and some books (including a recent one on wooden churches) explaining the fate that has befallen their homeland. Most of the members are post-World War II immigrants who experienced first

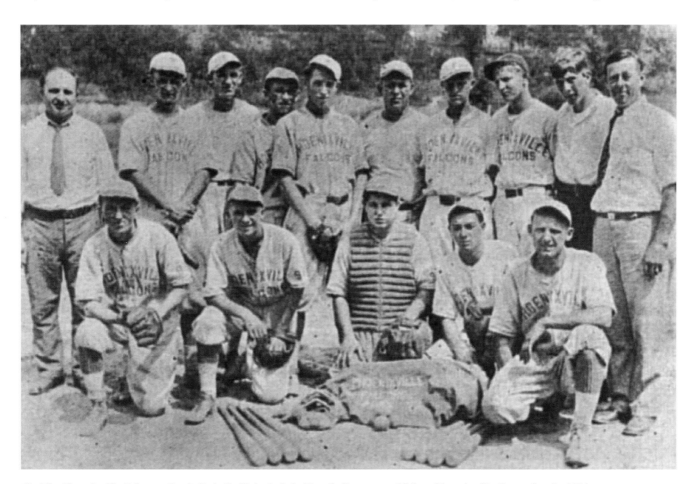

48. The Phoenixville Falcons, Greek Catholic Union's Sokol baseball team, no. 98 from Phoenixville, Pennsylvania, 1931

hand the displacement of the Lemko population from its ancestral Carpathian homeland in Galicia either eastward to the Soviet Ukraine or westward to other parts of Poland. Consequently, they are adamantly anti-Communist and anti-Polish, as well as Ukrainian in national orientation, factors which not surprisingly make them natural antagonists of the older Lemko Association. Since 1989, the pages of *Lemkivščyna* have also been filled with harsh criticism of the Rusyn national revival in Europe, and this attitude has further alienated pro-Ukrainian Lemkos from the larger Rusyn-American community.

Carpatho-Rusyns have also had their own sports and youth organizations. The oldest of these was the Sokol athletic organization of the GCU. Founded in 1910, the Sokol sponsored throughout the northeast United States a broad network of basketball teams and other sports activities. The Sokol also had its own newspaper, the *Amerikansky russky svokol* (Homestead, Pa., 1918-36), as well as a youth branch with its own organ, *Svit ditej/Children's World* (Homestead, Pa., 1917-38, 1946-75). These publications contained reports on sports activities and also articles designed to promote awareness of the Old-World culture.

Similarly, the Johnstown Diocese set up in 1937 the American Carpatho-Russian Youth organization, whose goals have been to promote social, cultural, and educational development among its approximately 1,000 members. This youth group has also had its own publications, often filled with articles stressing its "Carpatho-Russian" heritage: *Carpatho-Russian Youth* (Johnstown, Pa.; Binghamton, N. Y., 1938-41), *ACRY Annual and Church Almanac* (Ligonier, Pa.; Pittsburgh, 1949-present), and the *ACRY Guardian* (New York; Perth Amboy, N.J., 1957-62). For its part, the Byzantine Ruthenian Catholic Church has since the 1960s had a Byzantine Catholic Youth Organization. Branches exist at several parishes throughout the country and are concerned primarily with coordinating social functions for children, teenagers, singles, and young married couples. Among the most popular youth organizations are the performing folk groups, which will be discussed more extensively in Chapter 6.

49. The Greek Catholic Union's Sokol Girl's Basketball Team from Bridgeport, Connecticut, 1930-31.

Chapter 6

Culture

Carpatho-Rusyn culture in the United States has been expressed most naturally through the family unit, sometimes through fraternal organizations, but most especially through the church. Besides basic customs and habits, including language, learned from the family, it is really the religious context that is most important as a cultural identifier. In fact, the role of religion is so great that in the mind of most immigrants and their descendants, Carpatho-Rusyn culture is virtually synonymous with the Eastern-rite liturgy (originally sung in Church Slavonic) and the attendant rituals and family celebrations (births, marriages, funerals) associated with the church.

At the level of the family, it is cuisine and home handicrafts that symbolize most poignantly the "old country" culture. Recipes handed down from grandparents—stuffed cabbage *(holobci/holubki),* home-made noodles *(halušky),* stuffed peppers, and the generous use of garlic and sour cream in the preparation of many dishes—as well as embroidered or crocheted needlework and painted Easter eggs *(pysankŷ)* are still integral elements of Carpatho-Rusyn family life even after language and other cultural attributes have been long forgotten. The tradition of painted Easter eggs in their distinct Carpatho-Rusyn forms, which are generally symmetric short-stroke patterns using floral motifs and figures from life, has undergone a recent vogue. In some communities, classes have been organized to teach the skill to Americans of Rusyn and non-Rusyn background alike. The painted eggs and some of the traditional recipes are directly related to

the religious calendar. Easter, in particular, remains a memorable occasion, as the full gamut of Rusyn cuisine is again made available to palates that (if tradition is followed) have been especially whetted because of fasting during the preceding Lenten season.

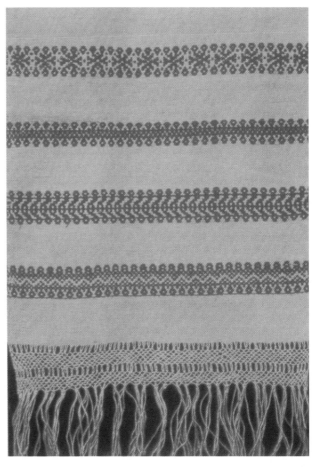

50. Embroidered ritual cloth *(ručnyk)* from the Prešov Region (former Zemplén county) in Czechoslovakia.

51. Rusyn hand-painted Easter eggs in (1) the geometric line style; and (2) the short-stroke pattern with real-life figures (photo by Anton Žižka).

52. Traditional Easter morning blessing of baskets filled with painted eggs (*pysankŷ*) and embroidered ritual cloths. The Reverend Alexis Toth outside St. Mary's Church, Minneapolis, Minnesota, circa 1890.

Even more striking evidence of the close ties between religion and Carpatho-Rusyn culture in America is the most important building outside of the familial home, the church. With regard to church architecture, many of the early structures first in wood and later in stone or brick were modeled on architectural prototypes brought from the homeland. These Old-World models reflected both the eastern and western influences that characterized Carpatho-Rusyn culture in Europe. Thus, while some Rusyn-American churches, especially among the Orthodox, were built according to the central-domed eastern style based on a Greek-cross ground plan, most were constructed on a hybrid pattern. This meant that their ground plans followed the western, basilica form, having a nave and transept and one or two towers dominating the westwork (western facade), while the towers themselves were often topped with golden, Baroque-style "onion" domes above which were placed three-barred Eastern-rite crosses. Many of these old "Russian" churches, as they are often incorrectly designated, are still standing and remain distinct landmarks in many urban centers of the northeastern United States. The eastern character of these structures was particularly noticeable in the interiors, which usually had icon screens (iconostases) separating the altar from the congregation. Such churches clearly reminded the parishioners of their cultural relations with the Carpatho-Rusyn homeland which, in turn, found its religious and artistic inspiration in Orthodox Byzantium.

At least until World War II, churches built by the Byzantine Ruthenian Catholic and Orthodox communities maintained traditional architectural styles. Since then, however, building costs and changing tastes have led to the construction of more "modern" structures, most often in a bland functional style that hardly distinguishes them externally—and in many cases internally as well—from other Catholic and even Protestant churches.

While construction of these simplistic, nondescript structures has become the rule in recent years,

53. Iconostasis, St. John the Baptist Byzantine Catholic Church, Lyndora, Pennsylvania, crafted by John Baycura, 1915.

54. St. George, later St. Nicholas Greek Catholic Church, Minersville, Pennsylvania, built 1896. An early example of the western-oriented basilica style.

55. St. Theodosius Russian Orthodox Greek Catholic Cathedral, Cleveland, Ohio, 1896. Early example of the eastern-oriented central-domed style.

there have nonetheless been a few exceptions. The Byzantine Ruthenian Catholic Church of St. Mary in New York City (lower Manhattan), completed in 1963, combines both the functionalism of the modern international school of architecture with many motifs of the Carpatho-Rusyn Eastern-rite heritage. Another adaptation of architectural tradition is to build entirely in wood, such as the striking Carpathian wooden church constructed for a new Byzantine Ruthenian parish in the Atlanta suburb of Roswell, Georgia.

The early immigrants have left other marks on the American cultural landscape, especially in local graveyards. Several cemeteries in towns where Carpatho-Rusyns settled contain gravestones with the visually distinct Eastern-rite three- or two-barred cross. Aside from the number of bars on the crosses, Rusyn graves are also easy to determine if their inscriptions are written in Cyrillic letters (using Rusyn phonetic transcription) or if they use Hungarian spellings in the Roman alphabet for Slavic names (for instance, Maczko, Zsatkovics).

Music has been a particularly important element in Carpatho-Rusyn culture. Secular music in the form

56. Holy Trinity Russian Orthodox Church, Chicago, Illinois, built 1903. Stylized central-domed style by the leading American architect, Louis Sullivan.

of Rusyn folk melodies was most often sung, and in some cases still is, although in a homogenized form at wedding receptions and other family gatherings. Social dancing to spirited Carpathian rhythms like the *karička* (girl's circle dance) and most especially the *čardaš* (the most popular "Rusyn" dance) were widespread during the first decades of this century, although they have been replaced by more "international" and stylized dances like the waltz or, for a more Slavic flavor, the Slovenian polka, the Polish polka, the Russian *kalinka,* and the Ukrainian *kozačok.*

The desire to perform the Old-World dances and songs in their original musical and lyrical form has become the goal of Rusyn-American folk ensembles. While many such groups existed during the earlier years of this century, by the 1950s they had begun to disappear. There was a revival, however, related in large part to the "roots fever" and general interest in ethnicity that swept much of the United States during the mid-1970s. Although often associated with a parish church or fraternal society, these ensembles were usually founded and led by young people interested in learning the dances and in making and donning the colorful costumes representative of the Carpatho-Rusyn heritage.

Not surprisingly, the new groups were based in the traditional centers of Rusyn-American settlement— the metropolitan areas of Pittsburgh, Cleveland, and Detroit. Often organized for several age levels and encouraging parent participation, the folk ensembles showed a real potential to draw and to maintain interest in popular Carpatho-Rusyn culture. Among the most effective activists in the folk ensemble movement during the 1970s and 1980s was Jerry Jumba, a professional musician and choreographer, who initiated and/or participated in many of the dozen new ensembles that came into being. Among these were the Carpathian Youth Choir and Dancers (Monessen, Pennsylvania), Rusynŷ (McKeesport, Pennsylvania), Karpaty (Ambridge, Pennsylvania), Kruzhok (Parma, Ohio), Beskidy Rusyns (Livonia, Michigan), Krajane (Sterling Heights, Michigan), and the Carpathians (Barberton, Ohio). By the late 1980s, however, most of these groups ceased functioning,

57. Former cathedral church of the Byzantine Ruthenian Catholic Archdiocese of Pittsburgh, built in 1903, Munhall, Pennsylvania. Since 2004 home to the Carpatho-Rusyn Society's National Carpatho-Rusyn Cultural Center.

58. Rusyn tombstones at the Rose Hill Cemetary, Butler, Pennsylvania (photo by Peter Bajcura).

either because the initial enthusiasm of the "roots fever" years had worn off, or because they were unable to find financial support from the established religious and secular organizations which, in general, remained unmoved by the ethnic revival. As a result, today only four of the groups founded since 1975 are still active—Slavjane (McKees Rocks, Pennsylvania), the Holy Ghost Choir and Dancers (Philadelphia, Pennsylvania), the Carpathians (Binghamton, New York), and the St. Michael's Youth Folk Dance Group (Chicago, Illinois).

While interest in secular music performed by Rusyn-American folk ensembles has risen and fallen at various times, church music has been more constant. The dominant feature of the church repertoire is the *prostopinije,* or liturgical plain chant, which is still used in both Byzantine Catholic and Orthodox churches. The *prostopinije* brought by the early immigrants from the Carpatho-Rusyn homeland was distinct from other Eastern-rite chant music because it incorporated numerous local folk melodies. This specific liturgical music has been preserved by generations of church choirs as well as by more formal programs, such as cantors' schools and the Carpatho-Rusyn Liturgical Chant Renewal Program run by Jerry Jumba for the Byzantine Ruthenian Metropolitan Archdiocese of Pittsburgh between 1984 and 1992.

Several choirs have also produced records with both religious and secular folk music, including renditions of the spirited Carpatho-Rusyn national anthem, "Podkarpatskij rusynŷ, ostavte hlubokyj son" (Subcarpathian Rusyns, Arise From Your Deep Slumber), and the even more popular "Ja rusyn bŷl, jesm' i budu" (I Was, Am, and Will Remain a Rusyn). Particularly well represented over the past three decades, with several recordings to their credit, are

59. Carpatho-Russian Orthodox Greek Catholic Church of St. John the Baptist, Mill Hill Avenue, Bridgeport, Connecticut, built 1946, by architect Jesse J. Hamblin. Neo-Byzantine basilica and central-domed hybrid modelled after the Church of the Madeleine in Paris.

60. St. Mary Byzantine Catholic Church, 15th Street and Second Avenue, Manhattan, New York City, built 1963, by architect Cajetan J.B. Baumann, OFM.

61. SS. Cyril and Methodius Church, American Carpatho-Russian Orthodox Diocesan Camp Nazareth, Mercer, Pennsylvania, built 2003. Stylized traditional Carpathian wooden church designed by Joseph P. Parimucha.

62. Holy Trinity Church, Wilkeson, Washington, typical white wooden clapboard rural church (photo by Orestes Mihaly).

the Holy Ghost Byzantine Choir of Philadelphia, directed by Daniel J. Kavka; St. Mary's Metropolitan Choir of New York City, directed by Gabriel Zihal; and the St. Mary Choir of Van Nuys, California, directed by Michael M. Bodnar—all associated with the Byzantine Ruthenian Catholic Church; Christ the Saviour Cathedral Choir of Johnstown, Pennsylvania, directed by Andrew Panchisin, and St. Michael's Church Choir of Binghamton, New York, directed by Edward Sedor—both with the Johnstown Diocese; and St. John the Baptist Russian Orthodox Church Choir of Passaic, New Jersey, directed by Michael Hilko, of the Orthodox Church in America.

The combination of music, spiritual devotion, and an appropriate architectural and natural setting is also expressed among those Carpatho-Rusyns in the United States who still actively maintain the Old-World custom of annual religious processions and retreats known as *otpusti*. These events are usually associated with retreats, such as those held at St. Tikhon's Monastery outside of Scranton, Pennsylvania among Orthodox in the OCA; at Holy Trinity Monastery in Jordanville, New York among the Orthodox in the Synod; at Christ the Saviour Seminary in Johnstown, Pennsylvania and at Camp Nazareth near Mercer, Pennsylvania for Orthodox in the Johnstown Diocese; and at the Monastery of the Basilian Fathers of Mariapoch in Matawan, New Jersey among Byzantine Ruthenian Catholics.

The oldest and largest of these religious processions/ retreats is held each August on the grounds of the Basilian Convent at Mount St. Macrina near Uniontown, Pennsylvania, south of Pittsburgh. Each Labor Day weekend since 1934, at times as many as 40,000 Byzantine Ruthenian Catholics have gathered to renew their faith, and by so doing to re-emphasize a sense of community among the group's members. The sisters at Mt. Macrina, in addition, have published for many years a periodical, *The Voice of Mount St. Macrina/Holos Hory Sv. Makriny* (Uniontown, Pa., 1948-present), which especially in its early years contained material on Carpatho-Rusyn culture. In 1975, during the height of the "roots fever" in America, the Basilian sisters sponsored a two-day cultural seminar on Carpathian Rus', which brought together secular and clerical scholars to lecture on several aspects of Rusyn history, language, and culture.

Another Old-World tradition that was begun and is still maintained among Carpatho-Rusyns in the United States is a celebration known as Rusyn Day *(Rus'kyj Den')*, held during the summer months and often at amusement parks. Rusyn Days have been geared to both people of Carpatho-Rusyn background as well as to the larger American public. Traditionally, the annual event includes speeches by Carpatho-Rusyn religious and secular leaders (joined sometimes by local politicians) as well as performances by folk choirs and dance groups. The oldest Rusyn Day celebration has been held since 1921 at Kennywood Park in Pittsburgh. From the 1920s until the 1950s, several towns in the northeast had annual Rusyn days, among the largest being those at Luna Park in Cleveland and at Idora Park in Youngstown, Ohio. From 1969 to the 1990s, the Lemkos held annual "Carpatho-Russian" festivals at their resort in Monroe, New York.

Among the various cultural characteristics associated with ethnic groups, language frequently has been considered the most important vehicle for transmitting and preserving group identity. With regard to language as a carrier of Carpatho-Rusyn culture in the United States, it would be useful first to emphasize the differences that exist between spoken and written languages. All languages are composed of several spoken dialects and of one, or even more than one, standard written form. Moreover, there is often a substantial difference between the standard written form of a language and the dialects that the written form ostensibly represents.

In the European homeland, Carpatho-Rusyns at the time of the largest migration to America before World War I communicated in a variety of speech which belonged to either the Prešov Region, Lemko Region, or Transcarpathian (Subcarpathian) dialectal groups, which together were classified by many linguists as part of the Ukrainian language. Living along the

63. Slavjane Folk Ensemble, McKees Rocks, Pennsylvania.

64. Carpathian Youth Choir and Dancers, Monessen, Pennsylvania (photo by George W. Shusta).

65. Otpust-religious procession at Mount St. Macrina, Uniontown, Pennsylvania, 1968.

66. Clergy lead the festivities on Rusyn Day *(Rus'kyj Den')*, Olympia Park, Cleveland, July 16, 1935.

The 34th Annual
RUSIN DAY

Sponsored by
THE RUSIN DAY ASSOCIATION OF GREATER CLEVELAND, INC.

SUNDAY
July 26, 1959

ST. JOHN'S GROVE
5822 BROADVIEW ROAD
PARMA, OHIO

REV. MYRON HORVATH, CHAIRMAN
RUSIN DAY COMMITTEE

PROCEEDS FOR BENEFIT OF THE
CLEVELAND BYZANTINE RITE DEANERY

67. Program to the annual Rusyn Day in the Cleveland area.

extreme western portion of the Ukrainian linguistic area, however, the Carpatho-Rusyns were strongly influenced by the Slovak, Polish, and Hungarian languages. The immigrants described their native speech in a variety of ways: (1) Rusyn *(rus'kyj),* which in English was frequently and incorrectly rendered as Russian or Carpatho-Russian; (2) "Slavish," a meaningless term which probably arose as a result of sharing with eastern Slovak dialect speakers many terms and expressions; and (3) *po-našomu,* meaning in our own way.

Despite what the immigrants actually spoke—various Rusyn dialects—and notwithstanding what they called their language, they also wrote and published in a wide variety of linguistic forms and alphabets. An analysis of their publications has revealed that basically three types of written languages were used. These may be classified as: (1) the Subcarpathian dialectal variant; (2) the Lemko dialectal variant; and (3) the Carpatho-Rusyn variant of Russian.

The Subcarpathian variant reflected the spoken language of immigrants from the Prešov Region of present-day northeastern Slovakia (sometimes with strong East Slovak dialectal influences) and from the Transcarpathian Oblast in Ukraine often with the addition of Russian and American English loanwords. This was the form used in the most widely read newspapers, such as the *Amerikansky russky viestnik*

(1892-1952), *Prosvita* (1917-1970s), *Vostok* (1919-50), *Russkij vistnik* (1917-1970s), and the only daily, *Den'* (1922-27). Some of these publications originally used the Cyrillic alphabet (including the old orthography distinguished by the letters ѣ and ы), but by the 1930s they changed to a Czech-based Latin alphabet (recognizable by use of the *haček* accent over certain letters—č=ch, š=sh, ž=zh—as well as apostrophes to indicate East Slavic soft signs usually at the end of words).

The Lemko variant reflected the spoken language of Lemko Rusyns from Galicia and was used in

most publications of the Lemko Association, such as *Karpatska Rus'* (1938-present), which still uses the Cyrillic alphabet in its modern orthography. The third written form, the Carpatho-Rusyn variant of Russian, represented the attempt of some Carpatho-Rusyn immigrants from various parts of Carpathian Rus' to write in Russian. The result was an unstandardized language using the Cyrillic alphabet (in the old orthography) that tried to follow the rudiments of literary Russian grammar but which invariably included numerous lexical and syntactical borrowings from Carpatho-Rusyn dialects. This linguistic form

(1)

V vašich rukach, dorohoj čitatel', jubilejnyj vypusk našeho official'noho organa "Vostoka", s uveličennym količestvom stranic.

Jubilejnyj nomer! Jubilej dvadcat' pjat' l'itňaho suščestvovanija odnoj iz nemnohich karpatorusskich zapomohovych organizacij v Sojedinennych Štatach — organizacii Svobody.

Dl'a postoronnaho čital'a sej jubilejnyj nomer ne označajet inšoho, jak uveličennoje količestvo stranic: bohato dobranyj material, snimki, stat'ji iz pod pera raznych lic, mnoho pozdravitel'nych i kommerčeskich privitstvij i proč. No dl'a členov-truženikov sej jubilej označajet zaveršenije dvadcat' pjat' l'itnaho truda na organizacijnim poprišči.

Každyj jubilej — eto obzor vseho toho, čto bylo sd'ilano za minuvšij srok. I tak, jak v nastojaščem misjaci my stavim točku v konci toj raboty, kotoru my končili v prot'aženii četvert' stol'itija, ne budet neumistnym ohl'anutis' nazad na projdennyj nami put' i dati sebi otčet iz našich dostiženij.

Vostok, July 1943

(2)

V New Yorku byla deržana konferencia meždu kompaniami mjahkoho uhl'a i zastupnikami majnerskej unii. Na začatku konferencii tak pokazovalosja, že iz toho nebude cilkom nič, poneže kompanie nijak nechotili pristati na sije, čtoby ot 1-ho april'a 1923, pod takima uslovijami byli majnery platene, jak teper polučajut za svoju robotu, a to dl'a klevlandskej konferencii rišenija. Konečno po dlukšom razbiraniju majnerskoho voprosa, na vlijanije pravitelstva iz Washingtonu, kompanie prijmajut to, že podpišu paktum klevelandskej konferencii na odin rok. To jest, ot 1-ho april'a 1923, do 1-ho april'a 1924. Zastupniki majnerskej unii chot'ili na dva roki, no to neudalosja. Tak samo i to bylo prijato ne newyorkskej konferencii, že načalom roku 1924 poderži sja znova taka konferencia, aby bylo obkerovano strajku ot 1-ho april'a 1924.

Slava Tebi Hospodi! — Chot'aj odno važnoje d'ilo pokojno rišeno i majnery budut spokojno prodolžati svoju robotu do 1-ho april'a 1924 hoda. Sija radostnaja sprava ne tol'ko pro majnerov, no i pro každoho obchodnika i urjadnika.

Russkij viestnik, January 25, 1923

(3)

"Карпатска Русь", яка пишеся нашым народным говором, чым одріжнятся од других газет, интересна и тым, што новостями, якы передає, дає можливость легше порозуміти значеніє світовых подий. Чытаючы нашу газету стає ясным, што ничого доброго народы світа не можут сподіватися од тых, што выділяют билионы и билионы доларов на вооруженіє, бо се означає убийство бідного, в ничом невиноватого народа. Се робится тоді, коли ищы не загоилися раны навет першой світовой войны, а про жертвы другой світовой войны навет не говорю, бо они свіжы в нашой памяти и очевидны, єсли отвидите ветеранскы шпыталі.

В першой світовой войні я был арестованый з небощыком татом, об, як и нашы покойны предки, мы голосилися до русской народности, мы осталися вірными сынами и дочками нашой православной віри и нашых звычайов. Батько стался жертвом переслідований врагами нашого народа. Умер от мук в Талергофі и там был похованый под соснами.

Карпатска Русь, July 6, 1980

(4)

Нерѣдко становится человѣку досадно, когда проѣзжая черезъ любую мѣстность, въ которой находятся промышленные заводы, или нефтяные рудники каковыхъ въ нашей русской части Галиціи особенно много, слышимъ все польскій или нѣмецкій говоръ работающихъ. А вѣдь если посмотрѣть мѣстоположеніе допустимъ таково всѣмъ почти заграничнымъ промышленникамъ извѣстнаго Борислава или Сходницы, такъ увидимъ, что кругомъ Русь; мало того, даже самые шахты помѣщаются на поляхъ русскихъ крестьянъ. Изъ нѣдръ этой отъ вѣковъ русской земли тысячи машинъ высасываютъ милліоны гектолитровъ нефты, которой питается чуть-ли не вся Европа.

Правда, February 16, 1923

68. Varieties of Carpatho-Rusyn written language from the press. (1) *Vostok*—Subcarpathian dialect using the Latin alphabet; (2) *Russkij viestnik*—Subcarpathian dialect using the Latin alphabet; (3) *Karpatska Rus'*—Lemko dialect; (4) *Pravda*—attempt to write in Russian.

CARPATHO-RUSYN IN THE CONTEXT
OF NEIGHBORING LANGUAGES AND DIALECTS

English translation

Soon my sister is getting married. I can't wait to see her in her wedding dress. All our family and friends will be in church and then we will all go to the wedding reception. Father says he will dance with my sister and mother and that there will be enough food, drink, and music to last all though the night. I only hope the weather will be nice.

SLOVAK

literary standard	East Slovak/Šariš dialect (Prešov)	Sotak dialect (Humenné)
Sestra sa mi bude zanedlho vydávat'. Nemôzem sa dočkat', až ju uvidím v svadobných šatách. Celá rodina a priatelia budú v kostole a potom pôjdeme na svadobnú hostinu. Otec hovorí, že bude tancovat' s mojou sestrou a mamou, a že bude dost' jedla i pitia a hudba bude vyhrávat' celú noc. Dúfam len, že počasie bude pekné.	Oňedluho śe mi budze śestra vidavic. Už śe ňemožem dočekac, kedi ju uvidim vof svadebnich (vešelnich, braltovskich) šatoch (lachoch). Cala rodzina a parcel'e budu v koscelě a potim pujdzeme na svadebnu hoscinu. Ocec (Apo) hutori, že budze tancovac z moju śestru i z maceru a že budze dosc jedzeňa I pijatiki a muzika budze hrac calu noc. L'em žebi chvil'a bula šumna.	Śestra šä mi budze skoro odavac. Juž šä ňemožu dočakac, so ju uvidzim u veśelných šatoch. Šỹčka rodzina i pajtaše budu v koscelě, a potym pujdzeme na hoscinu. Ocac povedaju, že vỹtancuju moju śestru i mac, a že jesc i pic budze nadosc a muzika budze vỹhravac calu noc. L'am ňaj bỹ čas bỹv dobrỹ.

CARPATHO-RUSYN

Prešov Region dialect (Svidník)	Lemko Region dialect (Dukla)	Transcarpathian dialect (Mukačevo)
Sestra sja mi bude neodovha vỹdavaty. Nemožu sja dočekaty, koly ju uvydžu vo vesil'ných šmatoch. Všỹtka rodyna I pryjatele budut v cerkvi, a potim pideme na vesil'nu hostynu. Ňaňo povidajut, že budut tancovaty zo sestrom i mamom, a že bude dost jisty i pyty a muzika bude vyhravaty cilu nič. L'em žebỹ chvil'a bỹla dobra.	Skoro moja sestra bude sja vỹdavaty. Ja ne možu dočekaty vydity jej slubne ubranja. Vsja rodyna pryjdut' do našej cerkvej a pak potomu mỹ ušytkỹ pideme na hostynu. Otec hvaryt', že vin iz sestrov i mamov bude tancuvaty i že bude dosta všỹtkoho jisty i pyty i pohuljaty od večera až do rana. Ja tilko žyču, žebỹ bula dobra pohoda.	Skoro moja sestra bude sja uddavaty. Ja ne honna dočekaty vydity jeji u molodyčnüj odeži. Usi naši rodyči taj znamnykỹ prejdut' do cerkvy a potüm mỹ ušỹtki püdeme na hostynu. Otec kaže, oš bude yhraty yz mamov taj sestrov, oš bude dosta isty j pyty taj banda bude bavyty do rana. Ja lem bỹch ljubyla obỹ bỹla krasna pohoda

CARPATHO-RUSYN IN THE CONTEXT
OF NEIGHBORING LANGUAGES AND DIALECTS
(cont'd)

UKRAINIAN		RUSSIAN
Galician dialect (Stanislaviv)	literary standard	literary standard
Skoro si bude viddavaty moja sestra. Ne možu si dočykaty zobačyty ji v šljubnim ubranju. Cila naši familija pryjde do cerkvy, a potim na vesilje. Tato kažut, žy budut huljaty z mamov i sestrov i žy bude dosta vs'oho jisty j pyty, a muzyky hratymut do samoho rani. Ja bym ino chtila, by bula fajna pohoda.	Nezabarom moja sestra vychodyt' zamiž. Ne možu dočekatysja, koly pobaču jiji v šljubnomu odjazi. Vsja naša ridnja ta znajomi pryjdut' do cerkvy na vinčannja, a potim na vesil'nu hostynu. Bat'ko kaže, ščo bude tancjuvaty z mamoju j sestroju, ščo na vesilli bude dosyt' vsjakoji jiži j napojiv, a muzyka hratyme do samoho ranku. Ja duže chotila b, ščob bula harna pohoda.	Moja sestra skoro vychodit zamuž. Ne mogu doždat'sja, kogda ja uvižu eë v podvenečnom plat'e. Vsja sem'ja i naši druz'ja budut v cerkvi, a zatem my vse pojdëm na svadebnyj užin. Otec govorit, čto on budet tancevat' s sestroj i materju i čto budet dostatočno edy, napitkpov i muzyki na vsju noč. Ja tol'ko nadejus', čto pogoda budet choroshaja.

Carpatho-Rusyn, Ukrainian, and Russian are written in the Cyrillic alphabet. The texts have been transliterated for those who may read only in Latin alphabet. For basic pronunciation: c=ts; ch=kh; j=y; ja=ya; ň=nye; š and ś=sh; ž=zh. The characteristic Carpatho-Rusyn (and Sotak) vowel ŷ is pronounced like *ea* in the word earth.

The dialectal forms in columns 2 through 7 have been transcribed from native speakers from villages near the cities that are indicated in the parentheses. Sotak is a transitional dialect between Slovak and Carpatho-Rusyn, and it is traditionally spoken in several villages between Humenné and Snina (old Zemplén county).

Dorohaya Marushka:

I guess ze ti dumala ze ya leave-vovala svit jak ja nye pisala sooner. Ale ja bula taka busy sos holidays, i ja mala mali mishap zhe ja neznala chi ja coming or going.

Tam tyi Thursday noch, ja bula babysitting, everything ishlo O.K., yak ja noticesovala zhe baby chokuje. Ja dostala so excited, ja grabuvala babu, i turnovala kid upside down, i trepem, i trepem, a ona estche chokuje.

Ja po callovala doctors, on prishol, i powil zati do hospitalya na X-rayse. X-rays buli O.K., i ya vzala jeh domy. Ja bula taka happy zhe nich ne yest wrong, i na druhu ruku taka mad zhe ona scareovala mene.

Ja learnovala taki lesson zhe never zabudem. Ja nihda budem watchovati kidsy anymore. Moji babysitting days pishle het.

Budte zdorovi, Helena

69. Rusyn-English pidgeon language as used in an amusing article from the *Orthodox Herald.*

dominated the early years of the newspapers *Svit* (1894-present) and *Pravda* (1902-present), and more recently appeared in the Cyrillic sections of *Carpatho-Russian Echoes/Karpatorusskije otzvuki* (1983-89).

To these three categories of Carpatho-Rusyn written language in the United States were added standard literary Ukrainian *(Karpats'ka zorja, Vistnyk)* and literary Russian *(Pravoslavnaja Rus', Svobodnoe slovo Karpatskoj Rusi)* used by post-World War II immigrants of the Ukrainian or Russian national orientations. But it is English which by far has become the most important language. Today, very few Carpatho-Rusyn immigrants or their descendants speak a language other than English in their daily lives and, with the exception of the Lemko Association newspaper *(Karpatska Rus')* and the now rare Rusyn columns in a few other newspapers *(Church Messenger,*

GCU Messenger), the group's religious and secular press is in English.

Even before English became the dominant linguistic form in the late 1950s and 1960s, it infiltrated Carpatho-Rusyn, so that both the spoken language as well as all three forms of written language rapidly acquired a high number of borrowings from English. This was particularly the case for words related to industrial and political situations not present in the old country at the time of the immigrant's departure. Among the more commonly used linguistic borrowings were: *bos* (boss), *kara* (car), *majna* (mine), *burder* (boarder), and *salun* (saloon). English loanwords also quickly entered everyday Carpatho-Rusyn speech—for example, *boysik* (boy), *štor* (store), *porč* (porch), *šusy* (shoes)—so that most first-generation immigrants and their offspring (if they retained their original language at all) spoke at best a kind of Rusyn-English hybrid. Today, the middle and retirement age children of the first immigrants may understand Carpatho-Rusyn, but they are unable to speak very much. The third-, fourth-, and fifth-generation descendants rarely know any Rusyn at all.

In the past, a few immigrant writers tried to provide some standards for their language. A grammar (1919) and a reader (1919, 1935), both by Father Joseph Hanulya, and three primers *(bukvary)* by Peter J. Maczkov (1921), Dmitry Vislocky (1931), and Stefan F. Telep (1938) all strove to provide "literary" forms which could be used in schools and by editors in their publications. In effect, each of these amateur linguists, who knew well only their own Carpatho-Rusyn dialect, tried to write in Russian, the result being highly individual varieties of the Carpatho-Rusyn variant of Russian. It is also interesting to note that, with the exception of Telep, these same authors did not try to write in Russian in their other publications, but rather used the Subcarpathian (Hanulya, Maczkov) or Lemko (Vislocky) Carpatho-Rusyn dialectal variants. Since World War II, there have been a few attempts to provide Carpatho-Rusyn texts for people who want to relearn or learn for the first time the language of their forefathers. The most recent of these are the two English-Rusyn phrasebooks by Paul R. Magocsi, *Let's Speak Rusyn (Bisidujme po-rus'kŷ,* 1976, 1978 and *Hovorim po-rus'kŷ,* 1979), based on the speech of individual villages in the Prešov Region and in

Subcarpathian Rus'.

In the end, spoken Carpatho-Rusyn has not survived, because there have been few formal means for preserving it. During the 1930s and 1940s, radio stations in cities like New York, Pittsburgh, and Cleveland offered short programs in Carpatho-Rusyn, and until the early 1960s most priests still gave brief homilies in the language, although the liturgy was sung in Church Slavonic, a classical language that functioned as Latin did until the 1960s in the Roman Catholic Church. For nearly three decades until his death in 1994, the "Byzantine Catholic Radio Bishop," John M. Bilock, used Carpatho-Rusyn in his homily on weekly church services broadcast from Pittsburgh. But today English is the predominant language in the Byzantine Ruthenian Catholic and Orthodox churches,

except in some parishes where Church Slavonic may still be used for the liturgy and in rare cases Rusyn for homilies.

There were educational facilities in Carpatho-Rusyn communities already during the last decade of the nineteenth century. These were usually "ethnic schools," called the *Rus'ka škola* (Rusyn school), that began first in church basements and in some cases later had their own buildings beside or near the church. The early "schools" were actually classes held after the public school day was over, and they were staffed more often than not by church cantors, who, because of their activity, popularly became known as "professors." By the 1940s, many of the after-public-school-classes were discontinued, while churches began to sponsor all-day parochial schools staffed, at

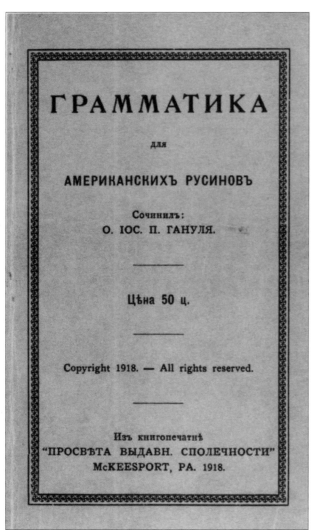

70. Title page of the first *Grammar for American Rusyns (Hrammatyka dlja amerykanskych rusynov)* by Father Joseph Hanulya.

71. Title page of a primer for American Lemkos, the *Carpatho-Russian Primer (Karpatorusskij bukvar')* by Vanja Hunjanka (pseud. of Dmitry Vislocky).

72. St. John's Greek Catholic School, Perth Amboy, New Jersey, built 1921.

least in the Byzantine Ruthenian Church, by sisters from the Order of St. Basil the Great. Although the Rusyn religious tradition was still stressed, language and other elements of the Old-World heritage were dropped from the curriculum.

Even during the early decades, when Carpatho-Rusyn language instruction was still offered, there were never any adequate textbooks nor, as we have seen, a clear decision as to what language should be taught—Rusyn vernacular, Russian, or a transitional East Slovak/Rusyn dialect. On the other hand, Carpatho-Rusyn had (and in some cases still has) a functional use in churches—whether in homilies, confessions, or general pastoral work—so that new priests assigned to older "ethnic" parishes are still expected to have some linguistic knowledge in order to communicate with the albeit ever-dwindling numbers of first-generation immigrants. Thus, since the 1950s, both the Byzantine Ruthenian Catholic Seminary in Pittsburgh and the Carpatho-Russian Orthodox Seminary in Johnstown, Pennsylvania have from time to time offered instruction in Carpatho-Rusyn, but this, too, has been largely ineffectual because of the lack of suitable texts and the restricted use of the language outside the classroom. For the Orthodox seminary course, a "Carpatho-Russian" text was prepared by Monsignor John Yurcisin, while for the Byzantine Catholic seminary course—offered during the mid-1970s in conjunction with Duquesne University and renewed in the 1990s—a "Ruthenian"

text was prepared by Father Athanasius Pekar. Neither of these instructional manuals was ever published.

The Carpatho-Rusyn immigration has produced a small corpus of belles-lettres. Short plays and collections of poetry were the most popular literary media. Plays describing village life in Europe or the American experience were particularly important, because they provided a repertoire for the adult and children's dramatic circles that before World War II were found in most local parishes and fraternal lodges. The most talented and prolific writer was Father Emilij A. Kubek, who published numerous short stories, poems, and the only novel produced in the Carpatho-Rusyn immigration: *Marko Šoltys: roman iz žit'ja Podkarpatskoj Rusi* (Marko Šoltys: A Novel About Life in Subcarpathian Rus', 1923), 3 volumes. Three other capable writers whose literary careers began in Europe but who also published in the United States were Dmitry Vislocky, author of short stories and plays in the Lemko dialect about life in the immigration and the homeland—*V Ameryki* (In America, 1932), *Šoltys* (1938), *Petro Pavlyk* (1937); the Russian-oriented Dmitry Vergun—*Karpatorusskie otzvuki* (Carpatho-Russian Echoes, 1920); and the Ukrainian-language lyric poet and Basilian monk, Sevastijan Sabol, who wrote under the pseudonym Zoreslav—*Z rannich*

73. Father Emilij A. Kubek.

74. Cast of the *Berecka svad'ba* (Bereg Wedding), performed in 1935 by the parishoners of the St. John the Baptist Church, Perth Amboy, New Jersey.

vesen (From Early Spring, 1963).

The remaining belletrists were amateurs, whose work had more sentimental, patriotic, and linguistic significance than literary value. Among the more popular writers were Peter P. Hatalak, Peter J. Maczkov, Stefan F. Telep, and several priests: Sigmund Brinsky, Valentine Gorzo, Orestes Koman, Ivan A. Ladižinsky, Jurion Thegze, and Stefan Varzaly.

A few belletrists of second-generation Carpatho-Rusyn background used autobiographical elements in some of their English-language works. The most well-known of these was the novelist and dramatist, Thomas Bell, whose father came from the Prešov Region in northeastern Slovakia. Several of Bell's novels dealt with the fate of Rusyn, Slovak, and other east-central European immigrants during the Great Depression. The best known of these was *Out of This Furnace* (1941). The hardships of the 1930s also served as the backdrop for the novel, *Icon of Spring* (1987) by Sonya Jason, the daughter of immigrants from Subcarpathian

Rus' who continues to incorporate Rusyn-American themes in her writings.

More widely read than belles-lettres was the large variety of polemical pamphlet literature. In a community that was continually rent by religious, political, and national controversy, it is not surprising that attacks and counterattacks were often the "literary order" of the day. And the environment was almost always one in which subtlety and persuasion by nuance were virtually unknown. Instead, blunt and aggressive though in retrospect colorful titles often summed up the "objective" and "truthful" arguments put forth by the avid polemicists. Typical in this genre for religious argumentation were pamphlets like: *Where to Seek the Truth* (1894) by Father Alexis Toth; *Whose Truth Is It? That of the Catholics or Non-Catholics?!* (1922) by Father Joseph P. Hanulya; *Why Am I a Greek Catholic of the Orthodox Faith?* (1939) by Father Peter J. Molchany; or *Should a Priest Be Married?* (1942) by Father Joseph Mihaly. The defense of "Rusynism"

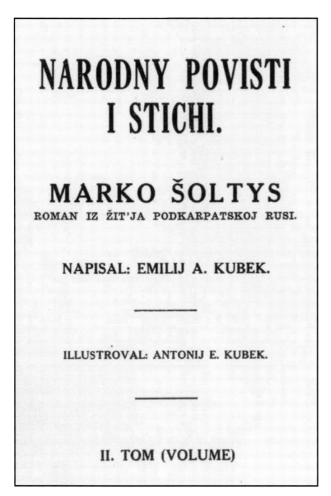

NARODNY POVISTI
I STICHI.

MARKO ŠOLTYS

ROMAN IZ ŽIT'JA PODKARPATSKOJ RUSI.

NAPISAL: EMILIJ A. KUBEK.

ILLUSTROVAL: ANTONIJ E. KUBEK.

II. TOM (VOLUME)

75. Title page of the novel *Marko Šoltys* by Emilij A. Kubek.

through anti-Czechoslovak attacks was most evident in *Wilson's Principles in Czechoslovak Practice: The Situation of the Czechoslovak People Under the Czech Yoke* (1929) by Michael Yuhasz, while Orthodox Russophile denials of the very existence of Ukrainians were summed up in *The Biggest Lie of the Century— 'the Ukraine'* (1952) and *Highlights of Russian History and the 'Ukrainian' Provocation (1955),* both by Father Peter G. Kohanik. Praise for the Soviet Union by leftist activists in the Lemko Associaton was best represented by Dmitry Vislocky, who under the pseudonym Van'o Hunjanka wrote *Pravda o Rossyy* (The Truth About Russia, 1935) and *Shto treba znaty Lemkam v Ameryki*: (What Lemkos in America Need to Know, 1962).

The largest percentage of Carpatho-Rusyn belles-lettres, polemical articles, and more serious historical and social commentaries did not come out as separate titles, but rather appeared in the more than 60 newspapers and annual almanacs that have appeared

since 1892 and have been published for the most part by the community's several churches and fraternal organizations. There was even a large format, though short-lived Rusyn-American literary monthly called *Niva* (Yonkers, N.Y., 1916).

Many of the individual titles were put out before the 1950s by publishing houses such as the Greek Catholic Union Typography (Homestead, Pennsylvania), the Vostok and Vestal Publishing Company (Perth Amboy, New Jersey), and George Sabo (Pearl River, New York) The problem of distribution during these early years was handled by bookdealers like Julius Egreczky of Cleveland, John Korman of Braddock, Pennsylvania, and George Sabo of Pearl River, New York and later Melbourne, Florida. The financial requirements of these businessmen were complemented by a sense of patriotism that prompted them to diffuse knowledge of Carpatho-Rusyn culture both within and beyond the community. With the changeover to English during the last three decades, two new publishing houses have come into existence: the Byzantine Seminary Press

76. Title page of the Rusyn-American literary and religious monthly, *Niva,* 11 issues (352 pages) of which appeared in 1916.

(Pittsburgh, Pennsylvania) publishes mostly religious-related materials, while the Carpatho-Rusyn Research Center (Ocala, Florida) is concerned primarily with works about the secular as well as religious heritage of the group both in Europe and in the United States.

The world of scholarship and the arts has also been enriched by a few Carpatho-Rusyn immigrants and their descendants. The history of the group itself in both Europe and America has quite naturally become the focus of attention. Several learned priests, in particular, have tried their hand at providing historical accounts of various aspects of Carpatho-Rusyn culture. Among the earliest was Father Joseph P. Hanulya, who wrote the first history in English of *Rusin Literature* (1941).

77. Title page of the *Carpatho-Rusyn American,* published quarterly (1978-1999) by the Carpatho-Rusyn Research Center.

He was followed by several other Byzantine Catholic priests, all of whom wrote on some aspect of Carpatho-Rusyn religious history: Stephen C. Gulovich, Julius Kubinyi, Basil Boysak, John Slivka, and among the most prolific, Basil Shereghy, Athanasius Pekar, and in Canada Alexander Baran.

There were also been a few self-trained laymen who chronicled certain aspects of Carpatho-Rusyn history. These included Simeon Pysh and Dmitry Vislocky, who wrote on the Lemko Region; Augustine Stefan and Vincent Shandor, who were concerned primarily with the era of Carpatho-Ukrainian autonomy (1938-1939); and Michael Roman, who prepared popular literature on the European heritage and life in America.

Beyond the perimeters of the community are several scholars of Carpatho-Rusyn background who have made their mark in American universities and research centers. Among them are: the physicist Oleksa M. Bilaniuk, Swarthmore College; the geographer George J. Demko, Dartmouth University; the historian Basil Dmytryshyn, Portland State University; the electrical engineer Nick Holonyak, University of Illinois; the Slavic bibliographer Edward Kasinec, New York Public Library; the Hindi linguist Colin S. Masica, University of Chicago; the astrophysicist Andrew Skumanich, National Center for Atmospheric Research; and the linguist Michael Zarechnak, Georgetown University. Several other university scholars of Carpatho-Rusyn background, especially in the humanities and social sciences, have published one or more works on their ancestral heritage: Paul Robert Magocsi, University of Toronto; Vasyl Markus, Loyola University; Richard Renoff, City University of New York; John Reshetar, University of Washington; Elaine Rusinko, University of Maryland; and Peter G. Stercho, Drexel University.

A few descendants of Carpatho-Rusyn immigrants have made successful careers in the world of American art and entertainment. The eminent choral director and arranger Peter J. Wilhousky began singing in the choir of a Carpatho-Rusyn parish in Passaic, New Jersey, but became best known for the now classic arrangements of the Yuletide "Carol of the Bells" and the stirring "Battle Hymn of the Republic," immortalized in recordings by the Morman Tabernacle Choir. Richard Dufallo, program director at the Julliard School of Music (New York City) and at the Aspen Music

78. Sandra Dee

Eat (1963), *Chelsea Girls* (1966), and *Trash* (1971).

Despite Andy Warhol's fame in the world of contemporary American art and film, there is another person of Carpatho-Rusyn background whose otherwise anonymous image is known to almost every American. He is Michael Strank, a Rusyn immigrant from the Prešov Region and later a sergeant in the United States Marine Corps. Strank was one of the six marines who raised the American flag atop a rugged mountain on Iwo Jima during the bitter battle against the Japanese for control of that Pacific Ocean island toward the end of World War II. Although killed in action within a week after the flag-raising (February 23, 1945), Strank was posthumously awarded numerous military decorations. He subsequently was immortalized because the wartime photograph of the flag raising was later transformed into the famous

79. Andy Warhol, *200 Campbell's Soup Cans,* 1962, one of the several versions of this painting that in the words of one critic "made Warhol's name almost as familar as Campbell's."

Festival in Colorado during the 1970s and 1980s, credited his predilection for Slavic classical music to his "Subcarpathian Ruthenian background."

Among other performers to achieve national success were a few Hollywood film stars. Lizabeth Scott (born Emma Matzo), the daughter of Carpatho-Rusyn immigrants from Subcarpathian Rus', played the role of a sultry leading lady in several films during the late 1940s and early 1950s. Somewhat later, Sandra Dee (born Alexandra Zuk), the granddaughter of Lemko immigrants, starred in roles as the prototypical American teenage girl in several Hollywood films of the early 1960s. More recently, Robert Urich, who is of mixed Rusyn-Slovak origin, starred during the 1980s and 1990s in a popular television series and several movies. But by far the most famous descendant of Carpatho-Rusyn immigrants (both parents were from a Rusyn village in the Prešov Region of northeastern Slovakia) was Andy Warhol, the artist, photographer, and film-maker, raised during the depression in Pittsburgh's Greenfield suburb still popularly known as Ruska *dolina* (Rusyn valley). This "enfant terrible" of the 1960s rocked the world of Pop Art with his famous paintings, *Two Hundred Campbell Soup Cans* (1962) and *Brillo Boxes* (1964), and then he shocked the underground film world with his award-winning—though often long and boring—motion pictures such as

"Iwo Jima Monument" that stands opposite the Lincoln Memorial in Washington, D.C., symbolizing American bravery during the last world conflict.

Finally, Carpatho-Rusyns and specifically their cultural experience in America have been the subject of attention in at least two works written by authors from outside the group. During the 1930s, the most outstanding twentieth-century Czech author, Karel Čapek, wrote a novel, *Hordubal* (1934), which analyzed the psychological and familial difficulties faced by a Carpatho-Rusyn immigrant who returned home to his native village after working several years in Pennsylvania.

More recently, the American script-writer E. M. Corder based a tale, the *Deerhunter* (1978), on a group of Rusyn Americans from Clairton, Pennsylvania, whose lives were brutally disrupted by the Vietnam War, in which several were wounded or died in particularly gruesome circumstances. The Rusyn Americans were used to typify those elements in the United States who, despite the numerous protests engendered by the war, served voluntarily and remained patriotic Americans even after their personal lives were so horribly damaged. The *Deerhunter* received national acclaim as an academy-award winning film, and although the term Carpatho-Rusyn is never used in the film (Russian is), the marriage scene was shot in St. Theodosius Orthodox Cathedral and the wedding reception *(hostyna)* in the Lemko Hall (both in Cleveland and with "locals" who uttered a few words in Rusyn dialect), so that the setting, dialogue, and action of the participants leave no doubt that the film is a contemporary saga about Americans of Slavic—and more precisely Carpatho-Rusyn—background.

80. United States commemorative postage stamp of the Iwo Jima Monument issued in 1945. Michael Strank is third from the left (under the upraised hand).

Chapter 7

Politics

For Carpatho-Rusyn immigrants and their descendants, politics has had a special connotation. It has generally not meant participation in the American political system, but rather refers to a concern with the fate of the homeland, to endless debates about the problem of ethnic or national self-identity, and to interaction with other ethnic groups of similar geographic background in the United States.

There were at least two reasons why the early Carpatho-Rusyn immigrants were reluctant to become involved in American political life. First, many of the newcomers believed they had come to the United States on a temporary basis, and therefore they had neither the time nor interest, let alone the linguistic skills or political experience, to take part in "American" matters. In fact, their only real experience in the American political process came as strikers (or sometimes hired strike-breakers) in the labor disturbances that often rocked the industrial centers they inhabited. Nonetheless, it should be pointed out that Carpatho-Rusyns were never singled out as a group, although they may have been castigated for their activity or tolerated for their existence along with their fellow eastern European immigrant workers, all of whom were lumped together under the opprobrious terms, *Bohunks, Hunkies,* or *Polaks*.

Even when it was clear that their permanent home really was to be the United States, the Old-World experience with politics in which the fate of Carpatho-Rusyns was usually decided by others led many of them to maintain a negative and pessimistic view of the political process. Their own newspapers and annual almanacs, which frequently featured success stories about political activists and national heroes like Presidents Washington and Lincoln, seemed to have little real impact. For the longest time it was not possible to recognize a Carpatho-Rusyn name on a list of local, state, or national elected officials.

There were a few attempts during the late 1930s and 1940s to enlist Carpatho-Rusyns to vote as a bloc in American political life, especially in the northeast where most lived. Although there was a Carpatho-Russian division in the Republican party in Pennsylvania, it was the Democratic party that attracted most members of the group. An American Rusin Democratic League and a Democratic Club headed by attorney Sigmund T. Brinsky functioned for a while in Ohio, while in New York a Carpatho-Russian division of the Democratic party was formed as early as 1932. Headed by businessman Michael Mahonic, the New York division claimed to be national in scope, but in practice it was limited to that state and to nearby Connecticut, where until the early 1950s it did help to elect local candidates on the Democratic ticket.

In general, however, the community never had any real impact on American politics and no politicians have ever talked about a Carpatho-Rusyn bloc of votes. Only since the 1970s have there been a few elected and appointed officials of Carpatho-Rusyn background: Joseph M. Gaydos, Democratic congressman from Pennsylvania; Orestes Mihaly, assistant attorney general of New York; and federal civil servants in the

Department of State: George J. Demko, Geographer, and Dimitry Zarechnak, Russian-language interpreter for Presidents Reagan, Bush, and Clinton at all U.S.-Soviet summit meetings. But the politician of Rusyn background with greatest prominence is former Republican governor of Pennsylvania Tom Ridge, who in the wake of the September 2001 terrorist attack on New York's World Trade Center became presidential advisor and later first cabinet Secretary for Homeland Security.

When we turn to the Rusyn-American involvement in European affairs, the picture is quite different. In 1904, the Greek Catholic Union's president Michael Yuhasz, Sr. and its editor Pavel Zatkovich participated with Slovaks in a congress which sent a memorandum to the Hungarian government protesting the treatment of their brethren in the homeland. For their part, both Hungary and Russia were greatly interested in immigrant activity, especially before World War I. Russia's tsarist government liberally supported the Orthodox movement, while Budapest, through local Austro-Hungarian consulates in Pittsburgh, New York City, and Cleveland as well as through its Trans-Atlantic Trust Company in New York City,

82. Homestead Resolution as it appeared on the pages of the *Amerikansky russky viestnik,* August 8, 1918.

tried to keep Carpatho-Rusyns loyal to Hungary and separated from fellow Slavs, especially from Slovaks and Galician Rusyns, whether of the Russophile or Ukrainophile orientation.

It was toward the end of World War I that the Rusyn-American community was to have its greatest impact on the fate of the homeland. Among the first to organize were the Orthodox Lemkos from Galicia, who under the leadership of the priest Joseph Fedoronko established in early 1917 the League for the Liberation of Carpatho-Russia (Sojuz Osvoboždenija Prikarpatskoj Rusi). The League published the newspaper *Prikarpatskaja Rus'* (New York, 1917-25) and collected funds to aid the war-torn homeland. To publicize its cause further, the League organized in New York City on July 13, 1917 the first Carpatho-Russian Congress (Karpatorusskij Kongress) in America. The goal of this and two subsequent congresses (1918, 1919) was to work for the "unification of all Carpatho-Russian lands"—that is, Galicia, Bukovina, and Hungarian or Subcarpathian Rus'—with a democratic Russia. Most of the supporters of the congress were Lemkos and other Russophiles from Galicia. The League addressed

81. Czechoslovak President Tomáš G. Masaryk.

83. Gregory I. Zatkovich as governor of Subcarpathian Rus',
autographed and dated 1920.

several memoranda and sent a delegation to the Paris
Peace Conference in an effort to argue its case before
that international forum.

Even more important was the arrival in the United
States of Professor Tomáš G. Masaryk, the Slavic
leader who was working on behalf of the creation of an
independent state of Czechoslovakia. While consulting
with Czech and Slovak immigrant leaders in Pittsburgh
in May 1918, Masaryk met with Nicholas Pachuta,
the head of an organization called the American
Russian National Defense (Amerikansko-Russka
Narodna Obrana). This group had been founded in
1915 in Braddock, Pennsylvania and drew most of
its supporters from the recent converts to Orthodoxy
led by Bishop Stephen (Dzubay). Although Pachuta
originally supported the idea of union with Russia,
he now urged that his countrymen in America should
favor instead the idea of joining with the Czechs and
Slovaks in their proposed new state.

What was to prove more significant, however,
was the gathering on July 23, 1918 of Byzantine
Ruthenian Catholic clerical and lay leaders from
the Greek Catholic Union and United Societies.

Meeting in Homestead, Pennsylvania (a suburb of
Pittsburgh), they formed the American National
Council of Uhro-Rusins (Amerikanska Narodna Rada
Uhro-Rusinov). Headed by Father Nicholas Chopey
and Julius Gardoš, this council proclaimed itself the
only legal representative of Carpatho-Rusyns in the
United States and proposed three possible political
alternatives for the homeland after the end of World
War I: (1) autonomy within Hungary; (2) unity with
fellow Rusyns in neighboring Galicia and Bukovina;
or (3) autonomy within an unspecified state.

Convinced that the United States, as a member of
the Entente, would play a decisive role in the postwar
redrawing of Europe's boundaries, and in order to be
confident of success while operating in an otherwise
alien American political environment, the American
Council of Uhro-Rusins engaged Gregory I. Zatkovich
to seek the best political alternative for the homeland.
Although born in Subcarpathian Rus', Zatkovich had
been educated from grade school through university
in the United States and was working at the time
as a lawyer for General Motors. Moreover, he was
thoroughly versed in Carpatho-Rusyn community
affairs since his recently deceased father, Pavel,
had been the founding editor of the Greek Catholic
Union's *Amerikansky russky viestnik,* and his brother,
Theophile, was a priest and later chancellor of the
Byzantine Ruthenian Catholic eparchy in Pittsburgh.
Aside from his important family connections, the then
32-year-old Gregory Zatkovich was an extremely
dynamic individual and clearly the best political

84. United States President Woodrow Wilson

lobbyist available to Carpatho-Rusyn Americans.

By October, Zatkovich had met with President Woodrow Wilson and other American officials, and he had registered the Uhro- (Subcarpathian) Rusyns as a separate people in the Mid-European Union organized in Philadelphia under the leadership of Masaryk. Zatkovich then convinced the Carpatho-Rusyn immigrants it would be best for Rusyns to join the newly established republic of Czechoslovakia. In order to legitimize the Czechoslovak orientation, a vote was taken throughout the lodges of the two largest Greek Catholic fraternal societies, the Greek Catholic Union and United Societies. The result was 68 percent of the lodges in favor of union with Czechoslovakia.

Satisfied with this result, Zatkovich led a Rusyn-American delegation in early 1919 to the Paris Peace Conference and to the homeland where local leaders, overjoyed with the decision of their brethren in America, formed a national council at Užhorod on May 8, 1919. The Užhorod council accepted the Rusyn-American proposal and called for the incorporation into Czechoslovakia of all Rusyn-inhabited territory south of the Carpathians. In September, the peacemakers in Paris approved the Czechoslovak solution to the Rusyn problem. Recognizing the role of Rusyn Americans in postwar international politics, Czechoslovakia's founding president, Tomáš Masaryk, in 1919 appointed Zatkovich—though he was still an

85.   Members of the Mid-European Union before a replica of America's Liberty Bell in Independence Hall, Philadelphia, October 1918. In the center (with glasses and white beard) is the union's chairman, Professor Tomáš G. Masaryk; standing in the back to the left of the bell is the Rusyn representative, Gregory Zatkovich. The bell was sent the following year as a memorial to Užhorod, the capital of Subcarpathian Rus'.

86. The Central Rusyn National Council in Užhorod greets the Rusyn-American delegation and proclaims its unity with Czechoslovakia, May 8, 1919. Alongside Gregory Zatkovich (behind the folk-costumed woman) is his successor as governor, Antonij Beskyd (on the right) and the future premier-minister of the Carpatho-Ukraine, Monsignor Avhustyn Vološyn (on the left).

87. The American Rusin National Congress, Homestead, Pennsylvania, September 15-16, 1919, greets Gregory Zatkovich before his return to the European homeland. Father Nicholas Chopey, chairman of the congress, is the third person seated to the right of the youthful Zatkovich (front row center). Photo by Fischer and Haller.

88. Third Carpatho-Russian Congress, New York City, December 28-31, 1919. Seated to the right center are the Russophile politicians from Galicia, Dr. Dmitry Markov (on the left) and Dmitry Vergun (on the right).

American citizen—as president of the Directorium and then, in 1920, as first governor of Subcarpathian Rus' (Czech: *Podkarpatská Rus)*.

But Zatkovich's European political career did not last long. In 1921, he resigned in protest after Czechoslovakia refused to grant the promised autonomy and to unite the approximately 100,000 Carpatho-Rusyns—living "temporarily" in eastern Slovakia—with the province of Subcarpathian Rus'. After returning to Pittsburgh, Zatkovich published various pamphlets criticizing Czechoslovakia, and he was soon joined by GCU president Michael Yuhasz, Sr., who organized the Rusin Council for National Defense at Pittsburgh on November 28, 1922. In the name of this council, Yuhasz sent several protests to the League of Nations in Geneva and to the Czechoslovak government in Prague. The original complaints had to do with administrative division and lack of autonomy for the Carpatho-Rusyn homeland. Now, too, were accusations that the Prague government was allowing Ukrainians from Galicia to dominate the cultural affairs of the province.

Since Zatkovich's experiences abroad had been well publicized, no Rusyn-American newspaper or organization during the 1920s and 1930s was willing to acknowledge the many economic, social, and cultural achievements brought about by the Prague government in the homeland. Instead, Rusyn-American publicists continued to harp on the supposed "injustices" of Czechoslovak rule. Furthermore, some Subcarpathian

politicians (Antonij Beskyd, Štefan Fencyk) travelled to the United States where they assured themselves of financial backing for their anti-Czechoslovak ventures.

By the 1930s, while Byzantine Catholic Carpatho-Rusyns were deeply involved in the celibacy issue, the initiative for political activity was taken up by Orthodox leaders. They kept up the criticism of Czechoslovakia through a new organization, the Carpatho-Russian Union (Karpatorusskij Sojuz), established in Pittsburgh in June 1933. This group was under the leadership of Dr. Aleksej Gerovsky, a staunch Orthodox spokesperson and recently arrived émigré, who had been forced to leave Czechoslovakia because of his anti-governmental and Russophile proselytizing activities among the Carpatho-Rusyns. In an attempt to rise above local Rusyn-American religious controversies, the Carpatho-Russian Union included Orthodox Rusyns as well as several leaders from the Greek Catholic Union. The dynamic Gerovsky also set up his own press agency in New York City under the name KARUS. Gerovsky's anti-Czechoslovak sentiment was so great that it was not long before his demands for Rusyn autonomy led to a call for border revisionism, thereby resulting in cooperation with Hungarian governmental representatives in the United States and western Europe as well as with pro-Hungarian Rusyn politicians from the homeland.

Among the latter was Štefan Fencyk, a Rusyn parliamentary deputy who was hosted by Gerovsky in

1935 on a grand tour of Rusyn-American communities, in order to raise funds for further anti-Czechoslovak political activity in the homeland. Gerovsky's influence reached its highest point in the summer of 1938, when he led a delegation of the Carpatho-Russian Union that held talks with the Czechoslovak government in Prague and then went eastward to Subcarpathian Rus' to foster, with some success, the formation of a political coalition between local Russophiles and Ukrainophiles who were working to achieve autonomy.

Considering the general Russophile and Rusynophile national orientations that prevailed during the 1930s among the majority of Rusyn-American spokespersons and their organizations, it is not surprising that most of the community expressed opposition to the "Ukrainian regime" headed by the Greek Catholic priest Avhustyn Vološyn and Minister Julian Revay, which came to power in Subcarpathian Rus' and renamed the region Carpatho-Ukraine during its few months of autonomy between October 1938 and March 1939. The only exception to the general anti-Ukrainian trend was the Committee for the Defense of Carpatho-Ukraine (Komitet Oborony Karpats'koji Ukrajiny), a small group headed by Father Emil Nevicky, which tried to convince Rusyn Americans to support Vološyn's Carpatho-Ukrainian goverment. But the Carpatho-Russian Union as well as the GCU and other Byzantine Catholic organizations were so angered by what they considered the Ukrainian "encroachment" that they did not even speak out against the forcible return of Hungarian rule in their homeland after March 1939.

In fact, the first group to protest the political changes in Europe was the Lemko Association, which under the leadership of Petro Guzlej, Michael Mahonec, Dmitry Vislocky, and Dr. Simeon Pysh, set up a Carpatho-Russian National Committee in New York City on February 11, 1939. In subsequent months, this committee called for the unification of all Carpatho-Rusyn lands—whether in Poland, Slovakia, or Hungary—with the Soviet Union. However, following the outbreak of World War II in September 1939, the pro-Soviet position of the Lemko Association and its National Committee became suspect in the eyes of American authorities, because at that time the Soviet Union was allied with Nazi Germany. Then came Germany's invasion of the Soviet Union in June 1941, as a result of which Stalin's "Communist Russians"

became allies of the United States. Now it was acceptable for Americans to praise Soviet Russia and still be patriotic.

Capitalizing on this new political situation, the Lemko Carpatho-Russian National Committee joined with the Carpatho-Russian Union (which by then had lost the support of the Byzantine Catholics and the Greek Catholic Union) to form, in July 1942, a new American Carpatho-Russian Congress (Amerikanskyj Karpatorusskij Kongress) headed by Peter Ratica. It was through this organization that Rusyn Americans (mostly Russophile-oriented Lemkos and Orthodox) contributed to the Russian War Relief, raising close to $100,000 for food, clothing, and other supplies destined for the Red Army. It is interesting to note, however, that the American Carpatho-Russian Congress did not call for the future unification of Carpathian Rus' with the Soviet Union, but only for political unity of all Rusyn-inhabited territory (the Lemko Region, Prešov Region, and Subcarpathian Rus') and for the unified territory's autonomy to be guaranteed in some unspecified state.

Meanwhile, it was not until three years into the war that the vast majority of Carpatho-Rusyns in

89.   Leaders of the American Carpatho-Russian Central Conference meet with officials of the Czechoslovak government-in-exile, May 23, 1943. Seated from left to right: Gregory Zatkovich, President Eduard Beneš, Dr. Paul Cibere, John Primich. The clergyman standing (second from the left) is Father Ivan Ladižinsky.

America (that is, those from the Prešov Region and Subcarpathian Rus') finally took a clear stand on the fate of their homeland south of the Carpathians. Following the disintegration of Czechoslovakia in March 1939, Subcarpathian Rus' was ruled by Hungary and the Prešov Region by the pro-German independent state of Slovakia. Gregory Zatkovich, head of the Byzantine Catholic American Carpatho-Russian Council of Pittsburgh, and Father Ivan A. Ladižinsky, head of the Orthodox Carpatho-Russian Unity of Gary, Indiana, dropped their differences and on March 22, 1942 united into one American Carpatho-Russian Central Conference. Based in Pittsburgh, this organization reversed the two decades of criticism against Czechoslovakia and instead agreed to work with that government's representatives in exile (led by former President Eduard Beneš and Minister Jan Masaryk) to restore Subcarpathian Rus' after World War II as an equal partner in a renewed Czechoslovak state. Such a policy also coincided with the war aims of the United States and its other allies, including the Soviet Union.

Hence, the Carpatho-Rusyns were very surprised to find at the end of the war that Subcarpathian Rus' did not become part of a restored Czechoslovakia, but rather was incorporated into the Soviet Union in June 1945. They were especially shocked to learn that the Soviet government had initiated a policy of Ukrainianization and that it had begun to undermine and before long to liquidate the Greek (or Byzantine-rite) Catholic Church. Protests to the United States State Department and to the newly founded United Nations Organization in San Francisco were sent in 1945, and the following year in August a special Carpatho-Russian Congress was convened in Munhall, Pennsylvania to protest Soviet rule in the homeland. But these acts proved to be of no avail. The most the immigrants could do was to deny money, food, clothing, and other supplies from the Carpatho-Russian Relief Fund to Soviet-held territory and to supply these only to Carpatho-Rusyns in northeastern Slovakia, which had not yet come under Soviet-inspired Communist rule.

In 1951, a Council of a Free Sub-Carpatho-Ruthenia in Exile (Rada Svobodnoj Podkarpatskoj Rusi v Exili) was founded in Hamilton, Ontario by Vasilij V. Fedinec, the former president of the Subcarpathian Bank in Užhorod and recent immigrant to Canada. This council worked closely with the Byzantine Ruthenian Catholic Church in the United States, and through its organ, *Rusin/Ruthenian* (New York and Hamilton, Ont., 1952-60), joined with other Czechoslovak émigré groups in protesting the Soviet annexation of Subcarpathian Rus' in 1945 and the imposition of Communist rule in Czechoslovakia in 1948. The Greek Catholic Union also continued to urge American authorities to help free their brethren in Subcarpathian Rus' *(Pod-Karpatskaja Rus'),* and at its 1964 convention it even adopted a resolution calling on the United Nations to act, "so that Carpatho-Russia be recognized and accepted into the free nations of the world as an autonomous state."[11] But none of these efforts were to have any impact. Clearly, the decisive political influence that Carpatho-Rusyn immigrants had once been able to exert over events in Europe following World War I was no longer possible in the post-1945 world.

The last organized attempt at political action was undertaken by the Lemko Relief Committee in the United States, founded in June 1946 by industrialist Peter S. Hardy and the Orthodox priest, Joseph Simko of Trumbull, Connecticut. Several thousand dollars were collected to aid Lemkos who, after their forced deportation in 1947 to various parts of Communist-ruled Poland, wanted to return to their Carpathian villages. After 1957, the Polish government allowed Hardy to visit the area and to distribute some funds which were used mainly to purchase food and clothing and to reconstruct damaged churches. The following year, through Hardy's personal intervention, the Polish government signed a fifteen-point document agreeing to continue the aid program. This unprecedented act for a Communist government—undertaken, moreover, at the height of the Cold War—was probably related to the fact that Hardy was a long-time supporter of the pro-Soviet Lemko Association in Yonkers, New York. Whatever the reason, the aid program had limited practical results, since the vast majority of Lemkos have until this day been unable to return from

---

[11] Cited in John Masich, "Highlights in the Glorious History of the Greek Catholic Union of the U.S.A.," in *Jubilee Almanac of the Greek Catholic Union of the U.S.A.,* LXXI, ed. Michael Roman (Munhall, Pa., 1967), p. 263.

other parts of Poland to their ancestral Carpathian homeland.

The aid program carried out by the Lemko Relief Committee after World War II points to another important aspect of Rusyn-American relations with the European homeland—the economic impact. Before World War I, but especially between 1919 and 1938, immigrant workers sent thousands of dollars in cash and goods to their families in Europe. This spontaneous, familial-based channelling of funds did in fact make a real difference. It helped numerous Rusyn families survive economic hardship, especially that brought on by the world depression of the 1930s.

More organized economic aid came in the form of bonds and other fund-raising activity carried out by Rusyn-American organizations. At least two financial institutions that operated at various times during the interwar years—the Subcarpathian Bank in Užhorod,

the administrative center of Subcarpathian Rus', and the Russian Bank in Mukačevo, the region's second largest city—were established, in part, with Rusyn-American investments.

Although immediately after World War II, Rusyn Americans could no longer send aid to Soviet-held Subcarpathian Rus' or to the Lemko Region in Poland (which at the time was being forcibly depopulated), they were able at least for a few years to send or purchase food, medicine, and clothing which was distributed mainly by the United Nations Relief and Recovery Administration (UNRRA) to Carpatho-Rusyns living in the Prešov Region of Czechoslovakia. Even though after 1948 the Cold War interrupted these contacts with Communist Czechoslovakia, by the 1960s the flow of money and goods on an individual basis was renewed. This has been supplemented further by United States social security and worker's compensation payments

90. A bond from the Subcarpathian Bank in Užhorod, designed by the noted Carpatho-Rusyn painter, Josyf Bokšaj, and made out to a Rusyn-American in the 1920s.

91. The Russian Bank in Mukačevo, Subcarpathian Rus', founded in 1930 primarily with Rusyn-American funding.

to the widows of the early immigrants. As a result, at least one region, eastern Slovakia, had in the last two decades of Communist rule (before 1989) acquired a reputation for affluence. It was not uncommon, for instance, to find elderly Rusyns in the Prešov Region with substantial bank accounts, or to hear tales of the "legendary *babas"* (grandmothers) who purchase new automobiles for their children and grandchildren with cash acquired "from America" as a result of the benefits (social security, worker's compensation) coming to them from the former employment of their long-deceased husbands.

Rusyn political involvement in Europe was essentially a first-generation phenomenon. Since World War II, the vast majority of the older immigrants and their descendants were basically apolitical and had virtually no concern with the fate of the homeland when it was part of Communist-ruled Czechoslovakia and the Soviet Union. Only among the Lemko immigrants from Polish Galicia (especially those who arrived after World War II) was there some political activism as expressed through publications and manifestations led at times by the Lemko Association, the Lemko Relief Committee, and most especially by the Organization for the Defense of the Lemko Land.

Apart from an interest in the fate of the European homeland, for most Carpatho-Rusyn immigrants and their descendants even before World War II, politics usually meant and still means the debates and controversies that surround national identity. This problem is, of course, intimately related to relations with other ethnic groups, especially Ukrainians

and Slovaks, and to a lesser degree, Russians and Hungarians.

Although it was quite understandable for the earliest newcomers to tell immigration officials that they were from Austria, or Hungary, or Poland, or Czechoslovakia, they at the same time knew very well that ethnically, linguistically, and culturally they were neither Austrian, nor Hungarian, nor Polish, nor Czech, nor Slovak. Their Rusyn dialectal speech and/or their Greek Catholic or Orthodox faith clearly set them off from the other groups. Thus, a Rusyn identity was the most common denominator among the pre-World War I immigrants.

Nonetheless, frequent interaction with related groups in the United States and the use from time to time of English often prompted a discussion, or at least self-reflection, on the question of national or ethnic identity. (In the European homeland, where one rarely left the native village, the question of national or ethnic identity hardly ever arose.) Assuming that the term *Rusyn* (or *Rusin*) was not acceptable usage in English, many community spokespersons and organizations began to describe themselves as Russian or sometimes Carpatho-Russian, even if they knew, at least initially, that they were different from the Russians of Russia (whom they often designated as Muscovites).

It was not too long before some leaders, especially from among the second generation, began to use the name *Russian* not simply as a self-perceived acceptable term in English, but as a description of the group's ostensible ethnic affiliation. To be sure, such Russophile views had also been prevalent in the European homeland both before and after World War I, that is, a belief that the Carpatho-Rusyns were a branch of one unified Russian people that inhabited an extensive territory stretching from the Carpathian Mountains to the Pacific Ocean. It was beliefs such as these that led some Rusyn-American editors to attempt to publish in Russian in the community's newspapers, attempts which generally resulted in a strange, uncodified, and often comical language.

For the most part, there have been at least four trends or orientations prevalent among Carpatho-Rusyn Americans regarding their national/ethnic identity: (1) that the group forms a distinct East Slavic nationality known as Rusyn, Rusnak, Ruthenian, Carpatho-Rusyn, or Uhro-Rusin; (2) that the group is part of either the Russian nationality; (3) the Slovak nationality; or (4) the Ukrainian nationality. It is interesting to note that for some individuals it is possible to be simultaneously a Rusyn and a Russian, or a Rusyn (Rusnak) and Slovak, or a Rusyn and Ukrainian.

Not surprisingly, in the United States, where there was never any official or legal need for the group to have a fixed identity, the situation remained from the outset very fluid. With regard to the community's organizational structure, it might be said that at least through World War I, the largest religious and secular organizations—the Greek (Byzantine Ruthenian) Catholic Church and the Greek Catholic Union— accepted the view that the group formed a distinct nationality. By the late 1920s and 1930s, however, the Greek Catholic Union's leaders, especially Peter Zeedick and Michael Roman, referred to the group as Russian and adopted a Russophile view. The Byzantine Catholic Church, meanwhile, although it adopted the term *Ruthenian*, more and more associated that name with a specific religious body (which could and did include Slovaks, Hungarians, and Croats as well as Rusyns) and preferred not to associate itself with any one ethnic group. Consequently, Ruthenian, and later by extrapolation Byzantine, became an identity, like Catholic or Jewish, and was perceived to be sufficient as an ethnic or national self-descriptor.

On the other hand, those Carpatho-Rusyns who joined Orthodox churches during the several waves of defections from Byzantine Catholicism, almost without exception adopted from the beginning the term *Russian* as an identifier, so that many so-called Russians, or persons of "Russian descent," in the United States have no awareness that their roots really go back to Subcarpathian Rus' or the Lemko lands north of the Carpathians, and that the Slavic population there is neither ethnically nor linguistically Russian.

There are also smaller groups of post-World War II immigrants and their descendants who identify as Ukrainians; while others, who know their parents or grandparents are from territories that are now within Slovakia, consider themselves Slovaks. Finally, beginning in the 1970s, with the general interest in ethnicity and the search for roots in American society, there has been a revival of the original term *Rusyn*, sometimes spelled *Rusin*. It is being used more and more in secular and religious (at least Byzantine Catholic) publications in the form *Carpatho-Rusyn* or *Carpatho-Ruthenian*, and with the connotation that it describes a distinct ethnic group.

As might be expected, the changing self-perceptions and the use of so many terms to describe the same people has caused controversy not only among Carpatho-Rusyns themselves but also friction and misunderstandings with the other groups whose identity "former" Rusyns may have been adopted. The Russian community, for instance, has generally ignored the specific characteristics of Carpatho-Rusyn culture, even though it is the Rusyns, whether from Subcarpathia and especially the Lemko Region, who make up significant portions of Russian Orthodox parishes. The traditional Russian view, after all, is that the population in question is just a dialectal branch of the Russian nation.

Ignorance and even conflict have often marked relations between Carpatho-Rusyns on the one hand and Slovaks or Ukrainians on the other. Slovak-American publications in the past (and some still today) have argued that the term *Rusnak* simply means a Byzantine-rite Catholic from Slovakia. Following that line of thinking, all Carpatho-Rusyns/Rusnaks whose ancestors stem from present-day Slovakia must be considered Slovaks. Views like these have prompted certain Slovak-American publications to describe the Byzantine Ruthenian Catholic Church and the Greek Catholic Union as Slovak organizations.

Relations between Carpatho-Rusyns and Ukrainians in the United States have been strained even more. Chapter 4 pointed out how regional and ethnic conflicts between immigrants from Subcarpathian Rus' and Galicia led, in 1916 and 1924, to the formal division of the Greek Catholic Church into separate Ruthenian and Ukrainian administrations, then eparchies, and subsequently metropolitanates. The two communities have continued to remain far apart. Ukrainians argue that *Rusyn* is just their own antiquated name, so that all Carpatho-Rusyns are simply Ukrainians, while Carpatho-Rusyns respond that Ukrainians are ethnically different and usually political extremists who are more concerned with nationalism than with religious concerns and Christian spirituality.

Arguments such as these have characterized public statements and private sentiments throughout the almost century-long interaction of Carpatho-Rusyns, Russians, Slovaks, and Ukrainians in the United States. On the other hand, it must be admitted that for most Carpatho-Rusyns who today are of the second-, third-, and fourth-generation, arguments over national or ethnic identity are at best academic if not irrelevant. Since World War I, the vast majority of the group's members have preferred to consider themselves first and foremost Americans, perhaps of the Byzantine Catholic or Orthodox faith. And if they need to think about their ethnic identity, a vague association with the concept Rus' or perhaps more generally Slavic is more than sufficient for their heritage and associational needs.

Chapter 8

Group Maintenance

The problem of the lack of a consistent identity, discussed at the end of the previous chapter, has had a significant impact on the ability of Carpatho-Rusyns to sustain a sense of ethnic commitment and group maintenance in the United States. In fact, the majority of third- and fourth-generation descendants of the original immigrants have at best only a vague idea of their heritage and very little awareness of its relationship to a specific territorial entity called Carpathian Rus' or Carpatho-Ruthenia.

The reasons for this are many. First, because the vast majority of Carpatho-Rusyn immigrants came here before World War I, their grandchildren and great-grandchildren more than half a century later are fully acculturated, even assimilated, into mainstream American society. In this context, it was the second generation—the sons and daughters of the original immigrants born or raised primarily in the United States—who were often the most active assimilators. While they were familiar with the Old-World heritage and at least had a passive if not active knowledge of some Carpatho-Rusyn dialect, these "American assimilators" more often than not deliberately chose to forget the past and to make sure that they and their children were just the same as all other Americans.

In the process of loosening ties to the past, language was the first characteristic to be lost. The first-generation immigrants still spoke their native Rusyn dialects, but these became laden with Americanisms quite quickly. In any case, English was urged upon the children, and the speech of the old country was denigrated as simply "our language" *(po-našomu).* It was not viewed as having any particular value in the "real," "American" world.

Even if the first or second generation did try to pass on some Old-World language to their children, more than likely they would tell them that they were speaking Russian (that is, "soft Russian" as opposed to "hard Russian") or "Slavish"/"Slavonic." The first interpretation was incorrect; the second meant nothing. Moreover, it is not surprising to find many younger descendants of Carpatho-Rusyns, who in recent years have gone to college in greater numbers, attending Russian language courses in which they were puzzled by encounters with American-trained teachers who ironically would refer to the few dialectal words or pronunciations they may remember from their family as "kitchen Russian."

Outside the home the use of Carpatho-Rusyn is hardly to be encountered anywhere. Church services are entirely in English, although a few liturgies are still being said in Church Slavonic (a liturgical language far from spoken Carpatho-Rusyn). We have also seen that, with the exception of the Lemko Association's newspaper *(Karpatska Rus'),* all other religious and fraternal publications are almost completely in English. Thus, when the now very old pre-World War I immigrants and their children will have passed on, spoken Carpatho-Rusyn in America will die as well. For Carpatho-Rusyns in the United States, as with many other similar groups, language maintenance is virtually non-existent.

Another difficulty for group maintenance is related to the larger American educational and social context. In effect, young people have had nothing concrete to relate to if they are ever exposed to the concept Carpathian Rus' or Ruthenia. Such names no longer appear on maps, and until very recently there were no adequate popular or scholarly books about the region written in English. In addition, it is extremely difficult, if not impossible, for Americans, even those with a higher education, to understand that ethnic or national identity is not necessarily coincident with the state in which one lives. Few are aware of the reality that not everyone who lives in France is French, or in Slovakia Slovak, or in the former Soviet Union Russian. To be sure, such misperceptions are not easy to change in an American social and educational context, which at the elementary, high school, and college level is woefully inadequate in terms of its coverage or exposure to east-central Europe.

Even the renewed contact with the homeland, which began slowly in the late 1960s, did not at first help very much. The reasons had to do with political policies and societal evolution. When the Soviet Union annexed Subcarpathian Rus' (Transcarpathia) to the Soviet Ukraine in 1945, the Communist authorities declared by fiat that the nationality problem was resolved. All Rusyns, regardless what they may have called themselves, were officially declared to be Ukrainian. This approach was adopted as well by the Soviet-influenced governments of Poland and (after 1948) Czechoslovakia. Therefore, officially—and for the most part in practice as well—Rusyns ceased to exit in the Carpathian homeland.

Consequently, when immigrants and their descendants did begin to visit the Europe they had once left or had heard about from parents, they were often struck by the fact that they could not understand the language of the people they met. In Soviet Transcarpathia, standard Ukrainian was generally spoken, while in the administrative center of Užhorod—where visitors were expected to stay and to meet their relatives from the villages—Russian was in most cases the language of formal and official communication. As for the Lemko Region north of the Carpathians in Poland, the indigenous Lemko Rusyns were deported in 1946-1947 and their places were taken by Poles. Finally, in the Prešov Region of northeastern

Slovakia, to which most American tourists flocked, the old people may have still spoken Rusyn dialects, but the younger generations used Slovak exclusively, most likely did not attend an Eastern-rite or any church, and more often than not were anxious to reject their Rusyn/Rusnak/East Slavic heritage in favor of a Slovak identity.

Thus, in a situation where the spoken Carpatho-Rusyn dialects in the United States were not being maintained, where the American educational system provided no suitable information, and where even travel to the homeland did not contribute to an understanding of the traditional culture, it was not surprising that second-, third-, and fourth-generation descendants of Carpatho-Rusyn immigrants, if they were conscious of their heritage at all, were likely to associate with groups that had some kind of concrete political existence, whether Russian, or Slovak, sometimes even Ukrainian. Even more likely, however, if asked about ethnic or national identity, a Carpatho-Rusyn American would simply respond with a religious affiliation—Byzantine Catholic (often raised to the category of national identity) or Orthodox.

For their part, the churches and their leaders always felt uneasy about the ethnic or national factor. On the one hand, it was ethnic or territorial specificity which made possible the existence of individual religious bodies. Otherwise, why should not all Byzantine-rite Catholics (Ruthenians, Ukrainians, Arabic Melkites) or all Orthodox (Carpatho-Russians, Belarusans, Greeks, Russians, and so forth) be united in a single Catholic or single Orthodox jurisdiction. It was ethnic and/or territorial distinctions, therefore, which often provided the justification, at least initially, for individual religious bodies, each of which today has its own bishops and jealously guarded hierarchical structures.

On the other hand, those same ethnic distinctions and, as we have seen, debates about identity often caused discord that frequently led to disunity, defections, and rivalry within and between churches. Therefore, church hierarchs frequently discussed religion and ethnicity or nationalism as mutually-exclusive phenomena. In simplest terms, religion and politics did not mix. It is not surprising, therefore, that the Byzantine Ruthenian hierarchs have at least since World War II spoken of all their parishioners (regardless of their ethnic origin) simply as Byzantine Catholics—the church's official name, *Ruthenian,* being understood as referring to rite, not nationality. Similarly, we have seen how historically the Russian Orthodox Church in the United States (both the Metropolia and Patriarchal Exarchate) repeatedly thwarted all attempts to set up a viable "Carpatho-Russian" diocese. And with the establishment of the Orthodox Church in America in 1970, the term *Russian* was dropped entirely from its name with the church following an official policy that de-emphasized ethnic differences in what was to be considered simply an American religious body of Orthodox Christian persuasion. In this regard, only the small "Johnstown" Orthodox diocese has been consistent in fostering a sense of "Carpatho-Russian" ethnic and cultural distinctiveness among its members.

Despite all the negative aspects regarding group maintenance and ethnic identity, it still must be said that an increasing number of Carpatho-Rusyns continue to cling in some way to their traditional heritage. It is true that the traditional mechanisms that have maintained ethnic awareness in the past— Rusyn language use in families, in churches, and in newspapers; ethnic schools; dramatic clubs—no longer exist. Nonetheless, both the churches and fraternal societies still provide settings in which old familial and friendship associational patterns are retained. Individual parishes bring together people for religious services, weddings, and other social functions such as dances, bingo nights, and "pirohy-making nights," the extensive income from which validates the often unrecognized fact that it is the women who have built and supported the churches. And despite the generally cautious attitude of the church toward ethnicity, it is still at the individual parish level, whether in the Byzantine Ruthenian Catholic Church, Orthodox Church in America, or "Johnstown" Orthodox diocese, where the new folk ensembles, with participation among children and parents, have been founded. Similarly, the fraternal societies, especially the widespread Greek Catholic Union, have through individual lodges continued to provide bowling and golf clubs and summer resorts where community ties are continually reinforced. Hence, in sociological terms, Carpatho-Rusyns in America still form a group or groups, whose members are united by common kinship, religion, and social ties, regardless of what individuals might call themselves.

There are, moreover, other factors which in the past two decades have contributed to raising the level of consciousness among Americans of Rusyn background. These factors are related to developments in the United States as well as in the European homeland. Since the 1970s, new cultural organizations like the Carpatho-Rusyn Research Center have flourished. For instance, during its first quarter century of existence (1978-2003), that center distributed over 47,000 books and maps and published 80 issues of a quarterly magazine, all of which have dealt specifically with the Carpatho-Rusyn past and present.

The larger North American society has discovered Carpatho-Rusyns as well. They figure as a distinct group with their own entry or volume in widely-distributed publications such as the *Harvard*

92. Cover of a popular book on Carpatho-Rusyns in America, published in 1989 with an introduction by Senator Daniel Patrick Moynihan.

Encyclopedia of American Ethnic Groups (1980), the Chelsea House *Peoples of North America Series* (1989), the volumes on America and Europe in Yale University's *Encyclopedia of World Cultures* (1992-93), the *Gale Encyclopedia of Multicultural America* (1995), the *Macmillan Encyclopedia on American Immigrant Cultures* (1997), and the *Encyclopedia of Canada's Peoples* (1999). Finally, the United States Census Bureau, after refining its ancestry categories, has since 1990 listed "Carpatho-Rusyn" as a distinct group in its decennial census reports. In short, for the first time Rusyn Americans have been recognized by the host society of which they are a part.

Political developments in Europe, especially since the rise to power in 1985 of Mikhail Gorbachev in the former Soviet Union and the revolutions of 1989 throughout east central Europe, have also had a profound impact on Rusyn-American life. In a real sense, during the century-long Carpatho-Rusyn presence in the United States, the degree of intensity of Rusyn self-awareness has been directly related to contacts with the homeland. When those contacts were strong, so was Carpatho-Rusyn group maintenance in the United States strong; when they were weak, a distinct Rusyn identity waned.

During the full half century that encompassed World War II and over four decades of Communist rule, Rusyn Americans were largely cut off from their relatives and friends in the European homeland. Even when travel was allowed, it was fraught with visa formalities and other restrictions that were characteristic of all Soviet-dominated police states. Then came Gorbachev and the revolutions of 1989. The proverbial iron curtain was lifted, familial contacts that had been broken off so many years before were restored, and new relationships were forged. The fear of travelling to Communist countries ended, visa requirements were simplified or entirely abolished, and for the first time visitors could travel wherever they wished in Ukraine's Transcarpathian region. Moreover, with the fall of Communism and the very disintegration of the Soviet Union in late 1991, the Rusyn nationality question became once again a real issue.

With the end of censorship and the introduction of freedom of speech in the Soviet Ukraine, Czechoslovakia, and Poland, local Rusyns felt that for the first time in forty years they could proclaim

93. Archbishop Thomas V. Dolinay of Pittsburgh meets for the first time in the European homeland with Bishop Ivan Semedij of the Eparchy of Mukačevo, February 1990.

openly that they were Rusyns and not Ukrainians. In the 1990s, six new Rusyn organizations were founded in each country where Rusyns live (including Hungary and most recently Romania), and Rusyn-language newspapers and magazines began to appear. The post-Communist governments of Czechoslovakia, Hungary, and Poland joined the former Yugoslavia in recognizing Rusyns as a distinct nationality and recording them as such in official censuses. Finally, the Greek Catholic Church, which for decades had been the bulwark of a Rusyn national identity, was legalized in Ukraine and Poland and fully reconstituted in Slovakia (where it at least had functioned since 1968).

In the course of these developments, Rusyns in each country where they live sought out and subsequently received encouragement and support from Carpatho-Rusyn religious and secular organizations in the United States. The Orthodox "Johnstown diocese" began already in 1989 to report on the plight of the Orthodox Church in eastern Slovakia. For its part, the Byzantine Ruthenian Catholic Church, led by Archbishops Kocisko and Dolinay and Bishop Dudick, played a particularly active role in the reconstitution of the Greek Catholic Church. The entire American hierarchy travelled to Slovakia to be present at the formal installation of the new Greek Catholic bishop in Prešov in early 1990. Soon after that they reestablished relations with the Eparchy of Mukačevo in Ukraine, which has included the donation of funds raised in a campaign among American Rusyns to construct a Greek Catholic seminary in Užhorod. In response to the political changes and new realities in the European homeland, the Byzantine Ruthenian Seminary in Pittsburgh has since 1991 offered scholarships to seminarians from Transcarpathia and the Prešov Region and has made the study of Rusyn language and Rusyn history required subjects in its own curriculum.

As for secular organizations, among the first to become active in assisting the Carpatho-Rusyn homeland was the Andy Warhol Foundation in New York City. Inspired by its vice-president John Warhola, who was concerned about his familial and Rusyn heritage, the foundation donated several paintings by Andy Warhol to a new Museum of Modern Art in the town of Medzilaborce, Slovakia, not far from the Carpatho-Rusyn village where both Warhol's parents were born. The Warhol Foundation also agreed to provide funds for an art school in Medzilaborce. The several gala functions surrounding the opening of the new museum, which took place in 1991 in the presence of the Warhol family and Slovak government officials, all stressed the Rusyn aspect of the artist's ancestral heritage.

The Carpatho-Rusyn Research Center has, in particular, been involved in the homeland's recent national revival. It has represented Rusyn Americans at all seven World Congresses of Rusyns held between 1991 and 2003 in each European country where Rusyns live. The center has co-sponsored scholarly seminars (1992) at local universities in Užhorod (Ukraine), Cracow (Poland), Prešov (Slovakia), and Novi Sad (Yugoslavia); it has cooperated in publishing books about Rusyns for readers in the homeland; and it has co-sponsored with the Rusyn Renaissance Society (Rusyns'ka Obroda) in eastern Slovakia the First (1992) and Second (1999) Congress of the Rusyn Language. In the wake of the civil war in former Yugoslavia, which beginning in 1991 destroyed several Rusyn communities in eastern Croatia and then divided the rest of Vojvodinian Rusyns into two countries, the Carpatho-Rusyn Research Center

94. Warhola Family Museum of Modern Art, Medzilaborce, Slovakia.

95. Members of the executive from Ukraine, Slovakia, Poland, Yugoslavia, and the United States at the First World Congress of Rusyns, held in Medzilaborce, Slovakia, March 1991 (photo by Alexander Zozul'ák).

initiated a Yugoslav Rusyn Youth fund to which American Rusyns generously donated. The goal was to assist the Ruska Matka organization in Ruski Kerestur (Vojvodina) to prepare new school textbooks and to provide scholarships for local Rusyn students to study abroad.

At the turn of the twenty-first century, the various chapters of the Carpatho-Rusyn Society have continued the tradition of assistance to Rusyns in Europe. The society established a special homeland fund, which since the late 1990s has coordinated the delivery of medical supplies (most especially to Subcarpathian Rus' in Ukraine), the dissemination of cultural awareness materials on the eve of the censuses in Slovakia (2001) and Ukraine (2002), and support for Rusyn-language and cultural classes in schools in Poland and Ukraine. At the more popular level, choreographers from the Slavjane Folk Ensemble train with their counterparts at the professional Rusyn PULS Ensemble in Prešov, Slovakia. The western Pennsylvania based Slavjane ensemble, sponsored by the Greek Catholic Union, participated en masse at the annual Rusyn folk festival in Medzilaborce in the summer of 1992.

Modern technology has contributed to closing the otherwise huge geographical gap that separates Rusyn Americans from their sisters and brothers in Europe. Individuals communicate instantaneously via e-mail (generally available to Rusyns in homeland) and there are today several Internet sites produced in North America and Europe which provide information about Carpatho-Rusyn culture and current events. For example, it is basically through e-mail that members of the youngest, pre-30-year-old generation (which in 2003 formed an organization called Rusyn Outpost: North America) stay in touch with their peers in Europe and are part of the International Forum of Rusyn Youth based in Slovakia.

Aside from the benefit such "American" contacts have for the homeland, they are particularly important for group maintenance in the United States. Today, Americans of Carpatho-Rusyn background, whether churchmen, scholars, cultural activists, or ordinary visitors, are able to travel easily to the ancestral homeland where they can see real places and real people who speak Rusyn and who are proud of their Rusyn heritage. As a result, Rusyn Americans now come back home with a sense that their ethnic heritage is not some vague fairy-tale like corpus of nostalgic reminiscences handed down by loving if somewhat mythologized grandparents, but rather that it is associated with a concrete place inhabited by real people of all ages and from all walks of life. Thus, the political changes in central and eastern Europe since 1989 have had, and are likely to continue to have, a positive impact on instilling in Rusyn Americans knowledge of and pride in their ancestral heritage.

Of course, it could also be argued that assimilation or, perhaps more appropriately, adaptation to American society is a healthy thing. Unlike some other related ethnic groups, whose members are frequently uncertain of just where they belong, second-, third-, fourth-, and fifth-generation descendants of Carpatho-Rusyn immigrants function most comfortably as Americans. As Americans, all of whose forefathers came at one time from another continent, some Carpatho-Rusyns may even have an interest in their particular heritage. After all, it was American society itself, which during the Bicentennial Year and the decade of the 1970s gave its official imprimatur to the roots fever that captured the imagination of much of the country.

In this context, Americans of Carpatho-Rusyn background continue to look to their past not as a substitute for what they already are—Americans—but as another way to enrich their lives. It is such a spirit that has led some observers to speak of a recent "Rusyn renaissance" in America. How else can one explain the rise of more than a dozen dance ensembles, a marked increase in publications about the group, the success of scholarly and community organizations such as the Carpatho-Rusyn Research Center and Carpatho-Rusyn Society, and the renewal of organizational and individual relations with the European homeland. Moreover, for the first time, all these activities are being carried out in a way in which the idea of a distinct Carpatho-Rusyn identity is accepted, even taken for granted. All things considered, it seems remarkable that several tens of thousands of poor, often illiterate immigrants arriving in America before World War I have produced offspring who several generations later, and several thousand miles from the European homeland, still in some way retain a sense of Carpatho-Rusyn identity.

96. Slavjane Folk Ensemble of McKees Rocks, Pennsylvania takes part in the parade prior to the Rusyn Festival of Sport and Culture, Medzilaborce, Slovakia, July 1992.

Chapter 9

Carpatho-Rusyns in Canada

As in the case of the United States, it is impossible to determine the exact number of Carpatho-Rusyns who immigrated to Canada. Estimates suggest that in the course of the twentieth century between 15,000 and 20,000 chose Canada as a new home. Most came after 1924, when immigration restrictions in the United States made entry there very difficult. It seems that the majority came from the Lemko Region in southern Galicia (then part of Poland), the rest from the Prešov Region of northeastern Slovakia, and a few even from the Vojvodina in former Yugoslavia.

Although land was still relatively cheap in Canada during the 1920s, the Carpatho-Rusyn immigrants gravitated to urban industrial centers. Some settled in Montreal, Quebec and farther west in Fort William (now part of Thunder Bay), Ontario and Winnipeg, Manitoba. But the vast majority went to the southern Ontario cities of Toronto, Hamilton, Brantford, and Windsor. By the 1990s, as many as three quarters of Canada's Carpatho-Rusyns and their descendants lived in Toronto, the largest urban complex in Canada. The vast majority have found employment in the industrial complex of southern Ontario, including its many factories and the steel plants of Hamilton.

As in the United States, Carpatho-Rusyns in Canada are divided along religious, national, and political lines. The Greek or Byzantine-rite Catholics have come primarily from the Prešov Region in eastern Slovakia, but because they were few in number they did not have their own Greek Catholic jurisdiction as in the United States. Rather, they came under the jurisdiction of the Ukrainian Catholic Church in Canada. But not wanting to assimilate with Ukrainians, they were able to maintain a few parishes which were exclusively or largely made up of Rusyns or Rusnaks, as they called themselves. For instance, the first of these Byzantine-rite Rusyn churches was established in 1921 in the southern Alberta farming town of Lethbridge by immigrants who came from three ethnolinguistic Rusyn villages (Slovinky, Poráč, and Závadka) located in the old county of Szepes (Spiš) in the Prešov Region.

While the Greek Catholic immigrants from eastern Slovakia who arrived before World War II were for the most part ethnically Rusyn, those who came subsequently, especially during and just after the liberalization period in Czechoslovakia in 1968, were Slovaks. Despite the presence of this Slovak element and some efforts to have Byzantine-rite religious services conducted in the Slovak language, the older Rusyn immigrants were able to maintain Church Slavonic for the liturgy, the only other language used being English.

The leadership of the Byzantine-rite Rusyns has opted for a Slovak identity, so that adherents of that religion (whether they are ethnically Rusyn or Slovak) have since World War II come to be known as Slovak Byzantine-rite Catholics. In 1964, one of their priests, Michael Rusnak, was made an auxiliary bishop within the Ukrainian Catholic jurisdiction for the "Slovak" parishes. Then, in 1980, the Vatican created a distinct Slovak Byzantine Catholic Eparchy headed by Bishop Rusnak. With financial assistance from the industrialist Stephan B. Roman, a monumental church was dedicated in 1984 in a Toronto suburb in the presence of Pope John Paul II and representatives from the Byzantine Ruthenian hierarchy and from Rusyn secular organizations in the United States. Despite its financial resources, the Slovak Byzantine Catholic Church was limited to only a few thousand members in six parishes and two missions, all in Ontario. In recent years, its Slovak and Rusyn membership has declined, and its official Slovak-language magazine, *Mária* (Toronto, 1961-88), ceased publication.

Much larger in number were Carpatho-Rusyns who came to Canada from the Lemko Region. The earliest of the Lemko immigrants actually were re-immigrants from the northeast United States to western Canada during the first three decades of the twentieth century. Known initially as "American Lemkos," they settled on farms in the prairie provinces of Saskatchewan, Manitoba, and Alberta, or in the cities of Winnipeg and Edmonton where they found work in factories and mills. A few went to eastern Canada as well, so that the oldest Greek Catholic (now Ukrainian Catholic) Church in Ontario, located in Brantford, was actually founded by immigrants from the Lemko village of Odrzechowa.

The Lemkos also comprised the majority of Orthodox Carpatho-Rusyns in Canada. As in the United States, they did not join Ukrainian Orthodox churches but rather Russian Orthodox churches, for the most part those under the jurisdiction of the Orthodox Church in America (formerly the Metropolia). Within such an environment, however, these people were not able to preserve a distinct Rusyn identity. Instead, they tended to think of themselves as simply Russians or, if they still had any awareness of their specific heritage, they might describe themselves as Carpatho-Russians.

Toward the close of World War I, the Orthodox Lemkos in western Canada joined with other East Slavs from Galicia who called themselves Russians to form organizations that were concerned with the political changes then occurring in the European homeland. They referred to their homeland in English as Carpatho-Russia, and in their own publications as "Prikarpatskaja Rus'" (literally: Rus' near the Carpathian Mountains). This meant, besides the Lemko Region and Subcarpathian Rus' (at the time in Hungary), all of Austrian Galicia east of the San River

97. Cathedral of the Transfiguration, Markham, Ontario, built in the 1980s. A large-scale replica of the church in Vel'ký Ruskov, Slovakia, the native village of the cathedral's main benefactor, Stephen B. Roman.

as well as northern Bukovina. Their first step was to form in July 1917 in Winnipeg, Manitoba and Mundare, Alberta a Congress of Russian People (Kongres russkogo naroda), which called for the unification of "Prikarpatskaja Rus'" with Russia. By the spring of 1919, when the Habsburg Empire had ceased to exist, the group convened on April 21, 1919 Canada's first Convention of Carpatho-Russians (Siezd Karpato-rossov) in Chapman, Alberta. This group made up primarily of Orthodox hierarchs and lay leaders led by Stefan Nai and Roman N. Samilo, requested that "the Paris Peace Conference unite Carpathian Rus' [*Prikarpatskaja Rus'*] with Russia, so that Carpathian Rus' would finally be liberated from 600 years of Polish and Austro-Hungarian oppression."[12]

The convention also dispatched the Winnipeg

[12] "Memorandum pervogo siezda karpato-rossov," in *Russkii narod* (Winnipeg), May 1, 1919.

Lemko newspaper publisher Victor Hladick as part of a three-person delegation from North America to the Paris Peace Conference, and it founded the League for the Liberation of Carpatho-Russia in order to collect funds for the Carpatho-Russian "Army" in Russia (refugees from Galicia who were fighting against Bolshevism) and to condemn all forms of what was described as "Ukrainian separatism." Cut off as they were from the European homeland, the Canada's Rusyn activists were unaware that by May and June 1919, "Prikarpatskaja Rus'" had already been divided between Poland (Galicia), Romania (Bukovina), and Czechoslovakia (Subcarpathian Rus').

By the end of the 1920s, when the new boundaries in east-central Europe were stabilized and when it became clear that many immigrants were in Canada to stay, the Lemko Rusyns decided to establish secular organizations that would respond to their needs in the New World. In 1929, they established the Lemko Association (Lemko Soiuz) in Winnipeg, Manitoba under the leadership of Theodore Kochan.

The center of Lemko activity quickly moved eastward to Toronto, however, where the largest concentration of Carpatho-Rusyn immigrants was located. In that same year, 1929, a Worker's Educational Carpathian Society (Robitnyčo-Osvitn'e Karpats'ke Tovarystvo) was established within the framework of the leftist Ukrainian Worker's Organization. Then, in 1931, on the initiative of Nestor Wolchak and Walter Cislak, a Toronto branch of the Lemko Association was set up, followed by other branches in Montreal, Hamilton, Windsor, Fort William, and Edmonton. These various branches joined in 1935 to form a united Lemko Association of Canada based in Toronto. They maintained close ties with their counterparts in the United States with whom they shared as an official organ, the newspaper *Lemko* (Philadelphia, Cleveland, New York, 1928-39) and later *Karpatska Rus'* (New York and Yonkers, 1938-present). Meanwhile, the Worker's Educational Carpathian Society of Toronto, which briefly published its own organ, *Holos Karpat* (Toronto, 1932-33), refused to join the Lemko

98. Carpatho-Russian Choir of Toronto, 1939.

99. Lemko Association's Carpatho-Rusyn Children's School, Toronto, 1937.

Association because of the latter's non-Ukrainian ethnic orientation and its less enthusiastic attitude toward Communism and the Soviet Union.

Whatever their internal differences, both organizations were perceived by the Canadian authorities to be leftist and therefore potentially subversive. Hence, with the outbreak of World War II in 1939 (at which time the Soviet Union was allied with Nazi Germany), the pro-Communist Workers Enlightenment Carpathian Educational Society was banned by the Canadian government. The largest branch of the Lemko Association in Toronto continued to survive, but under different names—beginning in 1940 as the Carpatho-Russian Society for the Struggle Against Fascism (Karpatorusske Obščestvo Bor'by s Fašyzmom), after World War II as the Carpatho-Russian Society of Canada (Karpatorusske Obščestvo Kanady), and since 1982 as the Alexander Duchnovich

Society of Carpatho-Russian Canadians (Obščestvo Karpatorusskich Kanadcev).

Under these various names, the group was most active from the late 1930s until the late 1950s, even though at its height it never had more than 200 registered members. In Toronto, it had its own Carpatho-Russian Choir, dance group, and dramatic circle, all of which gave frequent concerts and performances. After 1941, when the Soviet Union joined the Allies in fighting Germany, the Carpatho-Russian Society was permitted by Canadian authorities to cooperate with the Red Cross and Russian Relief Fund in collecting over $40,000 for clothing and medicine to be sent to the Soviet Union's Red Army. Toronto was also the base for a Carpatho-Russian Youth Organization with its own monthly, *Club 280* (Toronto, 1943-60). After World War II, the Carpatho-Russian Society opened national homes in Toronto and Hamilton and a food cooperative in Toronto.

Until the early 1960s, the Lemko Association and its successor, the Carpatho-Russian Society of Canada, maintained close ties with the Lemko Association in the United States. Both adamantly rejected interaction with Ukrainians and instead proclaimed a distinct "Carpatho-Russian" identity. Although the ethnic views of the group's members did not change, political and personality differences caused a split during the 1960s. The more left-wing members led by the former youth activist Michael Lucas broke with the supposedly "anti-Communist" and therefore "anti-progressivist" Lemko Association in the United States, because for a while the latter had become increasingly critical of Poland, Czechoslovakia, and the Soviet Union's past and present treatment of its Carpatho-Rusyn/Lemko minorities. Under Lucas' direction , the group in Toronto adopted a new name, the Society of Carpatho-Russian Canadians (Obščestvo Karpatorusskych Kanadcev), and began its own publication, *Naš holos* (Toronto, 1964-72), in order to show how "our people in the homeland live freely" and without any "national

100. Carpathian People's Home, Toronto, recently declared an historical monument.

discrimination" against them. Meanwhile, those members who were less enthusiastic about the pro-Communist orientation of the Society of Carpatho-Russian Canadians decided to revive the old branch of the Lemko Association in Toronto.

At present, both factions have dwindled to a few dozen members. Older members have died and young people, alienated by the pro-Communist orientation of the 1960s, do not join. The Carpathian People's Home in Toronto continued to host the sporadic meetings of the Society of Carpatho-Russian Canadians, although under the leadership of Lucas the building was renamed Friendship House. In an effort to attract leftist sympathizers regardless of ethnic origin, Lucas has used the Friendship House to operate the Canada-U.S.S.R Association, renamed in 1992 the Concerned Friends of Soviet People.

After World War II, a few hundred new immigrants arrived from the Rusyn homeland south of the Carpathians. Some of those from Subcarpathian Rus' and the Prešov Region supported the Council of a Free Sub-Carpatho-Ruthenia in Exile (Rada Svobodnoj Podkarpatskoj Rusi v Exili), founded in 1951 in Hamilton, Ontario by Vasilij V. Fedinec. This council joined with other Czechoslovak political émigrés in the Council of Free Czechoslovakia to protest the Soviet annexation of Subcarpathian Rus' in 1945 and to work for the re-creation of a democratic Czechoslovakia according to its pre-World War II boundaries. The council's organ, *Rusin/Ruthenian* (New York and Hamilton, Ont., 1952-60), was particularly critical of the policy of Ukrainianization and the forced liquidation of the Greek Catholic Church in the homeland. The council cooperated closely with the Byzantine Ruthenian Catholic Church in the United States. It also lobbied for Rusyn-language broadcasts to the homeland over Radio Free Europe which began in 1954, and it helped Carpatho-Rusyn displaced persons (DPs) then in camps in Germany to emigrate to North America through its affiliate organization, the Central Committee of Subcarpathian Political Emigrés (Centralnyj Komitet Podkarpatskich Političeskich Bižencev) in Ludwigsburg, Germany. The Hamilton-based council claimed at its height over 600 members in Canada and the United States.

An even greater proportion of post-World War II immigrants from north of the Carpathians and was comprised of nationally-conscious Ukrainian Lemkos. They joined Ukrainian Catholic or Ukrainian Orthodox churches and generally functioned within Canada's well-organized Ukrainian community. Some have set up specifically Lemko publications and organizations. Initially, the most active in this regard was the Ukrainian Lemko writer Julijan Tarnovyč (pseud. Julijan Beskyd), who after coming to Canada published several books and annual almanacs about the Lemko homeland and served as editor of the newspaper *Lemkivščyna-Zakerzonnja* (Toronto, 1949-53) and *Lemkivs'ki visti* (Yonkers, N.Y. and Toronto, 1958-79). The latter organ was subsequently published by the American-based Organization for the Defense of the Lemko Land, which in 1961 established its first Canadian branch in Toronto at the initiative of Ivan Olenych. In 1973, the few existing branches of the organization decided to form the Canadian Lemko's Association (Ob"jednannja Lemkiv Kanady), which still has several branches throughout the country and its main seat in Toronto. The Toronto branch of the Canadian Lemko's Association has been especially active in sponsoring lectures, concerts, and public protests in memory of the forced deportation of Lemkos from their Carpathian homeland carried out by the Communist government of Poland after World War II. Most recently, they have joined their pro-Ukrainian Lemko brethren in the United States in protest against the Rusyn national revival in the European homeland which they view as a threat to the unity of the Ukrainian people of which they consider Lemkos and all Rusyns an indelible part.

Toronto also became home to the Carpathian Sich Brotherhood (Bratstvo Karpats'kykh Sičovykiv), with branches in the United States as well as Canada. Founded in 1949 by Dr. Stepan Rosocha, the Sich brought together Ukrainian-oriented immigrants from Transcarpathia as well as those Galician Ukrainians who fought in that military unit during its struggle against the Hungarian invasion of Carpatho-Ukraine (Transcarpathia) in early 1939. During the early years of its existence, the Sich had its own Ukrainian-

101. Baèka/Vojvodinian Rusyns gather in Toronto for an evening of relaxation, ca. 1938.

language bulletin, *Karpats'ka Sič* (Toronto, 1949-53). In subsequent years, it was able to use the pages of the newspaper, *Vil'ne slovo* (Toronto, 1934-86), which under the editorship of Rosocha reported on the Ukrainian aspects of the Carpatho-Rusyn homeland. Following the death of the dynamic Rosocha in 1986, the Sich became inactive.

There was also a small group of Carpatho-Rusyns from the Bačka and Srem regions in the far south of the former Hungarian Kingdom, an area that after World War I became the Vojvodina of Yugoslavia. Already before World War I, there were in Canada over 50 Bačka Rusyns from one town alone, Ruski Kerestur in the Vojvodina. The Bačka/Vojvodinian, or Yugoslav Rusyns settled mostly in Montreal and especially in southern Ontario. During the 1930s, Vojvodinian Rusyns living in Windsor and other southwest Ontario towns participated in meetings of the only organization for Vojvodinian Rusyns in North America, the Rada Club in Detroit.

At present, Vojvodinian Rusyns form the most active group of Carpatho-Rusyns in Canada. This is because of the arrival of new families who started to immigrate in the 1980s and settle primarily in and around the town of Kitchener in southern Ontario. Newcomers continued to arrive in the wake of Yugoslavia's civil war during the mid-1990s, so that today there are about 75 families in southern Ontario and a few others scattered in the western provinces of Saskatchewan and Manitoba. Because of former Yugoslavia's recognition of a distinct Rusyn nationality and its widespread support after World War II of Rusyn culture and education, these immigrants arrived in Canada with a clear sense of a distinct identity. Their active community life, including an annual summer picnic and winter ball, has been spearheaded by a Kitchener businessman, Janko Sabadoš. At his initiative the Rusyn Society of North America was founded in late 1995; it publishes a newsletter in the Vojvodinian Rusyn language, *Hlasnïk* (Kitchener, Ont., 1996-present).

Canada has been home to a few individuals of Carpatho-Rusyn origin who did not otherwise fit into any of the existing religious or secular organizations. The Vojvodinian Rusyn Julijan Kolesar settled in Montreal in 1973, and for the next two decades he produced a substantive body of paintings, poetry, and scholarly works. He set up the Julijan Kolesarov

Rusnak Institute of America, for which he single-handedly wrote literally thousands of pages of historical, ethnographic, and linguistic works about Carpatho-Rusyns, including a 24-volume dictionary of Rusyn art. All of Kolesar's writings emphasized that Rusyns comprise a distinct nationality whose original homeland included not only the northcentral Carpathian region, but as well much of the Hungarian or Pannonian plain.

In 1987, the leading Greek Catholic dissident in Ukraine and a native of Transcarpathia (Subcarpathian Rus'), Josyf Terelya, was released from a prison camp as a result of high-level international diplomatic pressure on the Soviet Union's new government headed by Mikhail Gorbachev. Terelya settled in Toronto where he continued to work on behalf of the outlawed Greek Catholic Church in his homeland. Since the legalization of the church in Ukraine in 1990, Terelya has emphasized the mystical aspects of his persona, which through a well publicized autobiography (1991) have come to the attention of the larger Catholic world in Europe as well as North America. Perhaps the individual of Carpatho-Rusyn background with the highest profile in recent Canadian society was John Sopinka, whose parents immigrated from the Lemko Region in the 1920s. Following a successful career as an attorney in Toronto, Sopinka served as a justice to the Supreme Court of Canada from 1988 until his death in 1997.

But the Canadian who has had the most direct impact in promoting Carpatho-Rusyn culture not only in his own country but worldwide is the merchant banker based in Toronto, Steven Chepa. He is the son of immigrants from the Lemko Region and Subcarpathian Rus' who were active in the Lemko community in Hamilton, Ontario. Since the late 1990s, Chepa has been seriously committed to his Carpatho-Rusyn heritage. He has helped fund publications and projects related to the national revival in the homeland and has set up the annual Aleksander Duchnovyč Prize for the best work in Rusyn bellettres, an award for lifetime contributions to Rusyn culture, and a research fellowship in Rusyn studies at the University of Toronto. In 2002, he established the World Academy of Rusyn Culture, which operates an Internet site to disseminate information about past and present Rusyns in all walks of life.

With the exception of the Vojvodinian Rusyn community, today there is little if any organized group maintenance among the descendants of the earlier Carpatho-Rusyn immigrants to Canada. The organizations of the 1940s and 1950s have long since ceased to exist or have become moribund. All that remains are individuals who themselves or whose parents and grandparents came from Carpatho-Rusyn villages. At best a handful today claim a distinct Carpatho-Rusyn identity. The vast majority identify with no particular group or with more well-known groups, whether Russians, Slovaks, Poles, or the most influential Slavic group in Canada, the Ukrainians.

102. Award ceremony at the VI World Congress of Rusyns, Prague, October 2001. From left: Vasyľ Turok and Volodymyr Mykyta—laureates for Lifetime Service on behalf of Rusyns; donor Steven Chepa; Marija Maľcovska, Ivan Petrovc, Djura Papharhaji—laureates of the Duchnovynč Prize in Rusyn Literature.

Appendix

A Root Seeker's Guide to the Homeland

The following list of Carpatho-Rusyn villages is based on the 1910 Hungarian census for the Prešov Region and for Subcarpathian Rus'; that is, villages located today within Slovakia, Ukraine, and Romania, whose inhabitants had responded that their "mother tongue" (native language) was Rusyn. Data for the Lemko Region, that is, villages located today within Poland, are based on the 1921 Polish census.

Each main entry in this list includes the names of: (1) the village; (2) the pre-World War I Hungarian county *(megye)* or Austrian Galician district *(Bezirk)*; (3) the present administrative subdivision *(okres* in Slovakia, *rajon* in the Ukraine, *województwo* in Poland, *judeţe* in Romania); and (4) the present country. The name of the village in the main entry is given according to the official language of the country where it is presently located; that is, Polish in the Lemko Region of Poland, Romanian in Romania, Serbo-Croatian in Croatia and Serbia, Slovak in the Prešov Region of Slovakia, and Ukrainian in Subcarpathian Rus'. The main entry is followed by name variants including pre-1918 Hungarian names for villages south of the Carpathians; old Rusyn names that have later been altered; and the semi-official Ukrainian names for villages in the Prešov Region, Romania, and the Lemko Region. The language variants are explained by the following abbreviations: [H] Hungarian; [P] Polish; [Ro] Romanian; [Ru] Rusyn; [SC] Serbo-Croatian; [Sv] Slovak; and [U] Ukrainian. All name variants appear separately with appropriate cross references to the main entry.

With regard to the villages that are included in this list and which therefore define the territorial extent of Rusyn-inhabited lands, the Lemko Region north of the Carpathians in historic Galicia is problematic. Scholars disagree considerably as to what marks the eastern boundary of the Lemko Region, although the Solinka River is said by many to be the appropriate eastern border (see Map 2, page 4). American publicists from the Lemko Region, however, generally consider their group in America to comprise people who came from all villages as far east as the San River and as far north as the city of Sanok, even if, properly speaking, some of these are not ethnographically Lemko villages. Because of the American context of this book, the San River is being accepted as the eastern boundary of the Lemko Region, so that all villages west of that water body are included here.

As for the villages that do appear in this list, they have been primarily—though not exclusively—inhabited by Carpatho-Rusyns. In order to be included, at least 50 per cent of the inhabitants of the village had to claim Rusyn as their mother tongue. In fact, most of the villages in the list had 70 per cent or more Rusyn-speaking inhabitants according to the 1910 Hungarian census or 1921 Polish census.

Because of the fluctuating nature of ethnic/national self-identity in border areas, especially along the Rusyn-Slovak and Rusyn-Magyar ethnolinguistic boundary, there were a few villages whose inhabitants (50 per cent or more) did not claim that their mother tongue was Rusyn in the 1910 census, but who did claim Rusyn as their mother tongue or nationality in previous or subsequent censuses. There were 15 such Rusyn villages in the 1900 Hungarian census, which are listed here and marked with a single asterisk. There were another 37 such Rusyn villages in the 1921 Czechoslovak census, and these are also listed here

110

and marked with a double asterisk. This means that altogether there were during the first decades of the twentieth century a total of 1,102 Carpatho-Rusyn villages. Based on present-day boundaries, 468 of these are in Subcarpathian Rus' (Transcarpathia) in Ukraine; 324 in the Lemko Region of Poland; 291 in the Prešov Region of Slovakia; 11 in the Maramureş Region and 3 in the Banat region of Romania; 2 in the Vojvodina of Serbia; 2 in Croatia; and 1 in Hungary.

Finally, it should be noted that many Carpatho-Rusyns also lived in small towns and cities just beyond or even within the compact Rusyn ethnolinguistic territory depicted on Maps 1 and 2. In these places, Rusyns generally comprised only a small percentage of the inhabitants and for that reason do not appear on the larger list. The forebears of some Carpatho-Rusyn Americans may have come from such places. Among places that fall into this category and which, in 1910/1921, had at least 2 per cent of their inhabitants listed as Rusyn speakers are:

Town/City	Former Hungarian county or Galician district	Present country	Number of Rusyns 1910/1921	Rusyn percentage of total population
Bačinci [Ru, SC]	Szerem	Croatia	611	35
Baligród [P] (Baligrit [Ru]; Balyhorod [U])	Lesko	Poland	161	13
Berehovo [Ru, U] (Beregszász [H]; Berehove [U])	Bereg	Ukraine	221	3
Berkasovo [Ru, SC]	Szerem	Croatia	655	33
Cîmpulung la Tisa [Ro] (Dovhe Pole [Ru]; Hosszúmező [H])	Máramaros	Romania	2,588	9
Cireşu [Ro] (Cireşul [Ro]; Cserestemes [H]; Čeresne [Ru]	Krassó-Szőrény	Romania	102	11
Crăciuneşti [Ro] (Karácsonyfalva [H]; Kračunovo [Ru]; Kryčuniv[U]; Tiszakarácsonyfalva [H])	Máramaros	Romania	1,101	44
Dibrova [U] (Alsóapsa [H]; Nyžnja Apša [Ru])	Máramaros	Ukraine	407	7
Djurdjevo [SC] (Djurd'ov [Ru]; Sajkásgyörgye [H])	Bács-Bodrog	Serbia	1,476	31
Helcmanovce [Sv] (Helczmanócz [H]; Nagykunchfalu/ Nagykunczfalva [H])	Szepes	Slovakia	1,181	27

Town/City	Former Hungarian county or Galician district	Present country	Number of Rusyns 1910/1921	Rusyn percentage of total population
Kobylec'ka Poljana [U] (Gyertyánliget [H]; Kobŷlecka Poljana [Ru])	Máramaros	Ukraine	755	41
Krynica-Zdrój [P] (Krynycja Žyvec' [U])	Nowy Sącz	Poland	278	12
Kula [H, Ru, SC]	Bács-Bodrog	Serbia	456	5
Lesko [P] (Lisko [P, U])	Lesko	Poland	285	8
Levoča [Sv] (Lőcse [H])	Szepes	Slovakia	201	3
Michalovce [Sv] (Mychalivci/ Mychalovec' [Ru]; Nagymihály [H])	Zemplén	Slovakia	533	7
Mukačevo [U](Mukačeve/Mukačiv [U]; Mukačovo [Ru]; Munkács [H])	Bereg	Ukraine	1,394	8
Onokivci [U] (Felső-domonya [H]; Onokovci [Ru])	Ung	Ukraine	684	37
Peregu Mare [Ro] (Peregul-Mare [Ro]; Németpereg [H]; Velykyj Pereg [Ru]	Arad	Romania	381	28
Posada Jaśliska [P] (Posada Jasliska [Ru])	Sanok	Poland	888	27
Rakošyno [Ru, U] (Beregrákos/Rákos [H])	Bereg	Ukraine	2726	38
Sanok [P] (Sjanik [U])	Sanok	Poland	291	3
Scăiuş [Ro] (Bojtorjános [H]; Skejuš [Ru]; Szkejus [H]	Krassó-Szőrény	Romania	522	32
Seredne [U] (Seredn'oje [Ru]; Szerednye [H])	Ung	Ukraine	1867	34
Šid [Ru, SC] (Sid [H])	Szerem	Croatia	878	17
Sighetul Marmaţiei [Ro] (Máramarossziget [H]; Sigot' [Ru]; Syhit'[U])	Máramaros	Romania	532	3
Solotvyno [U] (Akna-Szlatina [H]; Solotvynskî Kopal'nî [Ru])	Máramaros	Ukraine	209	9

Town/City	Former Hungarian county or Galician district	Present country	Number of Rusyns 1910/1921	Rusyn percentage of total population
Stari Vrbas [SC] (Óverbász [H]; Verbas [Ru], today part of Vrbas	Bács-Bodrog	Serbia	571	12
Tisa [Ro] (Mikovo [Ru]; Tiszaveresmart/Veresmart [H]; Virişmort [Ro]	Máramaros	Romania	643	36
Tjačiv [U] (Técső [H]; Tjačovo [Ru])	Máramaros	Ukraine	855	14
Torysky [Sv, U] (Tárcafő [H]; Toriskŷ [Ru]; Toriszka [H])	Szepes	Slovakia	775	21
Užhorod [Ru, U] (Ungvár [H])	Ung	Ukraine	641	4
Velykyj Bereznyj [Ru, U] (Nagyberezna [H])	Ung	Ukraine	1,120	40
Vişeul de Sus [Ro] (Vyšovo [Ru]; Felsőviső [H])	Máramaros	Romania	318	3
Vynohradiv [U] (Nagyszőllős [H]; Sevljuš/Vynohradovo [Ru])	Ugocsa	Ukraine	1,266	16
Vyškovo [Ru] (Visk [H]; Vyškove [U];Vŷškovo nad Tysoju [Ru])	Máramaros	Ukraine	831	17
Žnjatyno [Ru, U] (Izsnyéte [H])	Bereg	Ukraine	1,465	40

NOTE TO THE USER

The letters in brackets refer to the languages in which villages have been named:

[H]	Hungarian	[Sc]	Serbo-Croatian
[P]	Polish	[Sv]	Slovak
[Ro]	Romanian	[U]	Ukraine
[Ru]	Rusyn		

The names of the former countries and districts are given in their Hungarian and Polish forms. Their equivalents in Rusyn are:

Hungarian	*Rusyn*	*Polish*	*Rusyn*
Bereg	Bereg	Gorlice	Gorlycŷ
Máramaros	Maramoroš	Grybów	Grŷbov
Sáros	Šaryš	Jaslo	Jaslo
Szepes	Spiš	Krosno	Krosno
Szerém	Srem	Lesko	Lisko
Ugocsa	Ugoča	Nowy Sącz	Novŷj Sanč
Ung	Ung	Nowy Targ	Novŷj Torh
Zemplén	Zemplyn	Sanok	Sjanok

SOURCES: Statistical data are based on *A magyar szent korona országainak 1910 évi népszámlálása,* Magyar statisztikai közlemények, új sorozat, Vol. XLII (Budapest, 1912) and *Skorowidz miejscowości Rzeczypospolitej Polskiej opracowany na podstawie . . . spisu ludności 1921 r.,* Vol. XII: *Województwo Krakowskie/Śląsk Cieszyński,* and Vol. XIII: *Województwo Lwowskie* (Warsaw, 1924-25).

Place name changes and supplemental statistical data were drawn from: *A magyar korona országainak 1900 évi népszámlálása,* Magyar statisztikai közlemények, új sorozat, Vol. I (Budapest, 1902); Stepan Tomashivs'kyi, "Etnohrafichna karta Uhors'koï Rusy," in V.I. Lamanskii, ed., *Stat'i po slavianovedeniiu,* Vol. III (St. Petersburg, 1910); *Statistický lexikon obcí v republice československé . . . na základě výsledků sčítání lidu z 15. února 1921,* Vol. III: *Slovensko,* and Vol. IV: *Podkarpatská Rus* (Prague, 1927-28); *Retrospektívny lexikon obcí československej socialistickej republiky 1850-1970,* Vol. II, pt. 2: *abecedný prehľad obcí a častí obcí v rokoch 1850-1970* (Prague, 1978); *Istoriia mist i sil Ukraïns'koï RSR: Zakarpats'ka oblast'* (Kiev, 1969); *Istoriia gorodov i sel Ukrainskoi SSR: Zakarpatskaia oblast'* (Kiev, 1982); *Shematyzm Hreko-*

katolyts'koho dukhoven'stva apostol'skoï administratsiï Lemkovshchyny 1936, 2nd ed. (Stamford, Conn., 1970); *Spis miejscowości Polskiej Rzeczypospolitej ludowej* (Warsaw, 1967); *Karpaty: obszar konwencji turystycznej* (Warsaw, 1967); *Bieszczady: mapa turystyczna, 1:75,000* (Warsaw, 1890); *Beskid Niski i Pogórze: mapa turystyczna, 1:125,000* (Warsaw, 1979); Volodymyr Kubijovych *Etnichni hrupy pivdennozakhidn'oï Ukraïny (Halychyny) na 1.1.1939* (Wiesbaden, 1983); Coriolan Suciu, comp., *Dicţionar istoric al localităţilor din Transilvania,* 2 vols. (Bucharest, 1968).

The Rusyn names, according to their official forms implemented in Subcarpathian Rus' in 1927, were taken from the 1921 Czechoslovak census (published in 1928). The Rusyn names for villages in Slovakia are taken from: Vasyl' Latta, *Atlas ukraïns'kykh hovoriv Skhidnoï Slovachchyny* (Bratislava and Prešov, 1991), pp. 24-26; for those in the Lemko Region from: Janusz Rieger, "Toponomastyka Beskidu Niskiego i Bieszczadów Zachodnich," in *Łemkowie: kultura—sztuka—język* (Warsaw and Cracow, 1987), pp. 135-168.

Village	Former Hungarian county or Galician district	Present administrative subdivision	Present country
Abranka [Ru, U] (Ábránka [H])	Bereg	Volovec'	Ukraine
Abroncsos, *see* Obručné			
Aklos, *see* Uklyn			
Akna-Szlatina, *see* Solotvyno, p. 112			
Alsóalmád, *see* Nižná Jablonka			
Alsóapsa, *see* Dibrova, p. 111			
Alsóbaskócz, *see* Baškovce			
Alsóbistra, *see* Nyžnij Bystryj			
Alsócsebény, *see* Nižné Čabiny			
Alsódomonya, *see* Domanynci			
Alsófenyves, *see* Nižná Jedl'ová			
Alsógereben, *see* Nyžnja Hrabivnycja			
Alsóhatárszeg, *see* Nyžnja Roztoka			
Alsóhidekpatak, *see* Nyžnij Studenyj			
Alsóhimes, *see* Nižná Pisaná			
Alsóhrabonica, *see* Nyžnja Hrabivnycja			
Alsóhunkócz, *see* Choňkovce			
Alsójedlova, *see* Nižná Jedl'ová			
Alsókálinfalva, *see* Kalyny			
Alsókalocsa, *see* Koločava			
Alsókaraszló, *see* Zaričcja			
Alsókerepec, *see* Nyžnij Koropec'			
Alsókomárnok, *see* Nižný Komárnik			
Alsóladács, *see* Nižná Vladiča			
Alsóladiskóc, *see* Nižné Čabiny			
Alsómerse, *see* Nižný Mirošov			
Alsónémeti, *see* Nižné Nemecké			
Alsóodor, *see* Nižný Orlík			
Alsóorlich, *see* Nižný Orlík			
Alsópagony, *see* Nižná Polianka			
Alsópásztély, *see* Behendets'ka Pastil'			
Alsópiszana, *see* Nižná Pisaná			
Alsópolyánka, *see* Nižná Polianka			
Alsóremete, *see* Nyžni Remety			
Alsósárad, *see* Nyžnje Bolotne			
Alsó-Schönborn, *see* Nyžnij Koropec'			
Alsószalánk, *see* Nižnie Slovinky			
Alsószelistye, *see* Nyžnje Selyšče			
Alsószinevér, *see* Synevyr			
Alsószlatina, *see* Nyžnje Solotvyno			
Alsószlovinka, *see* Nižnie Slovinky			
Alsószvidnik, *see* Nižní Svidník			
Alsótarócz, *see* Nižný Tvarožec			
Alsóvereczke, *see* Nyžni Vorota			
Alsóveresmart, *see* Mala Kopanja			
Alsóvizköz, *see* Nižní Svidník			
Alsóviznicze, *see* Nyžnja Vyznycja			
Alsóvladicsa, *see* Nižná Vladiča			
Andrásháza, *see* Andrijivka, Ung county			

Village	Former Hungarian county or Galician district	Present administrative subdivision	Present country
Andrasóc, *see* Andrijivka, Ung county			
Andrašovci, *see* Andrijivka, Ung county			
Andrejivka, *see* Nowy Sącz district			
see Andrzejówka			
Andrejová [Sv] (Andrijova [Ru, U];	Sáros	Bardejov	Slovakia
Endrevágása [H])			
Andrejovka [Sv], from 1850 to 1930			
and since 1961 part of Orlov			
Andrijivka, Nowy Sącz district,			
see Andrzejówka			
Andrijivka [U] (Andrásháza/Andrasóc [H];	Ung	Užhorod	Ukraine
Andrašovci [Ru])			
Andrijova, *see* Andrejová			
Andrivka, *see* Andrzejówka			
Andrzejówka [P] (Andrejivka [Ru];	Nowy Sącz	Nowy Sącz	Poland
Andrijivka [U]; Adrivka [Ru];			
Jedrzejówka [P])			
Antalócz, *see* Antalovci			
Antalovci [Ru, U] (Antalócz [H];	Ung	Užhorod	Ukraine
Antonivka [U])			
Antonivka, *see* Antalovci			
Apsica, *see* Vodycja			
Apšycja, *see* Vodycja			
Árdánháza, *see* Ardanovo			
Ardanove, *see* Ardanovo			
Ardanovo [Ru] (Árdánháza [H];	Bereg	Iršava	Ukraine
Ardanove [U])			
Ardovec', *see* Pidvynohradiv			
Árok, *see* Jarok			
Astrjabik/Astrjabyk, *see* Jastrzębik			
Bábafalva/Bábakút, see Babyči			
Bábakút, *see* Babyči			
Babyči [Ru, U] (Bábafalva/Bábakút [H])	Bereg	Mukačevo	Ukraine
Bachljava, *see* Bachlowa			
Bachlowa [P] (Bachljava [U];	Lesko	Krosno	Poland
Bachlova [Ru])			
Bachlova, *see* Bachlowa			
Bačinci, *see* p. 111			
Bačovo, *see* Chabanivka			
Bacsava, *see* Chabanivka			
Bácskeresztur, *see* Ruski Krstur			
Bacsó, *see* Chabanivka			
Bagniste [P] (Rudavka/Rodavka [Ru];	Sanok	Krosno	Poland
Rudavka Jaslys'ka [U];			
Rudawka Jaśliska [P])			
(ceased to exist after 1947)			
Bagolyháza, *see* Bilasovycja			
Bajerivci, *see* Bajerovce			

Village	Former Hungarian county or Galician district	Present administrative subdivision	Present country
Bajerovce [Sv] (Bajerivci [Ru, U]; Bajorvágás [H])	Sáros	Sabinov	Slovakia
Bajorvágás, *see* Bajerovce			
Balašovci [Ru, U] (Balázsfalva/ Ballósfalva [H])	Bereg	Sabinov	Ukraine
Balažijeve, *see* Kuz'myno			
Balázsfalva, *see* Balašovci			
Balázsvágás, *see* Blažov			
Baligrit, *see* Baligród, p. 111			
Baligród, *see* p. 111			
Ballósfalva, *see* Balašovci			
Balnica [P] (Balnycja [Ru]; Bal'nycja [U])	Lesko	Krosno	Poland
Balnycja/Bal'nycja, *see* Balnica			
Bałucianka [P] (Balutjanka [U]; Bavtjanka [Ru])	Sanok	Krosno	Poland
Balutjanka, *see* Bałucianka			
Balyhorod, *see* Baligród, p. 111			
Banica [P] (Banycja [Ru, U])	Gorlice	Nowy Sącz	Poland
Banica [P] (Banycja [Ru, U])	Grybów	Nowy Sącz	Poland
Banské [Sv] (Banske [Ru]; Bans'ke [U]; Bánszka/Bányapataka [H])	Zemplén	Vranov	Slovakia
Bánszka, *see* Banské			
Bányafalu, *see* Suskovo			
Bányavölgy, *see* Duplín			
Bányapataka, *see* Banské			
Banycja, *see* Banica			
Baranya, *see* Baranynci			
**Baranynci [Ru, U] (Baranya [H])	Ung	Užhorod	Ukraine
Barátlak, *see* Rohožník			
Barbovo [Ru, U] (Barbove [U]; Bárdháza [H]; Borodivka [U])	Bereg	Mukačevo	Ukraine
Bárdháza, *see* Barbovo			
Barkóczháza, *see* Ruská Volová			
Barnabás, *see* Kostylivka			
Bártfalva, *see* Dorobratovo			
Bartne [P, Ru] (Bortne [Ru, U])	Gorlice	Nowy Sącz	Poland
Barvinkoš, *see* Barvinok			
Barvinok [U] (Barvinkoš [U]; Bervînkoš [Ru])	Ung	Užhorod	Ukraine
Barwinek [P] (Barvinok [Ru, U])	Krosno	Krosno	Poland
Baskócz, *see* Baškovce			
**Baškovce [Sv] (Alsóbaskócz/ Baskócz [H])	Ung	Sobrance	Slovakia
Batár, *see* Botar			
Bátorhegy, *see* Krajná Bystrá			
Bavtjanka, *see* Bałucianka			
Becheriv, *see* Becherov			
Becherov [Sv] (Becheriv [U]; Beheró/Biharó [H])	Sáros	Bardejov	Slovakia

Village	Former Hungarian county or Galician district	Present administrative subdivision	Present country
Bedevlja [Ru, U] (Bedőháza [H])	Máramaros	Tjačiv	Ukraine
Bednarka [P] (Bodnarka [Ru, U])	Gorlice	Nowy Sącz	Poland
Bedőháza, *see* Bedevlja			
Begendját-Pásztély, see Behendets'ka Pastil'			
Begindjatska Pastîl', *see* Behendets'ka Pastil'			
Behendets'ka Pastil' [U] (Alsópásztély/ Begendját-Pásztély [H]; Begindjatska Pastîl' [Ru])	Ung	Velykyj Bereznyj	Ukraine
Beheró, *see* Becherov			
Bekrip, *see* Vel'krop			
Bélavézse, *see* Beloveža			
Belchivka/Bełchówka, *see* Borgówka			
Belebele, *see* Belebovo			
Belebova/Belebove, *see* Belebovo			
Belebovo [Ru] (Belebele/Belebova [H]; Belebove [U]; Kiscserjés [H]), now part of Kločky			
Belejivci, *see* Belejovce			
Belejócz, *see* Belejovce			
Belejovce [Sv] (Belejócz [H]; Belejivci [Ru, U])	Sáros	Svidník	Slovakia
Beloveža [Sv] (Bélavézse [H]; Biloveža [Ru, U])	Sáros	Bardejov	Slovakia
**Beňadikovce [Sv] (Benedekvágása/ Bendikóc [H]; Benjadŷkivci [Ru]; Benjadykivci [U])	Sáros	Svidník	Slovakia
*Beňatina [Sv] (Benetine [H]; Benjatyna [Ru, U]; Vadászfalva [H])	Ung	Sobrance	Slovakia
Benedeki, *see* Benedykivci			
Benedekvágása, *see* Beňadikovce			
Benedike, *see* Benedykivci			
Benedikóc, *see* Beňadikovce			
Benedykivci [U] (Benedeki [H]; Benedykovci [Ru])	Bereg	Mukačevo	Ukraine
Benetine, *see* Beňatina			
Beniowa [P] (Ben'ova [U]) (ceased to exist after 1947)	Turka	Krosno	Poland
Benjadykivci, *see* Beňadikovce			
Ben'ova, *see* Beniowa			
Bercsényifalva, *see* Dubrynyči			
Beregbárdos, *see* Bukovec', Bereg county			
Beregbükkös, *see* Bukovynka			
Beregfogaras, *see* Fogaraš			
Beregforrás, *see* Rodnykivka			
Bereghalmos, *see* Škurativci			
Beregkisalmás, *see* Zalužžja			
Beregkisfalud, *see* Sil'ce			
Beregkövesd, *see* Kamjans'ke			

Village	Former Hungarian county or Galician district	Present administrative subdivision	Present country
Beregleányfalva, *see* Lalovo			
Beregnagyalmás, *see* Jabluniv			
Beregpálfalva, *see* Volovycja			
Beregpapfalva, *see* Dilok			
Beregrákos, *see* Rakošyno, p. 112			
Beregrosztoka, *see* Velyka Roztoka			
Beregsárrét, *see* Kal'nyk			
Beregszász, *see* Berehovo, p. 111			
Beregszentmiklós, *see* Čynadijovo			
Beregsziklás, *see* Ščerbovec'			
Beregszilvás, *see* Kuz'myno			
Beregszőllős, *see* Lochovo			
Berehove, *see* Berehovo, p. 111			
Berehovo, *see* p. 111			
Berehy [U]	Máramaros	Mižhirja	Ukraine
Berehy Górne [P] (Berehy Horišni [U]; Brzegi Górne [P])	Lesko	Krosno	Poland
Bereščajska Vola, *see* Wola Matiaszowa			
Bereska, *see* Berezka			
Berest [P, Ru, U] nad Labirc'om	Grybów	Nowy Sącz	Poland
Berestiv nad Labirc'om, *see* Brestov nad Laborcem			
Berezka [P, U] (Bereska [P, Ru]; Brzozka [P])	Lesko	Krosno	Poland
Bereżki [P] (Bereżky [U])	Lesko	Krosno	Poland
Bereżky, *see* Bereżki			
Berezna, *see* Berezove			
Bereznek, *see* Bereznyky			
Bereżnica Niżna [P] (Berežnycja Nyžnja [U]) (ceased to exist after 1947)	Lesko	Krosno	Poland
Bereżnica Wyżna [P] (Bereznycja [Ru]; Berežnycja Vyžnja [U])	Lesko	Krosno	Poland
Bereznik, *see* Bereznyky			
Bereznycja, *see* Bereżnica Wyżna			
Berežnycja Nyžnja, *see* Bereżnica Niżna			
Berežnycja Vyžnja, *see* Bereżnica Wyżna			
Bereznyk, *see* Bereznyky			
Bereznyky [U] (Bereznek/Bereznik [H]; Bereznyk [Ru])	Máramaros	Svaljava	Ukraine
Berezócz, *see* Brezovec			
Berezóka, *see* Brezovka			
Berezova, *see* Brzezowa			
Berezove [U] (Berezna [H]; Berezovo [Ru])	Máramaros	Chust	Ukraine
Berezovec', Zemplén county, *see* Brezovec			
Berezovec/Berezovec', Lesko district, *see* Brzozowiec			
Berezovo, *see* Berezove			

Village	Former Hungarian county or Galician district	Present administrative subdivision	Present country
Berezowiec, *see* Brzozowiec			
Berkasovo, *see* p. 111			
Berkenyéd, *see* Jarabina			
Berlebaš, *see* Kostylivka			
Bértelek, *see* Breboja			
Bervînkoš, *see* Barvinok			
Besko [P] (Bos'ko [Ru, U])	Sanok	Krosno	Poland
Biała Woda [P] (Bila Voda [Ru, U])	Nowy Targ	Nowy Sącz	Poland
Bielanka [P] (Bilanka [Ru]; Biljanka [U])	Gorlice	Nowy Sącz	Poland
Bieliczna [P] (Bilična [Ru]; Bylyčna [U]) (ceased to exist after 1947)	Grybów	Nowy Sącz	Poland
Biharó, *see* Becherov			
Bila Voda, *see* Biała Woda			
Bilanka, *see* Bielanka			
Bilasovycja [Ru, U] (Bagolyháza [H])	Bereg	Volovec'	Ukraine
Bilászovica, *see* Bilasovycja			
Bil'careva, *see* Binczarowa			
Bilična, *see* Bieliczna			
Bilin, *see* Bilyn			
Biljanka, *see* Bielanka			
Bilke, *see* Bilky			
Bilky [Ru, U] (Bilke [H])	Bereg	Iršava	Ukraine
Bilovarci [U] (Bilovarec' [Ru]; Kiskirva [H])	Máramaros	Tjačiv	Ukraine
Bilovarec', *see* Bilovarci			
Biloveža, *see* Beloveža			
Bilŷj Potok, *see* Dilove			
Bilyn [Ru, U] (Bilin [H])	Máramaros	Rachiv	Ukraine
Binczarowa [P] (Bilcareva [Ru]; Bolcarjova/Borcalova [Ru])	Grybów	Nowy Sącz	Poland
Bistra [U] (Bisztra [H]; Bŷstrŷj [Ru]; Petrovabisztra [H])	Máramaros	Maramureş	Romania
Bisztra, *see* Bistra			
Bisztra-Verhovina, *see* Verchovyna-Bystra			
Blaživ, *see* Blažov			
Blažov [Sv] (Balázsvágás [H]; Blaživ [Ru, U]) (ceased to exist in 1950)	Sáros	Prešov	Slovakia
Blechnarka [P] (Blichnarka [Ru, U])	Gorlice	Nowy Sącz	Poland
Blichnarka, *see* Blechnarka			
Bobovo [Ru, U]	Máramaros	Tjačiv	Ukraine
Bobovyšči, *see* Bobovyšče			
Bobovyšče [U] (Bobovyšči [Ru]; Borhalom/ Bubuliska [H])	Bereg	Mukačevo	Ukraine
Bochivka, *see* Borgówka			
Bociocoiu Mare [Ro] (Bočkov [Ru]; Byčkiv [U]; Nagybocskó [H]); Velykŷj Bočkov [Ru}; Velykyj Byčkiv [U])	Máramaros	Maramureş	Romania

Village	Former Hungarian county or Galician district	Present administrative subdivision	Present country
Bočkov, *see* Bociocoiu Mare			
Bodaki [P] (Bodakŷ [Ru]; Bodaky [U])	Gorlice	Nowy Sącz	Poland
Bodakŷ/ Bodaky, *see* Bodaki			
Bodnarka, *see* Bednarka			
Bodružal' [Sv] (Bodrudžal' [Ru}; Bodružal [U]; Rózsadomb [H])	Sáros	Svidník	Slovakia
Bodzás, *see* Bžany			
Bogdány, *see* Bohdan			
Boglárka, *see* Bogliarka			
Bogliarka [Sv] (Boglárka [H]; Bogljarka [Ru, U])	Sáros	Bardejov	Slovakia
Bogusza [P] (Boguša [Ru]; Bohuša [U])	Grybów	Nowy Sącz	Poland
Boharevycja [U] (Boharovycja [Ru]; Falucska [H])	Bereg	Iršava	Ukraine
Bohdan [Ru, U] (Bogdány/ Tiszabogdány [H])	Máramaros	Rachiv	Ukraine
Bohuša, *see* Bogusza			
Bojtorjános, *see* Scăiuș, p. 112			
**Bokša [Ru, Sv, U]	Zemplén	Stropkov	Slovakia
Bolcarjova, *see* Binczarowa			
Bölcsős, *see* Kolibabovce			
Bonarivka, *see* Bonarówka			
Bonarówka [P] (Bonarivka [Ru, U])	Strzyżów	Rzeszów	Poland
Borcalova, *see* Binczarowa			
Borgówka [P] (Belchivka [U]; Bełchowka [P]; Bochivka [Ru]) (ceased to exist after 1947)	Sanok	Krosno	Poland
Borhalom, *see* Bobovyšče			
Boriv, *see* Borov			
Borkút, *see* Kvasy			
Boró, *see* Borov			
Boród, *see* Brid			
Borodivka, *see* Barbovo	Bereg	Volovec'	Ukraine
Borókás, *see* Jedlinka			
Borosnya, *see* Brusnica			
Borov [Sv] (Boró [H]; Boriv [Ru, U]), since 1970 part of Medzilaborce			
Borsučyna [Ru, U] (Borszucsina/ Borzfalva [H])	Bereg	Volovec'	Ukraine
Bortne, *see* Bartne			
Boržavs'ke [U] Nagycsongova [H]; Velyka Čengava [Ru]; Velyka Čynhava [U])	Ugocsa	Vynohradiv	Ukraine
Borzfalva, *see* Borsučyna			
Bos'ko, *see* Besko			
**Botar [Ru, U] (Batár [H]; Bratove/Bratovo [U])	Ugocsa	Vynohradiv	Ukraine
Breboja [Ru, U] (Bértelek [H])	Máramaros	Rachiv	Ukraine
Brestiv [U] (Brestov [Ru];	Bereg	Mukačevo	Ukraine

Village	Former Hungarian county or Galician district	Present administrative subdivision	Present country
Nagy-Bresztó/Ormód [H])			
Brestov, *see* Brestiv			
Brestov nad Laborcom [Sv] (Berestiv [Ru,U]; Berestiv nad Labirc'om [Ru]; Izbugyabresztó/ Laborczbér [H])	Zemplen	Medzilaborce	Slovakia
Breznička [Ru, Sv] (Breznyčka [U]; Kisberezsnye/Kisbrezsnyicze [H])	Zemplén	Stropkov	Slovakia
Breznyčka, *see* Breznička			
Brezova, *see* Brzezowa			
Brezovec [Sv] (Berezócz [H]; Berezovec' [Ru, U])	Zemplén	Snina	Slovakia
Brezovka [Sv] (Berezóka/Brezufka [H])	Sáros	Bardejov	Slovakia
Brezufka, *see* Brezovka			
Brid [U] (Boród [H]; Brod [H, Ru]; Brüd [H])	Bereg	Iršava	Ukraine
Brod, *see* Brid			
Bron'ka [U] (Bronyka/ Szuhabaranka [H])	Máramaros	Iršava	Ukraine
Bronyka, *see* Bron'ka			
Brüd, *see* Brid			
Brunarja Nyžnja, *see* Brunary Niżne			
Brunarja Vyšnja, *see* Brunary Wyżne			
Brunary Niżne [P] (Brunarja Nyžnja [Ru]; Brunary Nyžni [U])	Grybów	Nowy Sącz	Poland
Brunary Wyżne [P] (Brunarja Vyšnja [Ru]; Brunary Vyžni [U])	Grybów	Nowy Sącz	Poland
Brunary Vyžni, *see* Brunary Wyżne			
Brusnica [Ru, Sv] (Borosnya [H]; Brusnycja [U]; Brusnyicza [H])	Zemplén	Stropkov	Slovakia
Brusnycja, *see* Brusnica			
Brusnyicza, *see* Brusnica			
Brustov, *see* Lopušanka			
Brusturŷ, *see* Lopuchiv			
Brusztópatak, *see* Lopušanka			
Brustiv, *see* Lopušanka			
Brusztura, *see* Lopuchiv			
Brzegi Górne , *see* Berehy Górne			
Brzezowa [P] (Berezova [Ru, U]; Brezova [Ru])	Jasło	Krosno	Poland
Brzozka, *see* Berezka			
Brzozowiec [P] (Berezovec [Ru]; Berezovec' [U]; Berezowiec [P])	Lesko	Krosno	Poland
Bubuliska , *see* Bobovyšče			
Buk [P, U]	Lesko	Krosno	Poland
Bukivc'ovo [Ru, U] (Bukivcevo [U]; Bükkös/Bukócz/Ungbükkös [H])	Ung	Velykyj Bereznyj	Ukraine
Bukivci, *see* Bukovce			
Bükkös, Bereg county, *see* Bukovynka			

Village	Former Hungarian county or Galician district	Present administrative subdivision	Present country
Bükkös, Ung county, *see* Bukivc'ovo			
Bükköskő, *see* Potik			
Bükköspatak, *see* Bukovec', Máramaros county			
Bukócz, *see* Bukovec', Bereg county;			
Bukovec', Máramaros county			
Bukovce [Sv] (Bukivci [U])	Zemplén	Stropkov	Slovakia
Bukove [U] (Fakóbükk [H], Fakobŷky [Ru])	Ugocsa	Vynohradiv	Ukraine
Bukovec' [Ru, U] (Beregbárdos/ Bukócz [H])	Bereg	Volovec'	Ukraine
Bukovec' [Ru, U] (Bükköspatak/ Bukócz [H])	Máramaros	Mižhirja	Ukraine
Bukovec', Lesko county, *see* Bukowiec			
Bukovec', Turka county, *see* Bukowiec			
Bukovynka [Ru, U] (Beregbükkös/ Bükkös/Bukovinka [H])	Bereg	Mukačevo	Ukraine
Bukowiec [P] (Bukovec' [U])	Lesko	Krosno	Poland
Bukowiec [P] (Bukovec' [U]) (ceased to exist after 1947)	Turka	Krosno	Poland
Bustyaháza, *see* Buštyno			
Buštyno [U] (Bustyaháza [H]; Bužčyno [Ru])	Máramaros	Tjačiv	Ukraine
Byčkiv, *see* Bocicoiu Mare			
Bylyčna, *see* Bieliczna			
Bystrá [Sv] (Bŷstra [Ru]; Hegyesbisztra/Sztropkóbisztra [H])	Zemplén	Stropkov	Slovakia
Bystre [P, U] (Bŷstrŷj [Ru])	Lesko	Krosno	Poland
Bystrycja [U] (Repede [H]; Rjapid' [Ru])	Bereg	Mukačevo	Ukraine
Bystryj [U] (Bŷstrŷj [Ru]; Felsőbisztra/ Sebesfalva [H])	Bereg	Volovec'	Ukraine
Bŷstrŷj, Lesko district, *see* Bystre			
Bŷstrŷj, Máramaros county, *see* Bistra			
Bŷstrŷj, Ung county, *see* Verchovyna-Bystra			
**Bžany [Sv, U] (Bodzás [H]; Bžanŷ [Ru])	Zemplén	Stropkov	Slovakia
Čabalivci, *see* Čabalovce			
Čabalovce [Sv] (Čabalivci [Ru, U]; Csabalócz és Sterkócz [H])	Zemplén	Medzilaborce	Slovakia
Čabanivka [U] (Bačovo [Ru]; Bacsava/Bacsó [H])	Ung	Užhorod	Ukraine
Čabiny [Sv] (Čabynŷ [Ru]; Čabyny [U])	Zemplén	Medzilaborce	Slovakia
Čabyn [Ru, U] (Csabina [H])	Bereg	Mukačevo	Ukraine
Čabyny, *see* Čabiny			
Čapovci, *see* Čopivci			
Čarna, *see* Czarna			
Čarna Voda, *see* Czarna Woda			
Čarne, *see* Czarne			
Čarno, *see* Šarišské Čierne			

Village	Former Hungarian county or Galician district	Present administrative subdivision	Present country
Čarnŷj, *see* Czarne			
Caryns'ke, *see* Caryńskie			
Caryńskie [P] (Caryns'ke [U]) (ceased to exist after 1947)	Lesko	Krosno	Poland
Čašyn, *see* Czaszyn			
Čejšyn, *see* Czaszyn			
**Čepa [Ru, U] (Csepe [H])	Ugocsa	Vynohradiv	Ukraine
Čerejivci [U] (Čerejovci [Ru]; Cserejóc/Czerház [H])	Bereg	Mukačevo	Ukraine
Čerejovci, *see* Čerejivci			
Čeremcha, *see* Czeremcha			
Čerešne, see Cireşu, p. 111			
Cernina [Sv] (Cernyna [U]; Cernynŷ [Ru]; Czernina/Felsőcsernye [H])	Sáros	Svidník	Slovakia
Cernyna, *see* Cernina			
Cernynŷ, *see* Cernina			
Čertež, Máramaros county, *see* Čertiž			
Čertež, Sanok district, *see* Czerteż			
Čertež [Ru, U] (Čertiž [U]; Csertész/ Ungcsertész [H])	Ung	Užhorod	Ukraine
Čertiž, Sanok district, *see* Czerteż			
Čertiž [U] (Čertež [Ru])	Máramaros	Chust	Ukraine
Čertiž, Ung county, *see* Čertež			
Čertižné [Sv] (Čertižne [Ru]; Čertyžne [U]; Csertész/Nagycsertész [H])	Zemplén	Medzilaborce	Slovakia
Čertyžne, *see* Czertyżne			
Červen'eve, *see* Červen'ovo			
Červen'ovo [Ru, U] (Červen'eve [U]; Czerlenő [H])	Bereg	Mukačevo	Ukraine
Češyn, *see* Czaszyn			
Chmeliv [U] (Chmelî [Ru])	Máramaros	Rachiv	Ukraine
Chmel'ová [Sv] (Chmel'ova [Ru, U]; Komloša [Ru]; Komlósa/Komlóspatak [H])	Sáros	Bardejov	Slovakia
Chmil'nyk [Ru, U] (Komlós [H]; Komluš [Ru])	Bereg	Iršava	Ukraine
Choceń [P] (Chotin' [U]) (ceased to exist after 1947)	Lesko	Krosno	Poland
Cholmec' [Ru, U] (Helmec/ Korláthelmec/Putkahelmec [H])	Ung	Užhorod	Ukraine
Cholmovec' [U] (Cholmec' [Ru]; Homlőcz [H])	Ugocsa	Vynohradiv	Ukraine
Chon'kivci, *see* Choňkovce			
Choňkovce [Sv] (Alsóhunkócz [H]; Chon'kivci [U]; Hunkócz [H])	Ung	Sobrance	Slovakia
Chotin', *see* Choceń			
Chudl'ove, see Chud'lovo			
Chudl'ovo [Ru, U] (Chudl'ove [U]; Horlyó [H])	Ung	Užhorod	Ukraine
Chust [Ru, U] (Huszt [H])	Máramaros	Chust	Ukraine

Village	Former Hungarian county or Galician district	Present administrative subdivision	Present country
Chustec' [Ru, U] (Gernyésmező/ Husztec-Polyána [H])	Máramaros	Chust	Ukraine
Chyrowa [P] (Hŷrova [Ru]; Hyrova [U]; Hyrowa [P])	Krosno	Krosno	Poland
Chyža [U] (Chyži [Ru]; Kistarna/Tarna [H])	Ugocsa	Vynohradiv	Ukraine
Chyzi, *see* Chyža			
Cichania, *see* Ciechania			
Ciechania [P] (Cichania [P]; Tŷchanja [Ru]; Tychanja [U]) (ceased to exist after 1947)	Krosno	Krosno	Poland
Cigányóc, *see* Cyhanivci			
Cigel'ka [Sv] (Cigelka/Cigolka [Ru]; Cyhelka [U]; Czigelka [H])	Sáros	Bardejov	Slovakia
Cigla [Ru, Sv] (Cyhlja [U]; Czigla [H])	Sáros	Svidník	Slovakia
Cigolka, *see* Cigel'ka			
Cîmpulung la Tisa, *see* p. 111			
Činjad'ovo, *see* Čynadijovo			
Čirč [Ru, Sv] (Csércs [H]; Čyrč [U])	Sáros	Stará L'ubovňa	Slovakia
Cireşu, *see* p. 111			
Cisna [P] (Tisna [Ru, U])	Lesko	Krosno	Poland
Cisowiec [P] (Tysovec [Ru]; Tysivec' [U])	Lesko	Krosno	Poland
Čoma , *see* Zatysivka			
Čomal'ovo, *see* Čumal'ovo			
Copăcele [Ro] (Kopačele [Ru]) (until 1920s part of Mutnokszabadja/Ohaba Mutnik [H]; Ohaba-Mătnic [Ro])	Krassó-Szörény	Caraş-Severin	Romania
Čopivci [U] (Čapovci [Ru]; Csapóczka/Csapolcz [H])	Bereg	Mukačevo	Ukraine
Čorna [Ru, U] (Csarnató [H])	Ugocsa	Vynohradiv	Ukraine
Čorna Voda, *see* Czarna Woda			
Čorne, Gorlice county, *see* Czarne			
Čorne, Sáros county, *see* Šarišské Čierné			
Čornoholova [Ru, U] (Csornoholova/ Sóhát [H])	Ung	Velykyj Bereznyj	Ukraine
Čornoriky/Čornorikŷ, *see* Czarnorzeki			
Čornyj Potik [U] (Čornŷj Potok [Ru]; Feketepatak/Kenézpatak [H])	Bereg	Iršava	Ukraine
Crăciuneşti, *see* p. 111			
Crasna Vişeului [Ro] (Frumşeaua [Ro]; Krasna Vyšovs'ka [Ru]; Krasnyj [U]; Petrovakraszna [H])	Máramaros	Maramureş	Romania
Csabaháza, *see* Čabalovce			
Csabalócz és Sterkocz, *see* Čabalovce			
Csabina, *see* Čabyn			
Csapóczka, *see* Čopivci			
Csapolcz, *see* Čopivci			
Csarnató, *see* Čorna			
Csarnó, *see* Šarišské Čierné			

Village	Former Hungarian county or Galician district	Present administrative subdivision	Present country
Csendes, *see* Tyšiv			
Csendespatak, *see* Tichý Potok			
Csepe, *see* Čepa			
Csércs, *see* Čirč			
Cserejóc, *see* Čerejivci			
Cseres, *see* Dubová			
Cserestemes, *see* Cireşu, p. 111			
Csergőzávod, *see* Závadka, Sáros county			
Cserhalom, *see* Dibrivka, Bereg county			
Cserjés, *see* Lozjans'kyj			
Csertész, Ung county, *see* Čertež, Ung county			
Csertész, Zemplén county, *see* Čertižné			
Csillagfalva, *see* Knjahynja			
Csoma, *see* Čoma			
Csománfalva, *see* Čumal'ovo			
Csontos, *see* Kostryno			
Csornoholova, *see* Čornoholova			
Csukaháza, *see* Čukalovce			
Csuszka, *see* Tjuška			
Čukalivci, *see* Čukalovce			
Čukalovce [Sv] (Csukaháza [H]; Čukalivci [U]; Čukalovci [Ru])	Zemplén	Snina	Slovakia
Čuma, *see* Zatysivka			
Čumaleve, *see* Čumal'ovo			
Čumal'ovo [Ru, U] (Čomal'ovo [Ru]; [U]; Csománfalva [H])	Máramaros	Tjačiv	Ukraine Čumaleve
Cŷganovci, *see* Cyhanivci			
Cyhanivci [U] (Cigányóc [H]; Cŷganovci [Ru]; Czigányos [H])	Ung	Užhorod	Ukraine
Cyhelka, *see* Cigel'ka			
Cyhlja, *see* Cigla			
Čynadijeve, *see* Čynadijovo			
Čynadijovo [U] (Beregszentmiklós [H]; Činjad'ovo [Ru]; Čynadijeve [U]; Szentmiklós [H])	Bereg	Mukačevo	Ukraine
Čyrč, *see* Čirč			
Čyrna, *see* Czyrna			
Čystohorb, *see* Górna Wieś			
Czarna [P] (Čarna [Ru, U])	Grybów	Nowy Sącz	Poland
Czarna Woda [P] (Čarna Voda [Ru]; Čorna Voda [U])	Nowy Targ	Nowy Sącz	Poland
Czarne [P] (Čarne/Čarnŷj [Ru]; Čorne [Ru, U])	Gorlice	Nowy Sącz	Poland
Czarnorzeki [P] (Čornorikŷ [Ru]; Čornoriky [U])	Krosno	Krosno	Poland
Czaszyn [P] (Čašyn [U]; Čejšyn/ Češyn [Ru])	Sanok	Krosno	Poland
Czeremcha [P] (Čeremcha [Ru, U]) (ceased to exist after 1947)	Sanok	Krosno	Poland

Village	Former Hungarian county or Galician district	Present administrative subdivision	Present country
Czerház, *see* Čerejivci			
Czerlenő, *see* Červen'ovo			
Czernina, *see* Cernina			
Czerteż [P] (Čertež [U]; Čertiž [Ru])	Sanok	Krosno	Poland
Czertyżne [P] (Čertyžne [Ru, U])	Grybów	Nowy Sącz	Poland
Czigányos, *see* Cyhanivci			
Czigelka, *see* Cigel'ka			
Czigla, *see* Cigla			
Czirókaófalu, *see* Starina, Zemplén county			
Czyrna [P] (Čyrna [Ru, U])	Grybów	Nowy Sącz	Poland
Czystogarb/Czystohorb, *see* Górna Wieś			
Dąbrówka Ruska [P] (Dubrivka [Ru]; Dubrivka Rus'ka [U])	Sanok	Krosno	Poland
Dadafalva, *see* Dedačov			
Daliowa [P] (Dalova [Ru]; Dal'ova [U])	Sanok	Krosno	Poland
Dalova/Dal'ova, *see* Daliowa			
Danylove, *see* Danylovo			
Danylovo [Ru, U] (Danylove [U]; Husztófalva/Sófalva [H])	Máramaros	Chust	Ukraine
Dara [Ru, Sv, U] (since 1980 ceased to exist)	Zemplén	Snina	Slovakia
Darászvölgy, *see* Osava			
Dariv, *see* Darów			
Darócz, *see* Dravci			
Darov, *see* Darów			
Darów [P] (Dariv [Ru, U]; Darov [Ru]) (ceased to exist after 1947)	Sanok	Krosno	Poland
Darva, *see* Kolodne, Máramaros county			
Dávidfalva, *see* Zavydovo			
Dávidháza, *see* Stare Davydkovo			
Davidov [Sv] (Dávidvágása [H]; Davŷdiv [Ru]; Davydiv [U])	Zemplén	Vranov	Slovakia
Dávidvágása, *see* Davidov			
Davydiv/Davŷdiv, *see* Davidov			
**Dedačov [Sv] (Dadafalva/ Dedasócz [H]; Didačov [Ru]; Dydačiv [U])	Zemplén	Humenné	Slovakia
Dedasócz, *see* Dedačov			
Dengláz, *see* Denkovci			
*Denkovci [Ru] (Dengláz [H]), since 1920 part of Velyki Lazy			
Dér, *see* Mrazovce			
Deskófalva, *see* Deškovycja			
Deškovycja [Ru, U] (Deskófalva [H])	Bereg	Iršava	Ukraine
Desno, *see* Deszno			
Desznica [P] (Došnycja [Ru, U])	Jasło	Krosno	Poland
Deszno [P] (Desno [Ru]; Došno [U])	Sanok	Krosno	Poland
Detre, *see* Detrík			

Village	Former Hungarian county or Galician district	Present administrative subdivision	Present country
Detrík [Sv] (Detre [H]; Detryk [Ru, U])	Zemplén	Vranov	Slovakia
Detryk, *see* Detrík			
Dibrivka [U] (Cserhalom [H]; Dobróka [H]; Dubrovka nad Boržavoju [Ru]; Tölgyes [H])	Bereg	Iršava	Ukraine
Dibrivka [U] (Dubrovka [Ru])	Máramaros	Tjačiv	Ukraine
Dibrivka, Ung county, *see* Dubrivka, Ung county			
Dibrova, *see* p. 111			
Didačov, *see* Dedačov			
Dil [U] (Dîl [Ru]; Gyil/Hegyfok [H])	Máramaros	Mižhirja	Ukraine
Dilok [Ru, U] (Beregpapfalva/ Gyilok/Papfalva [H])	Bereg	Mukačevo	Ukraine
Dilok [Ru, U]	Máramaros	Chust	Ukraine
Dilove [U] (Bîlŷj Potok [Ru]; Fejérpatak/Terebesfejérpatak [H]; Trebušany [Ru])	Máramaros	Rachiv	Ukraine
Diskovycja, *see* Dyskovycja			
Djakovskyj, *see* Jakivs'ke			
Djurdjevo, *see* p. 111			
Djurd'ov, *see* Djurdjevo, p. 111			
Dlhoňa [Sv] (Dohun' [U]; Dolgonya [H]; Dolhoňa [Sv]; Dovhunja [Ru])	Sáros	Svidník	Slovakia
Długie [P] (Dovhe [Ru, U]; Dovhŷ [Ru]) (ceased to exist after 1947)	Gorlice	Nowy Sącz	Poland
Dobrjans'ke [U] (Njagovo [Ru]; Nyágova [H])	Máramaros	Tjačiv	Ukraine
Dobróka, *see* Dibrivka, Bereg county			
Dobroslava [Ru, Sv, U] (Dobroszló [H])	Sáros	Svidník	Slovakia
Dobroszló, *see* Dobroslava			
Dohun', *see* Dlhoňa			
Dolgonya, *see* Dlhoňa			
Dolha, *see* Dovhe			
Dolhoňa, *see* Dlhoňa			
Dolina [P] (Dolyny [U])	Gorlice	Nowy Sącz	Poland
Dolina [P] (Dolyna [U])	Sanok	Krosno	Poland
Dolyna, *see* Dolina, Sanok district			
Dolyny, *see* Dolina, Gorlice district			
Dołžyca [P] (Dołžycja [U]; Dovžycja [Ru, U])	Sanok	Krosno	Poland
Dołžyca [P] (Dołžyce [P]; Dołžycja [Ru, U]; Dovžycja [U])	Lesko	Krosno	Poland
Dołžyce, *see* Dołžyca, Lesko district			
Dołžycja, *see* Dołžyca, Lesko district; Sanok district			
Domafalva, *see* Domašyn			
Domanynci [Ru, U] (Alsódomonya [H]	Ung	Užhorod	Ukraine
Domašyn [Ru, U] (Domafalva/Domasina [H])	Ung	Velykyj Bereznyj	Ukraine

Village	Former Hungarian county or Galician district	Present administrative subdivision	Present country
Dombó, *see* Dubove			
Dombostelek, *see* Ploske			
Dorobratovo [Ru, U] (Bártfalva [H]; Dorobratove [U]; Dorohbratovo [Ru]; Drágabártfalva [H])	Bereg	Iršava	Ukraine
Dorohbratovo, *see* Dorobratovo			
Došno, *see* Deszno			
Došnycja, *see* Desznica			
Dovhe, Gorlice county, *see* Długie			
Dovhe [U] (Dovhoje [Ru]; Dolha [H])	Máramaros	Iršava	Ukraine
Dovhe Pole, Máramaros county, *see* Cîmpulung la Tisa, p. 112			
**Dovhe Pole [U] (Dovhoje [Ru]; Unghosszúmező [H])	Ung	Užhorod	Ukraine
Dovhoje, *see* Dovhe, Máramaros county; Dovhe, Ung county			
Dovhunja, *see* Dlhoňa			
Dovhŷ, *see* Długie			
Dovžycja, *see* Dołżyca, Lesko district; Dołżyca, Sanok district			
Drágabártfalva, *see* Dorobratovo			
Dragaszów, part of Ropica Górna			
Drahove, *see* Drahovo			
Drahovo [Ru, U] (Drahove[U]; Kövesliget /Liget [H])	Máramaros	Chust	Ukraine
*Dravci [Ru, U] (Darócz/Ungdarócz [H])	Ung	Užhorod	Ukraine
Drična/Dricsna, *see* Malá Driečna			
Driečna [Sv, U], since 1961 part of Vladiča			
Drienica [Sv] (Felsősom [H]; Drenicja [Ru]; Drjenycja [U]; Som [H]; Šoma [Ru])	Sáros	Sabinov	Slovakia
Drjenicja, *see* Drienica/Drjenycja			
Drotynci [U] (Sirma [Ru]; Szirma/Tiszaszirma [H])	Ugocsa	Vynohradiv	Ukraine
Drugetháza, *see* Zaričovo			
Dubina, *see* Dubyno			
Dubne [P, Ru, U]	Nowy Sącz	Nowy Sącz	Poland
Dubová [Sv] (Cseres [H]; Dubova [Ru, U])	Sáros	Svidník	Slovakia
Dubove [Ru, U] (Dombó [H])	Máramaros	Tjačiv	Ukraine
Dúbrava [Sv] (Dubrova [Ru, U]; Kistölgyes [H])	Zemplén	Snina	Slovakia
Dubrinics, *see* Dubrynyči			
Dubrivka [U] (Dibrivka [U]; Dubróka [H]; Dubrovka [Ru]; Ungtölgyes [H])	Ung	Užhorod	Ukraine
Dubrivka, Sanok district, *see* Dąbrówka Ruska			
Dubrivka Rus'ka, *see* Dąbrówka Ruska			
Dubróka, *see* Dubrivka			
Dubrova, *see* Dúbrava			
Dubrovka, *see* Dibrivka, Máramaros county;			

Village	Former Hungarian county or Galician district	Present administrative subdivision	Present country
Dubrivka, Ung county			
Dubrovka nad Boržavoju, *see* Dibrivka, Bereg county			
Dubrynyči [Ru, U] (Bercsényifalva/ Dubrinics [H])	Ung	Perečyn	Ukraine
Dubyno [U] (Dubina [H]; Dubyna [Ru]	Mukačevo	Bereg	Ukraine
Dudyńce, *see* Szybistów			
Dudynci, *see* Szybistów			
Dulfalva, *see* Dulove			
Dulove [U] (Dulfalva [H]; Dulovo [Ru])	Máramaros	Tjačiv	Ukraine
Dulovo, *see* Dulove			
Dunkófalva, *see* Obava			
Dunkovycja [Ru, U] (Nyiresfalva/ Nyiresújfalu [H])	Bereg	Iršava	Ukraine
Dušatyn, *see* Duszatyn			
*Duplín [Sv] (Bányavölgy [H]; Duplyn [Ru, U])	Sáros	Stropkov	Slovakia
Duplyn, *see* Duplín			
Dusyno [U] (Dusyna [Ru]; Duszina/ Zajgó [H])	Bereg	Svaljava	Ukraine
Duszatyn [P] (Dušatyn [U])	Sanok	Krosno	Poland
Duszina, *see* Dusyno			
Dvernyk, *see* Dwernik			
Dwernik, [P] (Dvernyk [U])	Lesko	Krosno	Poland
Dydačiv, *see* Dedačov			
Dyskovycja [U] (Dîskovycja [Ru]; Kisvadas/Vadas [H])	Bereg	Svaljava	Ukraine
Dziurdziów [P] (Dzjurdziv [Ru, U]; Žurdziv [Ru])	Lesko	Krosno	Poland
Dzjurdziv, *see* Dziurdziów			
Dzvynjam Horne, *see* Dźwiniacz Górny			
Dźwiniacz Górny [P] (Dzvynjam Horne [U]) (ceased to exist after 1945)	Turka	Krosno	Poland
Dzyndranova, *see* Zyndranowa			
Egereske, *see* Vil'chovycja			
Egres, *see* Olešnyk			
Egreske, *see* Vil'chovycja			
Egreshát, *see* Vil'šynky			
Endrevágása, *see* Andrejová			
Éralja, *see* Inovce			
Erdőludas, *see* Husnyj			
Erdőpatak, *see* Lisarnja			
Érfalu, *see* Potôčky			
Esztebnek, *see* Stebník			
Eszterág, *see* Stryčava			
Fagyalos, *see* Medvedivci			

Village	Former Hungarian county or Galician district	Present administrative subdivision	Present country
Fakóbükk/Fakobŷky, *see* Bukove			
Falkus, *see* Falkušovce			
Falkušivci, *see* Falkušovce			
**Falkušovce [Sv] (Falkus [H]; Falkušivci [U])	Zemplén	Michalovce	Slovakia
Falucska, *see* Boharevycja			
Fedelesfalva, *see* Fedelešovci			
Fedelesfalva, *see* Kryte			
Fedelešovci, see Kryte			
Fedelešovci [Ru, U] (Fedelesfalva [H])	Bereg	Mukačevo	Ukraine
Fejérpatak, part of Dilove			
Feketepatak, *see* Čornyj Potik			
Feketekut, *see* Šambron			
Felsőalmád, *see* Vyšná Jablonka			
Felsőapsa, *see* Verchnje Vodjane			
Felsőbisztra, *see* Bystryj			
Felsőcsebény, *see* Vyšné Čabiny			
Felsőcsernye, *see* Cernina			
Felsődomonya, *see* Onokivci, p. 112			
Felsőfenyves, *see* Vyšná Jedl'ová			
Felsőfricske, *see* Frička			
Felsőgereben, *see* Verchnja Hrabivnycja			
Felsőhalas, *see* Vyšná Rybnica			
Felsőhatárszeg, *see* Vyšnja Roztoka			
Felsőhidegpatak, *see* Verchnij Studenyj			
Felsőhimes, *see* Vyšná Pisaná			
Felsőhunkócz, *see* Hunkovce			
Felsőjedlova, *see* Vyšná Jedl'ová			
Felsőkalocsa, *see* Nehrovec'			
Felsőkánya, *see* Šarišské Jastrabie			
Felsőkaraszló, *see* Hreblja			
Felsőkázmér, *see* Ruský Kazimír			
Felsőkomárnok, *see* Vyšný Komárnik			
Felsőkrucsó, *see* Ruský Kručov			
Felsőladács, *see* Vladiča			
Felsőolsva, *see* Vyšná Ol'šava			
Felsőmerse, *see* Vyšný Mirošov			
Felsőnémeti, *see* Vyšné Nemecké			
Felsőneresznice, *see* Novoselycja, Máramaros county, Mižhirja rajon			
Felsőodor/Felsőorlich, *see* Vyšný Orlík			
Felsőpágony, *see* Vyšná Polianka			
Felsőpásztély, *see* Roztoc'ka Pastil'			
Felsőpiszana, *see* Vyšná Pisaná			
Felsőpolyánka, *see* Vyšná Polianka			
Felsőrákócz, *see* Rakovčík			
Felsőremete, *see* Verchni Remety			
Felsőribnyicze, *see* Vyšná Rybnica			
Felsőróna, *see* Rona de Sus			

Village	Former Hungarian county or Galician district	Present administrative subdivision	Present country
Felsősárad, *see* Šyroke, Ugocsa county			
Felsősom, *see* Drienica			
Felsőszalánk, *see* Vyšnie Slovinky			
Felsőszinevér, *see* Synevyrs'ka Poljana			
Felsőszlatina, *see* Verchnje Solotvyno			
Felsőszlovinka, *see* Vyšnie Slovinky			
Felsőszvidnik, *see* Vyšní Svidník			
Felsőtarócz, *see* Vyšný Tvarožec			
Felsőtokaj, *see* Tokajík			
Felsővargony, *see* Vagrinec			
Felsővereczke, *see* Verchni Vorota			
Felsőveresmart, *see* Velyka Kopanja			
Felsőviső, *see* Vişeul de Sus, p. 113			
Felsővízkőz, *see* Vyšní Svidník			
Felsőviznicze, *see* Verchnja Vyznycja			
Felsővladicsa, *see* Vyšná Vladiča			
Fenyves, see Stryhal'nja			
Fenyvestelep, *see* Stryhal'nja			
Fenyvesvőlgy, *see* Stavne			
Fias, *see* Fijaš			
Fijaš [Sv, Ru, U] (Fias [H])	Sáros	Svidník	Slovakia
Filipec, *see* Pylypec'			
Florynka [P, Ru] (Fl'orynka [U])	Grybów	Nowy Sącz	Poland
Fogaras/Fogaraš/Foharaš *see* Zubivka			
Foljuš, *see* Folusz			
Foluš, *see* Folusz			
Folusz [P] (Foljuš [U]; Foluš [Ru])	Jasło	Krosno	Poland
Folvark/Folyvárk, *see* Stráňany			
Fontenjasa, *see* Fontynjasy			
Fontynjasy [U] (Fontenjasa [Ru])	Máramaros	Tjačiv	Ukraine
Forrás, *see* Rodnykivka			
Forráshuta, *see* Rodnykova Huta			
Frička [Sv] (Felsőfricske [H]; Fryčka [U]; Frŷčka [Ru])	Sáros	Bardejov	Slovakia
Frumşeaua, *see* Crasna Vişeului			
Fryčka/Frŷčka, *see* Frička			
Fülöpfalva, *see* Pylypec'			
Füzesmező, *see* Loza			
Gajdos/Gajdoš, *see* Hajdoš			
Galambos, *see* Holubyne			
Gálfalva, *see* Kobalevycja			
Gánya, *see* Hanyči			
Ganyči, *see* Hanyči			
Gavranyecz, *see* Havranec			
Gázló, *see* Velyka Roztoka			
Gellért, *see* Geraltov			
Geraltiv, *see* Geraltov			

Village	Former Hungarian county or Galician district	Present administrative subdivision	Present country
Geraltov [Sv] (Gellért [H]; Geraltiv [Ru]; Heralt [U])	Sáros	Prešov	Slovakia
Geréb, *see* Hrabské			
Gerény, *see* Horjany			
Gerla, *see* Gerlachov			
Gerlachiv, *see* Gerlachov			
Gerlachov [Sv] (Gerla [H]; Gerlachiv [Ru]; Herlachiv [U])	Sáros	Bardejov	Slovakia
Gernyés, *see* Kopašnovo			
Gernyésmező, *see* Chustec'			
Gesztenyés, *see* Linci			
Gladyšiv, *see* Gładyszów			
Gładyszów [P] (Gladyšiv [Ru]; Hladyšiv [U])	Gorlice	Nowy Sącz	Poland
Gödrösolyka, *see* Krivá Ol'ka			
Gombás, *see* Hrybivci			
Gombástelep, *see* Zaperedillja			
Goncoš, *see* Honcoš			
Görbeszeg, *see* Uličské Krivé			
Górna Wies [P] (Čystohorb [U]; Czystogarb/Czystohorb [P]; Horb [Ru])	Sanok	Krosno	Poland
Görögfalu, *see* Závadka, Szepes county			
Gorond/Goronda, *see* Horonda			
Górzanka [P] (Horjanka [U])	Lesko	Krosno	Poland
Grab [P] (Hrab [Ru, U]; Hrap [Ru])	Jasło	Krosno	Poland
Grabówka [P] (Hrabivka [U])	Brzozów	Krosno	Poland
Gribov [Ru, Sv] (Hrybiv [U]; Kisgombas [H]	Sáros	Svidník	Slovakia
Gwoździanka [P] (Hvozdjanka [Ru, U])	Strzyżów	Rzeszów	Poland
Gyertyánliget, *see* Kobylec'ka Poljana, p. 112			
Gyertyánpatak, *see* Hrabovčík			
Gyil, *see* Dil			
Gyilok, *see* Dilok			
Györgyfölde, *see* Jurková Vol'a			
Habkivci, *see* Habkowce			
Habkowce [P] (Habkivci [U]; Hapkuvci [Ru])	Lesko	Krosno	Poland
Habov, *see* Hałbów			
Habur, *see* Habura			
Habura [Sv, U] (Habur [Ru]; Laborczfő [H])	Zemplén	Medzilaborce	Slovakia
Hajagos, *see* Klokočov			
Hajasd, *see* Volosjanka			
Hajdoš [U] (Gajdoš [Ru]; Nagygajdos [H])	Ung	Užhorod	Ukraine
Hajtivka, *see* Hajtovka			
Hajtivkŷ, *see* Hajtovka			
Hajtóka, *see* Hajtovka			

Village	Former Hungarian county or Galician district	Present administrative subdivision	Present country
Hajtovka [Sv] (Hajtivka [Ru, U]; Hajtivkŷ [Ru]; Hajtóka [H])	Sáros	Stará L'ubovňa	Slovakia
Halbiv, *see* Hałbow			
Hałbów [P] (Habov [Ru]; Halbiv [Ru, U]), now part of Desznica			
Halihivci/Halihovce, *see* Hlivištia			
Halmos, *see* Škurativci			
Hanajna, *see* Hnojné			
Hančova, *see* Hańczowa			
Hańczowa [P] (Hančova [Ru, U])	Gorlice	Nowy Sącz	Poland
**Handerovycja [Ru, U] (Klastromfalva [H])	Bereg	Mukačevo	Ukraine
Hanigivci, *see* Hanigovce			
Hanigovce [Sv] (Hanigivci [Ru]; Hanihivci [U]; Hönig [H])	Sáros	Sabinov	Slovakia
Hanihivci, *see* Hanigovce			
Han'kovycja [U] (Hankovycja [Ru]; Kisanna [H])	Bereg	Svaljava	Ukraine
Hanyči [Ru, U] (Gánya [H]; Ganyči [Ru])	Máramaros	Tjačiv	Ukraine
Hapkuvci, *see* Habkowce			
Harapás, *see* Kusín			
Harczos, *see* Zboj			
Hárs, *see* Lypovec'			
Hársád, *see* Litmanová			
Hársfalva, *see* Nelipyno			
Határhegy, *see* Zahorb, Ung county			
Határszög, *see* Verchovyna Bystra			
Hátmeg, *see* Zahattja			
Havaj [Ru, Sv, U]	Zemplén	Stropkov	Slovakia
Havasalja, *see* Tybava			
Havasköz, *see* Ljuta			
Havasmező, *see* Poienile de sub Munte			
Havranec [Sv] (Gavranyecz [H]; Havrjanec [Ru]; Havrjanec' [U]; Kishollód [H])	Sáros	Svidník	Slovakia
Havrjanec', *see* Havranec			
Hegyesbisztra, *see* Bystrá			
Hegyescsaba, *see* Horbokcsebinye			
Hegyfark, *see* Pidhorb			
Hegyfok, *see* Dil			
Hegygombás, *see* Hlivištia			
Hegyrét, *see* Hercivci			
Hegyvég, *see* Pritul'any			
Hegyzávod, *see* Závada			
Helcmanovce, *see* p.111			
Helczmanócz, *see* Helcmanovce, p. 111			
Helmec, *see* Cholmec'			
Heralt, *see* Geraltov			
Hercfalva, *see* Hercivci			

Village	Former Hungarian county or Galician district	Present administrative subdivision	Present country
Hercivci [U] (Hegyrét/Hercfalva [H]; Hercovci [Ru])	Bereg	Mukačevo	Ukraine
Hercovci, *see* Hercivci			
Herincse, *see* Horinčovo			
Herincsemonostor, *see* Monastyrec'			
Herlachiv, *see* Gerlachov			
Hetenja, *see* Hetynja			
Hetény, *see* Hetynja			
Hetonja, *see* Hetynja			
Hetynja [U] (Hetenja [Ru]; Hetény [H]; Hetonja [U]; Tiszahetény [H])	Ugocsa	Vynohradiv	Ukraine
Hičva, *see* Hoczew			
Hičvici, *see* Huczwice			
Hidegrét, *see* Paškivci			
Hilkócz, *see* Il'kivci			
Hil's'ke, *see* Stanisławów			
Hinkivci, *see* Hunkovce			
Hladyšiv, *see* Gladyszów			
Hlivištia [Sv] (Halihivci [U]; Halihovce [Ru]; Hegygombás [H])	Ung	Sobrance	Slovakia
Hlomča, *see* Hłomcza			
Hłomcza [P] (Hlomča [U])	Sanok	Krosno	Poland
Hlynjanec' [Ru, U] (Igléc/Pásztorlak [H])	Bereg	Mukačevo	Ukraine
Hlynjanyj [U] (Hlynjanŷj [Ru]	Máramaros	Tjačiv	Ukraine
Hnojne [Sv] (Hanajna [U])	Ung	Michalovce	Slovakia
Hočiv, *see* Hoczew			
Hoczew [P] (Hičva/Hočiv [Ru, U]; Hošiv [Ru])	Lesko	Krosno	Poland
Hodermark, *see* Stotince			
Holjatyn [Ru, U] (Tarfalu [H])	Máramaros	Mižhirja	Ukraine
Holubina, *see* Holubyne			
Holubyne [U] (Galambos/Holubina [H]; Holubynnoje [Ru])	Bereg	Svaljava	Ukraine
Holubynnoje, *see* Holubyne			
Hömlőcz, *see* Cholmovec'			
Homonnaolyka, *see* Ol'ka			
Homonnarokitó, *see* Humenský Rokytov			
Homonnazbojna, *see* Nižné Zbojné			
Honcoš [U] (Goncoš [Ru])	Máramaros	Chust	Ukraine
Hönig, *see* Hanigovce			
Horb [Ru, U] (Kalocsa Horb [H])	Máramaros	Mižhirja	Ukraine
Horb, Sanok district, *see* Górna Wies			
Horbky [Ru, U] (Rákospatak [H])	Ugocsa	Vynohradiv	Ukraine
Horbok [U] (Kissarkad/ Sarkad [H]; Šarkad' [Ru]	Bereg	Iršava	Ukraine
Horbok, Zemplén county, *see* Horbokcsebinye			
Horbokcsebinye [H] (Hegyescsaba [H]; Horbok [Ru]), since 1910 part of Vyšné Čabiny	Zemplén	Medzilaborce	Slovakia Horbok

Village	Former Hungarian county or Galician district	Present administrative subdivision	Present country
Horbokradvány, *see* Nižná Radvaň			
Horinčovo [Ru, U] (Herincse [H]; Horinčeve [U])	Máramaros	Chust	Ukraine
Horjanka, *see* Górzanka			
Horjany [U] (Gerény [H]; Horjanŷ [Ru])	Ung	Užhorod	Ukraine
Horlyó, *see* Chudl'ove			
Horodisko, *see* Hradisko			
Horodysko, *see* Hradisko			
Horonda [Ru, U] (Gorond [H]; Goronda [Ru])	Bereg	Mukačevo	Ukraine
Hošiv, *see* Hoczew			
Hosszúmező, *see* Cîmpulung la Tisa, p. 111			
Hosszúvágás, *see* Legnava			
Hostovice [Sv] (Hostovyci [Ru, U]; Vendégi [H])	Zemplén	Snina	Slovakia
Hostovyci, *see* Hostovice			
Hoverla [H, U] (Hoverlja [Ru]; Klauzura Howerla [H])	Máramaros	Rachiv	Ukraine
Hrab, *see* Grab			
Hrabivčik/Hrabivčyk, *see* Hrabovčik			
Hrabivka, *see* Grabówka			
Hrabová Roztoka [Sv]; Hrabovarosztoka [H]; Hrabova Roztoka [Ru, U]; Kisgereblyés [H])	Zemplén	Snina	Slovakia
Hrabovarosztoka, *see* Hrabová Roztoka			
Hrabovčik [Sv] (Gyertyánpatak [H]; Hrabivčik [Ru]; Hrabivčyk [U])	Sáros	Svidník	Slovakia
Hrabove, *see* Hrabovo			
Hrabovec, *see* Ruský Hrabovec			
Hrabovo [Ru, U] (Szidorfalva [H])	Bereg	Mukačevo	Ukraine
Hrabské [Sv] (Geréb [H]; Hrabske [Ru, U])	Sáros	Bardejov	Slovakia
Hradisko [Sv] (Horodisko [Ru]; Horodyško [U]; Radoskő[H]), since 1990s part of Terňa	Sáros	Prešov	Slovakia
Hrap, *see* Grab			
Hreblja [Ru, U] (Felsőkaraszló [H]; Verchnij Koroslov [U])	Ugocsa	Iršava	Ukraine
Hribócz, *see* Hrybivci			
Hrunyky [Ru, U]	Máramaros	Tjačiv	Ukraine
Hruševe, *see* Hrušovo			
Hrušovo [Ru, U] (Hruševe [U]; Körtvélyes/Szentmihalykörtvélyes [H])	Máramaros	Tjačiv	Ukraine
Hrybiv, *see* Gribov			
Hrybivci [Ru, U] (Gombás/Hribócz [H]; Hrybovci [Ru])	Bereg	Mukačevo	Ukraine
Hučyci, *see* Huczwice			
Huczwice [P] (Hičvici [Ru]; Hučyci [U]),			

Village	Former Hungarian county or Galician district	Present administrative subdivision	Present country
part of Rabe			
Huklyvyj [U] (Hukliva/Huklyvŷj [Ru]; Zugó [H])	Bereg	Volovec'	Ukraine
Hulskie [P] (Hil's'ke [U]) (ceased to exist after 1945)	Lesko	Krosno	Poland
Humenský Rokytov [Sv] (Homonnarokitó [H]; Humenskŷj Rokŷtiv [Ru]; Humens'kyj Rokytiv [U], since 1970 part of Rokytov pri Humennom			
Humenskŷj Rokŷtiv, *see* Humenský Rokytov			
Hunkócz, Sáros county, *see* Hunkovce			
Hunkócz, Ung county, *see* Choňkovce			
Hunkovce [Sv] (Felsőhunkócz [H]; Hinkivci [Ru, U]; Hunkócz [H])	Sáros	Svidník	Slovakia
**Husák [Sv] (Huszák /Ungludás [H])	Ung	Sobrance	Slovakia
Husnyj [U] (Erdőludas [H]; Husnŷj [Ru]; Huszna [H])	Ung	Velykyj Bereznyj	Ukraine
Huszák, *see* Husák			
Huszna, *see* Husnyj			
Huszt, *see* Chust			
Husztec-Polyána, *see* Chustec'			
Husztkőz, *see* Nankovo			
Husztófalva, *see* Danylovo			
Huta Samoklęska [P] (Huta Samokljaska [Ru]), part of Pielgrzymki			
Hutás, *see* Hutka			
Hutka [Ru, Sv, U] [Hutás [H]]	Sáros	Bardejov	Slovakia
Huzele [P] (Huzeli [U])	Lesko	Krosno	Poland
Huzeli, *see* Huzele			
Hvozdjanka, *see* Gwoździanka			
Hyrova/Hyrowa, *see* Chyrowa			
Igléc, *see* Hlynjanec'			
Iglinc, see Linci			
Ignécz, *see* Znjac'ovo			
lhl'any [Sv] (Ihljanŷ [Ru]; lhljany [U]; Száztelek [H])	Szepes	Kežmarok	Slovakia
Ihljanŷ, *see* Ih'lany			
Il'kivci [U] (Hilkócz/Ilkócz/Ilkó [H]; Il'kovci/Jivkovci [Ru])	Bereg	Mukačevo	Ukraine
Ilkó, *see* Il'kivci			
Ilkócz, *see* Il'kivci			
Il'kovci, *see* Il'kivci			
ll'nycja [Ru, U] (Iloncza [H])	Bereg	Iršava	Ukraine
Iloncza, *see* Il'nycja			
Ilonokújfalu, *see* Onok			
Ilosva, *see* Iršava			
Imsád/Imsadŷ, *see* Kosiv Verch			
Imstyčeve, *see* Imstyčovo			
Imstyčovo [Ru, U] (Imstyčeve [U];	Bereg	Iršava	Ukraine

Village	Former Hungarian county or Galician district	Present administrative subdivision	Present country
Miszticze [H])			
Inócz, *see* Inovce			
Inovce [Sv] (Éralja [H]; Inócz [H]; Inovec' [Ru, U])	Zemplén	Sobrance	Slovakia
Inovec', *see* Inovce			
Irhócz/Irholcz, *see* Vil'chivci			
Irljava [Ru, U] (Orlava/Orlyava/ Sasfalva/Ungsasfalva [H])	Ung	Užhorod	Ukraine
Iršava [Ru, U] (Ilosva [H])	Bereg	Iršava	Ukraine
Istvánd, *see* Štefurov			
Iszka, *see* Izky			
Ivanivci [U] (Ivanovci [Ru]; Iványi [H])	Bereg	Mukačevo	Ukraine
Ivanovci, *see* Ivanivci			
Iványi, *see* Ivanivci			
Iváskófalva, *see* Ivaškovycja			
Ivaškovycja [Ru, U] (Iváskófalva [H])	Bereg	Iršava	Ukraine
Iza [Ru, U]	Máramaros	Chust	Ukraine
Izbonya, *see* Zbyny			
Izbugyabéla, *see* Zbudská Belá			
Izbugyabresztó, *see* Brestov nad Laborcem			
Izbugyaradvány, *see* Vyšná Radvaň			
Izbugyarokitó, *see* Zbudský Rokytov			
Izbugyazbojna, *see* Vyšné Zbojné			
Izby [P] (Izbŷ [Ru])	Grybów	Nowy Sącz	Poland
Izdebki [P] (Izdebky [U])	Brzozów	Krosno	Poland
Izky [Ru, U] (Iszka [H])	Máramaros	Mižhirja	Ukraine
Izsnyéte, *see* Žnjatyno, p. 113			
Izvor, *see* Rodnykivka			
Izvorhuta, *see* Rodnykova Huta			
Izvorska Huta, *see* Rodnykova Huta			
Jablinky, *see* Jabłonki			
Jablonica Polska [P] (Jablonycja Pol's'ka)	Brzozów	Krosno	Poland
Jabłonki [P] (Jablinky [U]; Jablynkŷ [Ru])	Lesko	Krosno	Poland
Jablonovo, *see* Jabluniv			
Jablonycja Pol's'ka, *see* Jablonica Polska			
Jabluniv [U] (Beregnagyalmás [H]; Jablonovo [Ru]; Nagyalmás [H])	Bereg	Mukačevo	Ukraine
Jablynkŷ, *see* Jabłonki			
Jakabvölgye, *see* Jakušovce			
Jakivs'ke [U] (Djakovskyj [Ru])	Bereg	Svaljava	Ukraine
Jákórésze, *see* Jakovany			
Jakoris, *see* Jakovany			
Jakovany [Sv] (Jakovanŷ [Ru]; Jákórésze [H])	Sáros	Sabinov	Slovakia
Jakubany [Sv] (Jakubjany [U];	Szepes	Stará L'ubovňa	Slovakia

Village	Former Hungarian county or Galician district	Present administrative subdivision	Present country
Jakubjanŷ [Ru]; Szepesjakabfalva [H])			
Jakubjany/Jakubjanŷ, *see* Jakubany			
Jakušivci, *see* Jakušovce			
Jakusócz, *see* Jakušovce			
Jakušovce [Sv] (Jakabvölgye [H]; Jakušivci [Ru, U]; Jakusócz [H])	Zemplén	Stropkov	Slovakia
Jalová [Sv] (Jalova [Ru, U]; Jármos [H])	Zemplén	Snina	Slovakia
Jalove [Ru, U] (Jálovo/Jávor [H])	Bereg	Volovec'	Ukraine
Jálovo, *see* Jalove			
Jalyn, *see* Lalin			
Jalynka/Jalynky, *see* Jedlinka			
Jarabina [Sv] (Berkenyéd [H]; Jarembina [H, Ru]; Orjabyna [Ru]; Orjabyna [Ru, U])	Szepes	Stará L'ubovňa	Slovakia
Jarembina, *see* Jarabina			
Jármos, *see* Jalová			
Jarok [Ru, U] (Árok [H])	Ung	Užhorod	Ukraine
Jasel'/Jasel'ko, *see* Jasiel			
Jasiel [P] (Jasel' [U]; Jasel'ko [Ru, U]; Jaslo [Ru])	Sanok	Krosno	Poland
Jasinja, *see* Jasynja			
Jasionka [P] (Jasjunka [Ru]; Jas'onka [U])	Gorlice	Nowy Sącz	Poland
Jasiunka, *see* Jasionka			
Jaškova, *see* Jaśkowa			
Jaśkowa [P] (Jaškova [Ru, U]; Jaszkowa [P])	Grybów	Nowy Sącz	Poland
Jas'onka, *see* Jasionka			
Jaslo, *see* Jasiel			
Jastrabje, *see* Šarišské Jastrabie			
Jastrjabik/Jastrjabyk, *see* Jastrzębik			
Jastrzębik [P] (Astrjabik/Jastrjabik [Ru]; Astrjabyk/Jastrjabyk [U]	Grybów	Nowy Sącz	Poland
Jasynja [U] (Jasinja [Ru]; Kőrösmező [H])	Máramaros	Rachiv	Ukraine
Jaszkowa, *see* Jaśkowa			
Javirja/Javirje, *see* Jaworze			
Javirky, *see* Jaworki			
Javirnyk, *see* Jawornik			
Javŷrkŷ, *see* Jaworki			
Jávor, *see* Jalove			
Javorec', *see* Jaworzec			
Jaworki [P] (Javirky [U]; Javŷrkŷ [Ru])	Nowy Targ	Nowy Sącz	Poland
Jawornik [P] (Javirnyk [Ru, U]) (ceased to exist after 1947)	Sanok	Krosno	Poland
Jaworze [P] (Javirja [U]; Javirje [Ru])	Jasło	Krosno	Poland
Jaworzec [P] (Javorec' [U]) (ceased to exist after 1947)	Lesko	Krosno	Poland

Village	Former Hungarian county or Galician district	Present administrative subdivision	Present country
Jedlinka [H, Sv] (Borókás [H]; Jalynky [U]; Jalynka [Ru])	Sáros	Bardejov	Slovakia
Jedrzejówka, *see* Andrzejówka			
Jesztreb, *see* Šarišské Jastrabie			
Jizby, *see* Izby			
Jivkovci, *see* Il'kivci			
Jobbos, *see* Pravrovce			
Jósza, *see* Jovsa			
Jovra, *see* Storožnycja			
Jovsa [Sv] (Jósza [H])	Ung	Michalovce	Slovakia
Józsefvőlgy, *see* Juskova Vol'a			
Juhászlak, *see* Runina			
Juhos, *see* Parihuzovce			
Jurkova Vol'a [Sv, U] (Györgyfölde/ Jurkóvolya [H]; Jurkova Volja [Ru])	Sáros	Svidník	Slovakia
Jurkóvolya, *see* Jurkova Vol'a			
Jurivci, *see* Jurowce			
Jurowce [P] (Jurivci [U])	Sanok	Krosno	Poland
**Juskova Vol'a [Sv] (Józsefvőlgy/ Juszkóvolya [H])	Zemplén	Vranov	Slovakia
Juszkóvolya, *see* Juskova Vol'a			
Kabalas, *see* Kobylnice			
Kajdanó, *see* Kajdanovo			
Kajdanove, *see* Kajdanovo			
Kajdanovo [Ru, U] (Kajdanó [H]; Kajdanove [U])	Bereg	Mukačevo	Ukraine
Kajnja, *see* Ruská Kajňa			
Kaleniv, *see* Kalinov			
Kalenó, *see* Kalinov			
Kálinfalva, *see* Kalyny			
Kalinov [Sv] (Kalenó [H]; Kaleniv [Ru]; Kalyniv [Ru, U])	Zemplén	Medzilaborce	Slovakia
Kaliv [U] (Kalliv [U]; Kalov [Ru])	Mármaros	Chust	Ukraine
Kalliv, *see* Kaliv			
Kálnarosztoka, *see* Kalná Roztoka			
Kalná Roztoka [Sv] (Kálnarosztoka [H]; Kalna Rostoka [Ru]; Kalnoroztoky [U]; Kalnŷj [Ru])	Zemplén	Snina	Slovakia
Kalnica k. Lesko [P] (Kal'nycja Lis'ka [U])	Lesko	Krosno	Poland
Kalnica k. Cisnej [P] (Kal'nycja [U])	Lesko	Krosno	Poland
Kal'nycja, *see* Kalnica k. Cisnej			
Kal'nycja Lis'ka, *see* Kalnica k. Lesko			
Kalnŷj, *see* Kalna Roztoka			
Kal'nyk [U] (Beregsárrét [H]; Kalnyk [Ru]; Sárrét [H])	Bereg	Mukačevo	Ukraine
Kalocsa Horb, *see* Horb			
Kalocsa-Imsád, *see* Kosiv Verch			

Village	Former Hungarian county or Galician district	Present administrative subdivision	Present country
Kalocsa-Negrovec, see Nehrovec'			
Kalocsa-Ófalu, *see* Koločava			
Kalov, *see* Kaliv			
Kalŷčava, *see* Kiełczawa			
Kalyniv, *see* Kalinov			
Kalyny [U] (Alsókálinfalva/ Kálinfalva [H]; Kalynŷ [Ru])	Máramaros	Tjačiv	Ukraine
**Kamenna Porubá [Sv] (Kőporuba/ Kővágó [H])	Zemplén	Vranov	Slovakia
Kamennoj, *see* Kamienne			
Kamianna [P] (Kamjana [Ru]; Kamjanna [U])	Grybów	Nowy Sącz	Poland
Kamienka [Sv] (Kamjunka [Ru]; Kamjonka [U]; Kövesfalva [H])	Szepes	Stará L'ubovňa	Slovakia
Kamienne [P] (Kamennoj [Ru]; Kamjanne [U])	Sanok	Krosno	Poland
Kamionka [P] (Kamjanka [U]) (ceased to exist after 1947)	Sanok	Krosno	Poland
Kamionki [P] (Kamjanky [U]; Kamnjankŷ [Ru]) (ceased to exist after 1947)	Lesko	Krosno	Poland
Kamjana, *see* Kamianna			
Kamjanka, *see* Kamionka			
Kamjanky, *see* Kamionki			
Kamjanna, *see* Kamianna			
Kamjanne, *see* Kamienne			
Kamjans'ke [U] (Beregkövesd/ Kövesd [H]; Kyvjažd' [Ru])	Bereg	Iršava	Ukraine
Kamjanycja [U] (Kamjanycja nad Uhom [Ru]; Ókemencze [H])	Ung	Užhorod	Ukraine
Kamjanycja nad Uhom, *see* Kamjanycja			
Kamjonka, *see* Kamienka			
Kamjunka, *see* Kamienka			
Kamnjankŷ, *see* Kamionki			
Kanora [Ru, U]	Bereg	Volovec'	Ukraine
Kapás, *see* Priekopa			
Kapisó, *see* Kapišová			
Kapišová [Sv] (Kapisó [H]; Kapišova [Ru, U])	Sáros	Svidník	Slovakia
Kapuszög, *see* Voročevo			
Karácsenyfalva, see Crăciunești, p. 111			
Karlików [P] (Karlykiv [Ru, U])	Sanok	Krosno	Poland
Karlykiv, *see* Karlików			
Karpovtlaš [U] (Karputlaş [Ru])	Máramaros	Chust	Ukraine
Kaszópolyána, *see* Kosivs'ka Poljana			
Kaszómező, *see* Kosivs'ka Poljana			
Katlanfalu, *see* Kotel'nycja			
Kavicsos, *see* Livov			
Kazimierzowo [P] (Mučne [U];	Turka	Krosno	Poland

Village	Former Hungarian county or Galician district	Present administrative subdivision	Present country
Muczne [P])			
Kazimír, *see* Ruský Kazimír			
Kažmyrovo, *see* Ruský Kazimír			
Kečkivci, *see* Kečkovce			
Kečkovce [Sv] (Kečkivci [Ru, U]; Kecskőcz [H])	Sáros	Svidník	Slovakia
Kecskőcz, *see* Kečkovce			
Kel'čava, *see* Kiełczawa			
Kelecsény, *see* Kelečyn			
Kelečyn [Ru, U] (Kelecsény [H])	Máramaros	Mižhirja	Ukraine
Kelembér, *see* Klenov			
Kelemenfalva, *see* Klymovycja			
Kelen, *see* Klenová			
Kemencze, *see* Novoselycja, Ung county			
Kenderešiv [U] (Kendereske [H]; Kenderešov [Ru]; Konoplivci [U]	Bereg	Mukačevo	Ukraine
Kendereske, *see* Kenderešiv			
Kenderešov, *see* Kenderešiv			
Kenézpatak, *see* Čornyj Potik			
Kerecki, *see* Kerec'ky			
Kerec'ky [U] (Kerecki [Ru]; Kereczke [H])	Máramaros	Svaljava	Ukraine
Kereczke, *see* Kerec'ky			
Kerekhegy, *see* Okruhla			
Kereknye, *see* Korytnjany			
Kerešî, *see* Kireši			
Kereštvej, *see* Okružná			
Kervavčat Potok, *see* Potik			
Keselymező, *see* Košel'ovo			
Kičerely [U] (Kyčerela [Ru])	Máramaros	Chust	Ukraine
Kicsorna, *see* Kyčirnyj			
Kiesvőlgy, *see* Lubnja			
Kiełczawa [P] (Kalŷčava [Ru]; Kel'čava [U])	Lesko	Krosno	Poland
Kijó, *see* Kyjov			
Kinčeš [U] (Kynčeš [Ru])	Ung	Užhorod	Ukraine
Kins'ke, *see* Końskie			
Királyfiszállás, *see* Soločyn			
Királyháza, *see* Korolevo			
Királyhegy, *see* Piskorovce			
Kireši [U] (Kerešî [Ru])	Máramoros	Chust	Ukraine
Kirvavecpatak, *see* Potik			
Kisábránka, *see* Smolohovycja			
Kisalmás, *see* Zalužžja			
Kisanna, *see* Han'kovycja			
Kisapsa, *see* Vodycja			
Kisberezna, *see* Malyj Bereznyj			
Kisberezsnye, *see* Breznička			
Kisbrezsnyicze, *see* Breznička			
Kisbukócz, *see* Malé Bukovce			

Village	Former Hungarian county or Galician district	Present administrative subdivision	Present country

Kiscserjés, *see* Belebovo; Vil'chovaty
Kiscserjés, *see* Linturovycja
Kiscsongova, *see* Zavadka, Ugocsa county
Kisderencs, *see* Malá Driečna
Kisfagyalos, *see* Svidnička
Kisfalud, *see* Sil'ce
Kisgereblyés, *see* Hrabová Roztoka
Kisgombás, *see* Gribov
Kisgyertyános, *see* Vyšný Hrabovec
Kishárs, *see* Malý Lypník
Kishidvég, *see* Pasika
Kishollód, *see* Havranec
Kiskereszt, *see* Kríže
Kiskirva, *see* Bilovarci
Kiskökény, *see* Trnkov
Kiskolon, *see* Kolonica
Kiskőrösfő, *see* Okružná
Kiskupány, *see* Malakopanja
Kiskurima, *see* Kurimka
Kisléczfalva, *see* Lecovycja
Kislipnik, *see* Malý Lipník
Kislipoc, *see* Lypovec', Ung county
Kislonka, *see* Lunca la Tisa
Kislucska, *see* Novoselycja, Bereg county
Kismedvés, *see* Medvedzie
Kismihály, *see* Michajlov
Kismogyorós, *see* Mykulivci
Kisolysó, *see* Olšavka
Kispálos, *see* Pavlovo
Kispásztély, *see* Pastil'ky
Kispatak, *see* Rička
Kispereszlő, *see* Príslop
Kispetőfalva, *see* Petejovce
Kispolány, *see* Malá Pol'ana
Kisrákócz, *see* Malyj Rakovec'
Kisrétfalu, *see* Novoselycja, Bereg county
Kisrosztoka, *see* Vyšnja Roztoka
Kissarkad, *see* Horbok
Kisszabados, *see* Rus'ká Vol'a
Kisszlatina, *see* Verchnje Solotvyno
Kisszolyva, *see* Skotars'ke
Kistarna, *see* Chyža
Kistavas, *see* Malé Staškovce
Kistölgyes, *see* Dúbrava
Kistopolya, *see* Topol'a
Kisturica, *see* Turyčky
Kisturjaszög, *see* Turyčky
Kisvadas, *see* Dyskovycja
Kisvajszló, *see* Vislava

Village	Former Hungarian county or Galician district	Present administrative subdivision	Present country
Kisvalkó, *see* Valkov			
Kisvölgy, *see* Krišlovce			
Kjaton'/Kjatonja, *see* Kwiatoń			
Klacsanó, *see* Kljačanovo			
Klastromalja, *see* Pidmonastyr			
Klastromfalva, *see* Handerovycja			
Klauzura Howerla, *see* Hoverla			
Klembark/Klembarok, *see* Klenov			
Klembérk, *see* Klenov			
Klenov [Sv] (Kelembér [H]; Klembark [Ru]; Klembarok [Sv]; Klembérk [H])	Sáros	Prešov	Slovakia
Klenová [Sv] (Kelen [H]; Klenova [Ru, U])	Zemplén	Snina	Slovakia
Klimkówka [P] (Klymkivka [Ru, U])	Gorlice	Nowy Sącz	Poland
Kljačanovo [U] (Klacsanó [H]; Kljačanove [U]; Klyčanovo [Ru])	Bereg	Mukačevo	Ukraine
Ključarky [Ru, U] (Klucsarka/Várkulcsa [H])	Bereg	Mukačevo	Ukraine
Kločky [Ru, U] (Lakatosfalva [H])	Bereg	Mukačevo	Ukraine
Klokočov [Sv] (Hajagos [H]; Klokočovo [Ru]; Klokocsó [H])	Ung	Michalovce	Slovakia
Klopitnycja, *see* Kłopotnica			
Kłopotnica [P] (Klopitnycja [U]; Klopotnycja/Kvopitnycja [Ru])	Jasło	Krosno	Poland
Klucsárka, *see* Ključarky			
Klyčanovo, *see* Kljačanovo			
Klymkivka, *see* Klimkówka			
**Klymovycja [Ru, U] (Kelemenfalva [H])	Bereg	Iršava	Ukraine
Knjahynja [U] (Csillagfalva [H]; Knjahynyn [Ru])	Ung	Velykyj Bereznyj	Ukraine
Knjahynyn, *see* Knjahynja			
Kobalevycja [U] (Gálfalva [H]; Kobalovycja [Ru])	Bereg	Iršava	Ukraine
Kobalovycja, *see* Kobalevycja			
Kobasuv, *see* Kolbasov			
Kobivci, *see* Kolbovce			
Köblér, *see* Kybljary			
Kobulnicza, *see* Kobylnice			
Kobylec'ka Poljana, *see* p. 112			
Kobŷljarŷ, *see* Kybljary			
**Kobylnice [Sv] (Kabalas/ Kobulnicza [H]; Kobŷl'nicja/ Kobŷlnici [Ru]; Kobylnycja [U])	Sáros	Svidník	Slovakia
Kolbulnicza, *see* Kobylnice			
Kocur, *see* Kucura			
Koczkaszállás, *see* Kosyno			
Kokény, *see* Trnkov			
Kökényes, *see* Ternovo			
Kokyňa, *see* Trnkov			

Kobylec'ka Poljana, *see* p. 112

Village	Former Hungarian county or Galician district	Present administrative subdivision	Present country
Kolbasov [Sv] (Kobasuv [Ru]; Kolbaszó [H]; Kovbasiv [Ru, U]; Végaszó [H])	Zemplén	Snina	Slovakia
Kolbaszó, *see* Kolbasov			
Kolbivci, *see* Kolbovce			
Kolbócz, *see* Kolbovce			
Kolbovce [Sv] (Köves [H]; Kobivci [Ru]; Kolbivci [U]; Kolbócz [H])	Zemplén	Svidník	Slovakia
Kölcsén/Kolcsény, *see* Kol'čyno			
Kolčyne, *see* Kol'čyno			
Kol'čyno [U] (Kolcsény [H]; Kol'čyne [U]; Kolčyno [Ru])	Bereg	Mukačevo	Ukraine
Kolibabovce [Sv] (Bölcsős/Kolibabócz [H])	Ung	Sobrance	Slovakia
Koločava [Ru, U] (Alsókalocsa/ Kalocsa-Ófalu [H])	Máramaros	Mižhirja	Ukraine
Kolodne [U] (Kolodnoje [Ru]; Tökesfalu [H])	Bereg	Iršava	Ukraine
Kolodne [U] (Darva [H]; Kolodnoje [Ru])	Máramaros	Tjačiv	Ukraine
Kolodnoje, *see* Kolodne, Bereg county; Máramaros county			
Kolonica [Sv] (Kiskolon [H]; Kolonicja [Ru]; Kolonycja [U])	Zemplén	Snina	Slovakia
Kołonice [P] (Kolonyci [Ru, U])	Lesko	Krosno	Poland
Kolonicja, *see* Kolonica			
Kolonyci, *see* Kołonice			
Kolonycja, *see* Kolonica			
Koman'ča, *see* Komańcza			
Komańcza [P] (Koman'ča [Ru, U]; Kumanča [Ru])	Sanok	Krosno	Poland
Komját, *see* Velyki Komjaty			
Komlós, *see* Chmil'nyk			
Komlósa, *see* Chmel'ová			
**Komlóska [H] (Komloška [Ru])	Zemplén	Borsod-Abaúj-Zemplén	Hungary
Komlóspatak, *see* Chmel'ová			
Komluš, *see* Chmil'nyk			
Konečna, *see* Konieczna			
Konieczna [P] (Konečna [Ru, U])	Gorlice	Nowy Sącz	Poland
Konjuš, *see* Koňuš			
Konoplivci, *see* Kenderešiv			
Końskie [P] (Kins'ke [U])	Brzozów	Krosno	Poland
Koňuš [Sv] (Konjuš [Ru, U]; Konyus/ Unglovasd [H])	Ung	Sobrance	Slovakia
Konyus, *see* Koňuš			
Kopačele, *see* Copăcele			
Kopár, *see* Rosoš, Bereg county			
Kopašneve, *see* Kopašnovo			
Kopašnovo [Ru, U] (Gernyés [H];	Máramaros	Chust	Ukraine

Village	Former Hungarian county or Galician district	Present administrative subdivision	Present country
Kopašneve [U])			
Kőporuba, *see* Kamenná Poruba			
Kopynivci [U] (Kopynovci [Ru]; Mogyorós/Nagymogyorós [H])	Bereg	Mukačevo	Ukraine
Kopynovci, *see* Kopynivci			
Korejivci, *see* Korejovce			
Korejócz, *see* Korejovce			
Korejovce [Sv] (Korejivci [Ru, U]; Korejócz/Korócz [H])	Sáros	Svidník	Slovakia
Korláthelmec, *see* Cholmec'			
Körmös, *see* Kožuchovce			
Korócz, *see* Korejovce			
Koroleva Rus'ka, *see* Królowa Górna			
Korolevo [U] (Királyháza [H]; Kral'ovo nad Tysoju [Ru])	Ugocsa	Vynohradiv	Ukraine
Korolyk Volos'kyj, *see* Królik Wołoski			
**Koroml'a [U] (Koromlak/ Korumlya [H])	Ung	Sobrance	Slovakia
Koromlak, *see* Koroml'a			
Körösény, *see* Krušinec			
Kőrösfő, *see* Okružná			
Kőrösmező, *see* Jasynja			
Körtvélyes, *see* Hrušovo			
Korumlya, *see* Koroml'a			
Korunková [Sv] (Korunkova [Ru, U]; Puczák/Pusztaháza [H])	Zemplén	Stropkov	Slovakia
*Korytnjany [U] (Kereknye [H]; Korŷtnjanŷ [Ru])	Ung	Užhorod	Ukraine
Košeleve, *see* Košel'ovo			
Košel'ovo [Ru, U] (Keselymező [H]; Košeleve [U])	Máramaros	Chust	Ukraine
Kosiv Verch [U] (Imsád [H]; Imsadŷ [Ru]; Kalocsa-Imsád [H])	Máramaros	Mižhirja	Ukraine
Kosivs'ka Poljana [U] (Kaszómező/ Kaszópolyána [H]; Kosovska Poljana [Ru])	Máramaros	Rachiv	Ukraine
Kosovska Poljana, *see* Kosivs'ka Poljana			
Kostarivci, *see* Kostarowce			
Kostarowce [P] (Kostarivci [U])	Sanok	Krosno	Poland
Kosteva Pastil' [U] (Kost'ova Pastil'[Ru]; Kosztyova-Pásztély/Nagypásztély [H])	Ung	Velykyj Bereznyj	Ukraine
Kostryno [U] (Csontos [H]; Kostryna [Ru]; Kosztrina [H])	Ung	Velykyj Bereznyj	Ukraine
Kostryns'ka Roztoka [U]	Ung	Velykyj Bereznyj	Ukraine
Kostylivka [U] (Barnabás [H]; Berlebaš [Ru])	Máramaros	Rachiv	Ukraine
Kosyne, *see* Kosyno			
Kosyno [Ru, U] (Koczkaszállás [H])	Bereg	Mukačevo	Ukraine
Kosztrina, *see* Kostryno			

Village	Former Hungarian county or Galician district	Present administrative subdivision	Present country
Kosztyova-Pásztély, *see* Kosteva Pastil'			
Kotań [P] (Kotan [Ru]; Kotan' [U])	Jasło	Krosno	Poland
Kőtelep, *see* Kružlov			
Kotel'nycja [Ru, U] (Katlanfalu [H])	Bereg	Volovec'	Ukraine
Kotiv, *see* Kotów			
Kotów [P] (Kotiv [Ru, U])	Nowy Sącz	Nowy Sącz	Poland
Kovácsrét, *see* Kušnycja			
Kővágó, *see* Kamenná Poruba			
Kovászó, *see* Kvasovo			
Kovbasiv, *see* Kolbasov			
Kovbivci, *see* Kolbovce			
Köves, *see* Kolbovce			
Kövesd, *see* Kamjans'ke			
Kövesfalva, *see* Kamienka			
Kövesliget, *see* Drahovo			
Kožany [Sv, U] (Kožaný [Ru]; Kozsány [H])	Sáros	Bardejov	Slovakia
Kozsány, *see* Kožany			
Kozsuhócz, *see* Kožuchovce			
Kožuchivci, *see* Kožuchovce			
Kožuchovce [Sv] (Körmös/Kozsuhócz [H]; Kožuchivci [Ru, U])	Sáros	Stropkov	Slovakia
Kożuszne [P] (Kožušne [Ru, U])	Sanok	Krosno	Poland
Kračunovo, see Crăciuneşti, p. 111			
Krajna [U] (Krajnŷj [Ru])	Máramaros	Chust	Ukraine
Krajná Bystrá [Sv] (Bátorhegy [H]; Krajnja Bystra [U]; Krajnja Bŷstra [Ru])	Sáros	Svidník	Slovakia
Krajna Martinka/Martynka, *see* Krajnja Martynka			
*Krajná Pol'ana [Sv] (Krajnja Poljana [Ru, U]; Krajnópolyana/ Ladomérmező [H])	Sáros	Svidník	Slovakia
Krajná Porúbka [Sv] (Krajnja Porubka [Ru, U]; Krajnóporubka/Végortovány [H])	Sáros	Svidník	Slovakia
Krajné Čierno [Sv] (Krajnje Čorne [Ru, U]; Krajócsarnó/Végcsarnó [H])	Sáros	Svidník	Slovakia
Krajnja Bystra/Bŷstra, *see* Krajná Bystra			
Krajnja Martynka [U] (Krajna Martinka [H]; Krajna Martynka [Ru]; Végmártonka [H])	Bereg	Iršava	Ukraine
Krajnja Poljana; *see* Krajná Pol'ana			
Krajnja Porubka, *see* Krajná Porúbka			
Krajnja Čorne, *see* Krajné Čierno			
Krajnóbisztra, *see* Krajná Bystrá			
Krajnócsarnó, *see* Krajné Čierno			
Krajnópolyana, *see* Krajná Pol'ana			
Krajnóporubka, *see* Krajná Porúbka			
Krajnŷj, *see* Krajna			
Krajnykove, *see* Krajnykovo			

Village	Former Hungarian county or Galician district	Present administrative subdivision	Present country
Krajnykovo [Ru, U] (Krajnykove [U]; Mihálka [H]	Máramaros	Chust	Ukraine
Kral'ovo nad Tysoju, *see* Korolevo			
Krampna, *see* Krempna			
Krasna [P, Ru, U]	Krosno	Krosno	Poland
Krasna [Ru, U] (Krasznisora/ Taraczkraszna [H])	Máramaros	Tjačiv	Ukraine
Krasna Vyšovs'ka, *see* Crasna Vişeului			
Krásny Brod [Sv] (Krasnyj Brid [U]; Krasnŷj Brid [Ru]; Laborczrév [H])	Zemplén	Medzilaborce	Slovakia
Krasnyj, Máramaros county, *see* Crasna Vişeului			
Krasnyj, Zemplén county, *see* Krásny Brod			
Krasnŷj Brid, *see* Krásny Brod			
Krassogombás, *see* Zorile			
Krasznisora, *see* Krasna, Máramaros county			
Kremná [Sv] (Krempach [Ru, Sv]; Kremna [U]; Lublókorompa/ Lublókrempach [H])	Szepes	Stará L'ubovňa	Slovakia
Krempach, *see* Kremná			
Krempna [P] (Krampna [Ru, U])	Jasło	Krosno	Poland
Krenycja, *see* Krynica Wieś			
Kricsfalva, *see* Kryčovo			
Krilova Ruska, *see* Królowa Górna			
Krišlivci, *see* Krišlovce			
Krišlovce [Sv] (Kisvölgy [H]; Krišlivci [Ru]; Krizslócz [H]; Kryšlivci [U])	Zemplén	Stropkov	Slovakia
Krivá Ol'ka [Sv] [Gödrösolyka [H]; Kryva Ol'ka [U]; Kryve [Ru]), since 1961 part of Ol'ka			
Krivé [Sv] (Kryve [Ru, U]; Sárosgörbeny [H])	Sáros	Bardejov	Slovakia
Kríže [Sv] (Kiskereszt [H]; Križŷ [Ru]; Kryži [U]; Sárosgörbény [H])	Sáros	Bardejov	Slovakia
Križlova, *see* Kružl'ová			
Krizslócz, *see* Krišlovce			
Križŷ, *see* Kríže			
Królik Wołoski [P] (Korolyk Volos'kyj [U]; Krolyk Voloskŷj [Ru]; Krolyk Volos'kyj [U])	Sanok	Krosno	Poland
Królowa Górna [P] (Koroleva Rus'ka [U]; Koroleva Ruska/Krilova Ruska [Ru]; Królowa Ruska [P])	Grybów	Nowy Sącz	Poland
Królowa Ruska, *see* Królowa Górna			
Krolyk Voloskŷj/Volos'kyj, *see* Królik Woloski			
Krušinec [Sv] (Körösény [H]; Krušynec' [U]; Krušŷnec [Ru])	Sáros	Stropkov	Slovakia
Krušynec'/Krušŷnec, *see* Krušinec			
Kružliv, *see* Kružlov			
Kružlivs'ka Huta, *see* Kružlovská Huta			

Village	Former Hungarian county or Galician district	Present administrative subdivision	Present country
Kružlov [Sv] (Kőtelep [H]; Kružliv [Ru, U]; Kruzslyó [H])	Sáros	Bardejov	Slovakia
Kružlová [Sv] (Križlova [Ru]; Kružl'ova [U]; Ruzsoly [H])	Sáros	Svidník	Slovakia
Kružlovská Huta [Sv] (Kružlivs'ka Huta [U]; Kryžlivska Huta [Ru]), part of Kružlov			
Kruzslyó, *see* Kružlov			
Kryčove, *see* Kryčovo			
Kryčovo [Ru, U] (Kricsfalva [H]; Kryčove [U])	Máramaros	Tjačiv	Ukraine
Kryčuniv, *see* Crăciuneşti, p. 111			
Krynica Wieś [P] (Krenycja [Ru, U]; Krynycja [U]; Krŷnyca [Ru]; Krynycja Selo [U])	Nowy Sącz	Nowy Sącz	Poland
Krynica-Zdrój, *see* p. 112			
Krynycja, *see* Krynica Wieś			
Krynycja Selo, *see* Krynica Wieś			
Krynycja Žyvec', *see* Krynica-Zdrój, p. 112			
Kryšlivci, *see* Krišlovce			
Kryte [U] (Fedelesfalva [H]; Fedelešovci [Ru, U]	Bereg	Mukačevo	Ukraine
Kryva [Ru, U] (Tiszakirva [H])	Ugocsa	Chust	Ukraine
Kryva, Gorlice district, *see* Krzywa			
Kryva Ol'ka, *see* Krivá Ol'ka			
Kryve, Lesko district, *see* Krywe k. Cisnej			
Kryve, Sáros county, *see* Krivé			
Kryve [Ru, U] (Nagykirva [H])	Máramaros	Tjačiv	Ukraine
Kryve, Zemplén county, *see* Krivé Ol'ka; Uličské Krivé			
Kryve k. Tvoryl'noho, *see* Krzywe k. Tworylnego			
Kryvŷj, Máramaros county, *see* Repedea			
Kryvŷj, Zemplén county, *see* Uličské Krivé			
Kryvŷ, *see* Krywe k. Cisnej			
Krywe k. Cisnej [P] (Kryve [U]; Kryvŷ [Ru])	Lesko	Krosno	Poland
Krywe k. Tworylnego, *see* Krzywe k. Tworylnego	Lesko	Krosno	Poland
Kryži, *see* Kríže			
Kryživka, *see* Krzyżówka			
Kryžlivska Huta, *see* Kružlovská Huta			
Krzywa [P] (Kryva [Ru, U])	Gorlice	Nowy Sącz	Poland
Krzywe k. Tworylnego [P] (Kryve k. Tvoryl'noho [U]; Krywe k. Tworylnego [P])	Lesko	Krosno	Poland
Krzyżówka [P] (Kryživka [Ru, U])	Nowy Sącz	Nowy Sącz	Poland
Kucura [SC] (Kocur [Ru]; Kuczora [H])	Bács-Bodrog	Vojvodina	Serbia
Kuczora, *see* Kucura			

Village	Former Hungarian county or Galician district	Present administrative subdivision	Present country
Kula, *see* p. 112			
Kulaszne, *see* Międzygórze			
Kulašne, *see* Międzygórze			
Kulašnoj, *see* Międzygórze			
Kumanča, *see* Komańcza			
Kunkova, *see* Kunkowa			
Kunkowa [P] (Kunkova [Ru, U])	Gorlice	Nowy Sącz	Poland
Kurimka [Sv] (Kiskurima [H]; Kurymka [Ru, U])	Sáros	Svidník	Slovakia
Kuriv, *see* Kurov			
Kuró, *see* Kurov			
Kurov [Sv] (Kuriv [Ru, U]; Kuró [H])	Sáros	Bardejov	Slovakia
Kurucvár, *see* Likicary			
Kurymka, *see* Kurimka			
Kusín [Sv] (Harapás [H]; Kusyn [U]; Kuszin [H])	Ung	Michalovce	Slovakia
Kušnycja [Ru, U] (Kovácsrét [H])	Máramaros	Iršava	Ukraine
Kustánfalva, *see* Kuštanovycja			
Kuštanovycja [Ru, U] (Kustánfalva [H])	Bereg	Mukačevo	Ukraine
Kušyn, *see* Kusín			
Kuszin, *see* Kusín			
Kutkafalva, *see* Pokuttja			
Kutlaš [Ru, U]	Máramaros	Chust	Ukraine
Kuzmina, see Kuz'myno			
Kuzmyne, *see* Kuz'myno			
Kuz'myno [U] (Balažijeve [U]; Beregszilvás/Kuzmina [H]; Kuz'myne [U]; Kuzmyno [Ru]; Szilvás [H])	Bereg	Mukačevo	Ukraine
Kvasove, *see* Kvasovo			
Kvasovo [Ru, U] (Kovászó [H]; Kvasove [U])	Bereg	Berehovo	Ukraine
Kvasy [U] (Borkút [H]; Kvasŷ [Ru]; Tiszaborkút [H])	Máramaros	Rachiv	Ukraine
Kvjaton'/Kvjatonja, *see* Kwiatoń			
Kvopitnycja, *see* Kłopotnica			
Kwiatoń [P] (Kjaton'/Kjatonja [Ru]; Kvjaton' [Ru, U]; Kvjatonja [Ru])	Gorlice	Nowy Sącz	Poland
Kybljary [U] (Köblér [H]; Kobŷljarŷ /Kybral' [Ru])	Ung	Užhorod	Ukraine
Kyčerela, *see* Kičerely			
Kyčernŷj, *see* Kyčirnyj			
Kyčirnyj [U] (Kicsorna [H]; Kyčernŷj [Ru]; Nagycserjés [H])	Bereg	Volovec'	Ukraine
Kyjov [Sv, U] (Kijó [H]; Kŷjov [Ru])	Sáros	Stará L'ubovňa	Slovakia
Kynčes, *see* Kinčeš			
Kyvjažd', *see* Kamjans'ke			
Labivec', *see* Łabowiec			
Laborczbér, *see* Brestov nad Laborcom			

Village	Former Hungarian county or Galician district	Present administrative subdivision	Present country
Laborczfő, *see* Habura			
Laborczradvány, *see* Nižná Radvaň			
Laborczrév, *see* Krásny Brod			
Laborec, *see* Medzilaborce			
Labova, *see* Łabowa			
Labovec', *see* Łabowiec			
Łabowa [P] (Labova [Ru, U]; Vabova [Ru])	Grybów	Nowy Sącz	Poland
Łabowiec [P] (Labovec' [U]; Vabovec [Ru])	Nowy Sącz	Nowy Sącz	Poland
**Lačnov [Sv] (Lasciv [U]; Lacsnó [H]), since 1990s part of Lipovce	Sáros	Sabinov	Slovakia
Lacsnó, *see* Lačnov			
Ladomér, Sáros county, *see* Ladomirová			
Ladomér, Zemplén county, *see* Ladomirov			
Ladomérmező, *see* Krajná Pol'ana			
Ladomérvágása, *see* Ladomirová			
Ladomirov [Sv] (Ladomér [H]; Ladomyriv [Ru, U]; Ladomyrov [Ru])	Zemplén	Snina	Slovakia
Ladomirová [Sv] (Ladomér/ Ladomérvágása [H]; Ladomyrova [Ru, U])	Sáros	Svidník	Slovakia
Ladomyriv/Ladomyrov, *see* Ladomirov			
Ladomyrova, *see* Ladomirová			
Lagnó, *see* Legnava			
Lakatosfalva, *see* Klocky			
Lalin [P] (Jalyn [U]; Lalyn [U])	Sanok	Krosno	Poland
Lalove, *see* Lalovo			
Lalovo [H, U] (Beregleányfalva [H]; Lalove [U]; Leányfalva [H]; Ljal'ovo [Ru])	Bereg	Mukačevo	Ukraine
Lalyn, *see* Lalin			
Láposmező, *see* Luhy			
Lasciv, *see* Lačnov			
Latirka [U] (Latorczafő [H]; Latorka [Ru]; Láturka[H])	Bereg	Volovec'	Ukraine
Latorczafő, *see* Latirka			
Latorka, *see* Latirka			
Láturka, *see* Latorka			
Lauka, *see* Lavky			
Lavky [Ru, U] (Lauka/Lóka [H])	Bereg	Mukačevo	Ukraine
Lazák, *see* Lazy, Máramaroš county			
Lazeščyna [Ru, U] (Laziscsán [H])	Máramaros	Rachiv	Ukraine
Lazonpatak, *see* Podproč			
Lazy [U] (Lazŷ [Ru]; Timsor [H])	Bereg	Volovec'	Ukraine
Łazy [P] (Lazák [H]; Lazŷ [Ru]	Máramaros	Tjačiv	Ukraine
Leányfalva, *see* Lalovo			
Lecovycja [Ru, U] (Kisléczfalva/	Bereg	Mukačevo	Ukraine

Village	Former Hungarian county or Galician district	Present administrative subdivision	Present country
Léczfalva [H])			
Léczfalva, *see* Lecovycja			
Legnava [Ru, Sv] (Hosszúvágás/Lagnó [H]; Lehnava [U])	Sáros	Stará L'ubova	Slovakia
Lehnava, *see* Legnava			
Lehócz, *see* Ljachivci			
Leljuchiv, *see* Leluchów			
Leluchów [P] (Leljuchiv [Ru, U])	Nowy Sącz	Nowy Sącz	Poland
Lemkivci, see Ljachivci	Ung	Užhorod	Ukraine
Lengyelszállás, *see* Liskovec'			
Lesko, *see* p. 112			
Leszczyny [P] (Liščyny [U]; Liščŷnŷ [Ru])	Gorlice	Nowy Sącz	Poland
Leveles, *see* Lopušne			
Levoča, *see* p. 112			
Liget, *see* Drahovo			
Ligetes, *see* Luh, Ung county			
Likicary [U] (Kurucvár/ Likiczár [H]; Lîkicary [Ru])	Ung	Perečyn	Ukraine
Likiczár, *see* Likicary			
Limne, *see* Lomné			
Linci [Ru, U] (Gesztenyés/Iglinc Unggesztenyés [H])	Ung	Užhorod	Ukraine
Lipcse, *see* Lypča			
Lipcsemező, *see* Lypec'ka Poljana			
Lipcse Polyána, *see* Lypec'ka Poljana			
Lipna [P, Ru] (Lypna [U]) (ceased to exist after 1947)	Gorlice	Nowy Sącz	Poland
Lipová [Sv] (Lypova [Ru, U]; Tapolylippó [H])	Sáros	Bardejov	Slovakia
Lipowiec [P] (Lypovec [Ru]; Lypovec' [U])	Sanok	Krosno	Poland
Lisarnja [Ru, U] (Erdőpatak/ Liszárnya [H])	Bereg	Mukačevo	Ukraine
Liščyny/ Liščŷnŷ, *see* Leszczyny			
Lisko, *see* Lesko, p. 112			
Liskovec' [U] (Lengyelszállás [H]; Ljachovec' [Ru])	Máramaros	Mižhirja	Ukraine
Lisna/Lišna, *see* Liszna			
Liszárnya, *see* Lisarnja			
Liszna [P] (Lisna [Ru]; Lišna [U])	Lesko	Krosno	Poland
Litinye, *see* L'utina			
Litmanová [Sv] (Hársád [H]; Litmanova [Ru]; Lytmanova [U])	Szepes	Stará L'ubovňa	Slovakia
Liviv, *see* Livov			
Livivs'ka Huta, *see* Livovská Huta			
Livóhuta, *see* Livovská Huta			
Livov [Sv] (Kavicsos [H]; Liviv [Ru, U])	Sáros	Bardejov	Slovakia
Livovská Huta [Sv] (Livóhuta [H];	Sáros	Bardejov	Slovakia

Village	Former Hungarian county or Galician district	Present administrative subdivision	Present country
Livivs'ka Huta [U]; Livovska Huta [Ru])			
Ljachivci [U] (Lehócz [H]; Lemkivci [U]; Ljachovci [Ru])	Ung	Užhorod	Ukraine
Ljachovci, *see* Ljachivci			
Ljachovec', *see* Liskovec'			
Ljal'ovo, *see* Lalovo			
Ljumšory, *see* Lumšory			
Ljuta [Ru, U] (Havasköz/Ljucyna/ Lyuta [H])	Ung	Velykyj Bereznyj	Ukraine
Ljutyna, *see* L'utina			
Lochove, *see* Lochovo			
Lochovo [Ru, U] (Beregszőllős [H]; Lochove [U]; Nagylohó [H])	Bereg	Mukačevo	Ukraine
Lőcse, *see* Levoča, p. 112			
Lodyna, *see* Łodzina			
Łodzina [P] (Lodyna [U])	Sanok	Krosno	Poland
Lóka, *see* Lavky			
Lokit' [U] (Lokot' [Ru]; Nagyábránka [H])	Bereg	Iršava	Ukraine
Lokot', *see* Lokit'			
Lombos, *see* Lopušanka			
Lomna, *see* Lomné			
Lomné [Sv] (Limne [Ru, U]; Lomna [H])	Zemplén	Stropkov	Slovakia
Lonka, *see* Luh, Máramaros county			
Łopienka [P] (Lopjanka [U])	Lesko	Krosno	Poland
Lopjanka, *see* Łopienka			
Lopuchiv [U] (Brusturŷ [Ru]; Brusztura [H])	Máramaros	Tjačiv	Ukraine
Lopušanka[U] (Brustov [Ru, U]; Brusztópatak [H]; Brystiv [U]; Lombos [H])	Bereg	Svaljava	Ukraine
Lopušne [U] (Leveles/Lopusnya [H]; Lopušnŷj [Ru])	Máramaros	Mižhirja	Ukraine
Lopusnya, *see* Lopušne			
Lopušnŷj, *see* Lopušne			
Lőrinczvágaśa, *see* Vavrinec			
Łosie [P] (Losja [Ru]; Losje [U]; Vosje [Ru])	Gorlice	Nowy Sącz	Poland
Łosie [P] (Losje [U]; Vosje [Ru])	Nowy Sącz	Nowy Sącz	Poland
Losja/Losje, *see* Łosie, Gorlice district			
**Loza [Ru, U] (Füzesmező [H]; Polyánka [H])	Bereg	Iršava	Ukraine
Lozánszka, *see* Lozjans'kyj			
Lozjans'kyj [Ru, U] (Cserjés/ Lozánszka [H])	Máramaros	Mižhirja	Ukraine
Lublókorompa, *see* Kremná			
Lublókrempach, *see* Kremna			
Lubna, *see* Łubno			
Łubne [P]	Lesko	Krosno	Poland

Village	Former Hungarian county or Galician district	Present administrative subdivision	Present country
Lubno [P] (Lubna [U])	Brzozów	Przemyśl	Poland
Lubnja [Ru, U] (Kiesvőlgy/ Lubnya [H])	Ung	Velykyj Bereznyj	Ukraine
Lubnya, *see* Lubnja			
Lucina, *see* L'utina			
Ług [P] (Luh [U]; Uh/Vuh [Ru])	Gorlice	Nowy Sącz	Poland
Łuh [P] (Luh [U]) (ceased to exist after 1947)	Lesko	Krosno	Poland
Luh [Ru, U] (Lonka [H])	Máramaros	Rachiv	Ukraine
Luh [H, Ru, U] (Ligetes [H])	Ung	Velykyj Bereznyj	Ukraine
Luhy [Ru, U] (Láposmező [H])	Máramaros	Rachiv	Ukraine
Lukiv, Lesko district, *see* Łukowe			
Lukiv, Sáros county, *see* Lukov			
Lukó, *see* Lukov			
Lukov [Sv] (Lukiv [Ru, U]; Lukó [H])	Sáros	Bardejov	Slovakia
Lukova, *see* Lukovo			
Lukove, Bereg county, *see* Lukovo			
Lukove, Lesko district, *see* Łukowe			
Lukovo [Ru, U] (Lukova [H]; Lukove [U])	Bereg	Iršava	Ukraine
Łukowe [P] (Lukiv [Ru]; Lukove [U])	Lesko	Krosno	Poland
Lumšory [U] (Ljumsorŷ [Ru]; Lumsur/Ronafüred [H])	Ung	Perečyn	Ukraine
Lumsur, *see* Lumšory			
Lunca la Tisa [Ro] (Kislonka [H]; Luh nad Tysoiu [U])	Máramaros	Maramureş	Romania
Lunka [U]	Máramaros	Chust	Ukraine
Lupkiv, *see* Łupków			
Łupków [P] (Lupkiv [U])	Lesko	Krosno	Poland
L'utina [Sv] (Litinye [H]; Ljucyna [Ru]; Ljutyna [Ru, U]; Lucina [Ru, Sv])	Sáros	Sabinov	Slovakia
Lypča [Ru, U] (Lipcse [H])	Máramaros	Chust	Ukraine
Lypec'ka Poljana [Ru, U] (Lipesemező/ Lipcse Polyána [H])	Máramaros	Chust	Ukraine
Lypna, *see* Lipna			
Lypova, *see* Lipová			
Lypovec' [Ru, U]	Máramaros	Chust	Ukraine
Lypovec/Lypovec', Sanok district *see* Lipowiec			
Lypovec' [Ru, U] (Hárs/Kislipóc [H])	Ung	Perečyn	Ukraine
Lysyčeve, *see* Lysyčovo			
Lysyčovo [Ru, U] (Lysyčeve [U]; Rókamező [H])	Máramaros	Iršava	Ukraine
Lytmanova, *see* Litmanová			
Lyuta, *see* Ljuta			
Maciejowa [P] (Maciova/Macijova [Ru]; Matijeva [U])	Nowy Sącz	Nowy Sącz	Poland
Macina Velyka, *see* Męcina Wielka			
Maciova, *see* Maciejowa			

Village	Former Hungarian county or Galician district	Present administrative subdivision	Present country
Macyna Velyka, *see* Męcina Wielka			
Magyarkomját, *see* Velyki Komjaty			
Majdan [P, U]	Lesko	Krosno	Poland
Majdan [Ru, U] (Majdánka [H])	Máramaros	Mižhirja	Ukraine
Majdánka, *see* Majdan, Máramaros county			
Majurky	Ung	Perečyn	Ukraine
Makarja, *see* Makar'ovo			
Makarjovo, *see* Makar'ovo			
Makaro've, *see* Makar'ovo			
Makar'ovo [U] (Makaria [H]; Makarjovo [Ru])	Bereg	Mukačevo	Ukraine
Makivci, *see* Makovce			
Makócz, *see* Makovce			
Mákos, *see* Makovce			
Makovce [Sv] (Makivci [Ru, U]; Makócz/Mákos [H])	Zemplén	Stropkov	Slovakia
Mala Čengava, *see* Zavadka, Ugocsa county			
Mala Drična, *see* Malá Driečna			
Malá Driečna [Sv] (Dricsna/Kisderencs [H]; Mala Drična [Ru, U]; Zempléndricsna [H]), *see* Driečna			
Mala Kopanja [Ru, U] (Alsóveresmart/ Kiskupány [H])	Ugocsa	Vynohradiv	Ukraine
Mala Lunka [Ru], now part of Lunka			
Mala Martynka [Ru, U] (Mártonka [H])	Bereg	Svaljava	Ukraine
Malá Pol'ana [Sv] (Kispolány [H]; Mala Poljana [Ru, U]; Sztropkópolena [H])	Zemplén	Stropkov	Slovakia
Mala Poljana, *see* Malá Pol'ana			
Mala Roztoka [U] (Rosztoka [Ru]; Szőllősrosztoka/Ugocsa-Rosztoka [H])	Ugocsa	Iršava	Ukraine
Mala Uhol'ka [Ru, U]	Máramaros	Tjačiv	Ukraine
Malastiv, *see* Małastów			
Małastów [P] (Malastiv [Ru, U]; Mavastiv [Ru])	Gorlice	Nowy Sącz	Poland
Malcov [Ru, Sv, U] (Malczó [H])	Sáros	Bardejov	Slovakia
Malczó, *see* Malcov			
Malé Bukovce [Sv] (Kisbukócz [H]; Malyj Bukovec' [U]; Malŷj Bukovec [Ru]; Zemplénbukócz [H]), since 1964 part of Bukovce			
Malé Staškovce [Sv] (Kistavas [H]; Mali Staškivci [U]; Malŷ Staškivci [Ru]; Zemplénsztaskócz [H]), part of Staškovce			
Mali Staškivci, *see* Malé Staškovce			
Malmos, *see* Strojne			
Malý Lipník [Sv] (Kishárs/Kislipnik [H]; Malŷj Lypnyk [Ru]; Malyj Lypnyk [U])	Sáros	Stará L'ubovňa	Slovakia
Malŷ Staškivci, *see* Malé Staškovce			
Malý Sulín [Sv] (Malyj Sulyn [U];			

Village	Former Hungarian county or Galician district	Present administrative subdivision	Present country
Malŷj Sulyn [Ru]; Szulin [H]), since 1961 part of Sulín			
Malyj Bereznyj [U] (Kisberezna [H]; Malŷj Bereznŷj [Ru])	Ung	Velykyj Bereznyj	Ukraine
Malyj Bukovec', *see* Malé Bukovce			
Malyj/Malŷj Lypnyk, *see* Malý Lipník			
Malyj Rakovec' [U] (Kisrákócz [H]; Malŷj Rakovec' [Ru]	Ugocsa	Iršava	Ukraine
Malyj/Malŷj Sulyn, *see* Malý Sulín			
Manastŷr, *see* Monastyrec'			
Maniów [P] (Maniv [U])	Lesko	Krosno	Poland
Maniv, *see* Maniów			
Máramarossziget, *see* Sighetul Marmaţiei, p. 112			
Máriakút, *see* Rafajovce			
Mártonka, *see* Mala Martynka			
Maškivci, *see* Maškovce			
Maskócz, *see* Maškovce			
Maškovce [Sv] (Maškivci [Ru, U]; Maskócz [H]), since 1961 part of Vyšný Hrušov	Zemplén	Humenné	Slovakia
Maszárfalva, *see* Nehrovo			
Máté, *see* Matysová			
Mátévágasa, *see* Matovce			
Matiaška [Sv] (Matjaška [U]; Matjašok [Ru]; Mátyáska [H])	Zemplén	Vranov	Slovakia
Matijeva, *see* Maciejowa			
Mativciv, *see* Matovce			
Matjaška, *see* Matiaška			
Matjašok, *see* Matiaška			
Matovce [Sv] (Mátévágasa [H]; Mativci [Ru, U])	Sáros	Svidník	Slovakia
Mátyáska, *see* Matiaška			
Matysová [Sv] (Máté [H]; Matysova [U]; Matŷsova [Ru])	Sáros	Stará L'ubovňa	Slovakia
Mavastiv, *see* Małastów			
Mchava, *see* Mchawa			
Mchawa [P] (Mchava [U]; Muchava [Ru])	Lesko	Krosno	Poland
Męcina Wielka [P] (Macyna Velyka [Ru]; Mecyna Velyka [U])	Gorlice	Nowy Sącz	Poland
Mecyna Velyka, *see* Męcina Wielka			
Medencze, *see* Midjanycja			
Medved'ovci, *see* Medvedivci			
Medvedivci [U] (Fagyalos/Medvegyócz [H]; Medvjed'ovci [Ru])	Bereg	Mukačevo	Ukraine
Medvedzi, *see* Medvežyj, Máramaros county			
Medvedzie [Sv] (Kismedvés [H]; Medvedže/Medvidže [Ru]; Medviže [U])	Sáros	Svidník	Slovakia
Medvefalva, *see* Medvežyj, Bereg county			
Medvegyócz, *see* Medvedivci			

Village	Former Hungarian county or Galician district	Present administrative subdivision	Present country
Medvezsa, see Medvežyj, Bereg county			
Medvežyj [U] (Medvefalva/Medvezsa [H])	Bereg	Volovec'	Ukraine
Medveže see Medvedzie			
Medvežyj [U] (Medvedzi [H]; Medvežij [Ru])	Máramaros	Chust	Ukraine
Medvidže, see Medvedzie			
Medviže, see Medvedzie			
Medvjed'ovci, see Medvedivci			
Medžilabirci, see Medzilaborce			
*Medzilaborce [Sv] (Laborec [Ru]; Mezőlaborcz [H]; Medžilabirci [Ru]; Medžylabirci [U])	Zemplén	Medzilaborce	Slovakia
Medžylabirci, see Medzilaborce			
Meggyfalu, see Ol'šinkov			
Méhesfalva, see Pčoliné			
Mércse, see Myrča			
Meredély, see Príkra			
Merešor [Ru, U] (Meresul/ Rókarét [H])	Máramaros	Mižhirja	Ukraine
Meresul, see Merešor			
Mérfalva, see Mirol'a			
Mergeška, see Nová Polianka			
Mérgesvágása, see Nová Polianka			
Mészégető, see Vápeník			
Mezőhuta, see Poljans'ka Huta			
Mezőlaborcz, see Medzilaborce			
Mezőterebes, see Strabyčovo			
Michajlov [Sv] (Kismihály [H]; Michajluv [Ru]; Mihajló [H]; Mychajliv [U]; Mychajlov [Ru])	Zemplén	Snina	Slovakia
Michalovce, see p. 112			
**Midjanycja [U] (Medencze [H]; Mîdjanycja [Ru])	Bereg	Iršava	Ukraine
Międzygórze [P] (Kulašnoj [Ru]; Kulašne [Ru, U])	Sanok	Krosno	Poland
Mihajló, see Michajlov			
Mihálka, see Krajnykovo			
Mikloševci, see Miklusevci			
Miklósvágása, see Miklušovce			
Miklósvölgye, see Mikulášová			
Mikluševci [SC] (Mikloševci [Ru])	Szerém	Slavonia	Croatia
Miklušovce [Sv] (Miklósvágása [H]; Myklušivci [U])	Sáros	Prešov	Slovakia
Mikó, see Miková			
Mikovo, see Tisa, p. 113			
Miková [Sv] (Mikó [H]; Mykova [Ru, U])	Zemplén	Stropkov	Slovakia
Mików [P] (Mykiv [Ru, U])	Sanok	Krosno	Poland
Mikulášová [Sv] (Miklósvölgye [H]; Niklova [H, Sv]; Nikl'ova [U]; Nyklova [Ru])	Sáros	Bardejov	Slovakia

Village	Former Hungarian county or Galician district	Present administrative subdivision	Present country
Milik [P, Ru] (Mylyk [Ru, U])	Nowy Sącz	Nowy Sącz	Poland
Milpoš [Ru, Sv] (Mil'poš [U])	Sáros	Sabinov	Slovakia
Miňovce [Sv] (Minyevágása/Minyócz [H]; Mynivci [Ru, U])	Zemplén	Stropkov	Slovakia
Minyevágása, *see* Miňovce			
Minyócz, *see* Miňovce			
Mirča, *see* Myrča			
Mirol'a [Sv] (Mérfalva [H]; Myrolja [Ru, U])	Sáros	Svidník	Slovakia
Miskafalva, *see* Myškarovycja			
Miskarovica, *see* Myškarovycja			
Miszticze, *see* Imstyčovo			
Mižhirja [U] (Ökörmező [H]; Volovoje [Ru])	Máramaros	Mižhirja	Ukraine
Mlinarócz, *see* Mlynárovce			
Mlynarivci, *see* Mlynárovce			
Mlynárovce [Sv] (Mlinarócz [H]; Mlynarivci [Ru, U]; Molnáryágása [H])	Sáros	Svidník	Slovakia
*Mníšek nad Popradom [Sv] (Poprádremete [H])	Szepes	Stará L'ubovňa	Slovakia
Močar, *see* Rus'kyj Močar			
Močarne, *see* Moczarne			
Mochnačka, *see* Mochnaczka Niżna			
Mochnaczka Niżna [P] (Mochnačka/ Muchnačka Nyžnja [Ru, U])	Nowy Sącz	Nowy Sącz	Poland
Mochnaczka Wyżna [P] (Mochnačka/ Muchnačka Výšnja [Ru]; Muchnačka Vyžnja [U])	Nowy Sącz	Nowy Sącz	Poland
Moczarne [P] (Močarne [U]; Moczary [P]) (ceased to exist after 1947)	Lesko	Krosno	Poland
Moczary, *see* Moczarne			
Mogyorós, *see* Kopynivci; and Mykulivci			
Mokra [H, U] (Mokroje [Ru])	Ung	Perečyn	Ukraine
Mokre [P, U] (Mokroj/Mokrŷ [Ru])	Sanok	Krosno	Poland
Mokroj, *see* Mokre			
Mokroje, *see* Mokra			
Mokrŷ, *see* Mokre			
Molnáryágása, *see* Mlynárovce			
Monastyrec' [U] (Herinesemo-nostor [H]; Manastŷr [Ru])	Máramaros	Chust	Ukraine
Morochiw/Morochóv, *see* Mroczków			
Morochownica [P] (Zavadka [Ru]; Zavadka Morochivs'ka [U]; Zawadka Morochowska [P])	Sanok	Krosno	Poland
Moščanec/Moščanec', *see* Moszczaniec			
Moščenec, *see* Moszczaniec			
Moszczaniec [P] (Moščanec [Ru]; Moščanec' [U]; Moščenec [Ru])	Sanok	Krosno	Poland
Mrazivci, *see* Mrazovce			

Village	Former Hungarian county or Galician district	Present administrative subdivision	Present country
Mrázócz, *see* Mrázovce			
Mrázovce [Sv] (Dér [H]; Mrazivci [U]; Mrázócz [H])	Zemplén	Stropkov	Slovakia
Mroczków [P] (Morochiv [Ru, U]; Morochów [P])	Sanok	Krosno	Poland
Mšana, *see* Mszana			
Mszana [P] (Mšana [Ru, U])	Krosno	Krosno	Poland
Muchava, *see* Mchawa			
Muchnačka Nyžnja, *see* Mochnaczka Niżna			
Muchnačka Výšnja/Vyžnja, *see* Mochnaczka Wyżna			
Mučne/Muczne, *see* Kazimierzowo			
Mukačeve/Mukačiv/Mukačovo, *see* Mukačevo, p. 113			
Munkács, *see* Mukačevo, p. 112			
Munkácsváralja, *see* Pidhorod			
Mušynka, *see* Muszynka			
Muszynka [P] (Mušynka [Ru, U])	Nowy Sącz	Nowy Sącz	Poland
Mutnokszabadja, *see* Copăcele			
Mychajliv/Mychajluv, *see* Michajlov			
Mychalivci/Mychalovec', *see* Michalovce, p. 112			
Myczków [P] (Myčkiv [U])	Lesko	Krosno	Poland
Mykiv, *see* Mików			
Mykova, *see* Miková			
Myklušivci, *see* Miklušovce			
Mykulivci [U] (Kismogyorós/ Mogyorós [H]; Mykulovci [Ru])	Bereg	Mukačevo	Ukraine
Mykulovci, *see* Mykulivci			
Mylyk, *see* Milik			
Mynivci, *see* Miňovce			
Myrča [U] (Mércse [H]; Mirča [Ru])	Ung	Velykyj Bereznyj	Ukraine
Myrolja, *see* Mirol'a			
Myscova, *see* Myscowa			
Myscowa [P] (Myscova [Ru, U]; Mŷscova [Ru])	Krosno	Krosno	Poland
Myškarovycja [Ru, U] (Miskafalva/ Miskarovica [H])	Bereg	Volovec'	Ukraine
Nádaspatak, *see* Trostcjanycja			
Ňagov [Sv] (Njagiv [Ru]; Njahiv [U]; Nyágó [H])	Zemplén	Medzilaborce	Slovakia
Nagyábránka, *see* Lokit'			
Nagyalmás, *see* Jabluniv			
Nagyberezna, *see* Velykyj Bereznyj, p. 113			
Nagybocskó, *see* Bocicoiu Mare; Velykyj Byčkiv			
Nagybresztó, *see* Brestiv			
Nagybukócz, *see* Vel'ké Bukovce			
Nagycserjés, *see* Kyčirnyj			
Nagycsertész, *see* Čertižné			
Nagycsongova, *see* Boržavs'ke			

Village	Former Hungarian county or Galician district	Present administrative subdivision	Present country
Nagyderencs, *see* Vel'ka Driečna			
Nagygajdos, *see* Hajdoš			
Nagygereblyés, *see* Ruský Hrabovec			
Nagyhársas, *see* Vel'ký Lipník			
Nagykirva, *see* Kryve			
Nagykomját, *see* Velyki Komjaty			
Nagykunchfalu/Nagykunczfalva, *see* Helcmanovce, p. 111			
Nagyláz, *see* Velyki Lazy			
Nagylipnik, *see* Vel'ky Lipník			
Nagylohó, *see* Lochovo			
Nagylucska, *see* Velyki Lučky			
Nagymajor, *see* Stráňany			
Nagymihály, *see* Michalovce, 112			
Nagymogyorós, *see* Kopynivci			
Nagyolsva, *see* Ol'šavica			
Nagypásztély, *see* Kosteva Pastil'			
Nagypolány, *see* Vel'ká Pol'ana			
Nagyrákócz, *see* Velykyj Rakovec'			
Nagyrosztoka, *see* Nyžnja Roztoka			
Nagyruszka, *see* Vel'ky Ruskov			
Nagyruszkóc, *see* Rus'ke, Bereg county			
Nagyszlatina, *see* Nyžnje Solotvyno			
Nagyszőllős, *see* Vynohradiv, p. 113			
Nagyszulin, *see* Vel'ký Sulin			
Nagytavas, *see* Vel'ké Staškovce			
Nagyturjaszög, *see* Turycja			
Nagyugolyka/Nagyugolkavölgy, *see* Velyka Uhol'ka			
Nankove, *see* Nankovo			
Nankovo [Ru, U] (Husztkőz [H]; Nankove [U])	Máramaros	Chust	Ukraine
Nasičnje, *see* Nasiczne			
Nasiczne [P] (Nasičnje [U])	Lesko	Krosno	Poland
Nechval' Poljanky, *see* Nechválova Polianka			
Nechválova Polianka [Sv] (Nechval' Poljanky [U]; Nechval'ova Poljanka [Ru]; Nechválpolyánka [H]; Poljankŷ [Ru]; Szinnamező [H])	Zemplén	Humenné	Slovakia
Nechválpolyánka, *see* Nechválova Polianka			
Negrova, *see* Nehrovo			
Nehrove, *see* Nehrovo			
Negrovec', *see* Nehrovec'			
Negrovo, *see* Nehrovo			
Nehrove, *see* Nehrovo			
Nehrovec' [U] (Felsőkalocsa/ Kalocsa Negrovec [H]; Negrovec' [Ru])	Máramaros	Mižhirja	Ukraine
Nehrovo [U] (Maszárfalva/Negrova [H]; Negrovo [Ru]; Nehrove [U])	Bereg	Iršava	Ukraine

Village	Former Hungarian county or Galician district	Present administrative subdivision	Present country
Nelipeno/Nelipyne, *see* Nelipyno			
Nelipyno [U] (Hársfalva [H]; Nelipeno [Ru])	Bereg	Svaljava	Ukraine
Németpereg, *see* Peregu Mare, p. 112			
Németporuba, *see* Poruba pod Vihorlatom			
Németvágás, *see* Poruba pod Vihorlatom			
Neresnycja [Ru, U] (Nyerésháza [H])	Máramaros	Tjačiv	Ukraine
Nevickoje, *see* Nevyc'ke			
Neviczke, *see* Nevyc'ke			
Nevistka, *see* Niewistka			
Nevyc'ke [U] (Nevickoje [Ru]; Neviczke [H])	Ung	Užhorod	Ukraine
Neznajeva/Neznajova, *see* Nieznajowa			
Niewistka [P] (Nevistka [Ru, U])	Brzozów	Krosno	Poland
Nieznajowa [P] (Neznajeva [U]; Neznajova [Ru])	Gorlice	Nowy Sącz	Poland
Niklova, *see* Mikulášová			
Nižná Jablonka [Sv] (Alsóalmád [H]; Nyžnja Jablinka [Ru, U])	Zemplén	Humenné	Slovakia
Nižná Jedl'ová [Sv] (Alsófenyves/ Alsójedlova [H]; Nyžnja Jadlova [Ru, U])	Sáros	Svidník	Slovakia
Nižná Pisaná [Sv] (Alsóhimes/Alsópiszana [H]; Nyžnja Pysana [Ru, U])	Sáros	Svidník	Slovakia
Nižná Polianka [Sv] (Alsópagony/ Alsópolyánka [H]; Nyžnja Poljanka [Ru, U])	Sáros	Bardejov	Slovakia
Nižná Radvaň [Sv] (Horbokradvány/ Laborczradvány [H]; Nyžnja Radvan' [Ru, U]), since 1964 part of Radvaň nad Laborcom			
Nižná Vladiča [Sv] (Alsóladács/ Alsóvladicsa [H]; Nyžnja Vladyča [Ru, U], since 1964 part of Vladiča			
Nižné Čabiny [Sv] (Alsócsebeny [H]; Nyžni Čabyny [U]; Nyžni Čabynŷ [Ru]), since 1964 part of Čabiny			
Nižné Nemecké [Sv] (Alsónémeti [H])	Ung	Sobrance	Slovakia
Nižné Slovinky, *see* Nižnie Slovinky			
Nižné Zbojné [Sv] (Homonnazbojna [H]; Nyžnja Zbina [Ru]; Nyžnje Zbijne [U]; Óbajne [H]), since 1960 part of Zbojné			
Nižní Svidník [Sv] (Alsószvidnik/ Alsóvizköz [H]; Nyžnij Svydnyk [Ru]), since 1944 part of Svidník			
Nižnia Ol'ka, now part of Ol'ka			
*Nižnie Slovinky [Sv] (Alsószalánk/ Alsószlovinka [H]; Nyžni Slovinky [U]; Nyžni Slovynkŷ/ Slovinkŷ [Ru]), since 1943 part of Slovinky			
Nižný Komárnik [Sv] (Alsókomárnok [H];	Sáros	Svidník	Slovakia

Village	Former Hungarian county or Galician district	Present administrative subdivision	Present country
Nyžnij Komarnyk [Ru, U])			
Nižný Mirošov [Sv] (Alsómerse [H]; Nyžnij Myrošiv [Ru, U])	Sáros	Svidník	Slovakia
Nižný Orlík [Sv] (Alsóodor/Alsóorlich [H]; Nyžnij Orlyk [U]; Nyžnij Verlych [Ru])	Sáros	Svidník	Slovakia
Nižný Tvarožec [Sv] (Alsótarocz [H]; Nyžnij Tvarožec [Ru]; Nyžnij Tvarožec' [U])	Sáros	Bardejov	Slovakia
Njagiv, *see* Ňagov			
Njagovo, *see* Dobrjans'ke			
Njahiv, *see* Ňagov			
Nová Polianka [Sv] (Mergeška [Ru]; Mérgesvágása [H]; Nova Poljana [Ru, U])	Sáros	Svidník	Slovakia
Nova Poljana, *see* Nová Polianka			
Nova Roztoka [U] (Újrosztoka [H]), now part of Verbjaž			
Nová Sedlica [Sv] (Nova Sedlicja/ Novoselyca [Ru]; Novoselycja [U]; Novoszedlicza/Újszék [H])	Zemplén	Snina	Slovakia
Nova Stužycja [Ru, U] (Patakújfalu/ Újsztuzsica [H]), now part of Stužycja			
Nova Ves/Ves', *see* Nowa Wieś			
Nove Davydkovo [U] (Novoje Davydkovo [Ru]; Újdávidháza [H])	Bereg	Mukačevo	Ukraine
Noves, *see* Nowa Wieś			
Novobarovo [U] (Novoje Barovo [Ru]; Újbárd [H])	Máramaros	Tjačiv	Ukraine
Novoje Barovo, *see* Novobarovo			
Novoje Davydkovo, *see* Nove Davydkovo			
Novoselyca, *see* Nová Sedlica			
Novoselycja [Ru, U] (Kislucska/ Kisrétfalu/Rétfalu [H])	Bereg	Mukačevo	Ukraine
Novoselycja [Ru, U] (Felsőneresznice/ Taraczújfalu [H])	Máramaros	Mižhirja	Ukraine
Novoselycja [Ru, U] (Tarújfalu/ Újholyátin [H])	Máramaros	Tjačiv	Ukraine
Novoselycja [Ru, U] (Sósfalu/ Sós-Újfalu [H])	Ugocsa	Vynohradiv	Ukraine
Novoselycja [Ru, U] (Kemencze/ Újkemencze [H])	Ung	Perečyn	Ukraine
Novoselycja, Zemplén county, *see* Nová Sedlica			
Novosil'ci, *see* Nowosielce			
Novosilky, *see* Nowosiółki			
Novosivkŷ, *see* Nowosiółki			
Novoszedlicza, *see* Nová Sedlica			
Novycja, *see* Nowica			
Nowa Wieś [P] (Nova Ves [Ru]; Nova Ves' [U]; Noves [Ru])	Nowy Sącz	Nowy Sącz	Poland
Nowica [P] (Novycja [Ru, U])	Gorlice	Nowy Sącz	Poland
Nowosielce [P] (Novosil'ci [U])	Sanok	Krosno	Poland

Village	Former Hungarian county or Galician district	Present administrative subdivision	Present country
Nowosiółki [P] (Novosilky [U]; Novosivkŷ [Ru])	Lesko	Krosno	Poland
Nyágó, *see* Ňagov			
Nyágova, *see* Dobrjans'ke			
Nyerésháza, *see* Neresnycja			
Nyilas, *see* Roztoky, Máramaros county			
Nyiresfalva, *see* Dunkovycja			
Nyiresújfalu, *see* Dunkovycja			
Nyklova, *see* Mikulášová			
Nyžni Čabyny, *see* Nižné Čabiny			
Nyžni Remety [U] (Alsóremete [H]; Nyžni Remeta [Ru])	Bereg	Berehovo	Ukraine
Nyžni Remeta, *see* Nyžni Remety			
Nyžni Slovinky/Slovynkŷ, *see* Nižnie Slovinky			
Nyžni Verec'ky, *see* Nyžni Vorota			
**Nyžni Vorota [U] (Alsóvereczke [H]; Nyžni Verecky [Ru])	Bereg	Volovec'	Ukraine
Nyžnij Bystryj [U] (Alsóbistra [H]; Nyžnŷj Bŷstrŷj [Ru])	Máramaros	Chust	Ukraine
Nyžnij Dubovec' [U] (Nyžnŷj Dubovec' [Ru])	Máramaros	Tjačiv	Ukraine
Nyžnij Komarnyk, *see* Nižný Komárnik			
**Nyžnij Koropec' [U] (Alsó Kerepec [H]; Alsó Schönborn [H]; Nyžnŷj Koropec' [Ru])	Bereg	Mukačevo	Ukraine
Nyžnij Myrošiv, *see* Nižný Mirošov			
Nyžnij Orlyk, *see* Nižný Orlík			
Nyžnij Studenyj [U] (Alsóhidekpatak [H]; Nyžnŷj Studenŷj [Ru])	Máramaros	Mižhirja	Ukraine
Nyžnij Svydnyk, *see* Nižní Svidník			
Nyžnij Synevyr, *see* Synevyr			
Nyžnij Tvarožec/Tvarožec', *see* Nižný Tvarožec			
Nyžnij Verlych, *see* Nyžnij Orlyk			
Nyžnja Apša, *see* Dibrova, p. 111			
Nyžnja Hrabivnycja [U] (Alsógereben/ Alsóhrabonica [H])	Bereg	Svaljava	Ukraine
Nyžnja Jablinka, *see* Nižná Jablonka			
Nyžnja Jadlova, *see* Nižná Jedl'ová			
Nyžnja Pysana, *see* Nižná Pisaná			
Nyžnja Radvan', *see* Nižná Radvaň			
Nyžnja Roztoka [U] (Alsóhatárszeg/ Nagyrosztoka [H]), since 1960 part of Roztoka, Bereg county, Volovec' region			
Nyžnja Roztoka [Ru], Ung county part of Kostryns'ka Roztoka			
Nyžnja Vladiča, *see* Nižná Vladiča			
Nyžnja Vyznycja [U] (Alsóviznicze [H]; Nyžnja Vŷznycja [Ru])	Bereg	Mukačevo	Ukraine

Village	Former Hungarian county or Galician district	Present administrative subdivision	Present country
Nyžnja Zbina, *see* Nižné Zbojné			
Nyžnje Bolotne [U] (Alsósárad [H]; Nyžnŷj Šard [Ru])	Ugocsa	Iršava	Ukraine
Nyžnje Selyšče [U] (Alsószelistye [H])	Máramaros	Chust	Ukraine
Nyžnje Solotvyno [Ru, U] (Alsószlatina/ Nagyszlatina [H])	Ung	Užhorod	Ukraine
Nyžnje Zbijne, *see* Nižné Zbojne			
Nyžnŷj Bŷstrŷj, *see* Nyžnij Bystryj			
Nyžnŷj Koropec', *see* Nyžnij Koropec'			
Nyžnŷj Šard, *see* Nyžnje Bolotne			
Nyžnŷj Studenŷj, *see* Nyžnij Studenyj			
Óbajna, *see* Nižné Zbojné			
Obava [Ru, U] (Dunkófalva [H])	Bereg	Mukačevo	Ukraine
Oblaz [Ru, U]	Máramaros	Chust	Ukraine
Obručné [Sv] (Abroncsos [H]; Obručne [Ru, U]; Obrucsnó [H])	Sáros	Stará Ľubovňa	Slovakia
Obrucsnó, *see* Obručné			
Ődarma, *see* Storožnycja			
Ódavidháza, *see* Stare Davydkovo			
Odrechova/Odrychova, *see* Odrzechowa			
Odrzechowa [P] (Odrechova [U]; Odrychova [Ru])	Sanok	Krosno	Poland
Ohaba-Mătnik/Mutnik, *see* Copăcele			
Ókemencze, *see* Kamjanycja			
Ökörmező, *see* Mižhirja			
Ökröske, *see* Volica			
**Okruhla [Ru,U] (Kerekhegy [H])	Máramaros	Tjačiv	Ukraine
**Okružná [Sv] (Kereštvej [Ru]; Kiskőrösfő/Kőrösfő [H])	Sáros	Prešov	Slovakia
Ola, *see* Wola Michowa			
Oláhczertész, *see* Pidhirne			
Olajpatak, *see* Olejníkov			
Ol'chovec', *see* Olchowiec			
Olchowa [P] (Vilchova [Ru]; Vil'chova [U])	Lesko	Krosno	Poland
Olchowiec [P] (Ol'chovec'/ Vil'chivec' [U]; Vilchovec [Ru])	Krosno	Krosno	Poland
**Olejníkov [Sv] (Olajpatak/Olejnok [H]; Olejnykov [Ru]; Olijnyk [U])	Sáros	Sabinov	Slovakia
Olejnok, *see* Olejníkov			
Oleksandrivka [U] (Ósándorfalva/ Sándorfalva [H]; Šandorove [U]; Šandrovo [Ru])	Máramaros	Chust	Ukraine
Oleneve, *see* Olen'ovo			
Olen'ovo [Ru, U] (Olen'eve [U]; Szarvaskút [H])	Bereg	Svaljava	Ukraine
Olenyova, *see* Olen'ovo			
Olešnyk [Ru, U] (Egres/Szőllősegres [H])	Ugocsa	Vynohradiv	Ukraine

Village	Former Hungarian county or Galician district	Present administrative subdivision	Present country
Olijnyk, *see* Olejníkov			
Ol'ka [Ru, Sv, U] (Homonnaolyka/ Sztropkóolyka [H])	Zemplén	Medzilaborce	Slovakia
Ol'šany, *see* Vil'šany			
Ol'šavica [Ru, Sv] (Nagyolsva [H]; Ol'šavycja [U]; Vul'šavica [Ru])	Szepes	Levoča	Slovakia
Olšavka [Sv] (Kisolysó [H]; Ol'šavka [U]; Višavka [Ru])	Sáros	Stropkov	Slovakia
Ol'šavycja, *see* Ol'šavica			
Ol'šinkov [Sv] (Meggyfalu [H]; Ol'šŷnkiv [Ru]; Ol'šynkiv [U]; Vŷšŷnkiv [Ru])	Zemplén	Medzilaborce	Slovakia
Ol'šŷnkiv/Ol'šynkiv, *see* Ol'šinkov			
Ölyvös, *see* Vil'chivka			
Ondavafő, *see* Ondavka			
Ondavka [Ru, Sv, U] (Ondavafő [H])	Sáros	Bardejov	Slovakia
Onok [Ru, U] (Ilonokújfalu [H]; Onyk [Ru])	Ugocsa	Vynohradiv	Ukraine
Onokivci/Onokovci, *see* Onokivci, p. 112			
Onyk, *see* Onok			
Oparivka, *see* Oparówka			
Oparówka [P] (Oparivka [Ru, U])	Strzyżów	Krosno	Poland
Ördarma, *see* Storožnycja			
Ördögporuba, *see* Porúbka			
Ördögvágás, *see* Porúbka			
Őrhegyalja, *see* Pidhorjany			
Orichovycja [Ru, U] (Rahoncza [H])	Ung	Užhorod	Ukraine
Orjabyna, *see* Jarabina			
Orliv, *see* Orlov			
Orló, *see* Orlov			
Orlov [Ru, Sv] (Orliv [U]; Orló [H]; Virliv [Ru])	Sáros	Stará L'ubovňa	Slovakia
Orlova, *see* Irljava			
Orlyava, *see* Irljava			
Ormód, *see* Brestiv			
Orosvyhiv, *see* Rosvyhovo			
Oroszbisztra, *see* Ruská Bystrá			
Oroszhrabócz, Sáros county, *see* Vyšný Hrabovec			
Oroszhrabócz, Zemplén county, *see* Ruský Hrabovec			
Oroszkájnya, *see* Ruská Kajňa			
Oroszkázmér, *see* Ruský Kazimír			
Oroszkő, *see* Repedea			
Oroszkomoró/Oroszkomoróc, *see* Rus'ki Komarivci			
Oroszkrucsó, *see* Ruský Kručov			
Oroszkucsova, *see* Rus'ka Kučava			
Oroszmocsár, *see* Rus'kyj Močar			
Oroszmokra, Máramaros county, *see* Rus'ka Mokra, Máramaros county			

Village	Former Hungarian county or Galician district	Present administrative subdivision	Present country
Oroszpatak, *see* Ruský Potok			
Oroszporuba, *see* Ruská Poruba			
Oroszruszka, *see* Ruské			
Oroszsebes, *see* Ruská Bystrá			
Orosztelek, *see* Rus'ke			
Orosztokaj, *see* Tokajík			
Oroszvágás, *see* Ruská Poruba			
Oroszvég, *see* Rosvyhovo			
Oroszvolova, *see* Ruská Volová			
Oroszvolya, *see* Ruská Vol'a			
Oroszvolya, *see* Ruská Vol'a nad Popradom			
Ortutó, *see* Ortut'ová			
Ortut'ová [Sv] (Ortutó [H]; Ortutova [Ru, U])	Sáros	Bardejov	Slovakia
Osadné [Sv] (Osadne [Ru, U]; Telepivci [Ru]; Telepócz [H]; Telepovce [Sv])	Zemplén	Snina	Slovakia
Ósándorfalva, *see* Oleksandrivka			
Osava [Ru, U] (Darázsvölgy/ Oszáva [H])	Máramaros	Chust	Ukraine
Osij [U] (Osoj [Ru]; Szajkófalva [H])	Bereg	Iršava	Ukraine
Oslavyca/Oslavycja, *see* Osławica			
Osławica [P] (Oslavyca [Ru]; Oslavycja [U]; Uslavycja [Ru])	Sanok	Krosno	Poland
Osoj, *see* Osij			
Ostrožnica [Sv] (Ostružnica/Stružnica [Ru]; Stružnycja [U]; Szedreske [H]) (ceased to exist in 1980)	Zemplén	Snina	Slovakia
Osturňa [Sv] (Osturnja [Ru, U]; Osztornya [H])	Szepes	Kežmarok	Slovakia
Osturnja, *see* Osturňa			
Oszáva, *see* Osava			
Ószemere, *see* Simer			
Osztornya, *see* Osturňa			
Ósztuzsica, *see* Stara Stužycja			
Ötvösfalva, *see* Zolotar'ovo			
Óverbász, *see* Stari Vrbas, p. 113			
Owczary [P] (Rychvald [U]; Rŷchvald/ Rŷchvavt [Ru]; Rychwald [P])	Gorlice	Nowy Sącz	Poland
Ożenna [P] (Ožynna [Ru, U])	Jasło	Krosno	Poland
Ožoverch [Ru, U]	Máramaros	Chust	Ukraine
Ożynna, *see* Ożenna			
Packan'ove, *see* Packan'ovo			
Packan'ovo [Ru, U] (Packan'ove [U]; Patakos [H]; Patkan'ovo [Ru]; Patkanyócz [H])	Bereg	Užhorod	Ukraine
Padócz, *see* Podobovec'			
Pálfalva, *see* Volovycja			
Pálos, *see* Pavlovo			

Village	Former Hungarian county or Galician district	Present administrative subdivision	Present country
Pálosremete, *see* Remeți			
Palota [Sv] (Polata [Ru, U])	Zemplén	Medzilaborce	Slovakia
Panta, *see* Pętna			
Pankna, *see* Pętna			
Papfalva, *see* Dilok, Bereg county			
Parihuzócz, *see* Parihuzovce			
Parihuzovce [Sv] (Juhos/Parihuzócz [H]; Paryhuzovci [Ru]; Paryhuzivci [U])	Zemplén	Snina	Slovakia
Paryhuzivci, *see* Parihuzovce			
Pasika [Ru, U] (Kishidvég/ Paszika [H])	Bereg	Svaljava	Ukraine
Paškivci [U] (Hidegrét/Páskócz [H]; Paškovci [Ru])	Bereg	Volovec'	Ukraine
Páskócz, *see* Paškivci			
Paškovci, *see* Paškivci			
Pastil'ky [Ru, U] (Kispásztély [H])	Ung	Perečyn	Ukraine
Paszika, *see* Pasika			
Pásztorhegy, *see* Valaškovce			
Pásztorlak, *see* Hlynjanec'			
Pataki, *see* Potoky			
Patakófalu, *see* Stara Stužycja			
Patakos, *see* Packan'ovo			
Pataktanya, *see* Ploskyj Potok			
Patakújfalu, *see* Nova Stužycja			
Patkan'ovo/Patkanyócz, *see* Packan'ovo			
Pavlovo [Ru, U] (Kispálos/Pálos [H]; Pavlove [U])	Bereg	Svaljava	Ukraine
Pčalynŷ, *see* Pčoliné			
Pčoliné [Sv] (Méhesfalva [H]; Pčalynŷ [Ru]; Pčolyne [Ru, U])	Zemplén	Snina	Slovakia
Pčolyne, *see* Pčoliné			
Pčolyny *see* Pszczeliny			
Pelesalja, *see* Pidpleša			
Pelnja/Pel'nja, *see* Pielna			
Perechresnyj [U] (Perechrestna [Ru]; Pereháza /Perekreszna [H])	Bereg	Volovec'	Ukraine
Perechrestna/Perekreszna, *see* Perechresnyj			
Perecseny, *see* Perečyn			
Perečyn [Ru, U] (Perecseny [H])	Ung	Perečyn	Ukraine
Peregu Mare, *see* p. 112			
Pereháza, *see* Perechresnyj			
Perehonyna, *see* Przegonina			
Peregrymka/Perehrymka, *see* Pielgrzymka			
Perekreszna, *see* Perechresnyj			
Pereszlő, *see* Pryslip, Máramaros county			
Perunka, *see* Piorunka			
Peszternye, *see* Pstriná			
Petejivci, *see* Petejovce			
Petejovce [Sv] (Kispetőfalva [H];	Zemplén	Stropkov	Slovakia

Village	Former Hungarian county or Galician district	Present administrative subdivision	Present country
Petejivci [Ru, U]; Petőfalva [H]) (ceased to exist in 1965)			
Pętna [P] (Pankna [Ru]; Pantna [Ru, U])	Gorlice	Nowy Sącz	Poland
Petőfalva, *see* Petejovce			
Petrivci, *see* Petrovce nad Laborcem			
Petrócz, *see* Petrovce; Petrovce nad Laborcem			
Petrová [Sv] (Petrova [U]; Pitrova [H, Sv]; Pytrova [Ru]; Végpetri [H])	Sáros	Bardejov	Slovakia
Petrova Volja, *see* Wola Piotrowa			
Petrovabisztra, *see* Bistra			
Petrovakraszna, *see* Crasna Vişeului			
Petrovce [Sv] (Petrócz [H]; Petrovci [Ru]; Ungpéteri [H])	Ung	Sobrance	Slovakia
Petrovci [Ru, SC]	Szerém	Slavonia	Croatia
**Petrovce nad Laborcem [Sv] (Petrócz [H]; Petrivci [U]; Petrovce [Ru, Sv])	Ung	Michalovce	Slovakia
Petruša Volja, *see* Pietrusza Wola			
Petrušiv [U] (Petrušov [Ru])	Máramaros	Tjačiv	Ukraine
Petrušov, *see* Petrušiv			
Pichne [Sv] (Pychni [U]; Pŷchni [Ru]; Tüskés [H])	Zemplén	Snina	Slovakia
Pidčumal' [U] (Podčumal' [Ru])	Máramaros	Mižhirja	Ukraine
Pidhirne [U] (Oláhczertész [H]; Voloskoje [Ru])	Bereg	Iršava	Ukraine
Pidhorb [U] (Hegyfark [H]; Podhorb [Ru])	Ung	Užhorod	Ukraine
Pidhorjany [U] (Örhegyalja/Podhering [H]; Podhorjanŷ [Ru])	Bereg	Mukačevo	Ukraine
Pidhorod [U] (Munkácsváralja [H]; Podhorod [Ru]; Váralja [H])	Bereg	Mukačevo	Ukraine
Pidhorod', Ung county, *see* Podhorod'			
Pidpleša [U] (Pelesalja [H]; Podpleša [Ru]; Pudplesza [H])	Máramaros	Tjačiv	Ukraine
Pidmonastyr [U] (Klastromalja [H]; Podmanastŷr [Ru])	Bereg	Mukačevo	Ukraine
Pidpolozzja [U] (Podpolozja [Ru]; Pudpolócz/Vezérszállás [H])	Bereg	Volovec'	Ukraine
*Pidvynohradiv [U] (Ardovec' [Ru]; Szőllősvégardó/Végardó [H])	Ugocsa	Vynohradiv	Ukraine
Pielgrzymka [P] (Peregrymka [Ru]; Perehrymka [U])	Jasło	Krosno	Poland
Pielnia [P] (Pelnja [Ru]; Pel'nja [U])	Sanok	Krosno	Poland
Pietrusza Wola [P] (Petruša Volja [Ru, U])	Strzyżów	Krosno	Poland
Pilipec, *see* Pylypec'			
Pinkócz, *see* Pinkovce			
Pinkovce [Sv] (Pinkócz/Ungpinkócz [H])	Ung	Sobrance	Slovakia
Piorunka [P] (Perunka [Ru, U])	Grybów	Nowy Sącz	Poland
Piskorovce [Sv] (Királyhegy [H]; Piskurivci [Ru]; Piszkorcz [H];	Zemplén	Vranov	Slovakia

Village	Former Hungarian county or Galician district	Present administrative subdivision	Present country
Pyskurivci [U])			
Piskurivci, *see* Piskorovce			
Pistrjalove, *see* Pistrjalovo			
Pistrjalovo [Ru, U] (Pisztraháza [H])	Bereg	Mukačevo	Ukraine
Piszkorócz, *see* Piskorovce			
Pisztraháza, *see* Pistrjalovo			
Pitrova, *see* Petrová			
Plajuc' [U] (Plajec [Ru])	Máramaros	Rachiv	Ukraine
Plavja [U] (Zsilip [H])	Bereg	Svaljava	Ukraine
Płonna [P] (Plonna [U]; Polonna [Ru, U])	Sanok	Krosno	Poland
Ploskanovycja [Ru, U] (Ploszkan- falva [H])	Bereg	Mukačevo	Ukraine
Ploske [U] (Dombostelek/Ploszkó [H])	Bereg	Svaljava	Ukraine
Ploskyj Potok [U] (Pataktanya/ Ploszkópatak [H]; Potok [Ru])	Bereg	Svaljava	Ukraine
Ploszkanfalva, *see* Ploskanovycja			
Ploszkó, *see* Ploske			
Ploszkópatak, *see* Ploskyj Potok			
Podčumal', *see* Pidčumal'			
Podhering, *see* Pidhorjany			
Podhorb, *see* Pidhorb			
Podhorjanŷ, *see* Pidhorjany			
Podhorod, Bereg county, *see* Pidhorod			
**Podhorod' [Sv] (Pidhorod' [Ru, U]; Pudhorod' [Ru]; Tibaváralja/Váralja [H])	Ung	Sobrance	Slovakia
Podmanastŷr, *see* Pidmonastyr			
Podobócz, *see* Podobovec'			
Podobovec' [U] (Padócz/Podobócz [H])	Máramaros	Mižhirja	Ukraine
Podpleša, *see* Pidpleša			
Podpolozja, *see* Pidpolozzja			
Podproč [Sv] (Lazonpatak [H]; Popruč [Ru]), part of Ol'šavica			
Poienile de sub Munte [Ro] (Havasmező [H]; Rus'-Poljany [Ru, U]; Ruszpolyána [H])	Máramaros	Maramureş	Romania
**Pokuttja [U] (Kutkafalva [H]; Pokutja [Ru], part of Babyči	Bereg	Iršava	Ukraine
Polańczyk [P] (Poljančyk [U])	Lesko	Krosno	Poland
Polanki [P] (Poljanky [U])	Lesko	Krosno	Poland
Polany [P] (Poljany [U]; Poljanŷ [Ru])	Grybów	Nowy Sącz	Poland
Polany [P] (Poljany [U]; Poljanŷ [Ru])	Krosno	Krosno	Poland
Polany Surovickŷ/Surovičnŷ, *see* Polany Surowiczne			
Polany Surowiczne [P] (Poljany Surovyčni [U]; Poljanŷ Surovickŷ/Surovičnŷ [Ru]) (ceased to exist after 1947)	Sanok	Krosno	Poland
Polata, *see* Palota			
Polena, *see* Poljana, Bereg county			
Polena-huta, *see* Poljans'ka Huta			
Poljana [Ru, U] (Polena [H])	Bereg	Svaljava	Ukraine

Village	Former Hungarian county or Galician district	Present administrative subdivision	Present country
Poljana [Ru, U] (Polyána [H])	Máramaros	Chust	Ukraine
Poljančyk, *see* Polańczyk			
Poljanky, Lesko district, *see* Polanki			
Poljankŷ, Zemplen county, *see* Nechválova Polianka			
Poljans'ka Huta [Ru, U] (Mezőhuta/ Polena-huta [H])	Ung	Perečyn	Ukraine
Poljany/Poljanŷ, *see* Polany, Grybów district; Polany, Krosno district			
Poljany Surovčyni, *see* Polany Surowiczne			
Poljanŷ Surovičkŷ/Soruvičnŷ, *see* Polany Surowiczne			
Polonna, *see* Płonna			
Polyána, *see* Poljana, Máramaros county			
Poprádófalu, *see* Starina, Sáros county			
Poprádökrös, *see* Ruská Vol'a nad Popradom			
Poprádremete, *see* Mníšek nad Popradem			
Popruč, *see* Podproč			
Poráč [Sv] (Porač [Ru, U]; Vereshegy [H])	Szepes	Spišská Nová Ves	Slovakia
Poroskő, *see* Poroškovo			
Poroškov/Poroškove, *see* Poroškovo			
Poroškovo [U] (Poroškő [H]; Poroškov [Ru]; Poroskove [U])	Ung	Perečyn	Ukraine
Porszács, *see* Prosačov			
Poruba, *see* Ruská Poruba			
Poruba pod Vihorlatom [Sv] (Németporuba/ Németvágás [H])	Ung	Michalovce	Slovakia
Porúbka [Sv] (Ördögporuba/Ördögvágás [H])	Ung	Sobrance	Slovakia
Posada Jaśliska, *see* p. 112			
Posič [U] (Posîč [Ru])	Máramaros	Chust	Ukraine
Postoliv/Postolova/Postolovo, *see* Postołów			
Postołów [P] (Postoliv [U]; Postolova/ Postolovo [Ru])	Lesko	Krosno	Poland
Potašnja, *see* Potasznia			
Potasznia [P] (Potašnja [U]) (ceased to exist after 1947)	Turka	Krosno	Poland
Potičkŷ, *see* Potôčky			
Potik [U] (Bükköskő [H]; Kervavčat Potok [Ru]; Kirvavecpatak [H])	Máramaros	Mižhirja	Ukraine
Potôčky [Sv] (Érfalu [H]; Potičkŷ [Ru]; Potočky [U]; Potocska [H])	Zemplén	Stropkov	Slovakia
Potočok [Ru, U]	Máramaros	Chust	Ukraine
Potocska, *see* Potôčky			
Potok, *see* Ploskyj Potok			
Potoka, *see* Potoky			
**Potoky [Sv, U] (Potokŷ [Ru]), since 1921 part of Lúčka	Sáros	Sabinov	Slovakia
Potoky [Sv, U] (Pataki, Potoka [H]; Potokŷ [Ru])	Sáros	Stropkov	Slovakia

Village	Former Hungarian county or Galician district	Present administrative subdivision	Present country
Povalŷ, *see* Puławy			
Povoroznyk/Povroznyk, *see* Powroźnik			
Powroźnik [P] (Povoroznyk [Ru, U] Povroznyk [Ru])	Nowy Sącz	Nowy Sącz	Poland
Praurócz, *see* Pravrovce			
Pravrivci, *see* Pravrovce			
Pravrovce [Sv] (Jobbos/Praurócz [H]; Pravrivci [Ru, U]), since 1964 part of Repejov			
Pravukŷ, *see* Preluki			
Pregonina, *see* Przegonina			
Prehud', *see* Pryhid'			
Preluki [P] (Pravukŷ/Prelukŷ [Ru]; Preluky [U])	Sanok	Krosno	Poland
Prelukŷ, *see* Preluki			
Priekopa [Sv] (Kapás [H]; Prykopa [U])	Ung	Sobrance	Slovakia
Príkra [Sv] (Meredély [H]; Prykra [Ru, U])	Sáros	Svidník	Slovakia
Príslop [Sv] (Kispereszlő [H]; Pryslip [U]; Pryslop/Pryslup [Ru])	Zemplén	Snina	Slovakia
Priszlop, *see* Pryslip			
Pritul'any [Sv] (Hegyvég [H]; Pritulyán [H]; Prytuljany [U]; Prytuljanŷ [Ru])	Zemplén	Humenné	Slovakia
Pritulyán, *see* Pritul'any			
Procisne [P] (Protisne [U])	Lesko	Krosno	Poland
Prosačiv, *see* Prosačov			
Prosačov [Sv] (Porszács [H]; Prosačiv [Ru, U]; Proszács [H])	Sáros	Vranov	Slovakia
Protisne, *see* Procisne			
Protyven' [Ru, U]	Máramaros	Chust	Ukraine
Proszács, *see* Prosačov			
Prusiek [P] (Prusik [Ru, U])	Sanok	Krosno	Poland
Prusik, *see* Prusiek			
Pryboržavs'ke [U] (Zadn'oje [Ru]; Zádnya/Zárnya [H])	Máramaros	Iršava	Ukraine
Prybyšiv, *see* Przybyszów			
Pryhid' [U] (Prehud' [Ru])	Máramaros	Tjačiv	Ukraine
Prykopa, *see* Priekopa			
Prykra, *see* Príkra			
Pryslip, Lesko district, *see* Przysłup			
Pryslip, Zemplén county, *see* Príslop			
Pryslip [U] (Pereszlő/Priszlop [H]; Pryslop [Ru])	Máramaros	Mižhirja	Ukraine
Pryslop, Gorlice district, *see* Przysłop			
Pryslop, Zemplén county, *see* Príslop			
Pryslup, Lesko district, *see* Przysłup			
Pryslup, Zemplén county, *see* Príslop			
Prysvip, *see* Przysłóp			
Prytuljany/Prytuljanŷ, *see* Pritul'any			

Village	Former Hungarian county or Galician district	Present administrative subdivision	Present country
Przegonina [P] (Perehonyna [U]; Pregonina [Ru])	Gorlice	Nowy Sącz	Poland
Przybyszów [P] (Prybyšiv [Ru, U])	Sanok	Krosno	Poland
Przysłóp [P] (Pryslop [Ru, U];] Prysvip [Ru])	Gorlice	Nowy Sącz	Poland
Przysłup [P] (Pryslip [U]; Pryslup [Ru])	Lesko	Krosno	Poland
Pstrążne [P] (Pstružne [Ru, U])	Gorlice	Nowy Sącz	Poland
Pstriná [Sv] (Peszternye [H]; Pstryna [Ru, U])	Sáros	Svidník	Slovakia
Pstružne, *see* Pstrążne			
Pstryna, *see* Pstriná			
Puczák, *see* Korunková			
Pudhorod', *see* Podhorod'			
Pudplesza, *see* Pidpleša			
Pudpolócz, *see* Pidpolozzja			
Pulavy/Pulavŷ, *see* Puławy			
Puławy [P] (Povalŷ/Pulavŷ [Ru]; Pulavy [U])	Sanok	Krosno	Poland
Pusztaháza, *see* Korunková			
Pusztamező, *see* Vislanka			
Putkahelmec, *see* Cholmec'			
Puznjakivci [U] (Puznjakovci [Ru]; Puznyákfalva/Szarvasrét [H])	Bereg	Mukačevo	Ukraine
Puznjakovci, *see* Puznjakivci			
Puznyákfalva, *see* Puznjakivci			
Pychni/Pŷchni, *see* Pichne			
Pylypec' [Ru, U] (Filipec/Fülöpfalva/ Pilipec [H])	Máramaros	Mižhirja	Ukraine
Pyskurivci, *see* Piskorovce			
Pytrova, *see* Petrová			
Rabe [P] (Rabe ad Baligród [P]; Rjabe [Ru, U]; Rjabŷ [Ru]; Rjabe k. Balyhorodu [U])	Lesko	Krosno	Poland
Rachiv [U] (Rachov/Rahovo [Ru]; Rahó [H])	Máramaros	Rachiv	Ukraine
Rachov, *see* Rachiv			
Radejeva, *see* Radziejowa			
Radocyna [Ru, P, U]	Gorlice	Nowy Sącz	Poland
Radoskő, *see* Hradisko			
Radošyci, *see* Radoszyce			
Radoszyce [P] (Radošyci [Ru, U])	Sanok	Krosno	Poland
Radvan'-na-Labirci, *see* Radvaň nad Laborcom			
Radvan' nad Labirc'om, *see* Radvaň nad Laborcom			
Radvaň nad Laborcom [Sv]; Radvan'-na-Labirci [U];	Zemplén	Medzilaborce	Slovakia

Village	Former Hungarian county or Galician district	Present administrative subdivision	Present country
Radvan' nad Labirc'om [Ru])			
Radziejowa [P] (Radejeva [U]) (ceased to exist after 1947)	Lesko	Krosno	Poland
Rafajivci, *see* Rafajovce			
Rafajócz, *see* Rafajovce			
Rafajovce [Sv] (Máriakút [H]; Rafajivci [Ru, U]; Rafajócz [H])	Zemplén	Vranov	Slovakia
Rahó, *see* Rachiv			
Rahovo, *see* Rachiv			
Rahoncza, *see* Orichovycja			
Rajs'ke, *see* Rajskie			
Rajskie [P] (Rajs'ke [U])	Lesko	Krosno	Poland
Rakasz, *see* Rokosovo			
Rakivčik/Rakivčyk, *see* Rakovčík			
Rákó, *see* Rakovo			
Rákócz, *see* Rakovčík			
Rákócziszállás, *see* Zavadka, Bereg county			
Rákos, *see* Rakošyno, p. 112			
Rákospatak, *see* Horbky			
Rakošyno, *see* p. 113			
Rakov, *see* Rakovo			
Rakovčík [Sv] (Felsőrákócz [H]; Rakivčik [Ru]; Rakivčyk [U]; Rákócz [H])	Sáros	Svidník	Slovakia
Rakove [U]	Máramaros	Tjačiv	Ukraine
Rakovo [U] (Rákó [H]; Rakov/Turja Rakov [Ru])	Ung	Perečyn	Ukraine
Rászócska, *see* Rosiška			
Ratnavycja, *see* Ratnawica			
Ratnawica [P] (Ratnavycja [Ru, U])	Sanok	Krosno	Poland
Regetiv/Regetiv Nyžnij, *see* Regetów			
Regetiv Vŷšnij/Vyžnij, *see* Regetów Wyżny			
Regetovka [Sv] (Regetivka [Ru, U]; Regettő [H])	Sáros	Bardejov	Slovakia
Regetów [P] (Regetiv [Ru]; Regetów Niżny [P]; Regetiv Nyžnij [U])	Gorlice	Nowy Sącz	Poland
Regetów Wyżny [P] (Regetiv Vŷšnij [Ru]; Regetiv Vyžnij [U]) (ceased to exist after 1947)	Gorlice	Nowy Sącz	Poland
Regettő, *see* Regetovka			
Rekesz, *see* Zadil's'ke			
Rekettye, *see* Rekity			
Rekita, *see* Rekity			
Rekity [U] (Rekettye/Rekita [H]; Rekitŷ [Ru])	Máramaros	Mižhirja	Ukraine
Remeniny [Sv] (Remenynŷ [Ru]; Remenye [H]; Remenyny [U])	Sáros	Vranov	Slovakia
Remenye, *see* Remeniny			
Remenyny/Remenynŷ, *see* Remenye			

Village	Former Hungarian county or Galician district	Present administrative subdivision	Present country
Remete, *see* Remeți			
Remeți [Ro] (Pálosremete/ Remete [H]; Remety [U])	Máramaros	Maramureș	Romania
Remety, *see* Remeți			
Renčišiv, *see* Renčišov			
Renčišov [Sv] (Renčišiv [Ru]; Renčyšiv [U]; Szinyefő [H])	Sáros	Sabinov	Slovakia
Renčyšiv, *see* Renčisov			
Reped', *see* Rzepedź			
Repede, *see* Bystrycja			
Repedea [Ro] (Kryvŷj [Ru]; Oroszkő [H]; Rus'-Kryvyj [U])	Máramaros	Maramureș	Romania
Repejiv, *see* Repejov			
Repejő, *see* Repejov			
Repejov [Sv] (Repejiv [Ru, U]; Repejő [H]; Rjipiv [Ru])	Zemplén	Medzilaborce	Slovakia
Repenye, *see* Repynne			
Repid', *see* Rzepedź			
Repinne, *see* Repynne			
Repit, *see* Rzepedź			
Repynne [U] (Repenye [H]; Repinne [Ru])	Máramaros	Mižhirja	Ukraine
Réső, *see* Rešov			
Rešov [Sv] (Reső [H]; Rjašiv [Ru, U])	Sáros	Bardejov	Slovakia
Rétfalu, *see* Novoselycja, Bereg county			
Révhely, *see* Zabrid'			
Riabe, *see* Karolów			
Rička [Ru, U] (Kispatak/Ricska [H])	Máramaros	Mižhirja	Ukraine
Ricska, *see* Rička			
Ripky/Ripkŷ, *see* Ropki			
Ripnyk, *see* Rzepnik			
Rivne, *see* Rovné			
Rjabe/Rjabŷ, *see* Rabe			
Rjabe k. Balyhorodu, *see* Rabe			
Rjaped, *see* Rjapid', Máramaros county			
Rjapid', Bereg county, *see* Bystrycja			
Rjapid' [U] (Rjaped [Ru])	Máramaros	Chust	Ukraine
Rjašiv, *see* Rešov			
Rjipiv, *see* Repejov			
Rodavka, *see* Bagniste			
Rodnykivka [U] (Beregforrás/Forrás [H]; Izvor [Ru])	Bereg	Svaljava	Ukraine
Rodnykova Huta [U] (Forráshuta/ Izvorhuta [H]; Izvorska Huta [Ru])	Bereg	Svaljava	Ukraine
Rohožník [Sv] (Barátlak [H]; Rohožnyk [Ru, U]; Rohosznyik [H])	Zemplén	Humenné	Slovakia
Rohožnyk, *see* Rohožnik			
Rohosznyik, *see* Rohožnik			
Rókamező, *see* Lysyčovo			
Rókarét, *see* Merešor			

Village	Former Hungarian county or Galician district	Present administrative subdivision	Present country
Rokitó, *see* Rokytov pri Humennom			
Rokitócz, *see* Rokytovce			
Rokosiv/Rokosov, *see* Rokosovo			
Rokosovo [U] (Rakasz [H]; Rokosov [Ru]; Rokosiv [U])	Ugocsa	Chust	Ukraine
Rokŷtiv pry Humennim, *see* Rokytov pri Humennom			
Rokŷtivci, *see* Rokytovce			
Rokytov pri Humennom [Sv] (Rokitó [H]; Rokŷtiv pry Humennim [Ru])	Zemplén	Humenné	Slovakia
Rokytovce [Sv] (Rokitócz [H]; Rokytivci [U]; Rokŷtivci [Ru]), since 1961 part of Krásny Brod			
Romočevycja [Ru, U] (Romocsafalva/ Romocsaháza [H])	Bereg	Mukačevo	Ukraine
Romocsafalva, *see* Romočevycja			
Romocsaháza, *see* Romočevycja			
Róna, *see* Rovné			
Rona de Sus [Ro] (Felsőrona [H]; Vŷšna Runa [Ru]; Vyšnja Rivna/ Rona [U])	Máramaros	Maramureş	Romania
Rónafalu, *see* Žborivci			
Rónafüred, *see* Lumšory			
Rónapolyána, *see* Valea Vişeului			
Ropianka [P] (Ropjanka [Ru, U])	Krosno	Krosno	Poland
Ropica Górna [P] (Ropica Ruska [P]; Ropycja [Ru]; Ropycja Rus'ka [U]; Ruska Ropycja [Ru])	Gorlice	Nowy Sącz	Poland
Ropica Ruska, *see* Ropica Górna			
Ropjanka, *see* Ropianka			
Ropki [P] (Ripky [U]; Ripkŷ [Ru])	Gorlice	Nowy Sącz	Poland
Ropycja/Ropycja Rus'ka, *see* Ropica Górna			
Rosiška [U] (Rászócska [H]; Rozsoška [Ru]; Roszucska [H])	Máramaros	Rachiv	Ukraine
Roškivci, *see* Roškovce			
Roskócs, *see* Roškovce			
Roškovce [Sv] (Roškivci [Ru, U]; Roskócs [H])	Zemplén	Medzilaborce	Slovakia
Rosoš [U] (Kopár/Roszos [H]; Rozsošî [Ru])	Bereg	Svaljava	Ukraine
Rosoš [U]	Máramaros	Tjačiv	Ukraine
Rostajne, *see* Rozstajne			
Rostoka, *see* Roztoka Wielka			
Rostoka Mała, *see* Roztoka Mała			
Rostoka Velyka, *see* Roztoka Wielka			
Rostoka Wielka, *see* Roztoka Wielka			
Rostoki Dolne, *see* Roztoki Dolne			
Rostoki Górne, *see* Roztoki Górne			
Rostokŷ, Lesko district, *see* Roztoka Wielka;			

Village	Former Hungarian county or Galician district	Present administrative subdivision	Present country
Roztoki Dolne			
Rostokŷ, Sáros county *see* Roztoky			
Rostokŷ Horni, *see* Roztoki Górne			
Rostovjatnycja [U]	Bereg	Mukačevo	Ukraine
**Rosvyhovo [U] (Oroszvyhiv [U]; Oroszvég [H]; Rosvigovo [Ru]), since 1945 part of Mukačevo	Bereg	Mukačevo	Ukraine
Roszos, *see* Rosoš, Bereg county			
Rosztoka, Máramaros county, *see* Roztoka, Máramaros county			
Rosztoka, Sáros county, *see* Roztoky			
Rosztoka-Pásztély, *see* Roztoc'ka Pastil'			
Roszucska, *see* Rosiška			
**Rovné [Sv] (Róna [H]; Rivne [U]; Rovno [R, Sv])	Sáros	Svidník	Slovakia
Rozdziele [P] (Rozdilje [Ru, U])	Gorlice	Nowy Sącz	Poland
Rozdilje, *see* Rozdziele			
Rózsadomb, *see* Bodružal'			
Rozsošî, *see* Rosoš, Bereg county			
Rozsoši, *see* Rosoš, Máramaros county			
Rozsoška, *see* Rosiška			
Rozstajne [P] (Rostajne [P, Ru, U])	Jasło	Krosno	Poland
Roztoc'ka Pastil' [Ru, U] (Felsőpásztély/Rosztoka-Pásztély [H])	Ung	Velykyj Bereznyj	Ukraine
Roztoka [Ru, U]	Bereg	Volovec'	Ukraine
Roztoka, Bereg county, Iršava region, *see* Velyka Roztoka			
Roztoka [Ru, U] (Rosztoka [H])	Máramaros	Mižhirja	Ukraine
Roztoka, Ugocsa county, *see* Mala Roztoka			
Roztoka Mała [P] (Rostoka Mala [Ru, U])	Nowy Sącz	Nowy Sącz	Poland
Roztoka Velyka, *see* Roztoka Wielka			
Roztoka Wielka [P] (Rostoka/Rostoka Velyka [Ru]; Rostoka Wielka [P]; Rostokŷ [Ru]; Roztoka Velyka [U])	Nowy Sącz	Nowy Sącz	Poland
Roztoki Dolne [P] (Rostoki Dolne [P]; Rostokŷ [Ru]; Roztoky Dolišni [U])	Lesko	Krosno	Poland
Roztoki Górne [P] (Rostoki Górne [P]; Roztoky Horišne [U]; Rostokŷ Horni [Ru])	Lesko	Krosno	Poland
Roztoky [U] (Nyilas [H])	Máramaros	Rachiv	Ukraine
Roztoky [Sv, U] (Rostokŷ [Ru]; Rosztoka/ Végrosztoka [H])	Sáros	Svidník	Slovakia
Rostokŷ, *see* Rostoki Dolne			
Roztoky Dolišni, *see* Roztoki Dolne			
Rozotky Horišne, *see* Roztoki Górne			
Rudavka, *see* Bagniste; Rudawka Rymanowska			
Rudawka Jaslys'ka, *see* Bagniste			
Rudawka Rymanivs'ka, *see* Rudawka Rymanowska			
Rudawka Jaśliska, *see* Bagniste			

Village	Former Hungarian county or Galician district	Present administrative subdivision	Present country
Rudawka Rymanowska [P] (Rudavka [Ru]; Rudavka Rymanivs'ka [U])	Sanok	Krosno	Poland
Ruginosu [Ro] (Rugyinócz/Ruszinócz [H])	Krassó-Szőrény	Caraş-Severin	Romania
Runi, *see* Runina			
Runina [Sv] (Juhászlak [H]; Runi [Ru]; Runyina [H]; Runyna [Ru, U])	Zemplén	Snina	Slovakia
Runja [Ru, U]	Máramaros	Tjačiv	Ukraine
Runyina/Runyna, *see* Runina			
Rus'-Kryvyj, *see* Repedea			
Rus'-Poljany, *see* Poienile de sub Munte			
Ruscova [Ro] (Ruskovo [Ru, U]; Ruszkova/Visóoroszi [H])	Máramaros	Maramureş	Romania
Ruská Bystrá [Sv] (Oroszbisztra/ Oroszsebes [H]; Rus'ka Bystra [U]; Rus'ka Bŷstra [Ru])	Zemplén	Sobrance	Slovakia
Ruská Kajňa [Sv] (Kajnja [Ru]; Oroszkájnya [H]; Rus'ka Kajnja [Ru, U])	Zemplén	Humenné	Slovakia
Rus'ka Kučava [U] (Oroszkucsova [H]; Ruska Kučova [Ru])	Bereg	Mukačevo	Ukraine
Rus'ka Mokra [U] (Oroszmokra [H]; Ruska Mokra [Ru])	Máramaros	Tjačiv	Ukraine
**Ruská Nová Ves [Sv] (Rus'ka Nova Ves' [Ru]; Sósújfalu [H])	Sáros	Prešov	Slovakia
Ruská Poruba [Sv] (Oroszporuba/ Oroszvágás [H]; Poruba [Ru]; Rus'ka Poruba [Ru, U])	Zemplén	Humenné	Slovakia
Ruska Ropycja, *see* Ropica Górna			
Ruská Vol'a [Sv] (Kisszabados/ Oroszvolya [H]; Rus'ka Volja [Ru, U])	Sáros	Vranov	Slovakia
Ruská Vol'a nad Popradom [Sv] (Oroszvolya/Poprádökrös [H]; Rus'ka Volja [Ru, U])	Sáros	Stará L'ubovňa	Slovakia
Ruská Volová [Sv] (Barkóczháza/ Oroszvolova [H]; Rus'ka Volova [Ru, U])	Zemplén	Snina	Slovakia
Rus'ke [U] (Nagyruszkóc/Orosztelek [H]; Ruskoje [Ru]; Ruszkócz [H])	Bereg	Mukačevo	Ukraine
Rus'ke, Lesko district, *see* Ruskie			
Ruské [Sv] (Oroszruszka [H]; Rus'ke [U]; Rus'kŷj [Ru]; Zemplénoroszi [H]) (ceased to exist in 1980)	Zemplén	Snina	Slovakia
Rus'ke Pole [U] (Ruske Pole [Ru]; Úrmező [H])	Máramaros	Tjačiv	Ukraine
Ruski Kerestur, *see* Ruski Krstur			
Rus'ki Komarivci [U] (Oroszkomoró/ Oroszkomoróc [H]; Ruski Komarovci [Ru])	Ung	Užhorod	Ukraine
Ruski Krstur [SC] (Bácskeresztur [H]; Ruski Kerestur [Ru])	Bács-Bodrog	Vojvodina	Serbia
Ruskie [P] (Rus'ke [Ru, U]) (ceased to exist after 1945)	Lesko	Krosno	Poland

Village	Former Hungarian county or Galician district	Present administrative subdivision	Present country
Ruskoje, *see* Rus'ke			
Ruskovo, *see* Ruscova			
Ruský Hrabovec [Sv] (Hrabovec [Ru]; Nagygereblyés/Oroszhrabócz [H]; Rus'kŷj Hrabovec' [Ru]; Rus'kyj Hrabovec' [U])	Zemplén	Sobrance	Slovakia
*Ruský Kazimír [Sv] (Felsőkázmér [H]; Kazimír [Sv]; Kažmyrovo [Ru]; Oroszkázmér [H]; Rus'kyj Kažymyr [U]; Rus'kŷj Kažymyr [Ru])	Zemplén	Trebišov	Slovakia
Ruský Kručov [Sv] (Felsőkrucsó/ Oroszkrucsó [H]; Rus'kyj Kručiv [U]; Rus'kŷj Kručiv [Ru])	Zemplén	Stropkov	Slovakia
Ruský Potok [Sv] (Oroszpatak [H]; Rus'kŷj Potik [Ru]; Rus'kyj Potik [U]; Rus'kŷj Potuk [Ru])	Zemplén	Snina	Slovakia
Rus'kŷj, *see* Ruské			
Rus'kyj Hrabovec', *see* Ruský Hrabovec			
Rus'kyj Kažymyr, *see* Rusky Kazimír			
Rus'kyj/Rus'kŷj Kručiv, *see* Ruský Kručov			
Rus'kyj Močar [U] (Močar [Ru]; Oroszmocsár [H])	Ung	Velykyj Bereznyj	Ukraine
Rus'kyj Potik, *see* Ruský Potok			
Rus'kŷj Potuk, *see* Ruský Potok			
Ruszinócz, *see* Ruginosu			
Ruszkirva, *see* Repedea			
Ruszkova, *see* Ruscova			
Ruszkócz, *see* Rus'ke			
Ruszpolyána, *see* Poienile de sub Monte			
Ruzsoly, *see* Kružlová			
Rybne [P, U]), now part of Wołkowyja			
Rychvald/Rŷchvald, *see* Owczany			
Rŷchvavt, *see* Owczary			
Rychwałd, *see* Owczary			
Rypit, *see* Rzepedź			
Rzepedź [P] (Reped' [Ru]; Repid' [U]; Repit/Rypit [Ru])	Sanok	Krosno	Poland
Rzepnik [P] (Ripnyk [Ru, U])	Krosno	Krosno	Poland
Sajkásgyörgye, *see* Djurdjevo, p. 111			
Saldoboš, *see* Steblivka			
Šambron [Ru, Sv, U] (Feketekut [H])	Sáros	Stará Ľubovňa	Slovakia
Sándorfalva, *see* Oleksandrivka			
Šandorove, *see* Oleksandrivka			
Šandrovo, *see* Oleksandrivka			
Sanoczek [P] (Sjaničok [Ru, U])	Sanok	Krosno	Poland
Sanok, *see* p. 112			
Šapinec [Ru, Sv] (Sápony [H]; Šapynec' [U]), since 1961 part of Okrúhle	Sáros	Svidník	Slovakia
Sápony, *see* Šapinec			

Village	Former Hungarian county or Galician district	Present administrative subdivision	Present country
Šapynec', *see* Šapinec			
Šarbiv, *see* Šarbov			
Sarbó, *see* Šarbov			
Šarbov [Sv] (Šarbiv [Ru, U]; Sarbó [H])	Sáros	Svidník	Slovakia
Šarišske Čarne, *see* Šarišské Čierné			
Šarišské Čierné [Sv] (Čarno, Čorne [Ru]; Csarnó [H]; Šarišske Čarne [Ru]; Šarys'ke Čorne [U])	Sáros	Bardejov	Slovakia
Šarišské Jastrabie [Sv] (Felsőkanya [H]; Jastrabje [Ru]; Jesztreb [H]; Šaris'ke Jastrabje [Ru]; Šarys'ke Jastrabje [U])	Sáros	Stará L'ubovňa	Slovakia
**Šarišský Štiavnik [Sv] (Šarys'kyj Ščavnyk [U]; Ščavnik [Ru]; Scsavnyik/ Sósfüred [H]; Št'avník [Sv])	Sáros	Svidník	Slovakia
Sarkad/Šarkad', *see* Horbok			
Sárosbukócz, *see* Vel'ke Bukovce			
Sárosdricsna, *see* Vel'ká Driečna			
Sárosgörbény, *see* Krivé			
Sárossztaskócz, *see* Vel'ke Staškovce			
Sárosújlak, *see* Údol			
Sárrét, *see* Kal'nyk			
Šarys'ke Čorne, *see* Šarišské Čierné			
Šarys'ke Jastrabje, *see* Šarišské Jastrabie			
Šarys'kyj Ščavnyk, *see* Šarišský Štiavnik			
Sasivka [U] (Sasovka [Ru]; Szászóka [H])	Bereg	Svaljava	Ukraine
Sasfalva, *see* lrljava			
Sasó, *see* Šašová			
Sasov, *see* Sasovo, Máramaros county			
Šašová [Sv] (Sasó [H]; Šašova [Ru, U])	Sáros	Bardejov	Slovakia
Sasove, *see* Sasovo, Máramaros county; Sasovo, Ugocsa county			
Sasovka, *see* Sasivka			
Sasovo [U] (Sasov [Ru]; Sasove [U])	Máramaros	Tjačiv	Ukraine
Sasovo [Ru, U] (Sasove [U]; Szászfalu/ Tiszaszászfalu [H])	Ugocsa	Vynohradiv	Ukraine
Sasvár, *see* Trosnyk			
Savkivčyk, *see* Sawkowczyk			
Sawkowczyk [P] (Savkivčyk [U]), part of Rajskie			
Scăiuş, *see* p. 112			
Ščaslyve [U] (Serenčovci [Ru]; Szerencsfalva [H])	Bereg	Mukačevo	Ukraine
Ščavne/Ščavnej, *see* Szczawne			
Ščavnik, *see* Šarišský Štiavnik			
Ščavnoj/Ščavnŷj, *see* Szczawne			
Ščavnyk, Nowy Sącz district, *see* Szczawnik			
Ščavnyk, Sanok district, *see* Szczawne			
Ščerbanivka, *see* Szczerbanówka			
Ščerbovec' [U] (Beregsziklás/	Bereg	Volovec'	Ukraine

Village	Former Hungarian county or Galician district	Present administrative subdivision	Present country
Serbócz [H]; Šerbovec' [Ru]; Sziklás [H])			
Scsavnyik, *see* Šarišský Štiavnik			
Sebesfalva, *see* Bystryj, Bereg county			
Šelestove [U] (Šelestovo [Ru]; Seleszto/Szélestó [H]), since 1960 part of Kol'chyno	Bereg	Mukačevo	Ukraine
Šelestovo, *see* Šelestove			
Seleszto, *see* Šelestove			
Šemetkivci, *see* Šemetkovce			
Semetkócz, *see* Šemetkovce			
Šemetkovce [Sv] (Šemetkivci [Ru, U]; Semetkócz/Szemes [H])	Sáros	Svidník	Slovakia
Sen'kova Volja, *see* Wola Sękowa			
Serbócz, *see* Ščerbovec'			
Šerbovec', *see* Ščerbovec'			
Seredne, *see* p. 112			
Seredne Selo, *see* Średnia Wieś			
Seredni/Serednie Wielkie, *see* Średnie Wielkie			
Serednij, *see* Średnia Wieś			
Serednje Selo, *see* Średnia Wieś			
Serednje Velyke, *see* Średnie Wielkie			
Seredn'oje, *see* Seredne, p. 112			
Serenčovci, *see* Ščaslyve			
Sevljuš, *see* Vynohradiv, p. 112			
Sianki [P] (Sjanky [U]) (ceased to exist after 1945)	Turka	Krosno	Poland
Sid/Šid, *see* p. 112			
Sieniawa [P] (Sinjava [U]; Syniv [Ru]; Synjava [U]; Sŷnjava/Sŷn'ova [Ru])	Sanok	Krosno	Poland
Sighetul Marmaţiei, *see* p. 112			
Sigot', *see* Sighetul Marmaţiei, p. 112			
Sil' [U] (Sol'/ [Ru]; Sóslak [H]; Sul' [Ru]; Szolya [H])	Ung	Velykyj Bereznyj	Ukraine
Sil'ce [Ru, U] (Beregkisfalud/ Szilce/Kisfalud [H])	Bereg	Iršava	Ukraine
Simer [Ru, U] (Ószemere [H])	Ung	Perečyn	Ukraine
Simerky [Ru, U] (Újszemere [H])	Ung	Perečyn	Ukraine
Sinjava, *see* Sieniawa			
Sirma, *see* Drotynci			
Sitnyj [U] (Sytnŷj [Ru])	Máramaros	Rachiv	Ukraine
Sjaničok, *see* Sanoczek			
Sjanik, *see* Sanok, p. 112			
Sjanky, *see* Sianki			
Sjurjuk [U] (Surjuk [Ru])	Máramaros	Chust	Ukraine
Skejuš, *see* Scăiuş, p. 112			
Skladyste, *see* Składziste			
Składziste [P] (Skladyste [U]; Svadiste [Ru])	Nowy Sącz	Nowy Sącz	Poland

Village	Former Hungarian county or Galician district	Present administrative subdivision	Present country
Skljarŷ/Škljary, *see* Szklary			
Skotars'ke [U] (Kisszolyva [H]; Skotarskyj [Ru]); Szkotárszka [H])	Bereg	Volovec'	Ukraine
Skotarskyj, *see* Skotars'ke			
Škurativci [U] (Bereghalmos/Halmos/ Skuratócz [H]; Škuratovci [Ru])	Bereg	Mukačevo	Ukraine
Skuratócz, *see* Škurativci			
Škuratovci, *see* Škurativci			
Skvirtne/Skwirtne, *see* Skwierzyn			
Skwierzyn [P] (Skvirtne [Ru, U]; Škvirtne [Ru]; Skwirtne [P])	Gorlice	Nowy Sącz	Poland
Šlachtova, *see* Szlachtowa			
Šljachtova, *see* Szlachtowa			
Sloboda, *see* Svoboda			
Slopovyj [U] (Slopovŷj [Ru])	Máramaros	Chust	Ukraine
Słotwiny [P] (Solotvynŷ [Ru]; Solotvyny [U])	Nowy Sącz	Nowy Sącz	Poland
Slovinky [Sv, U] (Slovinkŷ [Ru])	Szepes	Spišská Nová Ves	Slovakia
Smerečne, *see* Smereczne			
Smereczne [P] (Smerečne [Ru, U]) (ceased to exist after 1947)	Krosno	Krosno	Poland
Smerek [P, Ru, U]	Lesko	Krosno	Poland
Smerekova/Smerekove, *see* Smerekovo			
Smerekovo [U] (Smerekova [Ru]; Smerekove [U]; Szemerekő/ Szmerekova [H])	Ung	Velykyj Bereznyj	Ukraine
Smerekovec', *see* Smerekowiec			
Smerekowiec [P] (Smerekovec [Ru]; Smerekovec' [U])	Gorlice	Nowy Sącz	Poland
Šmigovec [Sv] (Smugócz [H]; Šmŷgovec' [Ru]; Šmyhovec' [U]; Sugó [H])	Zemplén	Snina	Slovakia
Smilnyk/Smil'nyk, *see* Smolnik			
Smolnik [P] (Smilnyk [Ru]; Smil'nyk [U]; Smolnik k. Baligród [P])	Lesko	Krosno	Poland
Smolník [Sv] (Smulnyk [U]; Újszomolnok/ Zemplénszomolnok [H]) (ceased to exist in 1980)	Zemplén	Snina	Slovakia
Smolnik k. Baligród, *see* Smolnik, Lesko district			
Smolohovycja [Ru, U] (Kisábránka [H])	Bereg	Iršava	Ukraine
Smugócz, *see* Šmigovec			
Smulnyk, *see* Smolník			
Šmŷgovec', *see* Šmigovec			
Šmyhovec', *see* Šmigovec			
Snakiv, *see* Snakov			
Snakov [Sv] (Snakiv [Ru, U]; Szánkó [H])	Sáros	Bardejov	Slovakia
Śnietnica [P] (Snitnycja [Ru, U])	Grybów	Nowy Sącz	Poland
Snitnycja, *see* Śnietnica			
Sobatyn [Ru, U] (Szabátin/Szobatin/	Bereg	Iršava	Ukraine

Village	Former Hungarian county or Galician district	Present administrative subdivision	Present country
Szombati [H])			
Soboš [Ru, Sv, U] (Szobos [H])	Sáros	Svidník	Slovakia
Sófalva, *see* Danylovo			
Sóhát, *see* Čornoholova			
Sojmy [U] (Sojmŷ [Ru]; Szolyma/ Vizköz [H])	Máramaros	Mižhirja	Ukraine
Sokoliki Górskie [P] (Sokolyky Hirs'ki [U]) (ceased to exist after 1947)	Turka	Krosno	Poland
Sokolyky Hirs'ki, *see* Sokoliki Górskie			
Sokovata/Sokovate, *see* Sukowate			
Sokyrnycja [Ru, U] (Szeklencze [H])	Mármaros	Chust	Ukraine
Sol, *see* Sil'			
Solina [P] (Solyna [U])	Lesko	Krosno	Poland
Solja, *see* Sil'			
Solinka [P, Ru] (Solynka [Ru, U]) (ceased to exist after 1947)	Lesko	Krosno	Poland
Solník [Sv] (Solnyk [Ru, U]; Szálnik/ Szálnok [H])	Zemplén	Stropkov	Slovakia
Solnyk, *see* Solník			
Soločyn [Ru, U] (Királyfiszállás/ Szolocsina [H])	Bereg	Svaljava	Ukraine
Solone [U] (Solonŷj [Ru])	Mármaros	Tjačiv	Ukraine
Solonŷj, *see* Solone			
Solotvyno, *see* p. 112			
Solotvynskî Kopal'nî, *see* Solotvyno, p. 112			
Solotvyny/Solovynŷ, *see* Słotwiny			
Solyna, *see* Solina			
Solynka, *see* Solinka			
Som/Šoma, *see* Drienica			
Sopky [Ru, U] (Szopkó/Szopkótelep [H])	Máramaros	Mižhirja	Ukraine
Soročin/Soročyn, *see* Stročín			
Sorohiv Dolišnij, *see* Srogów Dolny			
Sorohiv Horišnij, *see* Srogów Górny			
Sorovycja, *see* Surowica			
Sósfalu, *see* Novoselycja, Ugocsa county			
Sósfüred, *see* Šarišsky Štiavnik			
Sósújfalu, see Novoselycja, Ugocsa county; and Ruská Nová Ves			
Sóslak, *see* Sil'			
Średnia Wieś [P] (Seredne Selo/ Serednij [Ru]; Seredne Selo [U])	Lesko	Krosno	Poland
Średnie Wielkie [P] (Seredni [Ru]; Serednie Wielkie [P]; Serednje Velyke [U])	Lesko	Krosno	Poland
Srogów Dolny [P] (Sorohiv Dolišnij [U])	Sanok	Krosno	Poland
Srogów Górny [P] (Sorohiv Horišnij [U])	Sanok	Krosno	Poland
Stakčianska Roztoka [Sv] (Staščyns'ka Roztoka [U]; Staščin'ska Roztoka [Ru]; Sztakcsinrosztoka/Zuhatag [H])	Zemplén	Snina	Slovakia

Village	Former Hungarian county or Galician district	Present administrative subdivision	Present country
Stakčín [Sv] (Staščyn [U]; Staščin [Ru]; Sztakcsin/Takcsány [H])	Zemplén	Snina	Slovakia
Stanove, *see* Stanovo			
Stanovec' [Ru, U]	Máramaros	Chust	Ukraine
Stanovo [Ru, U] (Stanove [U]; Szánfalva/ Sztánfalva [H])	Bereg	Mukačevo	Ukraine
Stara Stužycja [Ru, U] (Patakófalu [H]), now part of Stužycja			
Stare Davydkovo [U] (Dávidháza/ Ódavidháza [H]; Staroje Davydkovo [Ru])	Bereg	Mukačevo	Ukraine
Stari Vrbas, *see* p. 113			
Starina [Sv] (Poprádófalu [H]; Staryna [Ru, U]; Sztarina [H])	Sáros	Stará L'ubovňa	Slovakia
Starina [Sv] (Czirókaófalu [H]; Staryna [Ru, U]; Sztarina [H]) (ceased to exist in 1980)	Zemplén	Snina	Slovakia
Staroje Davydkovo, *see* Stare Davydkovo			
Staryna, *see* Starina, Sáros county; Starina, Zemplén county			
Staščyn, *see* Stakčín			
Staščyns'ka Roztoka, *see* Stakčianska Roztoka			
Stašinska Rostoka, *see* Stakčianska Roztoka			
Staškivci, *see* Staškovce			
Staškovce [Sv] (Staškivci [Ru, U]; Sztaskócz [H])	Zemplén	Stropkov	Slovakia
Stašyn, *see* Stakčín			
Stavne [U] (Fenyvesvőlgy [H]; Stavnoje [Ru]; Sztavna [H])	Ung	Velykyj Bereznyj	Ukraine
Šťavník, *see* Sarišský Štiavnik			
Stavnoje, *see* Stavne			
Stavyša, *see* Stawisza			
Stawisza [P] (Stavyša [Ru, U])	Grybów	Nowy Sącz	Poland
Steblivka [U] (Saldoboš [Ru]; Száldobos [H])	Máramaros	Chust	Ukraine
Stebník [Sv] (Esztebnek [H]; Stebnyk [Ru, U]; Sztebnek [H])	Sáros	Bardejov	Slovakia
Stebnyk, *see* Stebník			
Štefuriv, *see* Štefurov			
Štefurov [Sv] (Istvánd [H]; Štefuriv [Ru, U])	Sáros	Svidník	Slovakia
Štel'bach, *see* Tichý Potok			
Sterkivci, *see* Sterkovce			
Sterkócz, *see* Sterkove			
Sterkovce [Sv] (Sterkivci [Ru, U]; Sterkócz [H]), part of Čabalovce			
Stężnica [P] (Stežnycja [U]; Stýžnycja [Ru])	Lesko	Krosno	Poland
Stežnycja, *see* Stężnica			

Village	Former Hungarian county or Galician district	Present administrative subdivision	Present country
Storoži Mali, *see* Stróże Małe			
Storoži Velyki, *see* Stróże Wielkie			
**Storožnycja [U] (Jovra [Ru]; Ŏdarma [H])	Ung	Uzhhorod	Ukraine
Storožŷ, *see* Stróże Małe			
Storožŷ Velykŷ, *see* Stróże Wielkie			
Stotince [Sv] (Hodermark [H, Ru]; Stotynci [U]), since 1960 part of Ihl'hany			
Strabyčove, *see* Strabyčovo			
Strabyčovo [U] (Mezőterebes [H]; Strabyčove [U]; Sztrabicsó/Terebes [H])	Bereg	Mukačevo	Ukraine
Stráňany [Sv] (Folvark [Sv]; Fol'vark [Ru]; Folyvárk/Nagymajor [H]; Stranjanŷ [Ru]; Stranjany [U])	Szepes	Stará L'ubovňa	Slovakia
Stranjany, *see* Stráňany			
Strihovce [Sv] (Stryhovec' [Ru, U]; Szirtes/Sztriocz [H])	Zemplén	Snina	Slovakia
Strîmba, *see* Strymba			
Stročín [Sv] (Soročin [Ru]; Soročyn [U]; Szorocsány [H])	Sáros	Svidník	Slovakia
Strojne [U] (Malmos [H]; Strojno [Ru]; Sztrojna [H])	Bereg	Svaljava	Ukraine
Strojno, *see* Strojne			
Stróże Male [P] (Storoži Mali [U]; Storožŷ [Ru])	Sanok	Krosno	Poland
Stróże Wielke [P] (Storoži Velyki [U]; Storožŷ Velykŷ [Ru]) (ceased to exist after 1947)	Sanok	Krosno	Poland
Strubowiska [P] (Strubovyska [Ru, U])	Lesko	Krosno	Poland
Stružnica/Štružnycja, *see* Ostrožnica			
Stryčava [Ru, U] (Eszterág/Sztricsava [H])	Ung	Velykyj Bereznyj	Ukraine
Stryhal'nja [U] (Fenyves/Fenvestelep [H]; Stryhal'ni [Ru]; Sztrihánya [H])	Máramaros	Mižhirja	Ukraine
Stryhovec', *see* Strihovce			
Strymba [U] (Strîmba [Ru])	Máramaros	Rachiv	Ukraine
Strypa [Ru, U] (Sztrippa [H])	Ung	Užhorod	Ukraine
Studenne [P, U] (ceased to exist after 1947)	Lesko	Krosno	Poland
Studenyj Potik, *see* Nyžnij Studenyj			
Stuposiany [P] (Stuposjany [U]) (ceased to exist after 1945)	Lesko	Krosno	Poland
Stužycja [U]	Ung	Velykyj Bereznyj	Ukraine
Stŷžnycja, *see* Stężnica			
Suchá [Sv] (Sucha [Ru, U]; Szárazhegy/ Szuha [H]), since 1961 part of Vladiča			
Sucha [Ru, U] (Szucha-Bronyka/Szuha [H])	Máramaros	Iršava	Ukraine
Suchyj [Ru, U] (Szarazpatak [H])	Máramaros	Mižhirja	Ukraine
Suchyj [U] (Suchŷj [Ru]; Szucha/ Szuhapatak/Ungszuha [H])	Ung	Velykyj Bereznyj	Ukraine

Village	Former Hungarian county or Galician district	Present administrative subdivision	Present country
Sugó, *see* Šmigovec			
Sukiv, *see* Sukov			
Sukov [Sv] (Sukiv [Ru, U]; Szukó [H])	Zemplén	Medzilaborce	Slovakia
Sukovate, *see* Sukowate			
Sukowate [P] (Sokovata/Sokovate [Ru]; Sukovate [U]) (ceased to exist after 1947)	Lesko	Krosno	Poland
Sul', *see* Sil'			
Sulín [Sv] (Sulyn [Ru, U])	Szepes	Stará L'ubovňa	Slovakia
Sulyn, *see* Sulín			
Surjuk, *see* Sjurjuk			
Surovycja, *see* Surowica			
Surowica [P] (Sorovycja [Ru]; Surovycja [U]; Syrovycja [Ru, U]) (ceased to exist after 1947)	Sanok	Krosno	Poland
Suskove, *see* Suskovo			
Suskovo [Ru, U] (Bányafalu [H]; Suskove [U]; Szuszka [H])	Bereg	Svaljava	Ukraine
Svadiste, *see* Składziste			
*Svaljava [Ru, U] (Szolyva [H])	Bereg	Svaljava	Ukraine
Svaljavka [Ru, U] (Szvalyavka [H])	Ung	Perečyn	Ukraine
Svetlice [Sv] (Svetlici [Ru]; Svetlyci [U]; Világ [H]; Világy [Sv]; Vylagŷ [Ru])	Zemplén	Medzilaborce	Slovakia
Svetlici/Svetlyci, *see* Svetlice			
Svidnička [Sv] (Kisfagyalos [H]; Svidnyčka [Ru]; Svydnyčka [U]; Szvidnicska [H])	Sáros	Svidník	Slovakia
Svidník [Sv] (Svidnyk [Ru]; Svydnyk [U])	Sáros	Svidník	Slovakia
Svidnyčka, *see* Svidnička			
Svidnyk, *see* Svidník			
Sviržova, *see* Świerżowa Ruśka			
Sviržova Rus'ka, *see* Świerżowa Ruśka			
Svjatkivka, *see* Świątkowa Mała			
Svjatkova Mala, *see* Świątkowa Mała			
Svjatkova/Svjatkova Velyka, *see* Świątkowa Wielka			
Svoboda [U] (Sloboda [Ru]; Szloboda/ Szvoboda [H])	Máramaros	Mižhirja	Ukraine
Svydnyčka, *see* Svidnička			
Svydnyk, *see* Svidník			
Światkowa Mała [P] (Svjatkivka [Ru]; Svjatkova Mala [Ru, U])	Jasło	Krosno	Poland
Świątkowa Wielka [P] (Svjatkova [Ru]; Svjatkova Velyka [Ru, U])	Jasło	Krosno	Poland
Świerżowa Ruśka [P] (Sviržova/ Sviržova Ruska [Ru]; Sviržova Rus'ka [U]) (ceased to exist after 1947)	Jaslo	Krosno	Poland
Syhit', *see* Sighetul Marmaţiei, p. 112			

Village	Former Hungarian county or Galician district	Present administrative subdivision	Present country
Synevyr [U] (Alsószinevér [H]; Synŷvyr [Ru]; Szinevér [H])	Máramaros	Mižhirja	Ukraine
Synevyrs'ka Poljana [U] (Felsőszinevér/Szinevér-Polyana [H]; Vŷšnŷj Synŷvyr [Ru])	Máramaros	Mižhirja	Ukraine
Syniv, *see* Sieniawa			
Synjava/Sŷn'ova, *see* Sieniawa			
Synŷvyr, *see* Synevyr			
Šyroke [U] (Šyrokyj [Ru])	Máramaros	Chust	Ukraine
Šyroke [U] (Felsőárad [H]; Vŷšnŷj Šard [Ru])	Ugocsa	Vynohradiv	Ukraine
Šyrokyj, *see* Šyroke			
Šyrokyj Luh [Ru, U] (Széleslonka [H])	Máramaros	Tjačiv	Ukraine
Syrovycja, *see* Surowica			
Sytnŷj, *see* Sitnyj			
Szabátin, *see* Sobatyn			
Szajkófalva, *see* Osij			
Száldobos, *see* Steblivka			
Szállás, *see* Lischovec'			
Szálnik, *see* Solník			
Szálnok, *see* Solník			
Szánfalva, *see* Stanovo			
Szánkó, *see* Snakov			
Szárazhegy, *see* Suchá			
Szarazpatak, see Suchyj, Máramaros county			
Szarvasháza, *see* Ždenijevo			
Szarvaskút, *see* Olen'ovo			
Szarvasrét, *see* Puznjakivci			
Szászfalu, *see* Sasovo, Ugocsa county			
Szászóka, *see* Sasivka			
Száztelek, *see* Ihl'hany			
Szczawne [P] (Ščavne [U]; Ščavnej/ Ščavnoj/Ščavnŷj [Ru]; Ščavnyk [U])	Sanok	Krosno	Poland
Szczawnik [P] (Ščavnyk [Ru, U])	Nowy Sącz	Nowy Sącz	Poland
Szczerbanówka [P] (Ščerbanivka [Ru, U]) (ceased to exist after 1947)	Lesko	Krosno	Poland
Szécs-Tarnoka, *see* Trnvávka			
Szedreske, *see* Ostrožnica			
Szeklencze, *see* Sokyrnycja			
Széleslonka, *see* Šyrokyj Luh			
Szélestó, *see* Šelestove			
Szemerekő, *see* Smerekovo			
Szemes, *see* Šemetkovce			
Szénástelek, *see* Zavosyno			
Szentmihalykörtvélyes, *see* Hrušovo			
Szentmiklós, *see* Čynadijovo			
Szepesjakabfalva, *see* Jakubany			
Szerednye, *see* Seredne, p. 112			
Szerencsfalva, *see* Ščaslyve			

Village	Former Hungarian county or Galician district	Present administrative subdivision	Present country
Szidorfalva, *see* Hrabovo			
Sziklás, *see* Ščerbovec'			
Szilce, *see* Sil'ce			
Szilvás, *see* Kuz'myno			
Szinevér, *see* Synevyr			
Szinevér-Polyana, *see* Synevyrs'ka Poljana			
Szinnamező, Zemplén county, *see* Nechválova Polianka			
Szinyefő, *see* Renčišov			
Szirma, *see* Drotynci			
Szirtes, *see* Strihovce			
Szkejus, *see* Scăiuş, p. 112			
Szklary [P] (Skljarŷ/Škljarŷ [Ru]; Škljary [U])	Sanok	Krosno	Poland
Szlachtowa [P] (Šlachtova [Ru]; Šljachtova [U])	Nowy Targ	Nowy Sącz	Poland
Szloboda, *see* Svoboda			
Szmerekova, *see* Smerekovo			
Szobatin, *see* Sobatyn			
Szobos, *see* Soboš			
Szőllősegres, *see* Olešnyk			
Szőllősrosztoka, *see* Mala Roztoka			
Szőllősvégardó, *see* Pidvynohradiv			
Szolocsina, *see* Soločyn			
Szolya, *see* Sil'			
Szolyma, *see* Sojmy			
Szolyva, *see* Svaljava			
Szombati, *see* Sobatyn			
Szopkó/Szopkótelep, *see* Sopky			
Szorocsány, *see* Stročín			
Sztakcsin, *see* Stakčín			
Sztakcsinrosztoka, *see* Stakčianska Roztoka			
Sztánfalva, *see* Stanovo			
Sztarina, *see* Starina, Szepes county, and Zemplén county			
Sztaskócz, *see* Staškovce			
Sztavna, *see* Stavne			
Sztebnik, *see* Stebník			
Sztrabicsó, *see* Strabyčovo			
Sztricsava, *see* Stryčava			
Sztriócz, *see* Strihovco			
Sztrihánya, *see* Stryhal'nja			
Sztriócz, *see* Strihovce			
Sztrippa, *see* Strypa			
Sztrojna, *see* Strojne			
Sztropkóbisztra, *see* Bystrá			
Sztropkóhrabócz, *see* Vyšný Hrabovec			
Sztropkóolyka, *see* Ol'ka			
Sztropkópolena, *see* Malá Pol'ana			

Village	Former Hungarian county or Galician district	Present administrative subdivision	Present country
Szucha, *see* Suchyj			
Szucha-Bronyka, *see* Suchyj			
Szuha, *see* Suchá and Sucha			
Szuhabaranka, *see* Bron'ka			
Szuhapatak, *see* Suchyj			
Szukó, *see* Sukov			
Szulin, *see* Malý Sulín			
Szuszka, *see* Suskovo			
Szvalyavka, *see* Svaljavka			
Szvidnicska, *see* Svidnička			
Szvoboda, *see* Svoboda			
Szybistów [P] (Dudyńce [P]; Dudynci [Ru, U])	Sanok	Krosno	Poland
Takcsány, *see* Stakčín			
Talaborfalu, *see* Tereblja			
Tapolylippó, *see* Lipová			
Taraczkőz, *see* Teresva			
Taraczkraszna, *see* Krasna			
Taraczújfalu, *see* Novoselycja, Máramaros county, Mižhirja rajon			
Tarasivka [U] (Tereselpatak [H]; Teresova, Terešul [Ru])	Máramaros	Tjačiv	Ukraine
Tárcafő, *see* Torysky, p. 113			
Tarfalu, *see* Holjatyn			
Tarna, Ugocsa county, *see* Chyža			
Tarna, Zemplén county, *see* Trnava pri Laborci			
Tarnava, *see* Trnava pri Laborci			
Tarnavka, *see* Trnávka			
Tarnawa Niżna [P] (Nyžnja Tarnava [U])	Turka	Krosno	Poland
Tarnawa Wyżnia [P] (Vyšnja Tarnava [U]) (ceased to exist after 1947)	Turka	Krosno	Poland
Tarnawka [P] (Ternavka [Ru, U]) (ceased to exist after 1947)	Sanok	Krosno	Poland
Tarnkiv, *see* Trnkov			
Tarnóka, *see* Trnávka			
Tarújfalu, *see* Novoselycja, Máramaros county, Tjačiv rajon			
Técső, *see* Tjačiv, p. 113			
Telepivci, *see* Osadné			
Telepócz, *see* Osadné			
Telepovce, *see* Osadné			
Telova, *see* Tylawa			
Terebes, *see* Strabyčovo			
Terebesfejérpatak, *see* Dilove, Máramaros county			

Village	Former Hungarian county or Galician district	Present administrative subdivision	Present country
Tereblja [Ru, U] (Talaborfalu [H])	Máramaros	Tjačiv	Ukraine
Terepča, *see* Trepcza			
Tereselpatak, *see* Tarasivka			
Teresova/Terešul, *see* Tarasivka			
Teresva [Ru, U] (Taraczkőz [H])	Máramaros	Tjačiv	Ukraine
Terka [P, U]	Lesko	Krosno	Poland
Ternavka, Sanok county, *see* Tarnawka			
Ternavka, Zemplén county, *see* Trnávka			
Ternova/Ternove, *see* Ternovo			
Ternovo [U] (Kökényes/Ternova [H]; Ternove [U]; Ternovo nad Teresvoju [Ru])	Máramaros	Tjačiv	Ukraine
Ternovo nad Teresvoju, *see* Ternovo			
Terscjana/Terstjana, *see* Trzciana			
Tichý Potok [Sv] (Csendespatak [H]; Štel'bach [Ru]; Tychyj Potik [U]; Tychŷj Potik [Ru])	Sáros	Sabinov	Slovakia
Tibaváralja, *see* Podhorod'			
Ticha, *see* Tychyj			
Tiha, *see* Tychyj			
Timsor, *see* Lazy			
Tisa, *see* p. 113			
Tisna, *see* Cisna			
Tisova, *see* Tyšiv			
Tiszabogdány, *see* Bohdan			
Tiszaborkút, *see* Kvasy			
Tiszacsoma, *see* Čoma			
Tiszahetény, *see* Hetynja			
Tiszakarácsonyfalva, *see* Crăciuneşti, p. 111			
Tiszakirva, *see* Kryva			
Tiszasasvár, *see* Trosnyk			
Tiszaszászfalu, *see* Sasovo, Ugocsa county			
Tiszaszirma, *see* Drotynci			
Tiszaveresmart, *see* Tisa, p. 113			
Titkivci [U] (Tîtkovci [Ru]; Titokvölgy [H])	Máramaros	Mižhirja	Ukraine
Tîtkovci/Titokvölgy, *see* Titkivci			
Tjačiv, *see* p. 113			
Tjačovo, *see* Tjačiv, p. 113			
Tjuška [Ru, U] (Csuszka/Tyuska [H])	Máramaros	Mižhirja	Ukraine
Tócska, *see* Zaverchna Kyčera			
Tokajík [Sv] (Felsőtokaj/Orosztokaj [H]; Tokajik [Ru, U])	Zemplén	Stropkov	Slovakia
Tokarnia [P] (Tokarnja [Ru, U])	Sanok	Krosno	Poland
Tokarnja, *see* Tokarnia			
Tökesfalu, *see* Kolodne, Bereg county			
Tölgyes, *see* Dibrivka, Ung county			
Tölgyeshegy, *see* Zubné			
Topol'a [Sv] (Kistopolya [H]; Topolja [Ru, U])	Zemplén	Snina	Slovakia

Village	Former Hungarian county or Galician district	Present administrative subdivision	Present country
Topolja, *see* Topol'a			
Topolyn [Ru, U]	Máramaros	Chust	Ukraine
Toriszka, *see* Torysky, p. 113			
Torun' [U] (Toronya [H]; Torun [Ru])	Máramaros	Mižhirja	Ukraine
Toronya, *see* Torun'			
Torysky, *see* p. 113			
Tovčka, *see* Zaverchna Kyčera			
Trebušany, *see* Dilove			
Trepča, *see* Trepcza			
Trepcza [P] (Terepča/Trepča [Ru, U])	Sanok	Krosno	Poland
Trnava pri Laborci [Sv] (Tarna [H]; Tarnava [U])	Ung	Michalovce	Slovakia
**Trnávka [Sv] (Szécs-Tarnoka [H]; Tarnavka [U]; Tarnóka [H]; Ternavka [H])	Zemplén	Trebišov	Slovakia
**Trnkov [Sv] (Kiskökény/Kökény [H]; Kokyňa [Sv]; Tarnkiv [U])	Sáros	Prešov	Slovakia
*Trosnyk [U] (Sasvár/Tiszasasvár [H]; Trostnyk [Ru])	Ugocsa	Vynohradiv	Ukraine
Trostjanec' [Ru, U]	Máramaros	Rachiv	Ukraine
Trostjanycja [U] (Nádaspatak/ Trosztyanica [H])	Bereg	Mukačevo	Ukraine
Trostnyk, *see* Trosnyk			
Trosztyanica, *see* Trostnyk			
Trzciana [P] (Terscjana [Ru]; Terstjana [U]; Tŷrscjana [Ru])	Krosno	Krosno	Poland
Turjabisztra, *see* Turja-Bystra			
Turja-Bystra [U] (Turja Bŷstrŷj [Ru]; Turjabisztra/Turjasebes [H])	Ung	Perečyn	Ukraine
Turja Bŷstrŷj, *see* Turja Bystra			
Turjamező, *see* Turji-Poljana			
Turja-Pasika [Ru, U] (Turjapaszika/ Turjavágás [H])	Ung	Perečyn	Ukraine
Turjapaszika, *see* Turja-Pasika			
Turjapolena, *see* Turja-Poljana			
Turja-Poljana [Ru, U] (Turjamező/ Turjapolena [H])	Ung	Perečyn	Ukraine
Turja Rakov, *see* Rakovo			
Turja Remeta, *see* Turji Remety			
Turjaremete, *see* Turji-Remety			
Turjasebes, *see* Turja-Bystra			
Turjavágás, *see* Turja-Pasika			
Turji-Remety [U] (Turja Remeta [Ru]; Turjaremete [H])	Ung	Perečyn	Ukraine
Turycja [Ru, U] (Nagyturica/ Nagyturjaszög [H];Velyka Turycja [Ru])	Ung	Perečyn	Ukraine
Turyčky [Ru, U] (Kisturica/ Kisturjaszög [H])	Ung	Perečyn	Ukraine
Turyns'ke, *see* Turzańsk			

Village	Former Hungarian county or Galician district	Present administrative subdivision	Present country
Turzańsk [P] (Turyns'ke [U])	Sanok	Krosno	Poland
Tüskés, *see* Pichne			
Tvoryl'ne, *see* Tworylne			
Tworylne [P] (Tvoryl'ne [U]) (ceased to exist after 1947)	Lesko	Krosno	Poland
Tybava [U] (Havasalja [H]; Tŷbava [Ru])	Bereg	Svaljava	Ukraine
Tychanja, *see* Ciechania			
Tychyj [U] (Ticha/Tiha [H]; Tychŷj [Ru])	Ung	Velykyj Bereznyj	Ukraine
Tychyj/Tychŷj Potik, *see* Tichý Potok			
Tylawa [P] (Telova/Tŷljava [Ru]; Tyljava [U];Tŷlova [Ru])	Krosno	Krosno	Poland
Tylicz [P, Ru] (Tŷlyč [Ru]; Tylyč [U])	Nowy Sącz	Nowy Sącz	Poland
Tyljava, *see* Tylawa			
Tŷlova, *see* Tylawa			
Tylyč, *see* Tylicz			
Tyrscjana, *see* Trzciana			
Tyšiv [U] (Csendes/Tisova [H]; Tyšov [Ru])	Bereg	Volovec'	Ukraine
Tyskivec', *see* Cisowiec			
Tysolove, *see* Tysolovo			
Tysolovo [Ru, U] (Tysolove [U])	Máramaros	Tjačiv	Ukraine
Tyšov, *see* Tyšiv			
Tyskova, *see* Tyskowa			
Tysovec, *see* Cisowiec			
Tyskowa [P] (Tyskova [U]) (ceased to exist after 1947)	Lesko	Krosno	Poland
Tyuska, *see* Tjuška			
Ubl'a [Sv] (Ublja [Ru, U]; Ugar [H]; Vublja [Ru])	Zemplén	Snina	Slovakia
Ublja, *see* Ubl'a			
Údol [Ru, Sv] (Sárosújlak [H]; Udol' [U]; Ujak [Ru, Sv]; Uják [H])	Sáros	Stará L'ubovňa	Slovakia
Ugar, *see* Ubl'a			
Uglja/Uglya, *see* Uhlja			
Ugocsa-Rosztoka, *see* Mala Roztoka			
Uh, *see* Łuh			
Uhlja [U] (Uglja [Ru]; Uglya [H])	Máramaros	Tjačiv	Ukraine
Uhryń [P] (Uhryn [Ru, U])	Nowy Sącz	Nowy Sącz	Poland
Ujak/Uják, *see* Údol			
Újbajna, *see* Vyšné Zbojné			
Újbárd, *see* Novobarovo			
Újdávidháza, *see* Nove Davydkovo			
Ujholyátin, *see* Novoselycja, Máramaros county, Tjačiv rajon			
Újkemencze, *see* Novoselycja, Ung county			
Újrosztoka, *see* Nova Roztoka			
Ujsztuzsica, *see* Nova Stužycja			

Village	Former Hungarian county or Galician district	Present administrative subdivision	Present country
Újszék, *see* Nová Sedlica			
Újszemere, *see* Simerky			
Újszomolnok, *see* Smolník			
Uklina, *see* Uklyn			
Uklyn [Ru, U] (Aklos/Uklina [H])	Bereg	Svaljava	Ukraine
Ulič [Ru, Sv] (Ulics [H]; Ulyč [U]; Utczás [H]; Vulŷč [Ru])	Zemplén	Snina	Slovakia
Ulič-Kryve, *see* Uličské Krivé			
Ulics, *see* Ulič			
Ulicskriva, *see* Uličské Krivé			
Uličské Krivé [Sv] (Görbeszeg [H]; Kryve/Kryvŷj [Ru]; Ulič-Kryve [Ru]; Ulicskriva [H]; Ulyčs'ke-Kryve [U])	Zemplén	Snina	Slovakia
Ulyč, *see* Ulič			
Ulyčs'ke Kryve, *see* Uličské Krivé			
Ungbükkös, *see* Bukivceve			
Ungcsertész, *see* Čertež, Ung county			
Ungdarócz, *see* Dravci			
Unggesztenyés, *see* Linci			
Unghosszúmező, *see* Dovhe Pole			
Ungludás, *see* Husák			
Unglovasd, *see* Koňuš			
Ungordas, *see* Vovkove			
Ungpéteri, *see* Petrovce			
Ungsasfalva, *see* Irljava			
Ungszuha, *see* Suchyj			
Ungtölgyes, *see* Dubrivka, Ung county			
Ungvár, *see* Užhorod, p. 113			
Úrmező, *see* Rus'ke Pole			
Uście Gorlickie [P] (Uście Ruskie [P]; Ustje/Uscja/Uscjo Ruskje [Ru]; Ustje Rus'ke [U])	Gorlice	Nowy Sącz	Poland
Uście/Uscja/Uscjo Ruskie, *see* Uście Gorlickie			
Uslavycja, *see* Osławica			
Ustje Rus'ke, *see* Uście Gorlickie			
Ustrzyki Górne [P] (Ustryky Horišni [U])	Lesko	Krosno	Poland
Ustryky Horišni, *see* Ustrzyki Górne			
Utczás, *see* Ulič			
Užhorod, *see* p. 113			
Užok [Ru, U] (Uzsok [H])	Ung	Velykyj Bereznyj	Ukraine
Uzsok, *see* Užok			
Vabova, *see* Łabowa			
Vabovec, *see* Łabowiec			
Vadas, *see* Dyskovycja			
Vadászfalva, *see* Beňatina			
Vafka, *see* Wawrzka			
Văgaș [Ro] (Vagaš [Ru]; Vágás/ Vágástanya [H])	Ugocsa	Satu Mare	Romania

Village	Former Hungarian county or Galician district	Present administrative subdivision	Present country
Vagrinec [Sv] (Felsővargony [H]; Vagrynec [Ru]; Vagrynec' [U])	Sáros	Svidník	Slovakia
Vagrynec', *see* Vagrinec			
Vajkvágása, *see* Valkovce			
Vajnág, *see* Vonihovo			
Valaskócz, *see* Valaškovce			
Valaškovce [Sv] (Pásztorhegy/Valaskócz [H]; Valaškuvci/Valjaškuvci [Ru]; Valjaškivci [U]; Valyasboc [H])	Zemplén	Humenné	Slovakia
Valaškuvci, *see* Valaškovce			
Valea Vişeului [Ro] (Visóvölgy [H]; Vyšavs'ka Dolyna [U]; Vyšovs'ka Dolyna [Ru])	Máramaros	Vişeu	Romania
Valentivci, *see* Valentovce			
Valentócz, *see* Valentovce			
Valentovce [Sv], (Valentivci [Ru]; Valentócz [H]), between 1880 and 1930 part of Zbudská Belá	Zemplén	Medzilaborce	Slovakia
Valjaškivci/Valjaškuvci, *see* Valaškovce			
Valkaja, *see* Vovkove			
Val'kiv, *see* Valkov			
Valkivci, *see* Valkovce			
Valkó, *see* Valkov			
Valkov [Sv] (Kisvalkó [H]; Val'kiv [Ru, U]; Valkó [H]) (ceased to exist after 1965)	Zemplén	Svidník	Slovakia
Valkovce [Sv] (Vajkvágása [H]; Val'kivci [U]; Válykócz [H])	Sáros	Svidník	Slovakia
Valyasboc, *see* Valaškovce			
Válykócz, *see* Valkovce			
Vanivka, *see* Węglówka			
Vápeník [Sv] (Mészégető [H]; Vapenyk [U])	Sáros	Svidník	Slovakia
Vapenne, *see* Wapienne			
Vapenyk, *see* Vápeník			
Váradka [Sv] (Varadka [Ru, U])	Sáros	Bardejov	Slovakia
Váralja, *see* Pidhorod; Podhorod'			
Varechivci, *see* Varechovce			
Varechovce [Sv] (Varechivci [Ru, U]; Varehócz/Variháza [H])	Zemplén	Stropkov	Slovakia
Varehócz, *see* Varechovce			
Variháza, *see* Varechovce			
Várkulcsa, *see* Ključarky			
Vavrincz, *see* Vavrinec			
Vavrinec [Sv] (Lőrinczvágása/ Vavrincz [H]; Vavrinec' [Ru]; Vavrynec' [U])	Zemplén	Vranov	Slovakia
Vavrynec', *see* Vavrinec			
Végardó, *see* Pidvynohradiv			

Village	Former Hungarian county or Galician district	Present administrative subdivision	Present country
Végaszó, *see* Kolbasov			
Végcsarnó, *see* Krajné Čierno			
Végmártonka, *see* Krajnja Martynka			
Végortovány, *see* Krajná Porúbka			
Végpetri, *see* Petrová			
Végrosztoka, *see* Roztoky, Sáros county			
Veléte, *see* Veljatyno			
Velikij Ruskov, *see* Vel'ký Ruskov			
Veljatyno [U] (Veléte [H]; Veljatyn [Ru])	Ugocsa	Chust	Ukraine
Vel'ká Driečna [Sv] (Nagyderencs/ Sárosdricsna [H]; Velyka Drična [Ru, U], since 1960 part of Vladiča			
Vel'ká Pol'ana [Sv] (Nagypolány [H]; Velyka Poljana [Ru]; Velyki Poljany [U]) (ceased to exist in 1980)	Zemplén	Snina	Slovakia
Vel'ké Bukovce [Sv] (Nagybukócz/ Sárosbukócz [H]; Velykŷj Bukovec [Ru]; Velykyj Bukovec' [U]), since 1964 part of Bukovce			
Vel'ké Staškovce [Sv] (Nagytavas/ Sárossztaskócz [H]; Velyki Staškivci [U]; Velykŷ Staškivci [Ru]), part of Staškovce			
Velkő, *see* Vel'krop			
Vel'krop [Sv] (Bekrip [Ru]; Velkő [H]; Vel'krip [U])	Zemplén	Stropkov	Slovakia
Vel'ký Lipník [Sv] (Nagyhársas/ Nagylipnik [H]; Velykŷj Lypnyk [Ru]; Velykyj Lypnyk [U])	Szepes	Stará L'ubovňa	Slovakia
**Vel'ky Ruskov [Sv] (Nagyruszka [H]; Velikij Ruskov [Ru]), since 1964 part of Nový Ruskov	Zemplén	Trebišov	Slovakia
Vel'ký Sulín [Sv] (Nagyszulin [H]; Vel'kŷj Sulyn [Ru]; Velykyj Sulyn [U]), since 1961 part of Sulín			
Vel'kŷj Sulin, *see* Vel'ký Sulín			
Velšnja, *see* Wilsznia			
Velyka Čengava/Velyka Čynhava, *see* Boržavs'ke			
Velyka Drična, *see* Vel'ka Driečna			
Velyka Lunka [Ru], now part of Lunka			
Velyka Kopanja [Ru, U] (Felsőveresmart [H])	Ugocsa	Vynohradiv	Ukraine
Velyka Poljana, *see* Vel'ká Pol'ana			
Velyka Roztoka [U] (Beregrosztoka/ Gázló [H]; Roztoka [Ru])	Bereg	Iršava	Ukraine
Velyka Turycja, *see* Turycja			
Velyka Uhol'ka [Ru, U] (Nagyugolyka/ Nagyugnlyavölgy [H])	Máramaros	Tjačiv	Ukraine

Village	Former Hungarian county or Galician district	Present administrative subdivision	Present country
Velykopole, *see* Wielopole			
Velyki Komjaty [U] (Komját/Magyar-komját/Nagykomját [H]; Velykî Komnjata [Ru])	Ugocsa	Vynohradiv	Ukraine
Velyki Lazy [U] (Nagyláz [H]; Velyki Lazŷ [Ru])	Ung	Užhorod	Ukraine
Velyki Lučky [Ru, U] (Nagylucska [H])	Bereg	Mukačevo	Ukraine
Velyki Poljany, *see* Vel'ka Pol'ana			
Velyki Staškivci, *see* Vel'ke Staškovce			
Velykŷ Poljanŷ/Velyky Poljany, *see* Vel'ka Pol'ana			
Velykŷ Staškivci, *see* Vel'ke Staškovce			
Velykyj Bereznyj, *see* p. 113			
Velykyj Bočkov, *see* Bocicoiu Mare; Velykyj Byčkiv			
Velykyj Byčkiv [U] (Nagybocskó [H]; Velykyj Bočkov [Ru])	Máramaros	Rachiv	Ukraine
Velykŷj Lypnyk, *see* Vel'ký Lipník			
Velykyj Pereg, *see* Peregu Mare, p. 112			
Velykyj Rakovec' [Ru, U] (Nagyrákócz [H])	Ugocsa	Iršava	Ukraine
Velykyj Sulyn, *see* Vel'ký Sulín			
Vendági, *see* Hostovice			
Venecia [Sv] (Venecija [Ru, U]; Venécze [H]), since 1943 part of Lukov			
Venecija, *see* Venecia			
Venécze, *see* Venecia			
Verbas, *see* Stari Vrbas, p. 113			
Verbiás, *see* Verbjaž			
Verbjaž [Ru, U] (Verbiás/Verebes [H])	Bereg	Volovec'	Ukraine
*Verchni Remety [U] (Felsőremete [H]; Vŷšni Remeta [Ru])	Bereg	Berehovo	Ukraine
Verchni Verec'ky, *see* Verchni Vorota			
Verchni Vorota [U] (Felsővereczke [H]; Verchni Verecky [U]; Vŷšni Verecky [Ru])	Bereg	Volovec'	Ukraine
Verchnij Bystryj [U] (Vyšnij Bystryj [U]; Vŷšnyj Bŷstrŷj [Ru])	Máramaros	Mižhirja	Ukraine
Verchnij Dubovec' [U] (Vŷšnŷj Dubovec' [Ru])	Máramaros	Tjačiv	Ukraine
Verchnij Koroslov, *see* Hreblja			
Verchnij Studenyj [U] (Felsőhidegpatak [H]; Vŷšnŷj Studenŷj [Ru])	Máramaros	Mižhirja	Ukraine
Verchnja Apša, *see* Verchnje Vodjane			
Verchnja Hrabivnycja [U] (Felső-gereben [H]; Vŷšnja Hrabovnycja [Ru])	Bereg	Volovec'	Ukraine
Verchnja Roztoka, *see* Vŷšnja Roztoka			
Verchnja Vyznycja [U] (Felsőviznicze [H]; Vŷšnja Vŷznycja [Ru])	Bereg	Mukačevo	Ukraine
Verchnje Solotvyno [U] (Felsőszlatina/Kisszlatina [H];Vŷšnja Solotvyna [Ru])	Ung	Užhorod	Ukraine

Village	Former Hungarian county or Galician district	Present administrative subdivision	Present country
Verchnje Vodjane [U] (Felsőapsa [H]; Verchnja Apša [U]; Vŷšnja Apša [Ru])	Máramaros	Rachiv	Ukraine
Verchomlja Mala, *see* Wierchomla Mała			
Verchomlja Velyka, *see* Wierchomla			
Verchovnja, *see* Wierchomla			
Verchovyna-Bystra [U] (Bisztra-Verchovina [H]; Bŷstrŷj [Ru]; Határszög [H])	Ung	Velykyj Bereznyj	Ukraine
Verebes, *see* Verbjaž			
Verécze, *see* Verjacja			
Veremin', *see* Weremień			
Vereshegy, *see* Poráč			
Veresmart, *see* Tisa, p. 113			
Verjacja [Ru, U] (Verécze [H])	Ugocsa	Vynohradiv	Ukraine
Vertep [U] (Vertepa [Ru])	Ugocsa	Chust	Ukraine
Verymin, *see* Weremień			
Vetlyna, *see* Wetlina			
Vezérszállás, *see* Pidpolozzja			
Vidrány, *see* Vydraň			
Vidráspatak/Vîdyčka, *see* Vydryčka			
Viharos, *see* Vyška			
Vikova, *see* Wojkowa			
Világ/Világy, *see* Svetlice			
Vil'chivci [U] (Irhócz/Irholcz [H]; Vul'chovci [Ru])	Máramaros	Tjačiv	Ukraine
Vil'chivci-Lazy [U] (Lazŷ [Ru])	Máramaros	Tjačiv	Ukraine
Vil'chivčyk [U] (Vul'chovčyk [Ru])	Máramaros	Tjačiv	Ukraine
Vil'chivec', *see* Olchowiec			
Vil'chivka [U] (Ölyvös [H]; Vlachovo [Ru])	Ugocsa	Iršava	Ukraine
Vilchova/Vil'chova, *see* Olchowa			
Vil'chovaty [U] (Kiscserjés, Vilchovati, Vilhovati [H])	Máramaros	Rachiv	Ukraine
Vil'chovec', *see* Olchowiec			
Vil'chovycja [Ru, U] (Egereske/Egreske [H])	Bereg	Mukačevo	Ukraine
Vilhovati, *see* Vil'chovaty			
Vilka/Vil'ka, *see* Wólka			
Vil'šnja, *see* Wilsznia			
Vil'šynky [U] (Egreshát [H]; Vulsinka [H]; Vul'šynkŷ [Ru])	Ung	Perečyn	Ukraine
Virava, *see* Výrava			
Virchnja, *see* Wirchne			
Virchimka, *see* Wierchomla Mała			
Virchivka Mala, *see* Wierchomla Mała			
Virchovnja, *see* Wierchomla			
Virchovnja Velyka, *see* Wierchomla			
Virişmort, *see* Tisa, p. 113			
Virliv, *see* Orlov			

Village	Former Hungarian county or Galician district	Present administrative subdivision	Present country
Višavka, *see* Olšavka			
Vişeul de Sus, *see* p. 113			
Visk, *see* Vyškovo, p. 113			
Viska, see Vyška			
Viskó, *see* Vyškovce			
Vislanka [Sv] (Pusztamező [H]; Vŷslanka [Ru]; Vyslanka [U])	Sáros	Stará L'ubovňa	Slovakia
Vislava [Sv] (Kisvajszló [H];Vŷslava [Ru]; Vyslava [U])	Sáros	Stropkov	Slovakia
Visóbisztra, *see* Bistra			
Visóoroszi, *see* Ruscova			
Visóvölgy, *see* Valea Vişeului			
Vitrylv, *see* Witrylów			
Vizköz, *see* Sojmy			
Vlachovo, *see* Vil'chivka			
Vladiča [Sv] (Felsőladács [H]; Vladyč [U])	Zemplén	Stropkov	Slovakia
Vladyč, see Vladiča			
Vodycja [U] (Apsica [H]; Apšycja [Ru]; Kisapsa [H])	Máramaros	Rachiv	Ukraine
Vojkova, *see* Wojkowa			
Vojtivci, *see* Vojtovce			
Vojtócz, *see* Vojtovce			
Vojtovce [Sv] (Vojtivci [U]; Vojtócz/ Vojtvágása [H])	Zemplén	Stropkov	Slovakia
Vojtvágása, *see* Vojtovce			
Vola Ceklynska, *see* Wola Cieklińska			
Vola Michova, *see* Wola Michowa			
Vola Nŷžnja, *see* Wola Niżna			
Vola Petrova, *see* Wola Piotrowa			
Vola Synkova, *see* Wola Sękowa			
Vola Vŷšnja, *see* Wola Wyżna			
Volica [Sv] (Ökröske [H]; Volicja [Ru, U])	Zemplén	Medzilaborce	Slovakia
Volicja, *see* Volica			
Volja Ceklyns'ka, *see* Wola Cieklińska			
Volja Horjans'ka, *see* Wola Górzańska			
Volja Matijašova, *see* Wola Matiaszowa			
Volja Myhova, *see* Wola Michowa			
Volja Nyžnja, *see* Wola Niżna			
Volja Vyžnja, *see* Wola Wyżna			
Volkovŷja, *see* Wołkowyja			
Volócz, *see* Volovec', Bereg county			
Volosate, *see* Wołosate			
Volosjanka [Ru, U] (Hajasd/Voloszánka [H])	Ung	Velekyj Berznyj	Ukraine
Voloskoje, *see* Pidhirne			
Voloszánka, *see* Volosjanka			
Volovec' [Ru, U] (Volócz [H])	Bereg	Volovec'	Ukraine
Volovec/Volovec', Gorlice district, *see* Wołowiec			
Volovoje, *see* Mižhirja			

Village	Former Hungarian county or Galician district	Present administrative subdivision	Present country
Volovycja [Ru, U] (Beregpálfalva/ Pálfalva [H])	Bereg	Iršava	Ukraine
Voltušova, *see* Wołtuszowa			
Volyca/Volycja, *see* Wolica			
Vonihovo [Ru, U] (Vajnág [H]; Vonihove [U])	Máramaros	Tjačiv	Ukraine
Vorobik, *see* Wróblek Królewski; Wróblek Szlachecki			
Voroblyk Korolivs'kyj, *see* Wróblek Królewski			
Voroblyk Šljachets'kyj, *see* Wróblek Szlachecki			
Voročov/Vorocsó, *see* Voročevo			
Voročovo [U] (Kapuszög [H]; Voročov [Ru]; Vorocsó [H])	Ung	Perečyn	Ukraine
Vosje, *see* Łosie, Gorlice district; Łosie, Nowy Sącz district			
Vošovatyj, *see* Vyšovatyj			
Vovčyj [Ru, U]	Bereg	Svaljava	Ukraine
Vovkove [U] (Ungordas/Valkaja [H]; Vovkovoje/Vovkovŷî [Ru])	Ung	Užhorod	Ukraine
Vovkovyja, *see* Wołkowyja			
Vovkovŷî, *see* Vovkove			
Vrbas, *see* Stari Vrbas			
Vublja, *see* Ubl'a			
Vučkove [U] (Vučkovo [Ru]; Vucskómező [H])	Máramaros	Mižhirja	Ukraine
Vučkovo, *see* Vučkove			
Vucskómező, *see* Vučkove			
Vuh, *see* Łuh			
Vukovŷja, *see* Wołkowyja			
Vul'chovci, *see* Vil'chivci			
Vul'šavica, see Ol'šavica			
Vulsinka, *see* Vil'šynky			
Vul'šynkŷ, *see* Vil'šynky			
Vydraň [Sv] (Vidrány [H]; Vŷdran' [Ru]; Vydran' [U]), since 1961 part of Medzilaborce			
Vydryčka [U] (Vidráspatak [H]; Vîdryčka [Ru])	Máramaros	Rachiv	Ukraine
Vylagŷ, *see* Svetlice			
Vynohradovo, *see* Vynohradiv, p. 113			
Výrava [Sv] (Virava [H]; Vŷrava [Ru]; Vyrava [U])	Zemplén	Medzilaborce	Slovakia
Vyšavs'ka Dolyna, *see* Valea Vişeului			
Vyševatka, *see* Wyszowadka			
Vyška [U] (Viharos/Viska [H]; Vŷška [Ru])	Ung	Velykyj Bereznyj	Ukraine
Vyškivci, *see* Vyškovce			
Vyškovce [Sv] (Viskó [H]; Vŷškivci [Ru];	Sáros	Stropkov	Slovakia

Village	Former Hungarian county or Galician district	Present administrative subdivision	Present country
Vyškivci [U])			
Vyškove, *see* Vyškovo			
Vyškovo, *see* p. 113			
Vyškovo nad Tysoju, *see* Vyškovo			
Vyslanka/Výslanka, *see* Vislanka			
Vyslava/Výslava, *see* Vislava			
Vyslik Nyžij, *see* Wisłok Dolny			
Vyslik Velykŷj, *see* Wisłok Wielki			
Vyslik Vŷšnij, *see* Wisłok Gorny			
Vysločok, *see* Wisłoczek			
Vyslok Horišnyj, *see* Wisłok Górny			
Vyslok Nyžnyj, *see* Wisłok Dolny			
Vyslok Velykyj, *see* Wisłok Wielki			
Vyšná Jablonka [Sv] (Felsőalmád [H]; Vŷšnja Jablinka [Ru]; Vyšnja Jablinka [U])	Zemplén	Humenné	Slovakia
Vyšná Jedl'ová [Sv] (Felőfenyves/ Felsőjedlova [H]; Vŷšnja Jadlova [Ru]; Vyšnja Jadlova [U])	Sáros	Svidník	Slovakia
**Vyšná Ol'šava [Sv] (Felsőolsva [H]; Vyšnja Ol'šava [U]; Vŷšnja Vilšava [Ru])	Sáros	Stropkov	Slovakia
Vyšná Pisaná [Sv] (Felsőhimes/ Felsőpiszana [H]; Vŷšnja Pysana [Ru]; Vyšnja Pysana [U])	Sáros	Svidník	Slovakia
Vyšná Polianka [Sv] (Felsőpágony/ Felsőpolyanka [H]; Vŷšnja Poljanka [Ru]; Vyšnja Poljanka [U])	Sáros	Bardejov	Slovakia
Vyšná Radvaň' [Sv] (Izbugyaradvány [H]; Vŷšnja Radvan' [Ru], Vyšnja Radvan' [U]), since 1964 part of Radvaň nad Laborcem			
Vŷsna Runa, *see* Rona de Sus			
Vyšná Rybnica [Sv] (Felsőhalas/Felső- ribnyicze [H]; Vyšnja Rybnicja [U])	Ung	Sobrance	Slovakia
Vyšná Vladiča [Sv] (Felsővladicsa [H]; Vŷšnij Ladŷč [Ru]; Vyšnja Vladyča [U]), since 1964 part of Vladiča			
Vyšné Čabiny [Sv] (Felsőcsebeny [H]; Vŷšni Čabynŷ [Ru]; Vyšni Čabyny [U]), since 1964 part of Čabiny			
**Vyšné Nemecké [Sv] (Felsőnémeti [H])	Ung	Sobrance	Slovakia
Vyšné Zbojné [Sv] (Izbugyazbojna/Újbajna [H]); Vŷšnja Zbina [Ru]; Vyšnje Zbijne [U]), since 1960 part of Zbojné			
Vyšni Čabyny, *see* Vyšné Čabiny			
Vŷšni Čabynŷ, *see* Vyšné Čabiny			
Vŷšni Remeta, *see* Verchni Remety			
Vyšni Slovinky, *see* Vyšnie Slovinky			
Vŷšni Slovynkŷ, *see* Vyšnie Slovinky			
Vyšní Svidník [Sv] (Felsőszvidnik/			

Village	Former Hungarian county or Galician district	Present administrative subdivision	Present country
Felsővízkőz [H]; Vŷšnij Svydnyk [Ru]), since 1944 part of Svidník			
Vŷšni Verecky, *see* Verchni Vorota			
Vyšnia Ol'ka [Sv] (Vŷšnja Ol'ka [Ru]), part of Ol'ka			
Vyšnie Slovinky [Sv] (Felsőszalánk/ Felsőszlovinka [H]; Vŷšni Slovinkŷ [Ru]; Vyšni Slovinky [U]), since 1943 part of Slovinky			
Vyšnij Bystryj [U], *see* Verchnij Bystryj			
Vyšnij/Vŷšnij Hrabovec', *see* Vyšný Hrabovec			
Vyšnij/Vŷšnij Komarnyk, *see* Vyšný Komárnik			
Vŷšnij Ladŷč, *see* Vyšná Vladiča			
Vyšnij/Vŷšnij Myrošiv, *see* Vyšný Mirošov			
Vyšnij Orlyk, *see* Vyšný Orlík			
Vyšnij Svydnyk, *see* Vyšni Svidník			
Vyšnij/Vŷšnij Tvarožec', see Vyšný Tvarožec'			
Vŷšnij Verlych, *see* Vyšný Orlík			
Vŷšnja Apša, *see* Verchnje Vodjane			
Vŷšnja Hrabovnycja, *see* Verchnja Hrabivnycja			
Vyšnja/Vŷšnja Jablinka, *see* Vyšná Jablonka			
Vyšnja/Vŷšnja Jadlova, *see* Vyšná Jedl'ová			
Vŷšnja Ol'ka, *see* Vyšnia Ol'ka			
Vŷšnja Ol'šava, *see* Vyšná Ol'šava			
Vyšnja/Vŷšnja Poljanka, *see* Vyšna Polianka			
Vyšnja/Vŷšnja Pysana, *see* Vyšná Pisaná			
Vyšnja Radvan', *see* Vyšná Radvaň			
Vŷšnja Radvan, *see* Vyšná Radvaň			
Vŷšnja Rivna/Rona, *see* Rona de Sus			
Vŷšnja Roztoka [Ru] (Felsőhatárszeg/ Kisrosztoka [H]; Verchnja Roztoka [U]), since 1960 part of Roztoka, Bereg county, Volovec' region			
Vŷšnja Roztoka [Ru], Ung county, part of Kostryns'ka Roztoka			
Vyšnja Rybnicja, *see* Vyšná Rybnica			
Vŷšnja Solotvyna, *see* Verchnje Solotvyno			
Vŷšnja Vilšava, *see* Vyšná Ol'šava			
Vyšnja Vladyča, *see* Vyšná Vladiča			
Vŷšnja Vŷznycja, *see* Verchnja Vyznycja			
Vŷšnja Zbina, *see* Vyšné Zbojné			
Vyšnje Zbijne, *see* Vyšné Zbojne			
**Vyšný Hrabovec [Sv] (Kisgyertyános/ Oroszhrabócz/Sztropkóhrabócz [H]; Vŷšnij Hrabovec [Ru]; Vyšnij Hrabovec' [U]), since 1961 part of Turany nad Ondavou	Sáros	Stropkov	Slovakia
Vyšný Komárnik [Sv] (Felsőkomárnok [H]; Vŷšnij Komarnyk [Ru]; Vyšnij Komarnyk [U])	Sáros	Svidník	Slovakia

Village	Former Hungarian county or Galician district	Present administrative subdivision	Present country
Vyšný Mirošov [Sv] (Vŷšnij Myrošiv [Ru]; Vyšnij Myrošiv [U])	Sáros	Svidník	Slovakia
Vyšný Orlík [Sv] (Felsőodor/Felsőorlich [H]; Vyšnij Orlyk [U]; Vŷšnij Verlych [Ru])	Sáros	Svidník	Slovakia
Vyšný Tvarožec [Sv] (Felsőtarócz [H]; Vŷšnij Tvarožec [Ru]; Vyšnij Tvarožec' [U])	Sáros	Bardejov	Slovakia
Vŷšnyj Bŷstrŷj, *see* Verchnij Bystryj			
Vŷšnŷj Dubovec', *see* Verchnij Dubovec'			
Vŷšnŷj Šard, *see* Šyroke, Ugocsa county			
Vŷšnŷj Studenŷj, *see* Verchnij Studenyj			
Vŷšnŷj Synŷvyr, *see* Synevyrs'ka Poljana			
Vysočany/Vŷsočanŷ, *see* Wysoczany			
Vysova/Vŷsova, *see* Wysowa			
Vŷšovatka, *see* Wyszowadka			
Vyšovatyj [U] (Vošovatŷj [Ru])	Máramaros	Tjačiv	Ukraine
Vyšovo, *see* Vişeul de Sus, p. 113			
Vyšovs'ka Dolyna, *see* Valea Vişeului			
Vŷšŷnkiv, *see* Ol'šinkiv			
Wapienne [P] (Vapenne [Ru, U])	Gorlice	Nowy Sącz	Poland
Wawrzka [P] (Vafka [Ru, U])	Grybów	Nowy Sącz	Poland
Węglówka [P] (Vanivka [Ru, U])	Krosno	Krosno	Poland
Weremień [P] (Veremin' [U]; Verymin [Ru])	Lesko	Krosno	Poland
Wetlina [P] (Vetlyna [Ru, U])	Lesko	Krosno	Poland
Wielopole [P] (Velykopole [Ru, U])	Sanok	Krosno	Poland
Wierchomla [P] (Verchomlja Velyka/ Verchovnja/Virchovnja [Ru]; Virchovnja Velyka [Ru, U]; Wierchomla Wielka [P])	Nowy Sącz	Nowy Sącz	Poland
Wierchomla Mała [P] (Verchomlja Mala/ Virchimka [Ru]; Virchivka Mala [U])	Nowy Sącz	Nowy Sącz	Poland
Wierchomla Wielka, *see* Wierchomla			
Wilsznia [P] (Velšnja/Vilšnja [Ru]; Vil'šnja [U]) (ceased to exist after 1947)	Krosno	Krosno	Poland
Wirchne [P] (Virchnja [Ru, U]) (ceased to exist after 1947)	Gorlice	Nowy Sącz	Poland
Wisłoczek [P] (Vysločok [U])	Sanok	Krosno	Poland
Wisłok Dolny [P] (Vyslik Nyžnij [Ru]; Vyslok Nyžnyj [U]) (ceased to exist after 1947)	Sanok	Krosno	Poland
Wisłok Gorny [P] (Vyslik Vŷšnŷj [Ru]; Vyslok Horišnyj [U])	Sanok	Krosno	Poland
Wisłok Wielki [P] (Vyslik Velykŷj [Ru]; Vyslok Velykyj [U])	Sanok	Krosno	Poland
Witrylów [P] (Vytryliv [Ru, U])	Brzozów	Krosno	Poland
Wojkowa [P] (Vikova [Ru, U]; Vojkova [U])	Nowy Sącz	Nowy Sącz	Poland

Village	Former Hungarian county or Galician district	Present administrative subdivision	Present country
Wola Cieklińska [P] (Vola Ceklynska [Ru]; Volja Ceklyns'ka [U])	Jasło	Krosno	Poland
Wola Górzańska [P] (Volja Horjans'ka [U])	Lesko	Krosno	Poland
Wola Matiaszowa [P] (Bereščajska Vola [Ru]; Vola Matijošova [U])	Lesko	Krosno	Poland
Wola Michowa [P] (Ola/Vola Michova [Ru]; Volja Myhova [U])	Lesko	Krosno	Poland
Wola Niżna [P] (Vola Nŷznja [Ru]; Volja Nyžnja [U])	Sanok	Krosno	Poland
Wola Piotrowa [P] (Vola Petrova [Ru]; Petrova Volja [U])	Sanok	Krosno	Poland
Wola Sękowa [P] (Vola Synkova [Ru]; Sen'kova Volja [U])	Sanok	Krosno	Poland
Wola Wyżna [P] (Vola Vŷšnja [Ru]; Volja Vyžnja [U]), ceased to exist after 1947	Sanok	Krosno	Poland
Wolica [P] (Volyca [Ru]; Volycja [U])	Sanok	Krosno	Poland
Wólka [P] (Vilka [Ru]; Vil'ka [U]; Wulka [P]) (ceased to exist after 1947)	Sanok	Krosno	Poland
Wołkowyja [P] (Volkovŷja [Ru]; Vovkovyja [U]; Vukovŷja [Ru])	Lesko	Krosno	Poland
Wołosate [P] (Volosate [Ru, U])	Lesko	Krosno	Poland
Wołowiec [P] (Volovec [Ru]; Volovec' [U])	Gorlice	Nowy Sącz	Poland
Wołtuszowa [P] (Voltušova [U])	Sanok	Krosno	Poland
Wróblik Królewski [P] (Vorobik [Ru]; Voroblyk Korolivs'kyj [U])	Krosno	Krosno	Poland
Wróblik Szlachecki [P] (Vorobik [Ru]; Voroblyk Šljachets'kyj [U])	Sanok	Krosno	Poland
Wulka, *see* Wólka			
Wysoczany [P] (Vysočany [U]; Vŷsočanŷ [Ru])	Sanok	Krosno	Poland
Wysowa [P] (Vysova [U]; Vŷsova [Ru])	Gorlice	Nowy Sącz	Poland
Wyszowadka [P] (Vyševatka [U]; Vŷšovatka [Ru])	Jasło	Krosno	Poland
Za Rikoju, *see* Zarične			
Zabłotce [P] (Zabolotci [U])	Sanok	Krosno	Poland
Zabolotci, *see* Zabłotce			
Zabrid' [U] (Zabrod [Ru])	Máramaros	Chust	Ukraine
Zabrid' [U] (Révhely [H]; Zabrod [Ru])	Ung	Velykyj Bereznyj	Ukraine
Zabrod, *see* Zabrid'			
Zabrodja, *see* Zabrodzie			
Zabrodzie [P] (Zabrodja [U])	Lesko	Krosno	Poland
Zábrogy, *see* Zabrid'			
Zadil's'ke [U] (Zadil's'kj [Ru]; Rekesz/Zagyilszka [H])	Bereg	Volovec'	Ukraine
Zadil's'kŷj, *see* Zadil's'ke			

Village	Former Hungarian county or Galician district	Present administrative subdivision	Present country
Zadno'je, *see* Pryboržavs'ke			
Zádnya, *see* Pryboržavs'ke			
Zagyilszka, *see* Zadil's'ke			
Zahatja, *see* Zahattja			
Zahattja [U] (Hátmeg [H]; Zahatja [Ru])	Bereg	Iršava	Ukraine
Zahočevja, *see* Zahoczewie			
Zahoczewie [P] (Zahočevja [U]; Zalačyvja [Ru])	Lesko	Krosno	Poland
Zahorb [U]	Máramaros	Mižhirja	Ukraine
Zahorb [Ru, U] (Határhegy [H])	Ung	Velkyj Bereznyj	Ukraine
Zahutyń [P] (Zahutyn' [Ru, U])	Sanok	Krosno	Poland
Zajgó, *see* Dusyno			
Zalačyvja, *see* Zahoczewie			
Zalom [Ru, U]	Máarmaros	Chust	Ukraine
Zaluž, *see* Zalužžja			
Zalužžja [U] (Beregkisalmás/Kisalmás [H]; Zaluž [Ru])	Bereg	Mukačevo	Ukraine
Zandranova, *see* Zyndranowa			
Zaperedillja [U] (Gombástelep [H]; Zaperedîl [Ru])	Máramaros	Mižhirja	Ukraine
Zariča, Ugocsa county, *see* Zaričča			
Zarîča, Ung county, *see* Zaričovo			
Zaričča [U] (Alsókaraszló [H]; Zariča [Ru])	Ugocsa	Iršava	Ukraine
Zaričovo [U] (Drugetháza [H]; Zarîča/ Zaričov [Ru])	Ung	Perečyn	Ukraine
Zarične [U] (Za Rîkoju [Ru])	Máramaros	Chust	Ukraine
Zaricsó, *see* Zaričovo			
Zárnya, *see* Pryboržavs'ke			
Zaslav, *see* Zasław			
Zaslavje, *see* Zasław			
Zasław [P] (Zaslav [Ru]; Zaslavje [U]; Zasławie [P])	Sanok	Krosno	Poland
Zaslawie, *see* Zaslaw			
Žatkivci, *see* Žatkovce			
Žatkovce [Sv] (Žatkivci [Ru, U]; Zsetek [H]), since 1990s part of Geraltov	Sáros	Prešov	Slovakia
Zatvarnycja, *see* Zatwarnica			
Zatwarnica [P] (Zatvarnyca [Ru]; Zatvarnycja [U])	Lesko	Krosno	Poland
Zatysivka [U] (Čoma [Ru]; Čouma [U]; Čuma [Ru]; Csomafalva [H])	Ugocsa	Vynohradiv	Ukraine
Zauszina, *see* Zavosyno			
Závada [Sv] (Hegyzávod [H]; Zavada [Ru, U]	Zemplén	Humenné	Slovakia
Zavadka [Ru, U] (Rákócziszállás [H])	Bereg	Volovec'	Ukraine
Zavadka, Sanok district, *see* Morochownica			
*Závadka [Sv] (Csergőzávod [H]; Zavadka [Ru, U]), since 1990s part of Geraltov	Sáros	Prešov	Slovakia

Village	Former Hungarian county or Galician district	Present administrative subdivision	Present country
Závadka [Sv] (Görögfalu [H]; Zavadka [Ru, U])	Szepes	Gelnica	Slovakia
Zavadka [U] (Kiscsongova [H]; Mala Čengava [Ru])	Ugocsa	Vynohradiv	Ukraine
Zavadka Morochivs'ka, *see* Morochownica			
Zavadka Rymanivs'ka, *see* Zawadka Rymanowska			
Zavatka, *see* Zawadka Rymanowska			
Zavbuč	Ung	Perečyn	Ukraine
Zaverchnja Kyčera [U] (Tócska [H]; Tovčka [Ru])	Máramaros	Mižhirja	Ukraine
Zaviddja, *see* Závodie			
Zavidfalva, *see* Zavydovo			
Zavij, *see* Zawój			
Zaviz, *see* Zawóz			
Závodie [Sv] (Zaviddja [U]; Zavŷdja [Ru]), since 1961 part of Sulín			
Zavoj/Zavoji, *see* Zawoje			
Zavosyna, *see* Zavosyno			
Zavosyno [U] (Szénástelek/Zauszina [H]; Zavosyna [Ru])	Ung	Velykyj Bereznyj	Ukraine
Zavŷdja, *see* Závodie			
Zavydove, *see* Zavydovo			
Zavydovo [Ru, U] (Dávidfalva/ Zavidfalva [H]; Zavydove [U])	Bereg	Mukačevo	Ukraine
Zavyjka [U] (Határvölgy/Zavejka [H]; Zavojka [Ru])	Máramaros	Mižhirja	Ukraine
Zawadka Morochowska, *see* Morochownica			
Zawadka Rymanowska [P] (Zavadka Rymanivs'ka [U]; Zavatka [Ru])	Sanok	Krosno	Poland
Zawój [P] (Zavij [U]) (ceased to exist after 1947)	Lesko	Krosno	Poland
Zawoje [P] (Zavoj [Ru]; Zavoji [Ru, U]) (ceased to exist after 1947)	Sanok	Krosno	Poland
Zawóz [P] (Zaviz [U])	Lesko	Krosno	Poland
Zbij, *see* Zboj			
Zbijne, *see* Zbojné			
Zboiska [P, Ru] (Zbojis'ka [U])	Sanok	Krosno	Poland
Zboj [Ru, Sv] (Harczos [H]; Zbij [U]; Zbuj [Ru])	Zemplén	Snina	Slovakia
Zbojis'ka, *see* Zboiska			
Zbojné [Sv] (Zbijne [Ru, U])	Zemplén	Medzilaborce	Slovakia
Žborivci [U] (Rónafalu [H]; Žborovci [Ru])	Bereg	Mukačevo	Ukraine
Zbudská Belá [Sv] (Izbugyabéla [H]; Zbud'ska Bila [Ru]; Zbuds'ka Bila [U])	Zemplén	Medzilaborce	Slovakia
Zbudský Rokytov [Sv] (Izbugyarokitó [H]; Zbuds'kŷj Rokŷtiv [Ru]; Zbuds'kyj Rokytiv [U]), since 1970 part of Rokytov pri Humennom			

Village	Former Hungarian county or Galician district	Present administrative subdivision	Present country
Zbuj, *see* Zboj			
Zbun/Zbuna, *see* Zbyny			
Zbyny [U] (Izbonya/Zbun/Zbuna [H]; Zbŷnŷ [Ru])	Bereg	Volovec'	Ukraine
Ždenijevo [U] (Szarvasháza [H]; Ždeneve [U]; Ždjen'ovo [Ru]; Zsdenyova [H])	Bereg	Volovec'	Ukraine
Zdvyžen', *see* Zwierzyń			
Żdynia [P] (Ždynja [U]; Ždŷnja [Ru])	Gorlice	Nowy Sącz	Poland
Ždynja, *see* Żdynia			
Žegestiv, *see* Żegiestów			
Żegiestów [P] (Žegestiv [Ru, U])	Nowy Sącz	Nowy Sącz	Poland
Zelló, *see* Zvalá			
Zemplénbukócz, *see* Malé Bukovce			
Zempléndricsna, *see* Mala Driečna			
Zemplénoroszi, *see* Ruské			
Zemplénszomolnok, *see* Smolník			
Zemplénsztaskócz, *see* Malé Staškovce			
Żerdenka [P] (Žerdenka [U]; Žerdynka [Ru])	Lesko	Krosno	Poland
Żerdynka, *see* Żerdenka			
Żernica Niżna [P] (Žernycja [Ru]; Žernycja Nyžnja [U]) (after 1947 ceased to exist)	Lesko	Krosno	Poland
Żernica Wyżna [P] (Žernycja Vyžnja [U]) (after 1945 ceased to exist)	Lesko	Krosno	Poland
Žernycja Nyžnja, *see* Żernica Niżna			
Žernycja Vyžnja, *see* Żernica Wyżna			
Zgribest/Zgribeşti, *see* Zorile			
Zloc'ke, *see* Złockie			
Złockie [P] (Zloc'ke [U]; Zlockje [Ru])	Nowy Sącz	Nowy Sącz	Poland
Znjac'eve, *see* Znjac'ovo			
Znjac'ovo [Ru, U] (Ignécz [H]; Znjac'eve [U])	Bereg	Mukačevo	Ukraine
Žnjatyno, *see* p. 113			
Zolotareve, *see* Zolotar'ovo			
Zolotar'ovo [Ru, U] (Ötvosfalva [H]; Zolotareve [U])	Máramaros	Chust	Ukraine
**Zorile [Ro, Ru] (until 1920s part of Krassógombás/ Zgribest [H]; Zgribeşti [Ro])	Krassó-Szörény	Timiş	Romania
Žornava [U] (Žornavŷ [Ru])	Ung	Velykyj Bereznyj	Ukraine
Žovtneve [U]	Máramaros	Chust	Ukraine
Zsdenyova, *see* Ždenijevo			
Zsetek, *see* Žatkovce			
Zsilip, *see* Plavja			
Zsukó/Zsukova, *see* Žukovo			
Zubivka [U] (Beregforgaras/Fogaras [H]; Fogaraš [Ru]; Foharaš [U])	Bereg	Mukačevo	Ukraine
Zubeńsko [P] (Zubens'ko [U]) (ceased to exist after 1947)	Lesko	Krosno	Poland

Village	Former Hungarian county or Galician district	Present administrative subdivision	Present country
Zubna, *see* Zubné			
Zubné [Sv] (Tölgyeshegy/Zubna [H]; Zubnoj [Ru]; Zubnyj [U]; Zubnŷj [Ru])	Zemplén	Humenné	Slovakia
Zubnoj, *see* Zubné			
Zubnyj/Zubnŷj, *see* Zubné			
Zubrače, *see* Żubracze			
Żubracze [P] (Zubrače [U]; Zubrjači [Ru])	Lesko	Krosno	Poland
Zubrik, *see* Zubrzyk			
Zubrjači, *see* Żubracze			
Zubryk, *see* Zubrzyk			
Zubrzyk [P] (Zubrik [Ru]; Zubryk [U])	Nowy Sącz	Nowy Sącz	Poland
Zuella, *see* Zvala			
Zúgó, *see* Huklyvyj			
Zuhatag, *see* Stakčianska Roztoka			
Žukove, *see* Žukovo			
Žukovo [Ru, U] (Zsukó/Zsukova [H]; Žukove [U])	Bereg	Mukačevo	Ukraine
Žurdziv, *see* Dziurdziów			
Zvala [Ru, Sv, U] (Zelló/Zuella [H]) (ceased to exist in 1980)	Zemplén	Snina	Slovakia
Zwierzyń [P] (Zdvyžen' [U])	Lesko	Krosno	Poland
Żydivs'ke/Žŷdivskje, *see* Żydowskie			
Żydowskie [P] (Żydivs'ke [U]; Žŷdivskje/Žŷdivskŷj [Ru])	Jasło	Krosno	Poland
Żydivskŷj, *see* Żydowskie			
Zyndranova/Zŷndranova, *see* Zyndranowa			
Zyndranowa [P] (Dzyndranova/ Zandranova [Ru]; Zyndranova [U]; Zŷndranova [Ru])	Krosno	Krosno	Poland

For Further Reading

A. Bibliographical Guides and Historiography

There is no published bibliography devoted exclusively to Carpatho-Rusyns in the United States and Canada, although studies published since 1975 are referenced under the index entry, "Carpatho-Rusyns beyond the homeland," in Paul Robert Magocsi, *Carpatho-Rusyn Studies: An Annotated Bibliography*, Vol. I: *1975-1984* (New York and London: Garland Publishing, 1988), Vol. II: *1985-1994* (New York: Columbia University Press/ East European Monographs,1998), and Vol. III: *1995-1999* (New York: Columbia University Press/ East European Monographs, 2005). Research materials in libraries and other resource centers are discussed in Edward Kasinec, *The Carpatho-Ruthenian Immigration in the United States: A Preliminary Note on Sources in Some United States Repositories,* Harvard Ukrainian Research Institute Offprint Series, No. 6 (Cambridge, Mass., 1975); and in Robert Karlowich, *The Heritage Institute Museum and Library: A Description* (West Paterson, N. J.: Diocese of Passaic, 1995).

The basic source for the study of Carpatho-Rusyns in America are the more than 60 newspapers, journals, and annual almanacs published by various religious and secular organizations, which contain a wide variety of news reports, biographies of immigrant leaders, statistical data on organizations, and other valuable materials. Most of these serials have been preserved on microfilm and are listed in Frank Renkiewicz, *The Carpatho-Ruthenian Microfilm Project: A Guide to Newspapers and Periodicals* (St. Paul, Minn.: University of Minnesota Immigration History Research Center, 1979). An annotated bibliographical index to the oldest and most important Rusyn-American newspaper is found in the *Guide to the Amerikansky Russky Viestnik*, Vol. I: *1894-1914*, compiled by James M. Evans (Fairview, N. J.: Carpatho-Rusyn Research Center, 1979) and Vol.II: *1915-1929,* edited and revised by Robert A. Karlowich (New York: Columbia University Press/East European Monographs, 2000). There is also much information in individual parish memorial books and histories issued by a large number of churches.

The historiography produced in the European homeland and in North America about Carpatho-Rusyn immigration is surveyed in a few short studies: Dmytro Danyliuk "Emihratsiia iz Zakarpattia," in Iurii Iu. Slyvka, ed., *Ukraïns'ka emihratsiia: istoriia i suchasnist'* (L'viv: Kameniar, 1992), p. 369-377; Iu. M. Bysaha and V.V. Lemak "Emihratsiiia zakarpats'kykh rusyniv do Pivnichnoï Ameryky v istoriohrafiï," *Naukovyi visnyk Uzhhorods'koho universytetu, Seriia Istoriia,* Vol. I (Uzhhorod, 1995), pp. 36-38; and Paul Robert Magocsi, "Historiography: United States," *Encyclopedia of Rusyn History and Culture,* edited by Paul Robert Magocsi and Ivan Pop , 2nd rev. ed. (Toronto: University of Toronto Press, 2005), pp. 176-177. The encyclopedia just noted also includes several entries on Rusyn American organizations, churches, publications, and community activists, many which indicate further bibliographical references.

B. Documentary Sources

Although many of the items in this section deal with developments in Europe, they are listed here because they were published by Carpatho-Rusyns in the United States or Canada and reflect the political views held by the group at various times.

American Carpatho-Russian Congress. *Protest to the Honorable James F. Byrnes, Secretary of the U.S. State Department, Peace Conference, Paris, France (Europe). Re: Annexation of Podkarpatska Rus' (Ruthenia) to Soviet Union.* Munhall, Pa., 1946.

American League of Russians and Carpatho-Russians. *Memorandum Concerning the Russian People of Russia Rubra.* Philadelphia, Pa., [1945].

Carpatho-Russia, Clue to Soviet Policy?. Foreign Nationality Groups in the United States, No. 154. Washington, D.C.: Office of Strategic Services, Foreign Nationalities Branch, 11 October 1943.

Chornak, Orestes. *Documentae Appellationis.* Bridgeport, September 20, 1931.

Declaration and Memorandum of the Russian Council of Carpatho-Russia in Lwow, of the League for the Liberation of Carpatho-Russia in America, and of the League for the Liberation of Carpatho-Russia in Canada. n.p., 1919.

Fentsik, Stepan A. *Uzhgorod-Amerika: putevyia zamietki, 13.X. 1934-19.V.1935.* Uzhhorod: Nash put', 1935.

Gajdoš, Julij G. *Spravoizdanije predsidatel'a Amerkanskoj Narodnoj Rady Uhro-Rusinov na Pervyj Narodnyj Kongress.* Homestead, Pa.: Amerikansky russky viestnik, 1919.

[Gerovskij, Aleksij]. *Karpatskaja Rus' v česskom jarmi.* n.p., 1939.

Gladik, Viktor. *Proekt memoranduma amerikanskikh grazhdan karpatorusskago i voobshche russkago proiskhozhdeniia v dili vozsoedineniia vsekh russkikh zemel's Rossiei.* Philadelphia, 1941.

Jaka majet byti konstitucija Podkarpatskoj Rusi. Homestead, Pa.: Rusin Information Bureau, 192?

Karpatorossy v Amerike, ostavte hlubokij son: programa, resolucii Amerikanskoho Karpatorusskoho Jedinstva. Gary, Ind.: Amerikanskoje Karpatorusskoje Jedinstvo, [1941].

Karpatskij, Ivan. *Piznajte pravdu.* New York: Komitet oborony Karpatskoji Ukrajiny, 1939.

Krasovs'kyi, Ivan. *Do zemliakiv—za okean: zamitky z podorozhi do Kanady i SShA.* L'viv: Vyd-vo Kraj, 1993.

Krizis konstitucii i nikoli gubernatora Podkarpatskoj Rusi. Homestaed, Pa.: Rusin Information Bureau, 192?

Lemko Relief Committee in the U.S.A. Trumbull, Conn., 1962.

Lukach, Mykhayl; Lukach, Elena; Baran, Anna; Volchak, Mykhalyna. *Pravda o ridnim kraiu 1963: s podorozhy*

2-i delegatsyy Obshchestva karpatorusskykh kanadtsev do ChSSR, PNR y SSSR. Toronto: Tsentral'nyi komytet Obshchestva karpatorusskykh kanadtsev, 1964.

Memorandum in Behalf of Podkarpatskaja Rus. Pittsburgh: Greek Catholic Diocese, 1945.

Memorandum of the Carpatho-Russian Council in America Concerning Eastern Galicia with Lemkowschina and Bukovina. New York, 1921.

Memorandum Russkago kongressa v Amerikie, sozvannago 'Soiuzom osvobozhdeniia Prikarpatskoi Rusi', posviashchaemyi svobodnomu russkomu narodu v Rossii, Russkomu uchreditel'nomu sobraniu, Russkomu pravitel'stvu. n.p., [1917].

Michaylo, George. *A Memorandum in Behalf of Podkarpatskaja Rus to the State Department of the United States of America and Representatives of the U.S.A. at the World Security Conference.* Munhall, Pa., April 23, 1945.

Mushynka, Petro. *Iz tverdoho korenia: spohady na ridnyi krai i Kanadu.* Prešov: Fundatsiia Karpaty, 1996.

0 chîm radyly na Vsenarodnom vîchu d. 26 novembra 1903 v Yonkers, N.I. Scranton, Pa.: Amerykanskii russkii narodnyi fond, 1904.

Protest. Pittsburgh: Greek Catholic Diocese, 1945.

Protokol zapysnytsa zasîdaniia Narodnoho kongressa amerykanskykh rusynov pod okranoiu y rukovodstvom Amerykanskoi Narodnoi Radï Uhro-Rusynov poderzhannoho v Homsted, Pa., dnia 15, 16 sent. 1919-ho roka. Homestead, Pa., 1919.

Slivka, John, ed. *Historical Mirror: Sources of the Rusin and Hungarian Greek Rite Catholics in the United States of America, 1884-1963.* Brooklyn, N.Y., 1978.

Slovensko-podkarpatsko-ruska hranica. Homestead, Pa.: Rusin Information Bureau, 192?.

Statut Tovarystva "Rus'ko-amerykans'koy Radŷ" v Spoluche);khkh Derzhavakh Pôvn. Ameryky. Philadelphia, Pa., 1914.

Statuty Karpato-Russkoj Greko Kaftoličeskoj Jeparchii Voštočnaho Obrjada Cerkvi v Sojedinennych Štatach Ameriki/By-Laws of the Carpatho-Russian Greek Catholic Diocese of the Eastern Rite Church in the United States of America. n.p., n.d.

Takach, Basil. *Ot episkopa amerikanskich greko-katoličeskich rusinov.* Homestead, Pa., 1931.

Toth, Alexis. *Letters, Articles, Papers, and Sermons,* 4 vols. Edited and translated by George Soldatow. Chilliwack, British Columbia: Synaxis Press and Minneapolis, Minn.: AARDM Press, 1978-88.

——. *The Orthodox Church in America and Other Writing by St. Alexis.* Translated and edited by George Soldatow. Minneapolis, Minn.: AARDM Press, 1996.

——. *The Writing by St. Alexis Toth, Confessor and Defender of Orthodoxy in America.* Translated and edited by George Soldatow. Minneapolis, Minn.: AARDM Press, 1994.

Tretii vseobshchii Karpatorusskii kongress v Amerikie,

sostoiavshiisia v N'iu-Iorkie s 28-31 dekabria 1919 g. i 1-go ianvaria 1920 goda. New York: Karpatorusskaia narodnaia organizatsiia v Amerikie, 1920.

Tsentral'nŷi komitet Obshchestva karpatorusskikh Kanadtsev. *Mŷ za myr y druzhbu myzh narodamy.* Toronto: Obshchestvo karpatorusskykh Kanadtsev 1963.

Ustav Obshchestva Karpatorusskykh Kanadtsev/ Constitution of the Society of Carpatho-Russian Canadians [Toronto, 1961].

Vsenarodnyi Osvoboditel'nyi Kongress amerikantsev russkago karpatorusskogo proiskhozhdeniia . . . v Filadelfii . . . 8-go i 9-go oktiabria 1944 goda. Philadelphia, 1945.

Yuhasz, Michael. *Petition Concerning the Educational Complaints of the Autonomous Carpatho-Russian Territory South of the Carpathian Mountains . . . Presented by the Carpatho-Russian Council of National Defense in the United States of America to the League of Nations.* Homestead, Pa.: Amerikansky russky viestnik, 1932.

———. *Wilson's Principles in Czechoslovak Practice: The Situation of the Carpatho-Russian People Under the Czech Yoke.* Homestead, Pa.: Amerikansky russky viestnik, 1929.

Žatkovič, Gregory I. *Otkrytie-Exposé byvšeho gubernatora Podkarpatskoj Rusi, o Podkarpatskoj Rusi.* 2nd ed. Homestead, Pa.: Rusin Information Bureau, 1921.

———. *Spravoizdanije Predsidatel'a Direktoriuma Avtonomičnoj Rusinii, na Pervyj Narodnyj Kongress.* Homestead, Pa.: Amerikansky russky viestnik, 1919.

———. *The Rusin Question in a Nutshell.* n.p., 1923.

Zeedick, Peter Ivan and Smor, Adalbert Michael. *Naše stanovišče otnositel'no aktual'nych voprosov Amerikanskoj Gr. Kaftoličeskoj Russkoj Cerkvi Vostočnoho Obrjada.* Homestead, Pa.: Literaturnyj Komitet Sojedinenija Gr. Kaft. Russkich Bratstv, 1934.

Zhirosh, Miron. *Mili sinu moi: pisma Ani Papugovei sinovi Diurovi do Argentini, ioho pisma matseri do Ruskoho Kerestura i zapisi o zhivotse nashikh liudzokh u Argentini, Ziedinenykh Ameritskikh Derzhavakh i Kanadi.* Novi Sad: Ruske slovo/Hrekokatolïtska parokhiia sv. Petra i Pavla, 2002.

C. Secondary Sources

American Carpatho-Russian Orthodox Greek Catholic Diocese Commemorative Jubilee Journal: Fiftieth Golden Anniversary, 1938-1988. Johnstown, Pa.: American Carpatho-Russian Orthodox Greek Catholic Diocese, 1988.

American Carpatho-Russian Orthodox Greek Catholic Diocese of U.S.A. Silver Anniversary 1938-1963. Johnstown, Pa., 1963.

"Amerikanska Uhorska Rus': kratka historiia udaloscoch v minuvšom 1916 roku." In *Amerikansky russko-slovensky kalendar na rok 1917.* Homestead, Pa.: Sojedinenije Greko Kat. Russkych Bratstv, 1917, pp. 197-234.

Amerikanskaia Rus' voobshche. n.p., 1910.

"Amerikanskyi karpatoruskyi konhress." In Van'o Hunianka, ed. *Karpatorusskyi kalendar Lemko-Soiuza na 1943 hod.* Yonkers, N. Y. 1943, pp. 17-34.

Andrukhovych, K. *Z zhyttia rusyniv v Amerytsi: spomyn z rokiv 1889-1892.* Kolomyia, 1904.

Bachyns'kyi, Iuliian. *Ukraïns'ka immigratsiia v Z"iedynenykh Derzhavakh Ameryky.* L'viv, 1914.

Baran, Alexander. "Carpatho-Ukrainian Emigration, 1870-1914." In Jaroslav Rozumnyj, ed. *New Soil—Old Roots: The Ukrainian Experience in Canada.* Winnipeg: Ukrainian Academy of Arts and Sciences in Canada, 1983, pp. 252-275.

Barriger, Lawrence. *Glory to Jesus Christ: A History of the American Carpatho-Russian Orthodox Greek Catholic Diocese.* Brookline, Mass.: Holy Cross Orthodox Press, 2000.

———. *Good Victory: Metropolitan Orestes Chornock and the American Carpatho-Russian Orthodox Greek Catholic Diocese.* Brookline, Mass.: Holy Cross Orthodox Press, 1985.

Beck, Cheryl Weller et. al. *Opportunity Realized: The Greek Catholic Union's First One Hundred Years, 1892-1992.* Beaver, Pa.: Greek Catholic Union of the U.S.A., 1994.

Bed', Viktor. "Politychnyi portret H.Zhatkovycha—persohoho gubernatora Pidkarpats'koï Rusi." In Ivan Rebryk, ed. *Kul'tura ukraïns'kykh Karpat: tradytsiï i suchasnist'.* Uzhhorod: Grazhda, 1994, pp. 71-82.

Bensin, Basil M. *History of the Russian Orthodox Greek Catholic Church of North America.* New York, 1941.

Berezhnyi, Petro; Bek, Petro; Hiba, Mykhailo. *V im"ia pravdy: do uvahy Lemkam, prozhyvaiuchym v Amerytsi.* New York, 1962.

Bidwell, Charles E. *The Language of Carpatho-Ruthenian Publications in America.* Pittsburgh, Pa.: University of Pittsburgh Center for International Studies, 1971.

Bilak, Petro; Petryshche, Petro; Shvarts Peter. "Dolia i nedolia "Staroï kraïny: derzhavotvorchi kontseptsiï amerykans'kykh slovakiv ta rusyniv, 1900-1918 rr.," *Karpats'kyi krai,* IV, 5-6 [105] (Uzhhorod, 1994), pp. 23-26.

Blaško, Štefan. *Miriam Teresa, Faithful in a Little: Demjanovich Roots.* Toronto: Maria Magazine, 1984.

Bohiv, Oleksandr, "Ukraïns'ka (rusyns'ka) diaspora i pytannia pro nadannia Pidkarpats'kii Rusi avtonomiï (traven'—zhovten' 1938 r.)." In *Istorychna shkola profesora Volodymyra Zadorozhnoho: naukovyi zbirnyk,* Vol. I. Uzhhorod: Patent, 1999, pp.149-163.

Boruch, Ivan Gr. *Hospodarka ukrayno-radykal'nŷkh popov v 'Soiuzî'.* New York, 1903.

———. *Nashe tserkovno-narodnoe dielo v Amerikie ot nachala nashei emigratsii do nynieshnikh dnei.* New York, 1950.

Brinda, Mikhail. "Bekheroviane v Kanadi." In *Karpatorusskii kalendar Lemko-Soiuza na 1945.* Yonkers, N.Y., 1944, pp. 100-102.

Byzantine Slavonic Rite Catholic Diocese of Pittsburgh Silver Jubilee 1924-1949. McKeesport, Pa.: Prosvita, 1949.

Čapek, T. "Podkarpatští rusíni v Americe před valkou a za valky," *Naše revoluce,* IV (Prague, 1926), pp. 267-279.

Chambre, Renee. *Sister Miriam Teresa: Apostle of Unity.* Mahwah, N.J.: Unity League, 1970.

Conkin, Margaret M. *An American Teresa,* 2nd ed. Patterson, N.J.: Charles J. Demjanovich, 1946.

Custer, John S. "Byzantine Rite Slavs in Philadelphia, 1886-1916," *Records of American Catholic Society of Philadelphia,* CIV, 1-4 (Philadelphia, 1993), pp. 31-57.

Dancák, František. *Emil Kubek: kňaz, básnik, spisovatel', jazykovedec, rodol'ub.* Prešov: Petra, 1999.

——. "Z galéria našich rodol'ubov: Emil Kubek." In *Gréckokatolícky kalendár 1977.* Bratislava, 1976, pp. 151-155.

Danko, Joseph. "Natsional'na polityka Madiarshchyny sered rusyniv Zakarpattia v Spoluchenykh Shtatakh Ameryky," *Ukraïns'kyi istoryk,* XXXVI, 2-4 (New York, Toronto, Kiev, L'viv, and Paris, 1999), pp. 192-208.

——. "Plebiscite of Carpatho-Ruthenians in the United States Recommending Union of Carpatho-Ruthenia with Czechoslovakia," *Annals of the Ukrainian Academy of Arts and Sciences in the United States,* XI, 1-2 (New York, 1964), pp. 184-207.

——. "Rol' zakarpats'koï emihratsiï v SShA u vyrishenni doli Zakarpattia v 1918-1919 rokakh." In D.M. Fedaka, ed. *Ukraïns'ki Karpaty.* Uzhhorod: Karpaty, 1993, pp. 169-183.

Davis, Jerome. *The Russians and Ruthenians in America: Bolsheviks or Brothers?* New York: George H. Doran, 1922.

Dorko, Nicholas. "The Geographical Background of the Faithful of the Apostolic Exarchate of Pittsburgh," *Slovak Studies,* IV (Cleveland and Rome, 1964), pp. 217-226.

Duly, William. *The Rusyns of Minnesota.* Minneapolis, Minn.: Rusin Association of Minnesota, 1993.

Dushnyk, Walter. "Ukrainians and Ruthenians." In Joseph S. Roucek and Bernard Eisenberg, eds. *America's Ethnic Politics.* Westport, Conn. and London, England: Greenwood Press, 1982, pp. 367-385.

Dulichenko, Aleksander. "[Rusyn'skŷi] literaturnŷi iazŷk: Ameryka." In Paul Robert Magocsi, ed. *Rusyn'skŷi iazŷk.* Opole: Universytet Opolski, Instytut Filologii Polski, 2004, pp. 305-315.

"[Dvadtsiat'] 20-litye Lemko-Soiuza v Ameryki." In Symeon S. Pŷzh, ed. *Iubyleinŷi karpatorusskyi kalendar' Lemko-Soiuza na hod 1951.* Yonkers, N.Y., 1950, pp. 23-59.

Dyrud, Keith P. "East Slavs: Rusins, Ukrainians, Russians, and Belorussians." In June Drenning Holmquist, ed. *They Chose Minnesota: A Survey of the State's Ethnic Groups.* St. Paul, Minn.: Minnesota Historical Society, 1981, pp. 405-422.

——. *The Quest for the Rusyn Soul: The Politics of Religion and Culture in Eastern Europe and America, 1890-World War I.* Philadelphia, London, and Toronto: Associated University Preses for the Balch Institute Press, 1992.

Dzwonczyk, J. H., ed. *Iubileinyi al'manakh, 1900-1940, Obshchestva russkikh bratstv v S.Sh.A.* Philadelphia: Pravda, 1939.

[Fiftieth] 50th Anniversary Almanac of the Lemko Association of USA and Canada/Iubyleinŷi al'manakh 50-lityia Lemko Soiuza v SShA y Kanadi. [Yonkers, N.Y.: Lemko Soiuz, 1979].

First Pontifical Divine Liturgy and Solemn Installation of His Excellency, Most Reverend Orestes P. Chornock of the Carpatho-Russian Greek Catholic Diocese of the Eastern Rite in the United States. Bridgeport, Conn., 1938.

Fischer, Stanisław. "Wyjazdy Lemków nadosławskich na roboty zarobkowe do Ameryki," *Materiały Muzeum Budownictwa Ludowego w Sanoku,* No. 6 (Sanok, 1967).

Goga, Lawrence, ed. *The Establishment of the Rusins and the Greek Catholic Church in Minneapolis: A Recap of the First 50 Years, 1907-1957.* Minneapolis: Rusin Association, 1999.

Golden Jubilee: Sisters of St. Basil the Great, Mount St. Macrina, 1921-1971. Uniontown, Penn., 1971.

Goman, John D. *Galician-Rusins on the Iron Range.* Minneapolis, Minn.: p.a., 1990.

Gregorieff, Dimitry. "Historical Background of Russian Orthodoxy in America," *St. Vladimir's Theological Quarterly,* V, 1-2 (Crestwood, N.Y., 1961), pp. 2-53.

Gulanich, George. *Golden-Silver-Jubilee, 1896-1921-1946.* Uniontown, Pa., 1946.

Gulovich, Stephen C. "Byzantine Slavonic Catholics and the Latin Clergy," *Homiletic and Pastoral Review,* XLV, 7-9 (New York, 1945), pp. 517-527, 586-596, 675-680.

——. "The Rusin Exarchate in the United States," *Eastern Churches Quarterly,* VI (London, 1946), pp. 459-485.

——. *Windows Westward: Rome-Russia-Reunion.* New York: Declan X. McMullen, 1947.

Hardyi, Petro S. *Korotka istoriia Lemkovskoho relifovoho komiteta v SShA: moia podorozh' na Lemkovshchinu.* Yonkers, N.Y.: Lemko Soiuz, 1958.

Hightower, Michael J. "The Road to Russian Hill: A Story of Immigration and Coal Mining," *Chronicles of Oklahoma,* LXIII, 3 (Oklahoma City, 1985), pp. 228-249.

Himka, John-Paul. "Ivan Volians'kyi," *Ukraïns'kyi istoryk,* XII, 3-4 (New York, Toronto, and Munich, 1975), pp. 61-72.

Holy Synod of the Orthodox Church in America. "A Beloved Father, Leader, and Guide becomes a Saint: Father Alexis Toth is Glorified, " *Alive in Christ,* X, 1 (South Canaan, Penn., 1994), pp. 34-39.

Horbal', Bohdan. " Iosyf Fedoronko." In *Lemkivskii rich-*

nyk 2001. Krynica and Legnica, 2001. pp. 137-139.

——. "Osnovania pershoi lemkivskoi organizatsyi—Lemkivskoho Komitetu." In *Lemkivskii richnyk 2002*. Krynica and Legnica: Stovaryshŷnia Lemkiv, 2002, pp. 56-61.

——. "Stefan Kychura (1912-1997)." In *Lemkivskii richnyk 2002*. Krynica and Legnica, 2002, pp. 82-85.

——. "Viktor Hladyk." In *Lemkivskii richnyk 2003*. Krynica and Legnica: Stovaryshŷnia Lemkiv, 2003, pp. 132-142.

Hutnyan, Andrew, ed. *American Carpatho-Russian Orthodox Greek Catholic Diocese Commemorative Jubliee Journal Fiftieth Golden Anniversary, 1938-1988*. Johnstown, Pa: American Carpatho-Russian Orthodox Greek Catholic Diocese, 1988.

Iubileinyi sbornik v pamiat' 150-lietiia Russkoi pravoslavnoi tserkvi v Sievernoi Amerikie, 2 vols. New York: Iubileinaia komissiia, 1944-45.

Jankura, Stephen. *History of the Russian Orthodox Catholic Mutual Aid Society of the U.S.A.—Diamond Jubilee*. Wilkes Barre, Pa., 1970.

Janocsko, George M. " History of the Byzantine Catholic Metropolia of Pittsburgh." In *Byzantine-Ruthenian Metropolitas Church of Pittsburgh Directory*. Pittsburgh: Archeparchy of Pittsburgh, 1999, pp.17-26.

Johnson, Simeon, ed. *St. Mary's Orthodox Cathedral 100th Anniversary, 1887-1987*. Minneapolis, Minn.: St. Mary's Orthodox Cathedral, 1987.

Jorgeson, James. "Father Alexis Toth and the Transition of the Greek Catholic Community in Minneapolis to the Russian Orthodox Church," *St. Vladimir's Theological Quarterly*, XXXII, 2 (Crestwood, N. Y., 1988), pp. 119-137.

Jurchisin, Mitro. *Carpathian Village People: A Listing of Immigrants to Minneapolis, Minnesota from the 1880s to 1947*. Minneapolis, Minn.: p.a., 1981.

Kampov, Pavlo. "Politychna diial'nist' pidkarpats'kykh emihrantiv SShA u zlutsi Podkarpats'koï Rusi z Chekhoslovachchynoiu, 1918-1919 rr." In Ivan Hranchak, ed. *Zakarpattia v skladi Chekhoslovachchyny*. Uzhhorod: Uzhhorods'kyi dezhavnyi universytet, 1999, pp. 36-47.

"Karpatorusskaia sektsyia Mezhdunarodnoho Robochoho Ordena." In Van'o Hunianka, ed. *Karpatorusskyi kalendar Lemko-Soiuza na 1941 hod*. Yonkers, N. Y., 1941, pp. 114-118.

Kirshbaum, Joseph M. *Slovaks in Canada*. Toronto: Canadian Ethnic Press Association of Ontario, 1967, esp. "Slovak Greek Catholic Parishes and Missions," pp. 249-268.

Kohanik, Peter. *Do zahal'noi vîdomosty russkoho naroda v Spoluchennŷkh Derzhavakh*. n.p., 1916.

——. *Iubileinyi sbornik Soiuza pravoslavnykh sviashchennikov v Amerikie*. Passaic, N.J., 1960.

——. *Russkia Pravoslavnaia Tserkov i sovremennoe karpatorusskoe dvizhenie v Sievernoi Amerikie*. Passaic, N.J., 1946.

——. *The Most Useful Knowledge for the Russo-American Young People*. Passaic, N.J., 1934.

——. "Nachalo istorii Amerikanskoi Rusi." In Filipp I. Svistun, *Prikarpatskaia Rus' pod vladeniem Avstrii*. 2nd ed. Trumbull, Conn.: Peter S. Hardy, 1970, pp. 467-515.

——. *Rus' i pravoslavie v Sievernoi Amerikie: k XXV lietiiu Russkago pravoslavnago obshchestva vzaimopomoshchi*. Wilkes Barre, Pa.: Russkoe pravoslavnoe kafolicheskoe obshchestvo vzaimopomoshchi, 1920.

——. [Kohanik, Petr]. *Russkaia Pravoslavnaia Tserkov i sovremennoe karpatorusskoe dvizhenie v Sievernoi Amerikie*. Passaic, N.J., 1946.

——. [Kokhanik, Petr]. *Russkoe pravoslavnoe kafolicheskoe obshchestvo vzaimopomoshchi v sev.-amerikanskikh Soedinennykh Shtatakh: k XX-lietnemu iubileiu 1895-1915*. New York: Russkoe pravoslavnoe kafolicheskoe obshchestvo vzaimopomoshchi, 1915.

——. [Kokhanik, Petr Iur'evich]. *[Seventieth] 70th Anniversary: Russkoe Pravoslavnoe obshchestvo vzaimo-pomoshchi v sievierno-amerikanskikh Soedinennykh Shtatakh*. Wilkes-Barre, Pa.: Russkoe pravoslavnoe kafolicheskoe obshchestvo vzaimopomoshchi, 1965.

Kondratovics, Irén. "Az amerikai ruszinok," *Magyar szemle*, XLII, 1 (Budapest, 1942), pp. 21-24.

Konstankevych, I. and Bonchevs'kyi, A. *Uniia v Amerytsi*. New York, 1902.

"Korotka istorija jedinstvennoj organizacii Sobrania greko-katoličeskich cerkovnych bratstv." In *Kalendar' 'Rusina' dl'a členov 'Sobrania gr. kath. cerk. bratstv' na 1914 rok*. Uzhhorod: Unio, 1913, pp. 50-78.

Krafcik, Patricia A. and Rusinko, Elaine, eds. *Carpatho-Rusyn Research Center: The First Quarter Century*. Ocala, Flo.: Carpatho-Rusyn Research Center, 2004.

Kravcheniuk, Osyp. *Stezhkamy ottsia Ivana Volians'koho v Amerytsi*. Yorkton, Sask., 1981.

Lacko, Michael. "The Churches of Eastern Rite in North America," *Unitas*, XVI, 2 (Graymoor/Garrison, N.Y., 1964), pp. 89-115.

Ladižinsky, Ivan A. *Karpatorossy v Europi i Ameriki: primir Kamjonka*. Cleveland: Svet, 1940.

Lemak, Vasyl'. "Amerykans'ki rysyny I problema vyrishennia avtonomiï Podkarpats'koï Rusi 20—30-kh rokiv," *Karpats'kyi krai*, V, 9-12 [112] (Uzhhorod, 1995), pp. 62-65.

Lesko, David. "Eternal Memory: Bishop Stephen (Dzubay)," *Quarterly Newsletter*, Nos. 3-4 and 1-2 (Wexford, Pa., 1978-79), pp. 4, 4, 4, 3.

Litva, Felix, ed. *Stefan B. Roman: Človek v rozdvojenom svete/Man in a Divided World*. Cambridge, Ont.: Friends of Good Books, 1981.

Lowig, Evan. "The Historical Development of Ukrainians within the Orthodox Church in America: A Comparative Study." In David J. Goa. *The Ukrainian Religious Experience: Tradition and the Canadian Cultural Context*. Edmonton, Alta: Canadian Institute of Ukrainian

Studies, University of Alberta, 1989, pp. 209-218.

Loya, Joseph A. "'Cum Data Fuerit' Fallout: The Celibacy Crisis in the Byzantine Catholic Church, 1930-1940," *Records of the American Catholic Historical Society of Philadelphia,* LVI, 3-4 (Philadelphia, 1995), pp. 149-174.

Lukas [Lukáč], Michael. "Pät'desiat rokov vyst'ahovalectva z Karpát do Kanady." In *Vyst'ahovalectvo a život krajanov vo svete: k storočici začiatkov maseveho vyst'ahovalectva slovenského l'udu do zámoria.* Martin: Matica Slovenska, 1982, pp. 303-306.

——. *45 Anniversary, 1929-1974: Society of Carpatho-Russian Canadians.* Toronto, 1974.

——. *50 Anniversary, 1929-1979: Society of Carpatho-Russian Canadians/Obshchestvo karpato-russkykh kanadtsev.* Toronto, [1979].

Lutsyk, Ieronim Ia. [Roman Surmach]. *Narodnaia istoriia Rusi ot naidavnieishikh vremen do nynieshnikh dnei.* New York: Ivan Gr. Borukh, 1911, pp. 326-337.

Magocsi, Paul Robert. *The Carpatho-Rusyn Americans.* The Peoples of North America Series. New York and Philadelphia: Chelsea House Publishers, 1989. 2nd rev. ed., 2001.

——. "Carpatho-Rusyn Americans." In *Gale Encyclopedia of Multinational America,* Vol. I. Edited by Judy Galens, Anna Sheets, and Robyn V. Young. Detroit, Mich.: Gale Research, 1995, pp. 252-261. Reprinted in *Of the Making of Nationalities There is No End,* Vol. I, pp. 319-395.

——. "The Carpatho-Rusyn Press." In Sally M. Miller, ed. *The Ethnic Press in the United States.* Westport, Conn.: Greenwood Press, 1987, pp. 15-26. Reprinted in *Of the Making of Nationalities There is No End,* Vol. I, pp. 416-429.

——. "Carpatho-Rusyns." In *American Immigrant Cultures: Builders of a Nation,* Vol. I. Edited by David Levinson and Melvin Ember. New York: Macmillan Reference, 1997, pp. 141-148.

——. "Carpatho-Rusyns." In *Dictionary of American Immigrant History.* Edited by Francesco Cordasco, ed. *Dictionary of American Immigrant History.* Metuchen, N.J. and London: Scarecrow Press, 1990, pp. 105-109.

——. "Carpatho-Rusyns." In Dirk Hoerder, ed. *The Immigrant Labor Press in North America, 1840s-1970s: An Annotated Bibliography,* Vol. II. New York, Westport, Conn., and London: Greenwood Press, 1987, pp. 385-400.

——. "Carpatho-Rusyns." In *Encyclopedia of Canada's Peoples.* Edited by Paul Robert Magocsi. Toronto: University of Toronto Press, 1999, pp. 340-343.

——. "Carpatho-Rusyns." In *Encyclopedia of New York City.* Edited by Kenneth T. Johnson. New Haven, London and New York: Yale University Press/New York Historical Society, 1995, p. 182.

——. "Carpatho-Rusyns." In *Harvard Encyclopedia of American Ethnic Groups.* Edited by Stephan Thernstrom. Cambridge, Mass. and London, England: The Belknap

Press of Harvard University Press, 1980, pp. 200-210.

——. "Carpatho-Rusyns in Ontario." In Lubomyr Y. Luciuk and Iroida L. Wynnyckyj, eds. *Ukrainians in Ontario/Polyphony,* Vol. X. Toronto: Multicultural History Society of Ontario, 1988, pp. 177-190. Reprinted in *Of the Making of Nationalities There is No End,* pp.446-466.

——. "Carpatho-Ruthenian." In *The World's Written Languages: A Survey of the Degree and Modes of Use,* Vol. 1: *The Americas.* Québec: Université Laval, 1978, pp. 553-561.

——. "Immigrants from Eastern Europe: The Carpatho-Rusyn Community of Proctor, Vermont," *Vermont History,* XLII, I (Montpelier, Vt., 1974), pp. 48-52. Reprinted in *Rutland Historical Society Quarterly,* XV, 2 (Rutland, Vt., 1985), pp. 18-23.

——. "Karpato-rusyny u Ameryky," *Nova dumka,* VIII [20] (Vukovar, 1979), pp. 67-73; [21], pp. 97-100; [22], pp. 69-73.

——. "Made or Re-Made in America?: Nationality and Identity Formation Among Carpatho-Rusyn Immigrants and Their Descendants," *Coexistence—Special Issue: The Emigré Experience,* XXVIII (Dordrecht, Netherlands, 1991), pp. 335-348. Also in Paul Robert Magocsi, ed. *The Persistence of Regional Cultures: Rusyns and Ukrainians in Their Homeland and Abroad.* New York: Columbia University Press/East European Monographs, 1993, pp. 163-178; and Magocsi, *Of the Making of Nationalities There is No End,* Vol. I, pp. 467-482.

——. *Of the Making of Nationalities There is No End,* 2 vols. New York: Columbia University Press/East European Monographs, 1999.

——. "The Political Activity of Rusyn-American Immigrants in 1918," *East European Quarterly,* X, 3 (Boulder, Colo., 1976), pp. 347-365. Reprinted in *Of the Making of Nationalities There is No End,* Vol. I, pp. 394-415.

——. "Rusyn-American Ethnic Literature." In *Ethnic Literatures Since 1776: The Many Voices of America,* Vol. II. Lubbock, Texas: Texas Tech University, 1978, pp. 503-520. . Reprinted in *Of the Making of Nationalities There is No End,* Vol. I, pp. 430-445.

——. "Rusyn-Americans and Czechoslovakia." In Bohomír Bunža, ed. *Rada Svobodného Československa/Council of Free Czechoslovakia: Historie, program, činnost, dokumenty.* Toronto: Rada Svobodného Československa, 1990, pp. 206-211.

——. "Rusyn-Americans, Slovak-Americans, and Czecho-Slovakia." In Josef Stefka, ed. *Kalendár-Almanac National Slovak Society of the USA for the Year of 1990.* Pittsburgh, Pa., 1990, pp. 59-62.

——. "Rusyn Catholics in America." In Michael Glazier and Thomas J. Shelley, eds. *The Encyclopedia of American Catholic History.* Collegeville, Minn.: Liturgical Press, 1997, pp. 1221-1224.

——. "Sotsiolingvistichnŷi aspect [rusyn'skoho iazŷka]:

Ameryka." In Paul Robert Magocsi, ed. *Rusyn'skŷi iazŷk.* Opole: Universytet Opolski, Instytut Filologii Polski, 2004, pp. 383-390.

Mamatey, Victor S. "The Slovaks and Carpatho-Ruthenians." In Joseph P. O'Grady, ed. *The Immigrant's Influence on Wilson's Peace Policies.* Lewisburg, Ky.: University of Kentucky Press, 1967, pp. 224-249.

"Married Priests in the Eastern Catholic Churches, 1884-1998," *Eastern Churches Journal,* IX, 1 (Fairfax, Virginia, 2002), pp. 7-72.

Masich, John. "Highlights in the Glorious History of the Greek Catholic Union of the U.S.A." In *Jubilee Almanac of the Greek Catholic Union of the U.S.A.,* Vol. LXXI. Munhall, Pa.: Greek Catholic Union, 1967, pp. 33-95 and 258-263.

Matrosov, E.N. "Zaokeanskaia Rus'," *Istoricheskii viestnik,* LXVII, 1-5 (Moscow, 1897), pp. 131, 478, 853, 83, and 435. Reprinted in F. Svistun, *Prikarpatskaia Rus' pod vladeniem Avstrii.* 2nd. ed. Trumbull, Conn.: Peter S. Hardy, 1970, pp. 516-531.

Maynard, Theodore, *The Better Part: The Life of Teresa Demjanovich.* New York: Macmillan, 1952.

Medieshi, Liubomir. "Amerikantsi ruskoho pokhodzenia." In Diura Latiak, ed. *Narodni kalendar 1989.* Novi Sad: Ruske slovo, 1988, pp. 91-100.

———. "Ameritski Karpatoruski Vyhliedovatski Tsentr." In Diura Latiak, ed. *Narodni kalendar 1990.* Novi Sad: Ruske slovo, 1989, pp. 191-196.

———. "Ameritski Rusnatsi prez svoiu presu," *Shvetlosts,* XXVI, 2 (Novi Sad, 1988), pp. 199-225.

———. "'Podkorman'oshe'—putniki tvardei nadiï." In Diura Latiak, ed. *Narodni kalendar 1988.* Novi Sad: Ruske slovo, 1987, pp. 71-83.

———. "Rodoliubivi pisnï iuhoslavianskikh Rusnatsokh obiaveni u Ameriki," *Shvetlosts,* XXV, 5 (Novi Sad, 1987), pp. 691-705.

Michaylo, George. *Official Anniversary Volume 1902-1942: Forty Years in the Priesthood of his Excellency Basil Takach.* McKeesport: Prosvita, 1942.

Miliasevich, Iona. *Kratii istoricheskii ocherk zhizni Russkago pravoslavnago zhenskago obshchestva vzaimopomoshchi v S.Sh.S.A. so dnia osnovaniia obshchestva l-go iulia 1907 g. po l-e marta 1926 goda.* Coaldale, Pa., 1926.

Mushynka, Mykola. "Do 100-richchia z dnia narodzhennia ta 20-richchia z dnia smerti Dmytra Vyslots'koho/Vania Hunianky." In *Repertuarnyi zbirnyk,* No. 2. Prešov: Kul'turnyi soiuz ukraïns'kykh trudiashchykh, 1989.

———. "Emilii Kubek—pershyi romanist Zakarpattia." In *Ukraïns'kyi kalendar 1980.* Warsaw, 1980, pp. 213-215.

Mytsiuk, Oleksander. "Z emihratsiï uhro-rusyniv pered svitovoiu viinoiu," *Naukovyi zbirnyk tovarystva 'Prosvita',* XIII-XIV (Uzhhorod, 1937-38) pp. 21-32.

"Nasha Narodna budova v Iunkers: k 15-lityiu Karpatorusskoho amerykanskoho tsentra." In *Karpatorusskyi kalendar Lemko-Soiuza na 1954.* Yonkers, N. Y., 1954,
pp. 131-135.

"The New Republic of Rusinia, Mostly Made in America," *Literary Digest,* LXIX, 13 (New York, 1921), pp. 41-43.

Nowak, Jacek. "Konstruovanie etniczności." In his *Zaginiony świat?: nazywają ich Łemkami.* Cracow: Universitas, 2000, pp. 176-192.

Obushkevich, Feofan. *Ustroistvo russkikh gr. kaf. gromad tserkovnykh v Soed. Shtatakh Ameriki.* New York: Pravda, 1906.

Ol., M. "Deshcho z istoriï uhro-ruskoï parokhiï v Letbridzh, Alta." In *Iliustrovanyi kalendar kanads'koho ukraïntsia na rik 1925.* Winnipeg, 1924, pp. 93-94.

"Osnovanie Russkago Narodnago Soiuza, Russkago Pravoslavnago Obshchestva Vzaimopomoshchi i Obshchestva Russkikh Bratstv." In Filip Svistun. *Prikarpatskaia Rus' pod vladeniem Avstrii.* 2nd ed. Trumbull, Conn.: Peter S. Hardy, 1970, pp. 497-514.

Padokh, Iaroslav. "Emigratsiia." In Bohdan O. Strumins'kyi, ed. *Lemkivshchyna,* Vol. II. Zapysky Naukovoho tovarystva im. Shevchenka, Vol. 206. New York, Paris, Sydney, and Toronto, 1988, pp. 463-484.

Pahyria, Vasyl'. *Zakarpatsi u diaspori: narysy pro zakarpats'kykh emihrantiv.* Uzhhorod: Patent, 1997.

Palij, Michael. "Early Ukrainian Immigration to the United States and the Conversion of the Ukrainian Catholic Parish in Minneapolis to Russian Orthodoxy," *Journal of Ukrainian Studies,* VIII, 2 (Toronto, 1983), pp. 13-37.

Pamiatka k 20-lietiiu arkhiereiskago sluzheniia Arkhiepiskopa Lavra/An Album Commemorating the Twentieth Year of Hierarchical Service of Archbishop Laurus. [Jordanville, N.Y., 1987].

Pamiatkova kniha z nahody toržestvennaho posvjasčenija maternaho monastyra Sester Čina Sv. Vasilija Velikoho na Hori Sv. Makriny vo Uniontown, Penna. McKeesport, Pa.: Prosvita-Enlightenment, 1934.

Pamiatna knyzhka 10-lityia Lemko-Soiuza v Soed. Shtatakh y Kanadi y otkrŷtyia Karpatorus-skoho amerykanskoho tsentra maia 28, 1939. [Yonkers, N.Y.: Lemko Soiuz, 1939].

Papp, Alexander. "Korotkij perehlad istoriji Sobranija za 1903-1928 rr." In *Kalendar Sobranija na r. 1926.* McKeesport, Pa., 1929, pp. 136-152.

Pavlyk, Mykhailo. "Rusyny v Amerytsi," *Tovarysh,* No. 1 (L'viv, 1888), pp. 31-52.

Pekar, Athanasius B. "Historical Background of the Carpatho-Ruthenians in America," *Ukraïns'kyi istoryk,* XIII, 1-4 (New York, Toronto, and Munich, 1976), pp. 87-102 and XIV, 1-2 (1977), pp. 70-84.

———. *Our Past and Present: Historical Outlines of the Byzantine Ruthenian Metropolitan Province.* Pittsburgh, Pa.: Byzantine Seminary Press, 1974.

———. "Sheptyts'kyi and the Carpatho-Ruthenians in the United States." In Paul Robert Magocsi, ed. *Morality and Reality: the Life and Times of Andrei Sheptyts'kyi.* Edmonton: University of Alberta Canadian Institute of

Ukrainian Studies, 1989, pp. 363-374.

Pel'ts, Stepan A. "Do istoriï lemkivs'koï emigratsiï v ZDA." In *Lemkivs'kyi kalendar na 1965 rik*. Torotno and Pasaic, N.J.: Orhanizatsiia Oborony Lemkivshchyny, 1965, pp. 47-61.

Petras, David M. *Eastern Catholic Churches in America*. Parma, Ohio: Office of Religious Education, Diocese of Parma, 1987.

——. "The Liturgical Life of the Byzantine-Ruthenian Church: Its Past and Future,"*Diakonia,* XXV, 1 (Scranton, Pa., 1992), pp. 61-96.

Porter, Lorle. *The Immigrant Cocoon: Central Europeans in the Cambridge, Ohio Coalfield*. New Concord, Ohio: p.a., 1994.

Pospishil, Victor J. *Compulsory Celibacy for the Eastern Catholics in the Americas*. Toronto: Church of St. Demetrius Ukrainian Catholic Women's League, 1977.

Pravda ob ukrayntsiakh. Mahanoy City, Pa., 1903.

Procko, Bohdan P. "The Establishment of the Ruthenian Church in the United States, 1884-1907," *Pennsylvania History,* XLII, 2 (Bloomsburg, Pa., 1975), pp. 137-154.

——. "Soter Ortynsky: First Ruthenian Bishop in the United States, 1907-1916," *Catholic Historical Review,* LVIII, 4 (Washington, D.C., 1973), pp. 513-533.

Ramach, Liubomir. "Rusnatsi u Kanadi." *Khristiianskii kalendar za 1972 rok*. Ruski Krstur, 1972, pp. 106-110.

Ratica, Peter. "Korotka istorija Sojedinenija russkich pravoslavnych bratstv v Ameriki, 1916-1941." In *Iubileinyi kalendar' Pravoslavnoho Soedineniia na 1941 god*. Pittsburgh, Pa., 1941, pp. 37-44.

Renoff, Richard. "Carpatho-Ruthenian Resources and Assimilation, 1880-1924," *Review Journal of Philosophy and Social Science*, II, 1 (Meerut, India, 1977), pp. 53-78.

Renoff, Richard. " Changing Types of Church Dedications in the American Ruthenian Church," *Diakonia,* XXXIV, 2 (Scranton, Pa., 2001), pp.129-144.

——. "Community and Nationalism in the Carpatho-Russian Celibacy Schism: Some Sociological Hypotheses," *Diakonia,* VI, 1 (New York, 1971), pp. 58-68.

Renoff, Richard and Reynolds, Stephen, eds. *Proceedings of the Conference on Carpatho-Ruthenian Immigration, 8 June 1974*. Cambridge, Mass.: Harvard Ukrainian Research Institute Sources and Documents Series, 1975.

Roman, Jaroslav. "The Establishment of the American Carpatho-Russian Orthodox Greek Catholic Diocese in 1938: A Major Carpatho-Russian Return to Orthodoxy," *St. Vladimir's Theological Quarterly,* XX, 3 (Crestwood/ Tuckahoe, N.Y., 1976), pp. 132-160.

Roman, Michael. "Istorija Greko-Kaft. Sojedinenija." In *Zoloto-Jubilejnyj Kalendar' Greko Kaft. Sojedinenija v S.Š.A.,* XLVII. Munhall, Pa.: Greko Kaftoličeskoje Sojedinenije, 1942, pp. 39-74.

Russin, Keith S. "Father Alexis G. Toth and the Wilkes-Barre Litigations," *St. Vladimir's Theological Quarterly,*

XVI, 3 (Tuckahoe, N.Y., 1972), pp. 123-149.

St. Tikhon's Monastery: Center of Orthodoxy for the Russian Orthodox Greek Catholic Church of America, the Metropolia. South Canaan, Penn., [1968?].

St. Tikhon's Seminary 35th Year, 1938-1973. South Canaan, Penn., 1973.

Samielo, Roman N. "Amerikanskii Russkii Karpatorusskii Soiuz o sud'be Lemkoviny, Priashevschiny i Kholmshchiny." In I. Gr. Dzvonchik, comp. *Iubileinyi al'manakh 1900-1950*. Philadelphia, Pa.: Obshchestvo Russkikh Bratstv, [1950], pp. 161-170.

Schmal, Desmond A. "The Ruthenian Question," *American Ecclesiastical Review,* XCVII (Washington, D.C., 1937), pp. 448-461.

Sekellick, John T. "Catholic Ruthenians of the Byzantine Rite in the United States of America," *Diakonia,* XXV, 1 (Scranton, Pa., 1992) pp.19-60.

Seniuk, D. O. *Mitrofornyi protoierei Andrei Stepanovich Shlepetskii: kratkii ocherk zhizni i deiatel'nosti*. Prešov, 1967.

Serafim (Surrency), Archimandrite. *The Quest for Orthodox Church Unity in America*. New York: Boris and Gleb Press, 1973.

Shereghy, Basil. *Bishop Basil Takach `The Good Shepherd'*. Pittsburgh, Pa., 1979.

——. *Fifty Years of Piety: A History of the Uniontown Pilgrimages*. Pittsburgh, Pa.: Byzantine Seminary Press, 1985.

----., ed. *The United Societies of the U.S.A.: A Historical Album*. McKeesport, Pa., 1978.

Shipman, Andrew J. "Greek Catholics in America." In *The Catholic Encyclopedia,* Vol. VI. New York: The Gilmary Society, 1913, pp. 744-750.

Shlepetskii, Aleksander S. "Karpatorossi v Ameriki." In *Almanakh O.K.S. Vozrozhdenie*. Prague, 1936, pp. 81-86.

——. "Priashevtsi v Amerike." In Ivan S. Shlepetskii, ed. *Priashevshchina: istoriko-literaturnyi sbornik*. Prague: Khutor, 1948, pp. 255-262.

Shpontak, Mykhailo."Diial'nist' Karpats'koho soiuzu v ZSA." In Ivan Rebryk, ed. *Kultura ukraïns'kykh Karpat: tradytsiï i suchasnist'*. Uzhhorod: Grazhda, 1994, pp. 281-286.

Simirenko, Alex. "The Minneapolis Russian Community in Transition," *St. Vladimir's Seminary Quarterly,* V, 1-2 (Crestwood/Tuckahoe, N.Y., 1961), pp. 88-100.

——. *Pilgrims, Colonists, and Frontiersmen: An Ethnic Community in Transition*. New York: Free Press of Glencoe, 1964.

——. "The Social Structure of the Minneapolis Russian Community." In *Proceedings of the Minnesota Academy of Science for 1959*. Minneapolis, 1959, pp. 79-86.

Simon, Constantin. "Alexis Toth and the Beginnings of the Orthodox Movement among the Ruthenians in America (1891)," *Orientalia Christiana Periodica,* LIV, 2 (Rome, 1988), pp. 387-428.

——. "The First Years of Ruthenian Church Life in America," *Orientalia Christiana Periodica,* LV, 1 (Rome, 1994), pp. 187-232.

——. "In Europe and America: the Ruthenians between Catholicism and Orthodoxy," *Orientalia Christiana Periodica,* LIX, 1 (Rome, 1993), pp. 169-210.

——. "Uniates et Orthodoxes aux Étas-Unis," *Plamia,* No. 79 (Meudon, France, 1990) pp. 37-58.

Sister of Charity [M.Zita]. *Sister Miriam Teresa (1901-1927).* Convent Station, N.J.: Sister Miriam Teresa League of Prayer, 1936.

Smith, Raymond A. "Indigenous and Diaspora Elites and the Return of Carpatho-Ruthenian Nationalism, 1989-1992," *Harvard Ukrainian Studies,* XXI, 1-2 (Cambridge, Mass., 1997), pp. 141-160.

Souvenir Issued by the Rusin Peoples Home, Inc. on the Occasion of the Dedication of the Corner-Stone/ Pamiatnik izdan korporatsieiu Russkii Narodnyi Dom iz sluchai posviashcheniia kraeugol'nago kamen'ia. Homestead, Pa., 1919.

Stein, Howard F. "An Ethnohistory of Slovak-American Religious and Fraternal Associations: A Study in Cultural Meaning, Group Identity, and Social Institutions," *Slovakia,* XXIX (West Paterson, N.J., 1980-81), pp. 53-101.

Stryps'kyi, Hiiador. "Uhors'ki rusyny i slovaky v Amerytsi," *Zhytie i slovo,* VI (L'viv, 1897), pp. 414-420.

Tajtak, Ladislav. "Pereselennia ukraïntsiv Skhidnoï Slovachchyny do 1913 r.," *Duklia,* IX, 4 (Prešov, 1961), pp. 97-103.

——. "Východoslovenské výst'ahovalectvo do prvej svetovej vojny," *Nové obzory,* III (Prešov, 1961), pp. 221-247.

Tarasar, Constance J. and Erickson, John H. eds. *Orthodox America, 1794-1976: Development of the Orthodox Church in America.* Syosset, N.Y., 1975.

Tidick, Michail, ed. *Dumy o karpatorusskoj nivi: rieči skazannyja na Russkam Dňu, 29-ho oktjabrja 1933 h.* Cleveland: Karpatorusskyj sojuz v Sivernoj Ameriki, 1933.

"[Trydtsiata] 30-ta hodovshchyna Lemko-Soiuza." In Nykolai Tsysliak, ed. *Karpatorusskyi kalendar' Lemko-Soiuza na hod 1960.* Yonkers, N. Y., 1960, pp. 35-64 and 193-194.

Tsysliak, Nykolai. "[Desiat'] 10-litnyi iubylei Narodnoho Doma Lemko-Soiuza v Klyvlandi." In *Karpatorusskyi kalendar' Lemko-Soiuza na 1957.* Yonkers, N. Y., 1957, pp. 129-138.

——. "Lemkovska emyhratsyia v Kanadi." In Van'o Hunianka ed. *Karpatorusskyi kalendar' Lemko-Soiuza na 1937.* Cleveland, Ohio, 1963, pp. 93-97.

Turkevich, V. *Pravoslavnoe obshchestvo vzaimopomosh-chi v sievero-amerikanskikh Soedinennykh Shtatakh: k X-lietnemu iuvileiu, 1895-1905.* Bridgeport, Conn.: Pravoslavnoe obshchestvo vzaimo-pomoshchi, 1905.

Tverdyi Rusyn [0. Stetkevych]. *Bery y chytai.* New York: Svoboda, 1908.

Vidnianskyi, Stepan and Petryshche, Petro. "Politychna diial-nist' zakarpatskoï emihratsiï v SShA naprykintsi 19-ho—na pochatku 20-ho st. ta ïï vplyv na doliu ridnoho kraiu," *Ukraïnska diaspora,* II, 4 (Kiev, 1993) pp. 5-20.

Vigh, Kálmán. "Az Amerikai görög katolikus püspökség első évei," *Világtörténet,* No ? (Budapest, 1997), pp. 45-53.

Vostok—The East: Twenty-Fifth Anniversary, 1918-1943. Perth Amboy, N.J., 1945.

Vyslotskyi, D.F., ed. *Nasha knyzhka.* Yonkers: Lemko-Soiuz v ShSA y Kanadi, 1945.

Winslow, B. "Catholics of the Byzantine Rite," *Eastern Churches Quarterly,* V (London, 1944), pp. 319-324.

Warzeski, Walter C. *Byzantine Rite Rusins in Carpatho-Ruthenia and America.* Pittsburgh, Pa.: Byzantine Seminary Press, 1971.

——. "The Rusin Community in Pennsylvania." In John Bodnar, ed. *The Ethnic Experience in Pennsylvania.* Lewisburg, Pa.: Bucknell University Press, 1973, pp. 175-215.

"Ystorychne torzhestvo: chestovanye 25-litnoho iubileiu narodnoi orhanizatsyy Lemko-Soiuza v Klyvlandi." *Karpatorusskyi kalendar' Lemko-Soiuza na 1955.* Yonkers, N. Y., 1955, pp. 143-150.

Yurčišin, Joan. *Korotka cerkovna istorija karpatorusskaho naroda.* Johnstown, Pa.: Amerikanska Karpatorusska Pravoslavna Greko Kaftoličeskaja Jeparchija, 1954.

Zatkovich, Gregory. *The Tragic Tale.* Pittsburgh, Pa., 1926.

Zhirosh, Miron. "Ameritski men." In idem. *Bachvansko-srimski rusnatsi doma i u shvetse, 1745-2001,* Vol. V. Novi Sad: Ruske Slovo/Hreko-katolïtska parokhiia Sv. Petra i Pavla, 2003, pp. 129-245.

——. "Odkhod nashikh liudzokh do Kanadi i Argentini (u shvetle `Ruskikh novinokh', 1924-1933)." In Diura Latiak, ed. *Narodni kalendar 1984.* Novi Sad: Ruske slovo, 1983, pp. 46-59.

——. "Rusnak—ameritski men." In Iuliian Kamenitski, ed. *Ruski kalendar 1994.* Novi Sad: Ruske slovo, 1994, pp. 29-35.

Zięba, Andrzej. "Kanadyjcy rusofile a sprawa polskiej granicy południowo-wschodniej." In his *Ukraińcy w Kanadzie wobec Polaków i Polski, 1914-1939.* Cracow: Universytet Jagielloński, Instytut Polonjiny, 1988, pp. 201-210.

——. "Poland and Political Life in Carpatho-Rus and Among Carpatho-Rusyns in Emigration in North America, 1918-1939." In Paul J. Best, ed. *Contributions of the Carpatho-Rusyn Studies Group to the IV World Congress for Soviet and East European Studies.* New Haven, Conn.: Carpatho-Rusyn Studies Group, 1990, pp. 23-39. Reprinted in Paul Best and Jaroslaw Moklak, eds. *The Lemkos of Poland: Articles and Essays.* New Haven, Conn.: Carpatho-Slavic Studies Group, 2000, pp. 33-40.

Zsatkovics, Kalman. *Rules for the Spiritual Government of Greek-Ruthenian Catholics in the United States.* New York, n.d.

Index

Photograph Credits

The author and publisher wish to thank the following individuals, institutions, and publishers for supplying photographs and/or granting permission to reproduce them from existing publications. Their courtesy is gratefully acknowledged:

Connie Zatkovich Ash, Cornwall, Oregon—85; Peter Baycura, Butler, Pa.—53, 58; Byzantine Ruthenian Catholic Archdiocese of Pittsburgh—24, 25, 26, 65, 93; Carpatho-Rusyn Research Center, Ocala, Florida—77; Center for Research Libraries, Chicago—82; Chelsea House Publishers, Philadephia, Pa.—92; Cleveland Cultural Garden Federation—44; Greek Catholic Congregation of St. John the Baptist, Perth Amboy, N.J.—72, 74; Greek Catholic Union, Beaver, Pa.—17, 34, 36, 38, 39, 40, 48, 49, 63, 66, 96; Heritage Institute, Byzantine Ruthenian Catholic Diocese of Passaic—1, 2, 3, 8, 10, 11, 12, 16, 19, 35, 42, 54, 83, 87; Holy Trinity Monastery, Jordanville, N. Y.—31; Immigration History Research Center, St. Paul, Minn.—37, 43, 73, 76; Jerry Jumba, McKees Rocks, Pa.—67, 90; Paul Kobelak, Cleveland, Ohio—47; Lemko Association, Yonkers, N.Y.—45, 46; Mária Magazine, Toronto—29, 97; Ljubomir Medješi, Novi Sad, Yugoslavia—101; Orestes Mihaly, Armonk, N.Y.—15, 23, 55, 62; Orthodox Church in America Archives, Syosset, N.Y.—18, 30, 52; Osvìta Publishers, Martin, Slovakia—50; Pennsylvania Historical and Museum Commission, Harrisburg, Pa.—6; Princeton University Press, Princeton, N.J.—84; John Righetti, Pittsburgh, Pa.—64; Chetko Collection, Roberson Center for the Arts and Sciences, Binghamton, N.Y.—7; Russian Brotherhood Organization, Philadelphia, Pa.—33; St. Mary's Catholic Church of the Byzantine Rite, New York City—60; John Schweich, Reston, Va.—9; Society of Carpatho-Russian Canadians, Toronto—98, 99, 100; Universal-International Pictures, New York City—78; Reverend Stephen Veselenak, McKeesport, Pa.—57; University of Chicago Press, Chicago—56; Vostok Publishing Co., Perth Amboy, N.J.—91; Worldwide Church of God, Pasadena, Ca.—32; Msgr. John Yurcisin, Johnstown, Pa.—20, 21, 22, 27, 28, 41, 59; Anton Žižka, Prešov, Slovakia—51; Alexander Zozul'ák, Prešov, Slovakia—94, 95, 102.